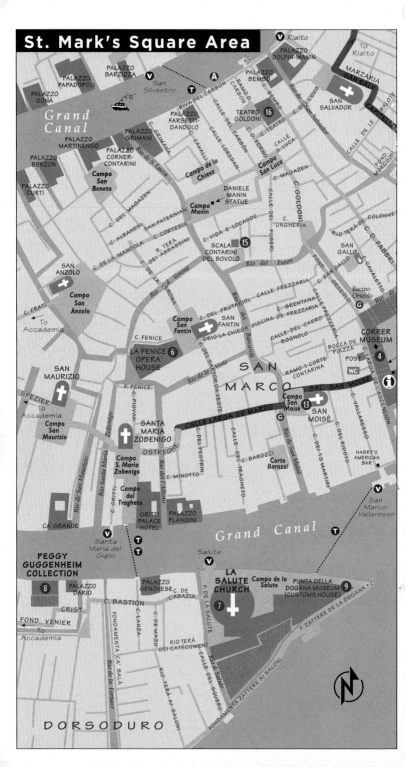

Rick Steves'

VENICE

Rick Steves & Gene Openshaw

2012

SIGHTS

1. Accademia Gallery
2. Bridge of Sighs
3. Ca' d'Oro
4. Ca' Pesaro Internat'l Gallery of Modern Art
5. Ca' Rezzonico
6. Campanile (Bell Tower)
7. Clock Tower
8. Correr Museum
9. Doge's Palace
10. Frari Church
11. Jewish Ghetto & Museum
12. La Fenice Opera House
13. La Salute Church
14. Palazzo Grassi
15. Palazzo Mocenigo Costume Museum
16. Peggy Guggenheim Collection
17. Piazzale Roma
18. Punta della Dogana Museum
19. Rialto Bridge
20. St. Mark's Basilica
21. St. Mark's Square
22. San Giorgio Maggiore Church
23. San Polo Church
24. San Zaccaria Church
25. Santa Maria Formosa Church
26. Scala Contarini del Bovolo
27. To Scuola Dalmata di San Giorgio
28. Scuola San Rocco
29. Train Station

200 Meters
200 Yards

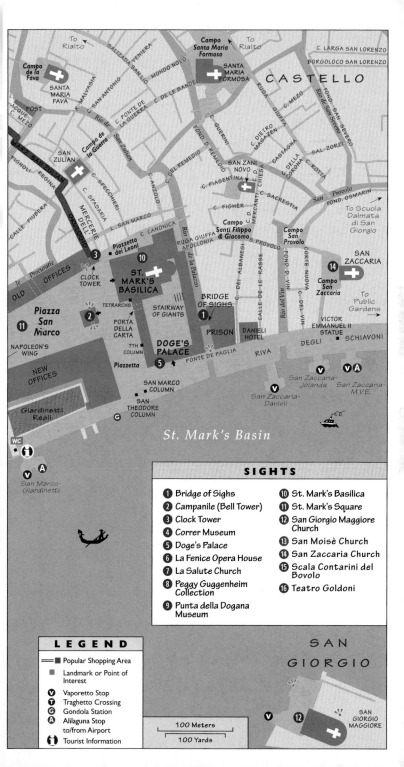

SIGHTS

1. Bridge of Sighs
2. Campanile (Bell Tower)
3. Clock Tower
4. Correr Museum
5. Doge's Palace
6. La Fenice Opera House
7. La Salute Church
8. Peggy Guggenheim Collection
9. Punta della Dogana Museum
10. St. Mark's Basilica
11. St. Mark's Square
12. San Giorgio Maggiore Church
13. San Moisè Church
14. San Zaccaria Church
15. Scala Contarini del Bovolo
16. Teatro Goldoni

LEGEND

- Popular Shopping Area
- Landmark or Point of Interest
- **V** Vaporetto Stop
- **T** Traghetto Crossing
- **G** Gondola Station
- **A** Alilaguna Stop to/from Airport
- Tourist Information

100 Meters
100 Yards

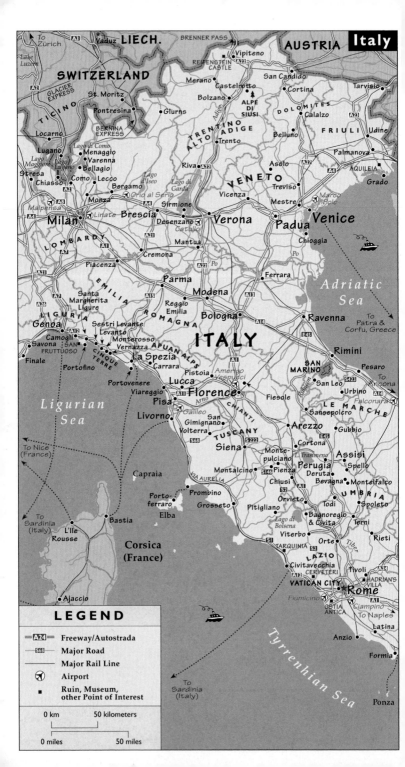

Rick Steves'

VENICE

2012

AVALON
TRAVEL

CONTENTS

Introduction 1

Planning 4

Practicalities. 8

Money .10

Sightseeing. 15

Traveling as a
  Temporary Local 17

Back Door
  Travel Philosophy. 19

▶ **Orientation** **20**

▶ **Sights in Venice** **39**

San Marco District 39

Across the Lagoon from
  St. Mark's Square 48

Dorsoduro District. 49

Santa Croce District 51

San Polo District. 52

Cannaregio District. 53

Castello District 57

Venice's Lagoon. 58

▶ **Self-Guided Tours**

Grand Canal Cruise 60

St. Mark's Square Tour 73

St. Mark's Basilica Tour . . . 84

Doge's Palace Tour 103

Correr Museum Tour. 118

Accademia Tour 132

Frari Church Tour. 146

Scuola San Rocco Tour . . .154

Ca' Rezzonico Tour 164

Peggy Guggenheim
  Collection Tour. 176

La Salute Church Tour 189

San Giorgio
  Maggiore Tour 194

Venice's Lagoon Tour. . . . 202

▶ **Self-Guided Walks**
St. Mark's to Rialto Walk . . 217
Rialto to Frari
 Church Walk 224
St. Mark's to
 San Zaccaria Walk 231
▶ **Sleeping in Venice** **237**
▶ **Eating in Venice** **265**
▶ **Venice with Children** **288**
▶ **Shopping in Venice** **292**
▶ **Nightlife in Venice** **296**
▶ **Venice Connections** **304**

**Day Trips
from Venice** **313**
▶ **Padua** **314**
Near Padua: Vicenza 341
▶ **Verona** **345**

Venetian History **366**

Appendix **377**
Tourist Information 377
Communicating 378
Transportation 386
Resources 402
Holidays and Festivals 406
Conversions and Climate . . 409
Hotel Reservation Form 412
Packing Checklist 413
Italian Survival Phrases 414

Index **417**
Map Index **428**

Venice Overview

INTRODUCTION

Engineers love Venice—a completely man-made environment rising from the sea, with no visible means of support. Romantics revel in its atmosphere of elegant decay, seeing the peeling plaster and seaweed-covered stairs as a metaphor for beauty in decline. And first-time visitors are often stirred deeply, awaking from their ordinary lives to a fantasy world unlike anything they've ever seen before.

Those are strong reactions, considering that Venice today, frankly, can also be an overcrowded, prepackaged, tacky tourist trap. But Venice is unique. Built on a hundred islands with wealth from trade with the East, its exotic-looking palaces are laced together by sun-speckled canals. The car-free streets suddenly make walkers feel big, important, and liberated.

By day, it's a city of museums and churches, packed with great art. Everything's within a half-hour walk. Cruise the canals on a vaporetto water bus. Climb towers for stunning seascape views. Shop for Venetian crafts (such as glass and lace), high fashions, or tacky souvenirs for your Uncle Eric. Linger over lunch, trying to crack a crustacean with weird legs and antennae. Sip a *spritz* at a café on St. Mark's Square while the orchestra plays "New York, New York."

At night, when the hordes of day-trippers have gone, another Venice appears. Dance across a floodlit square. Glide in a gondola through quiet canals while music echoes across the water. Pretend it's Carnevale time, don a mask—or just a clean shirt—and become someone else for a night.

About This Book

Rick Steves' Venice 2012 is a personal tour guide in your pocket. Better yet, it's actually two tour guides in your pocket: The

INTRODUCTION

Map Legend

𝓵 Viewpoint	✈ Airport	)⬛(Tunnel
↑ Entry Arrow	ⓣ Taxi Stand	▦▦ Pedestrian Zone
❶ Tourist Info	⬛ Tram Stop	—·—·— Railway
WC Restroom	Ⓑ Bus Stop	············ Ferry/Boat Route
🏰 Castle	⬛ Parking	⊢—⊢ Tram
🏠 Church	)(Mtn. Pass	▪▪▪▪▪ Stairs
Ⓥ Vaporetto Stop	Park	······ Walk/Tour Route
Ⓣ Traghetto Crossing	Statue/Point of Interest	------- Trail
Ⓖ Gondola Station		
Ⓐ Alilaguana Stop		

Use this legend to help you navigate the maps in this book.

co-author of this book is Gene Openshaw. Since our first "Europe through the gutter" trip together as high school buddies in the 1970s, Gene and I have been exploring the wonders of the Old World. An inquisitive historian and lover of European culture, Gene wrote most of this book's self-guided museum tours and neighborhood walks. Together, Gene and I keep this book current (though for simplicity, from this point "we" will shed our respective egos and become "I").

In this book, you'll find the following chapters:

Orientation includes specifics on public transportation, helpful hints, local tour options, easy-to-read maps, and tourist information. The "Planning Your Time" section suggests a schedule for how to best use your limited time.

Sights in Venice describes the top attractions and includes their cost and hours.

The **Self-Guided Tours** lead you through Venice's most fascinating museums and sights: the Grand Canal, St. Mark's Square, St. Mark's Basilica, Doge's Palace, Correr Museum, Accademia, Frari Church, Scuola San Rocco, Ca' Rezzonico (Museum of 18th-Century Venice), Peggy Guggenheim Collection, La Salute Church, San Giorgio Maggiore, and the islands in Venice's lagoon (including San Michele, Murano, Burano, and Torcello).

The **Self-Guided Walks** cover Venice's back streets. The walk from St. Mark's to Rialto follows a less touristy route between these two major landmarks than the one most tourists travel. The walk from Rialto to Frari Church (and its exquisite art) takes you through the bustling markets and by a mask-making shop. The walk from St. Mark's to San Zaccaria explores the area behind the basilica, featuring a historic church and a seldom-seen view of the famous Bridge of Sighs.

Sleeping in Venice describes my favorite hotels, from good-value deals to cushy splurges. I've focused on hotels conveniently

Key to This Book

Updates

This book is updated every year—but once you pin down Italy, it wiggles. For the latest, visit www.ricksteves.com /update. For a valuable list of reports and experiences—good and bad—from fellow travelers, check www.ricksteves.com /feedback.

Abbreviations and Times

I use the following symbols and abbreviations in this book: Sights are rated:

▲▲▲	**Don't miss**
▲▲	**Try hard to see**
▲	**Worthwhile if you can make it**
No rating	**Worth knowing about**

When you see a ✪ in a sight listing, it means that the sight is covered in much more detail in one of the tour chapters.

Tourist information offices are abbreviated as **TI,** and bathrooms are **WC**s. To categorize accommodations, I use a **Sleep Code** (described on page 239).

Like Europe, this book uses the **24-hour clock.** It's the same through 12:00 noon, then keep going: 13:00, 14:00, and so on. For anything over 12, subtract 12 and add p.m. (14:00 is 2:00 p.m.).

When giving **opening times,** I include both peak season and off-season hours if they differ. So, if a museum is listed as "May-Oct daily 9:00-16:00," it should be open from 9 a.m. until 4 p.m. from the first day of May until the last day of October (but expect exceptions).

For **transit** or **tour departures,** I first list the frequency, then the duration. So, a train connection listed as "2/hour, 1.5 hours" departs twice each hour and the journey lasts an hour and a half.

located near St. Mark's Square, the Rialto Bridge, and the Accademia—all handy to the sights in this compact city.

Eating in Venice serves up a range of options, from inexpensive cafés to fancy restaurants.

Venice with Children includes my top recommendations for keeping your kids (and you) happy in Venice.

Shopping in Venice gives you tips for shopping painlessly and enjoyably, without letting it overwhelm your vacation or ruin your budget.

Nightlife in Venice is your guide to after-dark Venice, including gondola rides, concerts, theaters, pubs, and clubs.

Venice Connections lays the groundwork for your smooth arrival and departure, covering transportation by train, bus, car, plane, and cruise ship. It provides detailed information on Venice's two airports (Marco Polo and Treviso), train station (Santa Lucia), and cruise port (Stazione Marittima).

Day Trips include art-filled Padua and romantic Verona.

Venetian History fills you in on the background of this fascinating city.

The **appendix** is a traveler's tool kit, with telephone tips, useful phone numbers, the basics on transportation in Italy, recommended books and films, a festival list, a climate chart, a handy packing checklist, a hotel reservation form, and Italian survival phrases.

Browse through this book and choose your favorite sights. Then have a *buono* trip! Traveling like a temporary local, you'll get the absolute most out of every mile, minute, and dollar. As you visit places I know and love, I'm happy you'll be meeting my favorite Venetians.

Planning

This section will help you get started on planning your trip—with advice on trip costs, when to go, and what you should know before you take off.

Travel Smart

Many people travel through Italy thinking it's a chaotic mess. They feel any attempt at efficient travel is futile. This is dead wrong—and expensive. Italy, which seems as orderly as spilled spaghetti, actually functions well. Only those who understand this and travel smart can enjoy Italy on a budget.

This book can save you lots of time and money. But to have an "A" trip, you need to be an "A" student. Read it all before your trip, noting holidays, specific advice on sights, and days when sights are closed. If you save St. Mark's Basilica for Sunday morning (when it's closed), you've missed the gondola. You can sweat in line at the Doge's Palace, or you can buy your pass at the nearby Correr Museum and zip right through the palace turnstile. Day-tripping to Verona on Monday, when the major sights are closed, is bad news. A smart trip is a puzzle—a fun, doable, and worthwhile challenge.

Be sure to mix intense and relaxed periods in your itinerary. Every trip—and every traveler—needs at least a few slack days (for picnics, laundry, people-watching, and so on). Pace yourself. Assume you will return.

Get online at Internet cafés or your hotel, and buy a phone card or carry a mobile phone: You can find tourist information, learn the latest on sights (special events, English tour schedule, etc.), book tickets and tours, make reservations, reconfirm hotels, research transportation connections, and keep in touch with your loved ones.

Enjoy the friendliness of the Venetian people. Connect with the culture. Set up your own quest for the best piazza, vaporetto ride, or gelato. Slow down and be open to unexpected experiences. Ask questions—most locals are eager to point you in their idea of the right direction. Keep a notepad in your pocket for organizing your thoughts. Wear your money belt, learn the currency, and figure out how to estimate prices in dollars. Those who expect to travel smart, do.

Trip Costs

Six components make up your trip costs: airfare, surface transportation, room and board, sightseeing/entertainment, shopping/miscellany, and gelato.

Airfare: A basic, round-trip flight from the US to Venice (or even cheaper, Milan) can cost $980-1,600, depending on where you fly from and when (cheaper in winter).

Surface Transportation: Venice's sights are within walking distance of each other, but vaporetto boat rides, while expensive ($9), are fun and save time. For a one-way trip between Venice's airport and the city, allow about $4 by bus, $20 by Alilaguna water bus, or $140 by water taxi (can be shared by up to 5 people).

The cost of round-trip, second-class train transportation to day-trip destinations is affordable and depends on the speed of the train (about $8 to Padua by slow train, and about $50 to Verona by fast train).

Room and Board: You can manage comfortably in Venice in 2012 on an average of $130 a day per person for room and board. This allows $15 for lunch, $25 for dinner, and $90 for lodging (based on two people splitting the cost of a $180 double room that includes breakfast). Students and tightwads can enjoy Venice for as little as $65 a day ($35 for a hostel bed, $30 for meals and snacks).

Sightseeing and Entertainment: Figure about $10-20 per major sight (Accademia, Doge's Palace, Guggenheim), $5-10 for smaller ones (museums, climbing church towers), and $25-30 or more for splurge experiences (e.g., tours and concerts). A gondola ride costs $110 (by day) or $140 (at night); split the cost by going with a pal. An overall average of $35 a day works for most people. Don't skimp here. After all, this category is the driving force behind your trip—you came to sightsee, enjoy, and experience Venice.

Shopping and Miscellany: Figure $2 per postcard and $4-5 per coffee, soft drink, or gelato. Shopping can vary in cost from nearly nothing to a small fortune. Good budget travelers find that this category has little to do with assembling a trip full of lifelong, wonderful memories.

When to Go

Venice's best travel months (also its busiest and most expensive) are May, June, September, and October. These months combine the convenience of peak season with pleasant weather.

Summer in Venice is more temperate (high 70s and 80s) than in Italy's scorching inland cities. Most mid-range Venetian hotels come with air-conditioning—a worthwhile splurge in the summer—but it's usually available only from May (at the earliest) through September. Spring and fall can be cool, and many hotels do not turn on their heat until winter.

Between November and April you can usually expect mild winter weather (with lows in the 30s and 40s), occasional flooding, shorter lines, lower prices, and fewer tourists (except during the Carnevale festival). While Carnevale comes with high hotel prices, it's a big party, with special concerts, lots of kids' events, fresh pastries, and costumed figures crowding through the city. March and April offer a good balance of low-season prices and comfortable weather. (For specifics, see the climate chart in the appendix.)

Venice has two main weather patterns: Wind from the southeast (the Balkans) brings cold and dry weather, while the sirocco wind from the south (north Africa) brings warm and wet weather, pushing more water into the lagoon and causing flooding *(acqua alta)*. This shouldn't greatly affect your sightseeing plans. *Tabacchi* (tobacco shops) and some souvenir shops sell boots to keep your feet dry. Elevated wooden walkways are sometimes set up in the busier, more flooded squares to keep you above the water. And it's worth a trip to St. Mark's Square to see waiters in fancy tuxes and rubber boots.

Off-Season Travel Tips: Off-season has none of the sweat and stress of the tourist season, but sights may have shorter hours, lunchtime breaks, and fewer activities. Here are several things to keep in mind if you visit Venice off-season, roughly November through March.

• Most sights close early, often at 17:00.

• The orchestras in St. Mark's Square may stop playing at 18:00 (and may not play at all in bad weather or during their annual vacations, usually in March).

• Vaporetto #2 (the Grand Canal fast boat) terminates at the Rialto stop before 9:00 and after 20:00, which means no stops at San Marco and Accademia early in the morning and late in the evening (you can take the slow boat, vaporetto #1, instead).

• Expect occasional flooding, particularly at St. Mark's Square and along Zattere (southern edge of Venice, opposite Giudecca Island).

• Room prices can be about 25-50 percent less than those quoted in this book.

Know Before You Go

Your trip is more likely to go smoothly if you plan ahead. Check this list of things to arrange while you're still at home.

You need a **passport**—but no visa or shots—to travel in Italy. You may be denied entry into certain European countries if your passport is due to expire within three to six months of your ticketed date of return. Get it renewed if you'll be cutting it close. It can take up to six weeks to get or renew a passport (for more on passports, see www.travel.state.gov). Pack a photocopy of your passport in your luggage in case the original is lost or stolen.

Book rooms well in advance if you'll be traveling during peak season and any major **holidays** (see page 406).

In Padua, reservations are mandatory to visit the **Scrovegni Chapel,** famous for its frescoes by Giotto, so book well in advance (easily done online; see page 324).

Call your **debit- and credit-card companies** to let them know the countries you'll be visiting, to ask about fees, and more (see page 11).

Do your homework if you want to buy **travel insurance.** Compare the cost of the insurance to the likelihood of your using it and your potential loss if something goes wrong. For more information, see www.ricksteves.com/insurance.

If you're bringing a mobile device, you can download free information from **Rick Steves Audio Europe,** featuring audio tours of major sights, hours of travel interviews on Venice, and more (via www.ricksteves.com/audioeurope, iTunes, or the Rick Steves Audio Europe smartphone app; for details, see page 402).

If you're planning on **renting a car** in Italy, you'll need your driver's license. An International Driving Permit is also required (see page 396). If you drive in restricted areas monitored by cameras, you can be fined without a cop ever stopping you (see page 399).

If you're taking an **overnight train** and need a couchette *(cuccetta)* or sleeper—and you must leave on a certain day—consider booking it in advance through a US agent (such as www.raileurope.com), even though it may cost more than buying it in Italy. Other Italian trains, like the high-speed ES trains, require a seat reservation, but for these it's usually possible to make arrangements in Italy just a few days ahead. (For more on train travel, see the appendix.)

Because **airline carry-on restrictions** are always changing,

visit the Transportation Security Administration's website (www
.tsa.gov/travelers) for an up-to-date list of what you can bring on
the plane with you...and what you have to check.

Practicalities

Emergency and Medical Help: In Italy, dial 113 for English-
speaking police help. To summon an ambulance, call 118.

If you get sick, do as the Venetians do and go to a pharmacist
for advice. Or ask at your hotel for help; they'll know the nearest
medical and emergency services. For the hospital, see page 26.

Theft or Loss: To replace a passport, you'll need to go in
person to a US embassy (see page 385). If your credit and debit
cards disappear, cancel and replace them (see "Damage Control for
Lost Cards" on page 12). File a police report, either on the spot or
within a day or two; it's required to submit an insurance claim for
lost or stolen railpasses or travel gear, and it can help with replacing your passport or credit and debit cards. For more information,
see www.ricksteves.com/help.

Time Zones: Italy, like most of continental Europe, is generally six/nine hours ahead of the East/West Coasts of the US. The
exceptions are the beginning and end of Daylight Saving Time:
Europe "springs forward" the last Sunday in March (two weeks
after most of the US), and "falls back" the last Sunday in October
(one week before US). For a handy online converter, try www
.timeanddate.com/worldclock.

Business Hours: Traditionally, Venice uses the siesta plan,
though many businesses have adopted the government's recommended 8:00 to 14:00 workday. In tourist areas, shops are open
longer. People usually work from about 9:00 to 13:00 and from
15:30 to 19:00. Some stores and restaurants close on Sunday.
Banking hours are generally Monday through Friday 8:30 to 13:30
and 15:30 to 16:30, but they can vary wildly.

Saturdays are virtually weekdays, with earlier closing hours.
Sundays have the same pros and cons as they do for travelers in the
US: Sightseeing attractions are generally open, while shops and
banks are closed. Rowdy evenings are rare on Sundays.

Watt's Up? Europe's electrical system is 220 volts, instead of
North America's 110 volts. Most newer electronics (such as lap-
tops, battery chargers, and hair dryers) convert automatically, so
you won't need a converter plug, but you will need an adapter plug
with two round prongs, sold inexpensively at travel stores in the
US. Avoid bringing older appliances that don't automatically convert voltage; instead, buy a cheap replacement in Europe.

Discounts: Venice's city museums offer youth and senior
discounts to Americans and other non-EU citizens (bring ID).

Venice Almanac

Population: Approximately 270,000 people

Currency: Euro

Nicknames: *La Serenissima* and The Queen of the Adriatic

City Layout: The city of Venice is built on 117 small islands in the Venetian Lagoon along the Adriatic Sea. The historic center is broken up into six districts that hold the city's main attractions. These *sestieri* include Cannaregio, Castello, Dorsoduro, San Polo, Santa Croce, and San Marco.

Tallest Structure: The Campanile on St. Mark's Square reaches 325 feet and offers a beautiful view of the city. Good news: It has an elevator.

Tourist Tracks: Nearly 20 million tourists flock to Venice each year, with 30,000 roaming the streets each day of the Carnevale festival. St. Mark's Square is the most popular sight and the Rialto Bridge is the top photo spot.

Culture Count: The Venice population is almost entirely Italian (91 percent), although there are a small percentage of Romanian and East/West Asian immigrants. While Italian is the official language of Italy, about 2 million people in the Veneto region speak the Venetian dialect. Venetians predominantly practice Roman Catholicism, but other religions include Eastern Orthodox, Hinduism, and Buddhism.

Fun Food Facts: Venice is known for its wine bars *(bacari)* that serve small bite-sized snacks called *cicchetti,* which are similar to Spanish tapas. During Carnevale, look for *fritola,* tiny sugar-covered doughnuts.

Oldest Café: Caffè Florian, on the south side of St. Mark's Square, opened in 1720. Famous visitors include Lord Byron and Charles Dickens.

Average Venetian: The average Venetian is 46 years old, has 1.4 children, and will live until the age of 82. Half of the Venetian population works in some sector of the tourism industry. Even though Venice is surrounded by water, the lack of a sewage system means that fewer than 20 Venetians are plumbers. Venetians are more likely to have a gondolier license than a driver's license.

These museums include the Doge's Palace, Correr Museum, Clock Tower on St. Mark's Square, Ca' Rezzonico, Ca' Pesaro, Palazzo Mocenigo Costume Museum, Murano's Glass Museum, and Burano's Lace Museum.

News: Americans keep in touch via the *International Herald Tribune* (published almost daily throughout Europe and online at www.iht.com). Another informative site is http://news.bbc.co.uk. Every Tuesday, the European editions of *Time* and *Newsweek* hit the stands with articles of particular interest to travelers in Europe. Sports addicts can get their daily fix online or from *USA Today*. Many hotels have CNN and BBC News television channels.

Money

This section offers advice on how to pay for purchases on your trip (including getting cash from ATMs and paying with plastic), dealing with lost or stolen cards, VAT (sales tax) refunds, and tipping.

What to Bring

Bring both a credit card and a debit card. You'll use the debit card at cash machines (ATMs) to withdraw local cash for most purchases, and the credit card to pay for larger items. Some travelers carry a third card as a backup, in case one gets demagnetized or eaten by a temperamental machine.

As an emergency backup, bring several hundred dollars in hard cash in easy-to-exchange $20 bills. Avoid using currency exchange booths (lousy rates and/or outrageous fees); if you have foreign currency to exchange, take it to a bank. Don't use traveler's checks—they're not worth the fees or long waits at slow banks.

Cash

Cash is just as desirable in Europe as it is at home. Small European businesses (hotels, restaurants, shops, etc.) prefer that you pay your bills with cash. Some vendors will charge you extra for using a credit card, and some won't take credit cards at all. Cash is the best—and sometimes only—way to pay for boats, buses, taxis, and local guides.

Throughout Europe, ATMs (which locals call a *bancomat*) are the standard way for travelers to get cash. Most ATMs in Venice are located outside of a bank. Try to use the ATM when the branch is open; if your card is munched by a machine, you can immediately go inside for help.

To withdraw money from an ATM, you'll need a debit card (ideally with a Visa or MasterCard logo for maximum usability), plus a PIN code. Know your PIN code in numbers; there are only numbers—no letters—on European keypads. For security, it's best to shield the keypad when entering your PIN at an ATM. Although you can use a credit card for ATM transactions, it's generally more expensive because it's considered a "cash advance" rather than a "withdrawal."

When using an ATM, try to withdraw large sums of money to reduce the number of per-transaction bank fees you'll pay. If the machine refuses your request, try again and select a smaller amount

Exchange Rate

1 euro (€) = about $1.40

To convert prices in euros to dollars, add about 40 percent: €20 = about $28, €50 = about $70. (Check www.oanda.com for the latest exchange rates.) Just like the dollar, one euro is broken down into 100 cents. You'll find coins ranging from €0.01 to €2, and bills ranging from €5 to €500.

Look carefully at any €2 coin you get in change. Some unscrupulous merchants give out similar-looking, gold-rimmed old 500-lire coins (worth $0) instead of €2 coins (worth $2.80). You are now warned!

(some cash machines limit the amount you can withdraw—don't take it personally). If that doesn't work, try a different machine. Also, be aware that some ATMs will tell you to take your cash within 30 seconds, and if you aren't fast enough, your cash may be sucked back into the machine...and you'll have a hassle trying to get it from the bank. It's easier to pay for purchases with smaller bills; if the ATM gives you big bills, try to break them at a bank or larger store.

To keep your cash safe, use a money belt—a pouch with a strap that you buckle around your waist like a belt and wear under your clothes. Pickpockets target tourists. A money belt provides peace of mind, allowing you to carry lots of cash safely. Don't waste time every few days tracking down a cash machine—withdraw a week's worth of money, stuff it in your money belt, and travel!

Credit and Debit Cards

For purchases, Visa and MasterCard are more commonly accepted than American Express. Just like at home, credit or debit cards work easily at larger hotels, restaurants, and shops. I typically use my debit card to withdraw cash to pay for most purchases. I use my credit card only in a few specific situations: to book hotel reservations by phone, to make major purchases (such as car rentals, plane tickets, and long hotel stays), and to pay for things near the end of my trip (to avoid another visit to the ATM). While you could use a debit card to make most large purchases, using a credit card offers a greater degree of fraud protection (because debit cards draw funds directly from your account).

Ask Your Credit- or Debit-Card Company: Before your trip, contact the company that issued your debit or credit cards.

• Confirm your card will work overseas, and alert them that you'll be using it in Europe; otherwise, they may deny transactions if they perceive unusual spending patterns.

• Ask for the specifics on transaction **fees.** When you use your credit or debit card—either for purchases or ATM withdrawals—you'll often be charged additional "international transaction" fees of up to 3 percent (1 percent is normal) plus $5 per transaction. If your card's fees are too high, consider getting a card just for your trip: Capital One (www.capitalone.com) and most credit unions have low-to-no international fees.

• If you plan to withdraw cash from ATMs, confirm your daily **withdrawal limit** (€300 is usually the maximum). Some travelers prefer a high limit that allows them to take out more cash at each ATM stop, while others prefer to set a lower limit in case their card is stolen.

• Ask for your credit card's **PIN** in case you encounter Europe's "chip and PIN" system; since they're unlikely to tell you your PIN over the phone, allow time for the bank to mail it to you.

Chip and PIN: If your card is declined for a purchase in Europe, it may be because of chip and PIN, which requires card-holders to punch in a PIN instead of signing a receipt. While chip and PIN is not yet common in Italy, much of Europe, including Great Britain, Ireland, France, Belgium, the Netherlands, and Scandinavia, is adopting it. Chip and PIN is used by some merchants, and also at automated payment machines—such as those at train and subway stations, toll roads, parking garages, luggage lockers, bike-rental kiosks, and self-serve pumps at gas stations. If you're prompted to enter your PIN (but don't know it), ask if the cashier can swipe your card or print a receipt for you to sign. If not, just pay cash. If you're dealing with an automated machine that won't take your card, look for a cashier nearby who can make your card work.

You can avoid potential hassles by getting your own chip-and-PIN card just for your trip, but I don't recommend it. Travelex offers US travelers a chip-and-PIN card, called "Cash Passport," preloaded with euros or British pounds (www.travelex.com). While handy, this service comes with exorbitant exchange rates; it's probably not worth it unless you're staying for several weeks in a country that's converted to chip-and-PIN cards, and you're willing to pay for the convenience.

Dynamic Currency Conversion: If merchants offer to convert your purchase price into dollars (called dynamic currency conversion, or DCC), refuse this "service." You'll pay even more in fees for the expensive convenience of seeing your charge in dollars.

Damage Control for Lost Cards

If you lose your credit, debit, or ATM card, you can stop people from using your card by reporting the loss immediately to the respective global customer-assistance centers. Call these 24-hour US numbers collect: Visa (410/581-9994), MasterCard (636/722-7111), and American Express (623/492-8427).

At a minimum, you'll need to know the name of the financial institution that issued you the card, along with the type of card (classic, platinum, or whatever). Providing the following information allows for a quicker cancellation of your missing card: full card number, whether you are the primary or secondary cardholder, the cardholder's name exactly as printed on the card, billing address, home phone number, details of the loss or theft, and identification verification (your birth date, your mother's maiden name, or your Social Security number—memorize this, don't carry a copy). If you are the secondary cardholder, you'll also need to provide the primary cardholder's identification-verification details. You can generally receive a temporary card within two or three business days in Europe (see www.ricksteves.com/help for more).

If you promptly report your card lost or stolen, you typically won't be responsible for any unauthorized transactions on your account, although many banks charge a liability fee of $50.

Tipping

Tipping in Italy isn't as automatic and generous as it is in the US, but for special service, tips are appreciated, if not expected. As in the US, the proper amount depends on your resources, tipping philosophy, and the circumstances, but some general guidelines apply.

Restaurants: A service charge *(servizio)* is usually already included in your bill. If you're pleased with the service, you can round up the bill by a euro or two (though Italians don't). For more on tipping in restaurants, see page 267.

Traghetti, **Gondolas, and Water Taxis:** There's no need to tip on a cheap *traghetto* ride (a stand-up ride in a gondola across the Grand Canal); it'd be a little like tipping for a city bus ride. You also don't need to tip for a romantic gondola ride; you're already paying plenty. Water taxi drivers don't expect tips, but if the driver hauls your bags and zips you to the airport to help you catch your flight, they won't say "no" if you toss in a little more. But if you feel like you got on the slow boat to nowhere, skip the tip.

Special Services: Tour guides at public sights sometimes hold out their hands for tips after they give their spiel. If I've already paid for the tour, I don't tip extra, unless they've really impressed me. At hotels, if you let the porter carry your luggage, it's polite to give them a euro for each bag (another reason to pack light). I don't tip the maid, but if you do, you can leave a euro per overnight at the end of your stay.

In general, if someone in the service industry does a super job for you, a small tip (the equivalent of a euro or two) is appropriate...but not required.

When in doubt, ask. If you're not sure whether (or how much) to tip for a service, ask your hotelier or the tourist information office; they'll fill you in on how it's done on their turf.

Getting a VAT Refund

Wrapped into the purchase price of your Italian souvenirs is a Value-Added Tax (VAT) of about 20 percent. You're entitled to get most of that tax back if you purchase more than €155 (about $220) worth of goods at a store that participates in the VAT-refund scheme. Typically, you must ring up the minimum at a single retailer—you can't add up your purchases from various shops to reach the required amount.

Getting your refund is usually straightforward and, if you buy a substantial amount of souvenirs, well worth the hassle. If you're lucky, the merchant will subtract the tax when you make your purchase. (This is more likely to occur if the store ships the goods to your home.) Otherwise, you'll need to:

Get the paperwork. Have the merchant completely fill out the necessary refund document, called a "cheque." You'll have to present your passport.

Get your stamp at the border or airport. Process your cheque(s) at your last stop in the EU (e.g., at the airport) with the customs agent who deals with VAT refunds. Before checking in for your flight, find the local customs office, and be prepared to stand in line. It's best to keep your purchases in your carry-on for viewing, but if they're too large or dangerous to carry on (such as knives), have your purchases easily accessible in the bag you're about to check, ready to show the customs agent. You're not supposed to use your purchased goods before you leave. If you show up at customs wearing your new gondolier outfit, officials might look the other way—or deny you a refund.

Collect your refund. You'll need to return your stamped document to the retailer or its representative. Many merchants work with a service, such as Global Blue (www.global-blue.com) or Premier Tax Free (www.premiertaxfree.com), which have offices at major airports, ports, or border crossings (after check-in and security, probably strategically located near a duty-free shop). These services, which extract a 4 percent fee, can refund your money immediately in cash or credit your card (within two billing cycles). If the retailer handles VAT refunds directly, it's up to you to contact the merchant for your refund. You can mail the documents from home, or quicker, from your point of departure (using a stamped, self-addressed envelope you've prepared or one that's been provided by the merchant). You'll then have to wait—it can take months.

Customs for American Shoppers

You are allowed to take home $800 worth of items per person duty-free, once every 30 days. You can also bring in duty-free a liter of alcohol. As for food, you can take home many processed and packaged foods: vacuum-packed cheeses, dried herbs, jams, chocolate, oil, vinegar, and honey. However, fresh fruits and vegetables and most meats are not allowed. Any liquid-containing foods must be packed in checked luggage, a potential recipe for disaster. To check customs rules and duty rates, visit www.cbp.gov.

Sightseeing

Sightseeing can be hard work. Use these tips to make your visits to Venice's finest sights meaningful, fun, fast, and painless.

Plan Ahead

Set up an itinerary that allows you to fit in all your must-see sights. For a one-stop look at opening hours, see "Venice at a Glance" (page 44; also see "Daily Reminder" on page 24). Most sights keep stable hours, but you can easily confirm the latest by checking with the TI or visiting museums' websites. If you plan to visit Padua's Scrovegni Chapel, make reservations in advance (see page 323).

Don't put off visiting a must-see sight—you never know when a place will close unexpectedly for a holiday, strike, or restoration. On holidays (see list on page 406), expect reduced hours or closures. Many museums have shorter hours off-season.

When possible, visit the major sights in the morning (when your energy is best) and save other activities for the afternoon. Hit the highlights first, then go back to other things if you have the stamina and time.

Going at the right time helps avoid crowds. This book offers tips on doing this at specific sights. Try visiting popular sights very early, at lunch, or very late. Evening visits are usually peaceful with fewer crowds (see the "Venice Early and Late" sidebar on page 49).

Study up. To get the most out of the self-guided tours and sight descriptions in this book, read them before you visit.

At Sights

Here's what you can typically expect:

Some important sights have metal detectors or conduct bag searches that will slow your entry, while others require you to check daypacks and coats. They'll be kept safely. If you have something you can't bear to part with, stash it in a pocket or purse. To avoid checking a small backpack, carry it under your arm like a purse as you enter. From a guard's point of view, a backpack is generally a problem while a purse is not.

Flash photography is sometimes banned, but taking photos without a flash is usually allowed. Look for signs or ask. Flashes damage oil paintings and distract others in the room. Even without a flash, a handheld camera will take a decent picture (or just buy postcards or posters at the museum bookstore). If photos are permitted, video cameras generally are okay, too.

You'll likely have to pay cash for the admission fee; few sights take credit cards. Museums may have special exhibits in addition to their permanent collection. Some exhibits are included in the entry price, while others come at an extra cost (which you may have to pay even if you don't want to see the exhibit).

Expect changes—artwork can be on tour, on loan, out sick, or shifted at the whim of the curator. To adapt, pick up any available free floor plans as you enter, and ask the museum staff if you can't find a particular item. Say the title or artist's name, or point to the photograph in this book and ask, *"Dov'è?"* (doh-VEH, meaning "Where is?").

Many sights rent audioguides, which generally offer excellent recorded descriptions in English (about €4-7). If you bring along your own pair of headphones and a Y-jack, you can sometimes share one audioguide with your travel partner and save money. Take advantage of my free downloadable audio tours of the major sights (see page 21).

Guided tours in English are most likely to be available during peak season (usually €5-15 and widely ranging in quality). Some sights also run short films featuring their highlights and history. These are generally well worth your time. I make it standard operating procedure to ask when I arrive at a sight if there is a film in English.

Important sights may have an on-site café or cafeteria (usually a good place to rest and have a snack or light meal). The WCs at many sights are free and generally clean (it's smart to carry tissues in case a WC runs out of TP).

Many sights sell postcards and guidebooks that highlight their attractions. Before you leave, scan the postcards and thumb through the biggest guidebook (or skim its index) to be sure you haven't overlooked something that you'd like to see.

Most sights stop admitting people 30-60 minutes before closing time, and some rooms close early (often about 45 minutes before the actual closing time). Guards usher people out, so don't save the best for last.

Every sight or museum offers more than what is covered in

How Was Your Trip?

Were your travels fun, smooth, and meaningful? If you'd like to share your tips, concerns, and discoveries, please fill out the survey at www.ricksteves.com/feedback. I value your feedback. Thanks in advance—it helps a lot.

---

this book. Use the information in this book as an introduction—not the final word.

Find Religion

Churches offer some amazing art (usually free), a cool respite from heat, and a welcome seat.

A modest dress code (no bare shoulders or shorts for anyone, even kids) is enforced at larger churches, such as St. Mark's Basilica and the Frari Church, but is often overlooked elsewhere. If you are caught by surprise, you can improvise, using maps to cover your shoulders and a jacket for your knees. (I wear a super-lightweight pair of long pants rather than shorts for my hot and muggy big-city Italian sightseeing.)

Some churches have coin-operated audioboxes that describe the art and history; just set the dial on English, put in your coins, and listen. Coin boxes near a piece of art illuminate the art (and present a better photo opportunity). I pop in a coin whenever I can. It improves my experience, is a favor to other visitors trying to appreciate a great piece of art in the dark, and is a little contribution to that church and its work. Whenever possible, let there be light.

Traveling as a Temporary Local

We travel all the way to Italy to enjoy differences—to become temporary locals. You'll experience frustrations. Certain truths that we find "God-given" or "self-evident," such as cold beer, ice in drinks, bottomless cups of coffee, hot showers, and bigger being better, are suddenly not so true. One of the benefits of travel is the eye-opening realization that there are logical, civil, and even better alternatives. A willingness to go local ensures that you'll enjoy a full dose of Italian hospitality.

Europeans generally like Americans. But if there is a negative aspect to Italians' image of Americans (apart from our foreign policy), it's that we are big, loud, aggressive, impolite, rich, and a bit naive. Think about the rationale behind "crazy" Italian decisions. For instance, many hoteliers turn off the heat in spring and can't turn on air-conditioning until summer. The point is to conserve energy, and it's mandated by the Italian government. You could complain about being cold or hot...or bring a sweater in winter, and in summer, be prepared to sweat a little like everyone else.

While Italians, flabbergasted by our Yankee excesses, say in disbelief, *"Mi sono cadute le braccia!"* ("I throw my arms down!"), they nearly always afford us individual travelers all the warmth we deserve.

Judging from all the happy feedback I receive from travelers who have used this book, it's safe to assume you'll enjoy a great, affordable vacation—with the finesse of an independent, experienced traveler.

Thanks, and *buon viaggio!*

Back Door Travel Philosophy
From *Rick Steves' Europe Through the Back Door*

Travel is intensified living—maximum thrills per minute and one of the last great sources of legal adventure. Travel is freedom. It's recess, and we need it.

Experiencing the real Europe requires catching it by surprise, going casual..."Through the Back Door."

Affording travel is a matter of priorities. (Make do with the old car.) You can eat and sleep—simply, safely, and enjoyably—anywhere in Europe for $120 a day plus transportation costs (allow more in bigger cities). In many ways, spending more money only builds a thicker wall between you and what you traveled so far to see. Europe is a cultural carnival, and time after time, you'll find that its best acts are free and the best seats are the cheap ones.

A tight budget forces you to travel close to the ground, meeting and communicating with the people. Never sacrifice sleep, nutrition, safety, or cleanliness to save money. Simply enjoy the local-style alternatives to expensive hotels and restaurants.

Connecting with people carbonates your experience. Extroverts have more fun. If your trip is low on magic moments, kick yourself and make things happen. If you don't enjoy a place, maybe you don't know enough about it. Seek the truth. Recognize tourist traps. Give a culture the benefit of your open mind. See things as different, but not better or worse. Any culture has plenty to share.

Of course, travel, like the world, is a series of hills and valleys. Be fanatically positive and militantly optimistic. If something's not to your liking, change your liking.

Travel can make you a happier American, as well as a citizen of the world. Our Earth is home to nearly seven billion equally precious people. It's humbling to travel and find that other people don't have the "American Dream"—they have their own dreams. Europeans like us, but with all due respect, they wouldn't trade passports.

Thoughtful travel engages us with the world. In tough economic times, it reminds us what is truly important. By broadening perspectives, travel teaches new ways to measure quality of life.

Globetrotting destroys ethnocentricity, helping us understand and appreciate other cultures. Rather than fear the diversity on this planet, celebrate it. Among your most prized souvenirs will be the strands of different cultures you choose to knit into your own character. The world is a cultural yarn shop, and Back Door travelers are weaving the ultimate tapestry. Join in!

ORIENTATION TO VENICE

The island city of Venice is shaped like a fish. Its major thoroughfares are canals. The Grand Canal winds through the middle of the fish, starting at the mouth where all the people and food enter, passing under the Rialto Bridge, and ending at St. Mark's Square (Piazza San Marco). Park your 21st-century perspective at the mouth and let Venice swallow you whole.

Venice is a car-less kaleidoscope of people, bridges, and odorless canals. There are six districts (*sestieri*, shown on map on page 22):

San Marco (from St. Mark's Square to the Accademia Bridge), Castello (the area east of St. Mark's Square), Dorsoduro (the belly of the fish, on the far side the Accademia Bridge), Cannaregio (between the train station and the Rialto Bridge), San Polo (west of the Rialto Bridge), and Santa Croce (the "eye" of the fish, across the canal from the train station).

To find your way, navigate by landmarks, not streets. Many street corners have a sign pointing you to *(per)* the nearest major landmark, such as San Marco, Accademia, Rialto, and Ferrovia (train station). Obedient visitors stick to the main thoroughfares as directed by these signs...and miss the charm of back-street Venice.

Beyond the city's core lie several other islands, including San Giorgio (with great views of Venice), Giudecca (more views), San Michele (old cemetery), Murano (famous for glass), Burano (lace-making), Torcello (old church), and the skinny Lido beach.

Rick Steves' Free Audio Tours

I've produced free, self-guided audio versions of my tours of the major sights in Venice (download them via www.rick steves.com/audioeurope, iTunes, or my Rick Steves Audio Europe smartphone app). These user-friendly, easy-to-follow, fun, and informative audio tours are available for the Grand Canal, St. Mark's Square, St. Mark's Basilica, and Frari Church. Compared to live tours, these audio tours are hard to beat: Nobody will stand you up, the quality is reliable, you can take the tour exactly when you like, and they're free.

ORIENTATION

Planning Your Time

Venice is remarkably small. You can walk across it, from head to tail, in about an hour. Nearly all of your sightseeing is within a 20-minute walk of the Rialto Bridge or St. Mark's Square. Remember that Venice itself is its greatest sight. Make time to wander, explore, shop, and simply be.

Key considerations: Maximize your evening magic, and avoid the midday crowds around St. Mark's Basilica and the Doge's Palace. If you arrive in Venice at the end of the day, try taking the Grand Canal Cruise and St. Mark's Square Tour. These sights are more romantic and much less crowded after dark—and they provide a wonderful welcome to the city. (Also see "Crowd Control" tips in the "Daily Reminder" sidebar, later.)

Depending on when you visit, you may have to juggle the itineraries below, as sights' visiting hours will vary by season and day of the week.

Venice in One Busy Day

9:00 Take the Grand Canal Cruise, hopping off two times—first at the Mercato Rialto stop to enjoy the market action, and then at the San Tomà stop to tour the Frari Church.

12:00 Lunch near the Frari.

13:00 Catch the vaporetto (boat) to St. Mark's Square to explore.

14:30 Correr Museum (ticket bought here includes Doge's Palace).

15:30 St. Mark's Basilica (closes at 17:00).

17:00 Doge's Palace (closes at 18:30).

Venice's Districts

18:00   Tour St. Mark's Square.
19:00   Dinner—pub crawl or restaurant.
21:00   Gondola ride.
22:00   Enjoy the dueling orchestras with a drink on St. Mark's Square.

Venice in Two or More Days
Day 1
9:00   Walk to the train station and over the Calatrava Bridge to Piazzale Roma. Then catch the slow boat vaporetto (line #1) to take my self-guided Grand Canal Cruise.
10:30   Interrupt the tour, hopping off at Mercato Rialto to explore the market. Eat an early lunch of *cicchetti* (Venetian tapas) at the bars recommended on page 280.
13:00   Continue the Grand Canal Cruise, ending at St. Mark's Square.
13:30   Tour St. Mark's Square.
14:30   Correr Museum (ticket here includes Doge's Palace).
15:30   St. Mark's Basilica (closes at 17:00).
17:00   Doge's Palace (closes at 18:30).
19:00   Go up the Campanile bell tower for the city view (July-Sept only, when it's open until 21:00; in other months, squeeze it in on the afternoon of Day 2).
20:00   Dinner (make a reservation).
22:00   Enjoy the dueling orchestras with a drink on St. Mark's Square.

Day 2
9:00   Shopping or exploring.

10:00   Visit the Frari Church.

11:30   Tour Ca' Rezzonico (Museum of 18th-Century Venice).

13:00   Lunch (pizza near Accademia Bridge?).

14:00   Your choice: Tour Accademia, explore Dorsoduro neighborhood (wander back lanes to the Zattere promenade), or visit La Salute Church or Peggy Guggenheim Collection.

18:00   Commence pub crawl (perhaps on a pub tour with Alessandro—see page 35), eating dinner along the way.

20:00   Concert and/or gondola ride.

Day 3—Lagoon Tour

10:00   Catch boat at Fondamente Nove to San Michele (old cemetery), then continue to Murano.

11:00   Tour Murano, see glassworks.

13:00   Boat to Burano for lunch and browsing.

15:00   Shuttle boat to Torcello, tour church, back to Burano.

18:00   Take the long way back by boat via the Lido (but don't stop there—just enjoy a cruise on the lagoon).

20:00   Dinner and/or concert in Venice.

Day 4 and Beyond

Take a Venicescapes tour or other tour.

Visit the Church of San Giorgio Maggiore.

Follow additional self-guided neighborhood walks in this book.

Side-trip to Padua (30 minutes away by train).

Overview

Tourist Information

With this book, a free city map from your hotel, and the free *Shows & Events* booklet (described below), there's little need to visit a TI in Venice. That's fortunate, because the city's TIs are crowded and clunky. If you need to check or confirm something, TIs are located at the **train station** (daily 8:00-18:30), on **St. Mark's Square** (daily 9:00-15:30, in far-left corner with your back to the basilica), nearby at the **San Marco-Vallaresso vaporetto stop** (daily 11:00-18:00), and at the **airport** (daily 9:00-21:00). You can save time by phoning the TI at 041-529-8711 or visiting www.turismovenezia.it.

The TI publishes a useful, free booklet called *Shows & Events*, available at hotels and on the TI website (click on "Venezia"). It lists upcoming events and nightlife, museum hours, and emergency telephone numbers, and includes a vaporetto route map.

For a creative travel guide written by young Venetians,

Daily Reminder

Sunday: While anyone is welcome to worship, sightseers are asked to avoid Mass—which means that today, many churches are open to visitors only in the afternoon, including St. Mark's Basilica (14:00-17:00, until 16:00 Nov-March), Frari Church (13:00-18:00), and the Church of San Zaccaria (16:00-18:00). The Church of San Polo is closed all day. Today, the Rialto open-air market consists mainly of souvenir stalls (fish and produce sections closed). It's a bad day for a pub crawl, as most pubs are closed.

Monday: All sights are open except the Rialto produce market, Ca' Pesaro, and Torcello Museum (on the island of Torcello). The Accademia and Ca' d'Oro close at 14:00. Don't side-trip to Verona today, as most sights there are closed in the morning, if not all day.

Tuesday: All sights are open except the Peggy Guggenheim Collection, Ca' Rezzonico (Museum of 18th-Century Venice), Punta della Dogana, and the Lace Museum (on the island of Burano).

Wednesday/Thursday/Friday: All sights are open.

Saturday: All sights are open except the Jewish Museum.

Notes: The Accademia is open earlier (daily at 8:15) and closes later (19:15 Tue-Sun) than most sights in Venice. Some sights close earlier off-season (such as the Correr Museum, Campanile bell tower, St. Mark's Basilica, and the Church of **San Giorgio Maggiore**). Modest dress is recommended at churches and required at St. Mark's Basilica—no bare shoulders, shorts, or short skirts.

Crowd Control: The city is inundated with cruise-ship crowds and tours from mainland hotels daily from 10:00 to about 17:00. Crowds can be a serious problem at **St. Mark's Basilica.** Try going early or late, or even better, you can bypass the line if you have a bag to check (see page 85).

At the **Doge's Palace,** avoid the long line by purchasing your ticket at the less-crowded Correr Museum. You can also visit late in the day, buy your ticket online, or book a tour (see Doge's Palace Tour chapter).

For the **Campanile,** ascend late (it's open until 21:00 July-Sept), or skip it entirely if you're going to the similar San Giorgio Maggiore bell tower.

For the **Accademia,** go early or late—or you can reserve a ticket at least a day in advance by phone or online (see Accademia Tour chapter).

The sights that have crowd problems get even more crowded when it rains.

consider *My Local Guide Venice,* for its neighborhood histories, self-guided walking tours, and recommendations on sights and activities (sold at TIs for €13).

Maps: Of all places, you need a good map in Venice. Hotels give away freebies (no better than the small color ones at the front of this book). The TI sells a decent €2.50 map and miniguide—but you can find a wider range at bookshops, newsstands, and postcard stands. The cheap maps are pretty bad, but if you spend €5, you'll get a map that shows you everything. Investing in a good map can be the best €5 you'll spend in Venice. Map lovers should look for the book *Calli, Campielli e Canali,* sold at bookstores for €22.50, with 1:2000 maps of the whole city.

Arrival in Venice

For a rundown on Venice's train station and airport, and tips for drivers, see the Venice Connections chapter.

Sightseeing Passes for Venice

Venice offers an array of passes. For most people, the best choice is the combo-ticket, which covers entry into the Doge's Palace and more. Note that some major sights (Accademia, Peggy Guggenheim Collection, Scuola San Rocco, Campanile, and the three sights within St. Mark's Basilica that charge admission) are not covered on any pass.

Combo-Ticket: The combo-ticket for the Doge's Palace or Correr Museum, at opposite ends of St. Mark's Square, always gets you into the other museum as well (and includes two other museums within the Correr: the National Archaeological Museum and the Monumental Rooms of Marciana National Library). From April through October, this ticket costs €14 and gives you a single bonus entry into your choice of one of these other city-run museums: Ca' Rezzonico (Museum of 18th-Century Venice); Palazzo Mocenigo Costume Museum; Casa Goldoni (home of the Italian playwright); Ca' Pesaro (modern art); Museum of Natural History in the Santa Croce district; the Glass Museum on the island of Murano; and the Lace Museum on the island of Burano (full details at www.museiciviciveneziani.it; this €14 version is technically called the San Marco Museum Plus ticket). In winter (Nov-March), this ticket costs €13 and covers only the Doge's Palace and Correr Museum. To bypass the long line at the Doge's Palace, buy your combo-ticket at the Correr Museum or at any other included museum. Note that you can't buy an individual ticket for just the Doge's Palace or solely for the Correr.

Museum Pass: Busy sightseers may prefer this more expensive pass, which covers all eleven museums listed in the preceding paragraph, including the Doge's Palace and Correr Museum (€18, available all year). In general, this pass saves you money only if you visit five or more sights; before you buy, make sure they're sights you really want to see.

Chorus Pass: This pass gives church-lovers admission to 16 of Venice's churches and their art (generally €3 each)—including the Frari Church—for €10 (€20 family pass, www.chorusvenezia.org).

Venice Card: This pass combines the 11 city-run museums and the 16 churches covered by the Chorus Pass, plus a few minor discounts, for €40, but it's hard to make it pay off if you're over 29 (€30 for anyone under 30, valid 7 days, info at www.hellovenezia .com). Don't confuse this pass with CartaVenezia, a discount transit card used mainly by locals.

Rolling Venice: This youth pass offers discounts at dozens of sights and shops, but its best deal is for transit. If you're under 30 and want to buy a three-day transit pass, it'll cost you just €18—rather than €33—with the Rolling Venice pass (€4 for anyone 14-29, sold at TIs and HelloVenezia shops).

Venice Connected: This confusing web-based system allows you to buy vouchers exchangeable for sightseeing and transport tickets; it's generally not worth the trouble (www.veniceconnected .com).

Transportation Passes: Venice sells transit-only passes that cover *vaporetti* and mainland buses. For a rundown on these, see "Getting Around Venice," later.

Helpful Hints

Theft Alert: The dark, late-night streets of Venice are safe. Even so, pickpockets (often elegantly dressed) work the crowded main streets, docks, and *vaporetti* (wear your money belt, zip up your valuables, and watch your purse or day bag). Your biggest risk of pickpockets is inside St. Mark's Basilica.

A handy Polizia station is on the right side of St. Mark's Square (near Caffè Florian). To call the police, dial 113. The Venice TI handles complaints—which must be submitted in writing—about local crooks, including gondolier, restaurant, or hotel rip-offs (fax 041-523-0399, complaint.apt@turismovenezia.it).

It's illegal for street vendors to sell knock-off handbags and it's also illegal for you to buy them; both you and the vendor can get big fines.

Medical Help: Venice's Santi Giovanni e Paolo hospital (tel. 118) is a 10-minute walk from both the Rialto and San Marco neighborhoods, located on Fondamenta dei Mendicanti toward Fondamente Nove. You can take vaporetto #4.1 from San Zaccaria-Jolanda, or #5.2 from the train station or Piazzale Roma, to the Ospedale stop.

Be Prepared to Splurge: Venice is expensive for residents as well as tourists, as everything must be shipped in and hand-trucked to its destination. Perhaps the best way to enjoy Venice is just to succumb to its charms and blow a little money.

Take Breaks: Venice's endless pavement, crowds, and tight spaces are hard on tourists, especially in hot weather. Schedule breaks in your sightseeing. Grab a cool place to sit down, relax, and recoup—meditate on a pew in an uncrowded church, or stop in a café.

Etiquette: Walk on the right and don't loiter on bridges. On St. Mark's Square, a "decorum patrol" admonishes snackers and sunbathers. Picnicking is forbidden (keep a low profile). The only place for a legal picnic is in Giardinetti Reali, the small park along the waterfront west of the Piazzetta near St. Mark's Square.

Dress Modestly: Men should keep their shirts on. When visiting St. Mark's Basilica or other major churches, men, women, and even children must cover their shoulders and knees (or risk being turned away). Remove hats when entering a church.

Public Toilets: Handy public WCs (€1.50) are near major landmarks, including: St. Mark's Square (one is behind the Correr Museum, to the left of the post office; another is at the waterfront park, Giardinetti Reali), Rialto, and at the Accademia Bridge. Use free toilets whenever you can—in a museum you're visiting or a café you're eating in. Like Mom always said, "Just try."

Best Views: While the best views of Venice may be from water level, several upper-altitude viewing spots are also worth the ascent: On St. Mark's Square, try the soaring Campanile or St. Mark's Basilica (specifically the balcony of the San Marco Museum, requires admission). The Rialto and Accademia bridges provide free, expansive views of the Grand Canal, along with a cooling breeze. Or get off the main island for a view of the Venetian skyline: Ascend the Church of San Giorgio Maggiore's bell tower, or venture to La Giudecca island to visit the swanky bar of the Molino Stucky Hilton Hotel (free shuttle boat leaves from a dock near the San Zaccaria-M.V.E. vaporetto dock).

Pigeon Poop: If your head is bombed by a pigeon, resist the initial response to wipe it off immediately—it'll just smear into your hair. Wait until it dries, and it should flake off cleanly. But if the poop splatters on your clothes, wipe it off immediately to avoid a stain.

Water: I carry a water bottle to refill at public fountains. Venetians

ORIENTATION

pride themselves on having pure, safe, and tasty tap water piped in from the foothills of the Alps. You can actually see the mountains from Venice's bell towers on crisp, clear winter days.

Services

Internet Access: Almost all hotels have Wi-Fi, many have a computer that guests can use, and most provide these services for free. If Internet access is important to you, choose a hotel that doesn't charge for it. Otherwise, look for one of the handy, if pricey, little Internet places scattered around town, usually on back streets and marked with an @ sign. The going rate is €5/hour—more expensive than in other Italian cities. Ask your hotelier for the nearest place.

Post Office: The main post office is on Marzaria San Salvador, a few blocks toward St. Mark's Square from the Rialto, just beyond the Bata shoe store at #5016 (Mon-Fri 8:30-18:30, Sat 8:30-13:00, closed Sun). Branch offices (open shorter hours) are at Piazzale Roma, behind the Correr Museum, and elsewhere. Use post offices only as a last resort, as simple transactions can take 45 minutes if you get in the wrong line. You can buy stamps from tobacco shops and mail postcards at any of the red postboxes around town.

Bookstores: In keeping with its literary heritage, Venice has classy and inviting bookstores. The small **Libreria Studium,** a block behind St. Mark's Basilica, has a carefully chosen selection of new English books, including my guidebooks (Mon-Sat 9:00-19:30, Sun 9:30-13:30 & 14:00-18:00, on Calle de la Canonica at #337—see map on page 75, tel. 041-522-2382).

Used-bookstore lovers shouldn't miss the funky **Acqua Alta** ("high water") bookstore, whose quirky owner Luigi has prepared for the next flood by displaying his wares in a selection of vessels, including bathtubs and a gondola (daily 9:00-21:00, large and classically disorganized selection includes prints of Venice, just beyond Campo Santa Maria Formosa on Calle Longa Santa Maria Formosa at #5176, tel. 041-296-0841, mobile 340-680-0704). For a solid selection of used books in English, visit **Marco Polo,** on Calle del Teatro Malibran at #5886a, close to the St. Mark's side of the Rialto Bridge on the way to Corte del Milion (Mon-Sat 10:00-19:00, closed Sun, mobile 348-569-1125, www.booksmarcopolo .com).

Laundry: You'll find coin-operated launderettes near the train station and off Campo Santa Maria Formosa. I've listed details for a self-service *lavanderia* and a competitively-priced full-service laundry near St. Mark's Square (see page 245), and for a self-serve laundry near the train station (page 262). Or ask your hotelier for the nearest launderette.

Travel Agencies: If you need to get train tickets, make seat reservations, or arrange a *cuccetta* (koo-CHET-tah—a berth on a night train), save a time-consuming trip to Venice's crowded train station by using a downtown travel agency. Most trains between Venice, Florence, and Rome require reservations, even for railpass-holders. A travel agency can also give advice on cheap flights (book at least a week in advance for the best fares).

Near St. Mark's Square, **Oltrex Change and Travel** sells train and plane tickets and books train reservations for a €4 fee (tickets sold daily May-Oct 9:00-18:00, Nov-April 9:00-16:30; on Riva degli Schiavoni, one bridge past the Bridge of Sighs, at #4192—see map on page 75; tel. 041-524-2828, Luca and Beatrice).

Near Rialto, **Kele & Teo Travel** sells train tickets for a €4 per-person service charge (Mon-Fri 9:00-18:00, Sat 9:00-12:00, closed Sun; leaving the Rialto Bridge heading for St. Mark's, it's half a block away, tucked down a side street on the right at #5097; tel. 041-520-8722).

English Church Services: The **San Zulian Church**—the only church in Venice that you can actually walk around—offers a Mass in English (generally May-Sept Mon-Fri at 9:30 and Sun at 11:30, Sun only Oct-April, 2 blocks toward Rialto off St. Mark's Square, tel. 041-523-5383). **St. George's Anglican Church** welcomes all Christians to its English-language Eucharist (Sun at 10:30, located on Campo San Zio in Dorsoduro, midway between Accademia and Peggy Guggenheim Collection, www.stgeorgesvenice.com).

Haircuts: I've been getting my hair cut at **Coiffeur Benito** for nearly two decades. Benito has been keeping men and women trim for 28 years. He's an artist—actually a "hair sculptor"—and a cut here is a fun diversion from the tourist grind (about €20 for women or men, Tue-Fri 8:30-13:00 & 15:30-19:30, Sat 8:30-13:00 only, closed Sun-Mon; between St. Mark's Square and

Rialto, on Calle San Zulian Già del Strazzariol, by back corner of San Zulian Church at #592a; tel. 041-528-6221).

Getting Around Venice

On Foot

The city's "streets" are narrow pedestrian walkways connecting its docks, squares, bridges, and courtyards. To navigate, look for yellow signs on street corners pointing you to *(per)* the nearest major landmark. The first landmarks you'll get to know are San Marco (St. Mark's Square), Rialto (the bridge), Accademia (another bridge), Ferrovia (the train station), and Piazzale Roma (the bus station). Determine whether your destination is in the direction of a major signposted landmark, then follow the signs through the maze.

Dare to turn off the posted routes and make your own discoveries. While 80 percent of Venice is, in fact, not touristy, 80 percent of the tourists never notice. Escape the crowds and explore on foot. Walk and walk to the far reaches of the town. Don't worry about getting lost—in fact, get as lost as possible. Keep reminding yourself, "I'm on an island, and I can't get off." When it comes time to find your way, just follow the arrows on building corners or simply ask a local, *"Dov'è San Marco?"* ("Where is St. Mark's?") People in the tourist business (that's most Venetians) speak some English. If they don't, listen politely, watch where their hands point, say *"Grazie,"* and head off in that direction. If you're lost, refer to your map, or pop into a hotel and ask for their business card—it probably comes with a map and a prominent "You are here."

If you need to find a specific address, it helps to know its district, street, house number, and nearby landmarks. Every building in Venice has a house number, which is usually stenciled in red letters surrounded by a black oval above the doorway. The numbers relate to the district (each with about 6,000 address numbers), not the street. For example, say you wanted to find the recommended Acqua Alta bookstore at Castello 5176 (that is, in the Castello district, at house number 5176). It's on a street called Calle Longa Santa Maria Formosa, near the square called Campo Santa Maria Formosa, which in turn is near two major landmarks: the Rialto Bridge and St. Mark's Square. Once you've found Campo Santa Maria Formosa, you can look for a painted sign on one corner (like the one in this photo) which marks where the street begins. If you can find the Rialto Bridge and then the square—you can find the bookstore.

CALLE DE LA VERONA

Some helpful street lingo: *Campo* means square, *campiello* is a small square, *calle* is a street, *fondamenta* is the embankment along a canal or the lagoon, *rio* is a small canal, *rio terà* is a street that was once a canal and has been filled in, *sotoportego* is a covered passageway, and *ponte* is a bridge. Don't get hung up on the exact spelling of street and square names, which may sometimes appear in the Venetian dialect and other times in standard Italian. (Where streets and squares have Venetian names that differ significantly from the Italian, I list both.)

By Vaporetto

Venice's public transit system, run by a company called ACTV, is a fleet of motorized bus-boats called *vaporetti*. They work like city buses except that they never get a flat, the stops are docks (cheerfully painted yellow and white), and if you get off between stops, you might drown.

For most travelers, only two vaporetto lines matter: line #1 and line #2. These lines leave every 10 minutes (less frequently off-season) and go up and down the Grand Canal, between the "mouth of the fish" at one end and San Marco at the other. Line #1 is the slow boat, taking 45 minutes and making every stop along the way. Line #2 is the fast boat that zips down the Grand Canal in 25 minutes, stopping only at Tronchetto (parking lot), Piazzale Roma (bus station), Ferrovia (train station), San Marcuola, Rialto Bridge, San Tomà (Frari Church), Accademia Bridge, San Marco (west end of St. Mark's Square), and San Zaccaria (east end of St. Mark's Square).

Catching a vaporetto is very much like catching a city bus. You can buy either single-ride tickets (valid for 1 hour) or passes (valid for a variety of durations, from 12 hours to 7 days) from any ticket window or HelloVenezia office. HelloVenezia, run by ACTV, is a string of shops selling tickets and passes at the same prices as ticket windows (www.hellovenezia.com).

Before you board, validate your ticket by holding it up to the small white machine on the dock until you hear a pinging sound. The machine readout shows how long your ticket is valid—and inspectors do come by now and then to check tickets. If you board without a ticket (because ticket windows at odd hours or small stops may be closed), seek out the conductor immediately to buy a single ticket on board (or risk a €50 fine).

Large stops—such as San Marco, San Zaccaria, and Piazzale Roma— have multiple docks, and each dock has its own name,

Handy Vaporetti from San Zaccaria, near St. Mark's Square

Several *vaporetti* leave from the San Zaccaria docks, located 150 yards east of St. Mark's Square. There are four separate San Zaccaria docks spaced about 70 yards apart: Danieli, Jolanda, M.V.E., and Pietà. Although I list which specific dock these lines leave from, they often change from season to season—confirm before boarding.

- Line #1 goes up the Grand Canal, making all the stops, including San Marco-Vallaresso, Rialto, Ferrovia (train station), and Piazzale Roma (but it does not go as far as Tronchetto). In the other direction, it goes to the Lido. Line #1 departs from the San Zaccaria stop (usually from the Danieli dock).
- Line #2 zips over to San Giorgio Maggiore, the island church across from St. Mark's Square (5 minutes, €3 ride). From there, it continues on to the parking lot at Tronchetto (departs from the San Zaccaria stop, generally from the M.V.E. dock).
- Line #4.1 goes to San Michele and Murano in 45 minutes (departs from San Zaccaria stop, usually from the Jolanda dock).
- The #12 heads to Burano (70 minutes, from San Zaccaria stop, usually from the Pietà dock).
- The Molino Stucky shuttle boat takes even non-guests to the Hilton Hotel, with its popular view bar (free, 20-minute ride, leaves at 0:20 past the hour from near the San Zaccaria-M.V.E. dock).
- Lines #5.1 and #5.2 are the *circulare* (cheer-koo-LAH-ray), making a loop around the perimeter of the island, with a stop at the Lido—perfect if you just like riding boats. Line #5.1 goes counterclockwise (departs from San Zaccaria stop, generally from the Danieli dock), and #5.2 goes clock-

such as San Marco-Vallaresso, San Zaccaria-Jolanda, and Piazzale Roma-Parisi. Helpful electronic boards at larger stops display which boats are coming next and when, and give information for all docks at that stop.

At smaller stops, check the charts and signs to figure out which dock your boat will use. Signs on each dock show the vaporetto lines that stop there and the direction they are headed: Along the Grand Canal, a #1 or #2 boat might be headed toward St. Mark's Square wise (also departs from San Zaccaria, but usually from the Jolanda dock).

- The Alilaguna airport shuttle to and from the airport stops at the San Zaccaria stop (generally at the Jolanda dock).

(signposted *San Marco*), or back toward the mainland (signposted *Ferrovia, Piazzale Roma,* or *Tronchetto*). Sorting out the different directions of travel can be confusing, especially as boats on some circular routes travel in one direction (true for lines #5.1 and #5.2, plus the non-Murano sections of lines #4.1 and #4.2).

To clear up any confusion, ask a ticket-seller or conductor for help (sometimes they're stationed on the dock to help confused tourists), or look at the most current ACTV timetable (in English and Italian, free at ticket booths but often unavailable—can be downloaded from the ACTV website, tel. 041-2424, www.actv.it).

These are your ticket and pass options:

Individual Vaporetto Tickets: A single ticket costs a whopping €6.50. (Don't worry—cheaper passes are described below.) Tickets are good for one hour in one direction; you can hop on and off at stops and change boats during that time. Technically, you're not allowed a round-trip (though in practice, a round-trip is allowed if you can complete it within a one-hour span). Tickets are electronic and refillable. The fare is reduced to €3 for a few one-stop runs that are hard to do by foot, including the route from San Marco to La Salute, from Fondamente Nove to Murano-Colonna, and from San Zaccaria-M.V.E. to San Giorgio Maggiore.

Vaporetto Passes: You can buy a pass for unlimited use of *vaporetti* and ACTV buses: €16/12 hours, €18/24 hours, €23/36 hours, €28/48 hours, €33/72 hours, €50/7-day pass; pass must be validated once, before use. Because single tickets cost a hefty €6.50 a pop, these passes can pay for themselves in a hurry. Think through your Venice itinerary before you step up to the ticket booth to pay for your first vaporetto trip. The 48-hour pass pays for itself with five rides (e.g., to your hotel, on a Grand Canal joyride, into the lagoon and back, to the train station). And it's fun to be able to hop on and off spontaneously, and avoid long ticket lines. On the other hand, many tourists just walk and rarely use a boat.

Anyone under 30 years old can get a 72-hour pass for €18 if they also buy a **Rolling Venice** discount card for €4 (available from TIs, larger ticket windows, and HelloVenezia shops). Those settling in for a longer stay can ride like a local by buying the **CartaVenezia** ID card (€40/year, which lets you ride for about €1 per trip). See www.actv.it for details.

Passes are also valid on ACTV's mainland buses, including bus #5 to the airport (but not the airport buses run by ATVO, a separate company).

Vaporetto Tips: For fun, take the Grand Canal Cruise (see that chapter). Boats can be literally packed during the tourist rush hour. Morning rush hour (8:00-10:00) is headed in the direction of St. Mark's Square, as tourists and commuters arrive. Afternoon rush hour (about 17:00) is when they're headed in the other direction for the train station. Riding at night, with nearly empty boats and chandelier-lit palace interiors viewable from the Grand Canal, is an entirely different experience.

By Traghetto

Only four bridges cross the Grand Canal, but *traghetti* (gondola-like rowboats) shuttle locals and in-the-know tourists across the Grand Canal at eight handy locations (marked on the color map of Venice at the front of this book). Venetians stand while riding, but you shouldn't (€0.50, don't tip—

literally). Note that some *traghetti* stop running as early as 13:00 and all stop by 18:00.

By Water Taxi

Venetian taxis, like speedboat limos, hang out at busy points along the Grand Canal. Prices are regulated and listed in the TI's *Shows & Events* brochure: €13 for the first seven minutes plus €1.80 per minute thereafter; €5 per person for more than two passengers; and €8 between 22:00 and 6:00. Large bags cost €3 apiece. To the airport, a flat fee of about €100 for up to five people is common (for more information see the Venice Connections chapter). Despite regulation, prices can be soft; negotiate and settle on the price or rate before stepping in. For travelers with lots of luggage or small groups who can split the cost, taxi boat rides can be a worthwhile and time-saving convenience—and skipping across the lagoon in a classic wooden motorboat is a cool indulgence. For a little more than €100 an hour, you can have a private, unguided taxi-boat tour.

By Gondola

If you're interested in hiring a gondolier for your own private cruise, see the Nightlife in Venice chapter.

Tours in Venice

Avventure Bellissime Venice Tours—This company offers several two-hour walks, including a basic St. Mark's Square introduc-

tion called the "Original Venice Walking Tour" (€21.50, includes church entry, most days at 11:00, Sun at 14:00; 45 minutes on the square, 15 minutes in the church, one hour along back streets). Other walks include Cannaregio/Jewish Ghetto, "Hidden Venice," ghost stories and legends, and a Doge's Palace tour (€20, group size 8-22, English-language only, tel. 041-970-499, www.tours-italy.com, info@tours-italy.com, Monica or Jonathan). Their 70-minute Grand Canal boat tour is timed for good late-afternoon light (€40, daily at 16:30, 8 people maximum). They also offer small-group excursions to the Dolomites and Veneto hill towns. For a 10 percent discount on certain tours, say "Rick sent me."

Classic Venice Bars Tour—Debonair guide Alessandro Schezzini is a connoisseur of Venetian *bacari*—classic old bars

Is Venice Sinking?

Venice has battled rising water levels since the fifth century. But today, the water seems to be winning. Several factors, both natural and man-made, cause Venice to flood about 100 times a year—usually from October until late winter—a phenomenon called the *acqua alta*.

Simply put, Venice is sinking and the water is rising. Venice sits atop sediments deposited at the ancient mouth of the Po River, which are still compacting and settling. Early industrial projects, such as offshore piers and the railroad bridge to the mainland, affected the sea floor and tidal cycles in ways that made the city more vulnerable to flooding. Twentieth-century industry worsened things by pumping out massive amounts of groundwater from the aquifer beneath the lagoon for nearly 50 years before the government stopped the practice in the 1970s. In the last century, Venice has sunk by about nine inches.

Meanwhile, the waters around Venice are rising, a phenomenon that's especially apparent in winter. The highest so far was in November 1966, when a huge storm (the same one that famously flooded Florence) raised Venice's water level to more than six feet above the norm. The notorious *acqua alta* happens when an unusually high tide combines with strong sirocco winds and a storm. Although tides are miniscule in the Mediterranean, the narrow, shallow Adriatic Sea has about a three-foot tidal range. When a storm—an area of low pressure—travels over a body of water, it pulls the surface of the water up into a dome. As strong sirocco winds from Africa blow storms north up the Adriatic, they push this high water ahead of the front, causing a surging storm tide. Add to that the world-wide sea-level rise that's resulted from recent climate change (melting ice caps, thermal expansion of the water, more frequent and more powerful storms) and it makes a high sea that much higher.

If the *acqua alta* appears during your visit, you'll see the

serving wine and traditional *cicchetti* snacks. He organizes two-hour Venetian pub tours (€30, any night on request at 18:00, depart from the top of the Rialto Bridge, better to book by email—alessandro@schezzini.it—than by phone, mobile 335-530-9024, www.schezzini.it). Alessandro's tours include sampling *cicchetti* with wines at three different *bacari*, plus he'll answer all of your questions about Venice. (If you think of this tour as a light dinner with a local friend, you can consider it part of your eating budget.)

first puddles farthest from the sea—not near overflowing canals but in the center of paved squares, pooling around the limestone grates at the square's lowest point. These grates cover cisterns that long held Venice's only source of drinking water. That's right: Surrounded by the lagoon and beset by constant flooding, this city had no natural source of fresh water. For centuries, residents carried water from the mainland with much effort and risk. In the ninth century, they devised a way to collect rainwater

by using paved, cleverly sloped squares as catchment systems, with limestone filters covering underground clay tubs. Venice's population grew markedly once citizens were able to access fresh water by simply dropping buckets down into these "wells." Several thousand cisterns provided the city with drinking water up until 1886, when an aqueduct was built (paralleling the railroad bridge) to bring in water from nearby mountains. Now the wells are capped, the clay tubs are rotted out, and rain drains from squares into the lagoon—or up from it, as the case may be.

So what is Venice doing about the flooding? Since the 1966 flood, officials knew something had to be done, but it took about four decades to come up with a solution that some are still unhappy about. In 2003, a consortium of engineering firms began construction on the MOSE Project, which is expected to be operational by 2014. Named for the acronym of its Italian name, *Modulo Sperimentale Elettromeccanico*, it's also a nod to Moses and his (albeit temporary) mastery over the sea.

Underwater "mobile" gates are being built on the floor of the sea that will lie flat at the entrances of the three inlets that lead into Venice's lagoon. When the seawater rises above a certain level, air will be pumped into the gates, causing them to rise, and shutting out the Adriatic.

Will it work? Time...and tides...will tell.

Artviva: The Original and Best Walking Tours—This company offers a number of group and private tours, including a Venice in One Glorious Day Special and four themed tours (Grand Canal, Venice Walk, Doge's Palace, Gondola Tour). The 1.25-hour Gondola Tour (€66) includes a 35-minute gondola ride, followed by a 40-minute walk culminating at St. Mark's Square, while the two-hour "Learn to Be a Gondolier" tour teaches the ancient craft of rowing Venetian-style (€80, 4 people maximum). See the tour details and Rick Steves readers' discounts on their website (book in advance, tours run March-Nov, tel. 055-264-5033, www.italy .artviva.com, staff@artviva.com).

Venicescapes—Michael Broderick's private theme tours of Venice are intellectually demanding and beyond the attention span of most mortal tourists. But those with a keen interest and a desire to gain a solid understanding of Venice find him passionate and engaging. Rather than a "sightseeing tour," your time with Michael is more like a rolling, graduate-level lecture. See his website for descriptions of his various itineraries (book well in advance, tours last 4-6 hours: $250-290 for 2 people, $60/person after that, pay in dollars or the current euro equivalent, price includes maps and printed info but not admissions or transportation, tel. 041-520-6361, www.venicescapes.org, info@venicescapes.org).

Local Guides—Plenty of licensed, trained guides are available. If you organize a small group from your hotel at breakfast to split the cost (figure on roughly €70/hour with a 2-hour minimum), the fee becomes more reasonable. The following companies and guides give tours to individuals, families, and small groups.

Elisabetta Morelli guides many of my tour groups around Venice (€65/hour with this book in 2012, 2-hour minimum, tel. 041-526-7816, mobile 328-753-5220, www.elisabettamorelli.it, bettamorelli@inwind.it).

Walks Inside Venice is a group of three women enthusiastic about teaching (€70/hour per group with this book, 3-hour minimum; Roberta: mobile 347-253-0560; Cristina: mobile 348-341-5421; Sara: mobile 335-522-9714; www.walksinsidevenice.com, info@walksinsidevenice.com). They also do regularly scheduled small-group walking tours (see details on their site).

Venice with a Guide is a co-op of 10 equally good guides (www.venicewithaguide.com).

Alessandro Schezzini, mentioned earlier for his Classic Venice Bars Tour, isn't a licensed Italian guide and therefore can't take you into sights. But his relaxed, two-hour, back-streets "Rick Steves" tour does a great job of getting you beyond the clichés and into off-beat Venice (€15/person, see page 35 for contact info).

Tour Leader Venice, a.k.a. **Treviso Car Service,** offers small-group tours beyond Venice to 16th-century villas, wine-and-cheese tastings, and the Dolomites. Within Venice, their guided excursions include visits to the Rialto produce market, the lagoon, artisan shops, and a one-hour gondola tour (also provides airport transfers—see page 309, mobile 348-900-0700 or 333-411-2840; in Venice: www.tourleadervenice.com, info@tourleadervenice.com; beyond Venice: www.trevisocarservice.com, tvcarservice@gmail .com; Igor, Andrea, and Marta).

SIGHTS IN VENICE

Venice's greatest sight is the city itself. As well as seeing world-class museums and buildings, make time to wander narrow lanes, linger over a meal, or enjoy evening magic on St. Mark's Square. One of Venice's most delightful experiences—a gondola ride, worth ▲▲▲—is covered in the Nightlife in Venice chapter.

In this chapter, don't judge a listing by its length. Some of Venice's most important sights have the shortest listings and are marked with a ✪. These sights are covered in much greater detail in the individual tour chapters later in this book.

For information on sightseeing passes, see page 25. Venice's city museums offer youth and senior discounts to Americans and other non-EU citizens; see page 8.

San Marco District

▲▲▲**St. Mark's Square (Piazza San Marco)**—This grand square is surrounded by splashy, historic buildings and sights: St. Mark's Basilica, the Doge's Palace, the Campanile bell tower, and the Correr Museum. The square is filled with music, lovers, pigeons, and tourists by day, and is your private rendezvous with the Venetian past late at night, when Europe's most magnificent dance floor is *the* romantic place to be.

For a slow and pricey evening thrill, invest about €12-20 (including the cover charge for the music) for a drink at one of the elegant cafés with the dueling orchestras (see "Cafés on St. Mark's Square," page 78). For an unmatched experience that offers the best people-watching, it's worth the small splurge.

The **Clock Tower** (Torre dell'Orologio), built during the Renaissance in 1496, marks the entry to the main shopping drag, called the Mercerie (or "Marzarie," in Venetian dialect), which connects St. Mark's Square with the Rialto. From the piazza, you

can see the bronze men (Moors) swing their huge clappers at the top of each hour. In the 17th century, one of them knocked an unsuspecting worker off the top and to his death—probably the first-ever killing by a robot. Notice one of the world's first "digital" clocks on the tower facing the square (with dramatic flips every five minutes). You can go inside the Clock Tower with a pre-booked guided tour that takes you close to the clock's innards and out to a terrace with good views over the square and city rooftops. Reserve by calling 848-082-000, booking online at www.musei civiciveneziani.it, going in person at the Correr Museum a day in advance, or even just showing up at the Correr prior to a scheduled tour to see if space is available (€12 combo-ticket includes Correr Museum, where tour starts; tours in English Mon-Wed at 10:00 and 11:00, Thu-Sun at 14:00 and 15:00; no kids under age 6).

A good **TI** is on the square (with your back to the basilica, it's in the far-left, southwest corner; daily 9:00-15:30), and a €1.50 WC is 30 yards beyond the square (see *Albergo Diorno* sign marked on pavement, WC open daily 9:00-17:30). Another TI is on the lagoon near the San Marco-Vallaresso vaporetto stop (daily 10:00-18:00, walk toward the water by the Doge's Palace and go right, €1.50 WCs nearby).

For more about the square, ✪ see the St. Mark's Square Tour chapter.

▲▲▲St. Mark's Basilica (Basilica di San Marco)—Built in the 11th century to replace an earlier church, this basilica's dis-

tinctly Eastern-style architecture underlines Venice's connection with Byzantium (which protected it from the ambition of Charlemagne and his Holy Roman Empire). It's decorated with booty from returning sea captains—a kind of architectural Venetian trophy chest. The interior glows mysteriously with gold mosaics and colored marble. Since about A.D. 830, the saint's bones have been housed on this site.

Cost and Hours: Basilica entry is free, three interior sights charge admission, open Mon-Sat 9:45-17:00, Sun 14:00-17:00 (Sun until 16:00 Nov-March), St. Mark's Square, vaporetto stops: San Marco or San Zaccaria, tel. 041-270-8311, www.basilicasanmarco.it.

Billboards

As part of Venice's ongoing renovation, you may see not only scaffolding covering major monuments, but also advertising covering the scaffolding. Cash-strapped Venice is seeking funding from corporations in exchange for advertising space. Might there be Coca Cola ads covering St. Mark's Square? The mayor of Venice said of the possibility of more billboards: "It's not beautiful. It's not ugly. It's necessary."

The dress code is strictly enforced for everyone (no bare shoulders or bare knees). Lines can be long, and bag check is mandatory, free, and can save you time in line; for details, see the "Orientation" section in the St. Mark's Basilica Tour chapter. No photos are allowed inside.

Three separate exhibits within the church charge admission: the **Treasury** (€3, includes free audioguide), **Golden Altarpiece** (€2), and **San Marco Museum** (€4). The San Marco Museum has the original bronze horses (copies of these overlook the square), a balcony offering a remarkable view over St. Mark's Square, and various works related to the church.

○ See the St. Mark's Basilica Tour chapter.

▲▲▲**Doge's Palace (Palazzo Ducale)**—The seat of the Venetian government and home of its ruling duke, or doge, this

was the most powerful half-acre in Europe for 400 years. The Doge's Palace was built to show off the power and wealth of the Republic. The doge lived with his family on the first floor, near the halls of power. From his once-lavish (now sparse) quarters, you'll follow the one-way tour through the public rooms of the top floor, finishing with the Bridge of Sighs and the prison. The place is wallpapered with masterpieces by Veronese and Tintoretto. Don't worry much about the great art. Enjoy the building.

Cost and Hours: €14 combo-ticket includes admission to the Correr Museum and a third city museum of your choice; from Nov-March the combo-ticket is €13 and covers only the Doge's Palace

SIGHTS

Venice at a Glance

▲▲▲**St. Mark's Square** Venice's grand main square. **Hours:** Always open. See page 39.

▲▲▲**St. Mark's Basilica** Cathedral with mosaics, saint's bones, treasury, museum, and viewpoint of square. **Hours:** Basilica—Mon-Sat 9:45-17:00, Sun 14:00-17:00 (until 16:00 Nov-March); Treasury and Golden Altarpiece close 15 minutes before church; San Marco Museum—daily 9:45-16:45. See page 42.

▲▲▲**Doge's Palace** Art-splashed palace of former rulers, with prison accessible through Bridge of Sighs. **Hours:** Daily April-Oct 8:30-18:30, Nov-March 8:00-17:30. See page 43.

▲▲▲**Rialto Bridge** Distinctive bridge spanning the Grand Canal, with a market nearby. **Hours:** Bridge—always open; market—souvenir stalls open daily, produce market closed Sun-Mon, fish market closed Sun. See page 51.

▲▲**Correr Museum** Venetian history and art. **Hours:** Daily April-Oct 10:00-19:00, Nov-March 10:00-17:00. See page 46.

▲▲**Accademia** Venice's top art museum. **Hours:** Mon 8:15-14:00, Tue-Sun 8:15-19:15. See page 49.

▲▲**Peggy Guggenheim Collection** Popular display of 20th-century art. **Hours:** Wed-Mon 10:00-18:00, closed Tue. See page 50.

▲▲**Frari Church** Franciscan church featuring Renaissance masters. **Hours:** Mon-Sat 9:00-18:00, Sun 13:00-18:00. See page 52.

▲▲**Scuola San Rocco** "Tintoretto's Sistine Chapel." **Hours:** Daily 9:30-17:30. See page 52.

▲**Campanile** Dramatic bell tower on St. Mark's Square with elevator to the top. **Hours:** Daily Easter-June and Oct 9:00-19:00, July-Sept 9:00-21:00; Nov-Easter 9:30-15:45 except closed from Christmas to mid-Jan. See page 46.

▲**Bridge of Sighs** Famous enclosed bridge, part of Doge's Palace, near St. Mark's Square. **Hours:** Generally viewable, but covered with scaffolding during renovation. See page 47.

▲**La Salute Church** Striking church dedicated to the Virgin Mary. **Hours:** Daily 9:00-12:00 & 15:00-17:30. See page 50.

▲**Ca' Rezzonico** Posh Grand Canal palazzo with 18th-century Venetian art. **Hours:** Wed-Mon April-Oct 10:00-18:00, Nov-March 10:00-17:00, closed Tue year-round. See page 50.

▲**Punta della Dogana** Museum of contemporary art. **Hours:** Wed-Mon 10:00-19:00, closed Tue. See page 50.

▲**Ca' Pesaro International Gallery of Modern Art** in a canalside palazzo. **Hours:** Tue-Sun 10:00-18:00, closed Mon. See page 51.

▲**Scuola Dalmata di San Giorgio** Exquisite Renaissance meeting house. **Hours:** Mon 14:45-18:00, Tue-Sat 9:15-13:00 & 14:45-18:00, Sun 9:15-13:00. See page 57.

Church of San Zaccaria Final resting place of St. Zachariah, plus a Bellini altarpiece and an eerie crypt. **Hours:** Mon-Sat 10:00-12:00 & 16:00-18:00, Sun 16:00-18:00. See page 48.

Church of San Polo Ninth-century church with works by Tintoretto, Veronese, and Tiepolo. **Hours:** Mon-Sat 10:00-17:00, closed Sun. See page 53.

Nearby Islands

▲**San Giorgio Maggiore** Island across the lagoon featuring church with Palladio architecture, Tintoretto paintings, and fine views back on Venice. **Hours:** May-Sept Mon-Sat 9:30-12:30 & 14:30-18:00, Sun 8:30-11:00 & 14:30-18:00; Oct-April until 16:30. See page 48.

San Michele Cemetery island on the lagoon. **Hours:** Daily April-Sept 7:30-18:00, Oct-March 7:30-16:30. See page 58.

Murano Island famous for glass factories and glassmaking museum. **Hours:** Glass Museum open daily April-Oct 10:00-18:00, Nov-March 10:00-17:00. See page 59.

Burano Sleepy island known for lacemaking and a lace museum. **Hours:** Lace Museum open Tue-Sun April-Oct 10:00-18:00, Nov-March 10:00-17:00, closed Mon year-round. See page 59.

Torcello Near-deserted island with old church, bell tower, and museum. **Hours:** Most sights open daily March-Oct 10:30-18:00, Nov-Feb 10:00-16:30, museum closed Mon. See page 59.

and Correr Museum; both sights also covered by €18 Museum Pass. If the line is long at the Doge's Palace, buy your ticket or pass at the Correr Museum across the square; then you can go directly through the Doge's turnstile without waiting in line. Open daily April-Oct 8:30-18:30, Nov-March 8:00-17:30, last entry one hour before closing, tel. 041-271-5911, www.museicivicineziani.it. It's next to St. Mark's Basilica, just off St. Mark's Square. Vaporetto stops: San Marco or San Zaccaria.

Tours: The audioguide costs €5. For a 1.25-hour live guided tour, consider the Secret Itineraries Tour, which takes you into palace rooms otherwise not open to the public (€18 includes Doge's Palace admission but not Correr Museum admission; €12 with combo-ticket or Museum Pass; two or three English-language tours each morning). Reserve ahead for this tour in peak season— it can fill up as much as a month in advance. Book online at www .museicivicineziani.it or reserve by phone (tel. 848-082-000, from the US dial 011-39-041-4273-0892), or ask at the info desk.

✪ See the Doge's Palace Tour chapter.

▲▲Correr Museum (Museo Correr)—This uncrowded museum gives you a good overview of Venetian history and art. The doge memorabilia, armor, banners, statues (by Canova), and paintings (by the Bellini family and others) re-create the festive days of the Venetian Republic. There are English descriptions and breathtaking views of St. Mark's Square throughout the museum.

Cost and Hours: €14 combo-ticket also includes the Doge's Palace; from Nov-March the combo-ticket is €13 and covers only the Correr Museum and Doge's Palace; both sights also covered by €18 Museum Pass; open daily April-Oct 10:00-19:00, Nov-March 10:00-17:00, last entry one hour before closing; enter at far end of square directly opposite basilica, no photos, tel. 041-240-5211, www.museicivicineziani.it.

✪ See the Correr Museum Tour chapter.

▲Campanile (Campanile di San Marco)— This dramatic bell tower replaced a shorter lighthouse, part of the original fortress that guarded the entry of the Grand Canal. The lighthouse crumbled into a pile of bricks in 1902, a thousand years after it was built. Today you'll see construction work being done to strengthen the base of the rebuilt tower. Ride the elevator 300 feet to the top of the bell tower for the best view in Venice (especially at sunset). For an ear-shattering experience, be on top when the bells ring. The golden archangel Gabriel at the top always faces into the wind. Lines are longest at midday; beat the crowds and enjoy the crisp morning air at 9:00 or the cool evening breeze at 18:00.

Cost and Hours: €8, daily Easter-June and Oct 9:00-19:00, July-Sept 9:00-21:00, Nov-Easter 9:30-15:45, closed from Christmas to mid-Jan, tel. 041-522-4064, www.basilicosanmarco.it.

For more on the Campanile, see page 79 of the St. Mark's Square Tour chapter.

La Fenice Opera House (Gran Teatro alla Fenice)—During Venice's glorious decline in the 18th century, this was one of

seven opera houses in the city, and one of the most famous in Europe. For 200 years, great operas and famous divas debuted here, applauded by ladies and gentlemen in their finery. Then in 1996, an arson fire completely gutted the theater. But La Fenice ("The Phoenix") has risen from the ashes, thanks to an eight-year effort to rebuild the historic landmark according to photographic archives of the interior. To see the results at their most glorious, attend an evening **performance** (theater box office open daily 9:30-18:30, tel. 041-2424 answered daily 9:00-18:00, www.teatrolafenice.it).

You can also **tour the opera house** during the day. All you really see is the theater itself; there's no "backstage" tour of dressing rooms, or an opera museum. The auditorium, ringed with box seats, is impressive: pastel blue with sparkling gold filigree, muses depicted on the ceiling, and a starburst chandelier. It's also a bit saccharine and brings sadness to Venetians who remember the place before the fire. Other than a minor exhibit of opera scores and Maria Callas memorabilia, there's little to see from the world of opera. A dry 45-minute audioguide recounts two centuries of construction.

Cost and Hours: €8 tours, generally open daily 9:30-13:30, but can vary wildly, depending on the performance schedule—from being closed, open only an hour or two, or being open all day—so confirm in advance (call box office number listed above, schedule not posted on web). La Fenice is on Campo San Fantin, between St. Mark's Square and the Accademia Bridge. Nearest vaporetto stops: Santa Maria del Giglio and San Marco.

Behind St. Mark's Basilica
▲Bridge of Sighs—Connecting two wings of the Doge's Palace high over a canal, this enclosed bridge is currently surrounded by scaffolding for restoration.

Travelers popularized this bridge in the Romantic 19th century. Supposedly, a condemned man would be led over this bridge on his way to the prison, take one last look at the glory of Venice, and sigh. Though overhyped, when it's uncovered the Bridge of Sighs is undeniably tingle-worthy—especially after dark, when the crowds have dispersed and it's just you and floodlit Venice. A local legend says that lovers will be assured eternal love if they kiss on a gondola at sunset under the bridge.

The Bridge of Sighs is around the corner from the Doge's Palace: Walk toward the waterfront, turn left along the water, and look up the first canal on your left. You can walk across the bridge (from the inside) by visiting the Doge's Palace.

❂ See the Doge's Palace Tour chapter.

Church of San Zaccaria—This historic church is home to a sometimes-waterlogged crypt, a Bellini altarpiece, a Tintoretto painting, and the final resting place of St. Zachariah, the father of John the Baptist.

Cost and Hours: Free, €1 to enter crypt, €0.50 coin to light up Bellini's altarpiece, Mon-Sat 10:00-12:00 & 16:00-18:00, Sun 16:00-18:00 only, 2 canals behind St. Mark's Basilica.

❂ See the St. Mark's to San Zaccaria Walk chapter.

Across the Lagoon from St. Mark's Square

▲**San Giorgio Maggiore**—This is the dreamy church-topped island you can see from the waterfront by St. Mark's Square.

The striking church, designed by Palladio, features art by Tintoretto, a bell tower, and good views of Venice.

Cost and Hours: Free entry to church; May-Sept Mon-Sat 9:30-12:30 & 14:30-18:00, Sun 8:30-11:00 & 14:30-18:00; Oct-April until 16:30. The bell tower costs €3 and is accessible by elevator (runs from 30 minutes after the church opens until 30 minutes before the church closes).

Getting There: To reach the island from St. Mark's Square, take the five-minute ride on vaporetto #2 (€3, 6/hour, ticket valid for one hour; leaves from San Zaccaria-M.V.E. stop located east of Bridge of Sighs by equestrian statue, direction: Tronchetto).

❂ See the San Giorgio Maggiore Tour chapter.

Venice Early and Late

Most sightseeing in Venice is restricted to the hours between 10:00 and 18:00. Here are some exceptions:

Sights Open Early

Accademia: Daily at 8:15.

Doge's Palace: Daily April-Oct at 8:30, Nov-March at 8:00.

Campanile: Daily Easter-Oct at 9:00, Nov-Easter at 9:30.

Frari Church: Mon-Sat at 9:00.

La Salute Church: Daily at 9:00.

Scuola Dalmata di San Giorgio: Tue-Sun at 9:15.

San Giorgio Maggiore: Mon-Sat at 9:30, Sun at 8:30.

Scuola San Rocco: Daily at 9:30.

St. Mark's Basilica: Mon-Sat at 9:45.

San Marco Museum: Daily at 9:45.

Sights Open Late

Doge's Palace: April-Oct daily until 18:30.

Correr Museum: April-Oct daily until 19:00.

Campanile: Daily Easter-June and Oct until 19:00, July-Sept until 21:00.

Accademia: Tue-Sun until 19:15.

Punta della Dogana: Wed-Mon until 19:00.

Always Open

St. Mark's Square and the Rialto Bridge are always open, uncrowded in the early morning and magical at night.

SIGHTS

Dorsoduro District

▲▲**Accademia (Galleria dell'Accademia)**—Venice's top art museum, packed with highlights of the Venetian Renaissance, features paintings by the Bellini family, Titian, Tintoretto, Veronese, Tiepolo, Giorgione, Canaletto, and Testosterone. It's just over the wooden Accademia Bridge from the San Marco action.

Cost and Hours: €6.50, Mon 8:15-14:00, Tue-Sun 8:15-19:15, last entry 45 minutes before closing, no photos allowed. At Accademia Bridge, vaporetto: Accademia, tel. 041-522-2247, www.gallerieaccademia.org.

Avoiding Crowds: Expect long lines in the late morning, because they allow only 300 visitors in at a time; visit early or late to miss the crowds, or make a reservation at least a day in advance (€1 fee; calling 041-520-0345 is easier than reserving online at their clunky website; calls answered Mon-Fri 9:00-18:00, Sat 9:00-14:00, closed Sun).

○ See the Accademia Tour chapter.

▲▲Peggy Guggenheim Collection—The popular museum of far-out art, housed in the American heiress' former retirement palazzo, offers one of Europe's best reviews of the art of the first half of the 20th century. Stroll through styles represented by artists whom Peggy knew personally—Cubism (Picasso, Braque), Surrealism (Dalí, Ernst), Futurism (Boccioni), American Abstract Expressionism (Pollock), and a sprinkling of Klee, Calder, and Chagall.

Cost and Hours: €12, usually includes temporary exhibits, Wed-Mon 10:00-18:00, closed Tue, last entry 15 minutes before closing, free and mandatory baggage check, no photos inside, Dorsoduro 704, vaporetto: Accademia or Salute, tel. 041-240-5411, www.guggenheim-venice.it.

○ See the Peggy Guggenheim Collection Tour chapter.

▲La Salute Church (Santa Maria della Salute)—This impressive church with a crown-shaped dome was built and dedicated to the Virgin Mary by grateful survivors of the 1630 plague.

Cost and Hours: Free entry to church, daily 9:00-12:00 & 15:00-17:30. Sacristy—€2, may have shorter hours than church. It's a 10-minute walk from the Accademia Bridge; the Salute vaporetto stop is at its doorstep, tel. 041-241-1018, www.seminariovenezia.it.

○ See the La Salute Church Tour chapter.

▲Ca' Rezzonico (Museum of 18th-Century Venice)—This grand Grand Canal palazzo offers the best look in town at the life of Venice's rich and famous in the 1700s. Wander under ceilings by Tiepolo, among furnishings from that most decadent century, enjoying views of the canal and paintings by Guardi, Canaletto, and Longhi.

Cost and Hours: €8, covered by Museum Pass—see page 25, Wed-Mon April-Oct 10:00-18:00, Nov-March 10:00-17:00, closed Tue year-round, last entry one hour before closing, free and mandatory baggage check, at Ca' Rezzonico vaporetto stop, tel. 041-241-0100, www.museiciviciveneziani.it.

○ See the Ca' Rezzonico Tour chapter.

▲Punta della Dogana—This new museum of contemporary art makes the Dorsoduro a major destination for art-lovers. Housed in the former Customs House at the end of the Grand Canal, it features cutting-edge 21st-century art in spacious rooms. This isn't Picasso and Matisse, or even Pollock and Warhol—those guys are ancient history. But if you're into the likes of Jeff Koons, Cy Twombly, Rachel Whiteread, and a host of newer artists, the museum is world-class. The displays change completely about every year, drawn from the museum's large collection. In fact, the art spreads over two locations—the triangular Customs House and Palazzo Grassi.

Cost and Hours: €15 for one locale, €20 for both; Wed-Mon 10:00-19:00, closed Tue, last entry one hour before closing; audioguide-€5 (€8/2 people), small café; in Italy call 199-139-139, otherwise use tel. 041-523-0313; www.palazzograssi.it. Punta della Dogana is near La Salute Church (Dogana *traghetto* or vaporetto: Salute). Palazzo Grassi is a bit upstream, on the east side of the Grand Canal (vaporetto: San Samuele).

Santa Croce District

▲▲▲**Rialto Bridge**—One of the world's most famous bridges,

this distinctive and dramatic stone structure crosses the Grand Canal with a single confident span. The arcades along the top of the bridge help reinforce the structure...and offer some enjoyable shopping diversions, as does the **market** surrounding the bridge (souvenir stalls open daily, produce market closed Sun-Mon, fish market closed Sun).

○ See the St. Mark's to Rialto Walk chapter.

▲**Ca' Pesaro International Gallery of Modern Art**—This museum features 19th- and early 20th-century art in a 17th-century canalside palazzo. The collection is strongest on Italian (especially Venetian) artists, but also presents a broad array of other well-known artists. The highlights are in one large room: Klimt's beautiful/creepy *Judith II,* with eagle-talon fingers; Kandinsky's *White Zig Zags* (plus other recognizable shapes); the colorful *Nude in the Mirror* by Bonnard that flattens the 3-D scene into a 2-D pattern of rectangles; and Chagall's surprisingly realistic portrait of his hometown rabbi, *The Rabbi of Vitebsk.* The adjoining Room VII features small-scale works by Matisse, Max Ernst, Mark Tobey, and a Calder mobile. Admission also includes an Oriental Art wing.

Cost and Hours: €8, covered by Museum Pass—see page 25, Tue-Sun 10:00-18:00, closed Mon, last entry one hour before closing, 2-minute walk from San Stae vaporetto stop, tel. 041-524-0662, www.museiciviciveneziani.it.

Palazzo Mocenigo Costume Museum—The Museo di Palazzo Mocenigo offers a walk through six rooms of a fine 17th-century mansion with period furnishings, family portraits, ceilings painted (c. 1790) with family triumphs (the Mocenigos produced seven doges), Murano glass chandeliers in situ, and a paltry collection of costumes with sparse descriptions (€5, covered by Museum Pass—see page 25, Tue-Sun 10:00-17:00, closed Mon, last entry one hour before closing, a block in from San Stae vaporetto stop, tel. 041-721-798, www.museiciviciveneziani.it).

San Polo District

If you'll be walking from the Rialto Bridge to the following sights, note that they're all stops on the Rialto to Frari Church Walk (see that chapter).

▲▲**Frari Church (Basilica di Santa Maria Gloriosa dei Frari)**—My favorite art experience in Venice is seeing art in the

setting for which it was designed—as it is at the Frari Church. The Franciscan "Church of the Brothers" and the art that decorates it are warmed by the spirit of St. Francis. It features the work of three great Renaissance masters: Donatello, Giovanni Bellini, and Titian—each showing worshippers the glory of God in human terms.

Cost and Hours: €3, Mon-Sat 9:00-18:00, Sun 13:00-18:00, last entry 30 minutes before closing, no visits during services, modest dress recommended. On Campo dei Frari, near San Tomà vaporetto and *traghetto* stops.

Concerts: The church occasionally hosts evening concerts (€20, buy ticket at church, no concerts in winter). For concert details, look for fliers, check www.basilicadeifrari.it, or call the church at 041-272-8611.

○ See the Frari Church Tour chapter.

▲▲**Scuola San Rocco**—Sometimes called "Tintoretto's Sistine Chapel," this lavish meeting hall (next to the Frari Church) has some 50 large, colorful Tintoretto paintings plastered to the walls and ceilings. The best paintings are upstairs, especially the *Crucifixion* in the smaller room. View the neck-breaking splendor with one of the mirrors available at the entrance.

Cost and Hours: €7, daily 9:30-17:30, last entry 30 minutes before closing, tel. 041-523-4864, www.scuolagrandesanrocco.it.

A Dying City?

Venice's population (about 60,000) is half what it was just 30 years ago, and people are leaving at a rate of a thousand a year. Of those who stay, 25 percent are 65 or older.

Sad, yes, but imagine raising a family here: Apartments are small, high up, and expensive. Humidity and occasional flooding make basic maintenance a pain. Home-improvement projects require navigating miles of red tape, and you must follow regulations intended to preserve the historical ambience. Everything is expensive because it has to be shipped in from the mainland. You can easily get glass and tourist trinkets, but it's hard to find groceries or get your shoes fixed. Running basic errands involves lots of walking and stairs—imagine crossing over arched bridges while pushing a child in a stroller and carrying a day's worth of groceries.

With millions of visitors a year (150,000 a day at peak times), on any given day Venetians are likely outnumbered by tourists. Despite government efforts to subsidize rents and build cheap housing, the city is losing its residents. The economy itself is thriving, thanks to tourist dollars and rich foreigners buying second homes. But the culture is dying. Even the most hopeful city planners worry that in a few decades Venice will not be a city at all, but a museum, a cultural theme park, a decaying Disneyland for adults.

○ See the Scuola San Rocco Tour chapter.

Church of San Polo—This nearby church, which pales in comparison to the two sights just listed, is only worth a visit for art-lovers. One of Venice's oldest churches (from the ninth century), San Polo features works by Tintoretto, Veronese, and Tiepolo and son.

Cost and Hours: €3, Mon-Sat 10:00-17:00, closed Sun, last entry 15 minutes before closing.

Cannaregio District

Jewish Ghetto—Tucked away in the Cannaregio District is the ghetto where Venice's Jewish population once lived, segregated from their non-Jewish neighbors. While today's Jewish population is dwindling, the neighborhood still has centuries of history, not to mention Jewish-themed sights and eateries.

Getting There: From either the San Marcuola vaporetto

Jewish Ghetto

N

GHETTO

Rio de San Girolamo

FONDAMENTE DEI ORMESINI

PONTE DE GHETO NOVO

JEWISH SENIOR/ COMMUNITY CENTER

Rio del Batelo

HOLOCAUST MEMORIALS

PONTE DEL GHETO VECHIO

Campo de Gheto Novo

SOTOPORTEGO DEL GHETO NOVO

GHETO VECHIO

Rio di Gheto Novo

JEWISH COMMUNITY INFOPOINT

JEWISH MUSEUM & SYNAGOGUE

CALLE DEL FORNO

Corte Scala Mata

SYNAGOGUE

CALLE GHETO NOVISSIMO

Campo de la Scuola

To Rio Terà Farsetti & Rialto

C. DE LA MASENA

C. DE TIRACANA

C. DEL CONTERIE

GHETO VECHIO

To Ponte de le Guglie & Train Station

50 Meters

50 Yards

stop or the train station, walk five minutes to the Ponte de Guglie bridge that crosses the Cannaregio Canal. Cross the bridge and turn left. About 50 yards north of the bridge, a small covered alleyway (Calle del Gheto Vechio) leads between the *farmacia* and the Gam-Gam Kosher Restaurant, through a newer Jewish section, across a bridge, and into the historic core of the ghetto at Campo de Gheto Novo.

🟢 **Self-Guided Tour: Campo de Gheto Novo** must have been quite a scene in the 17th century, ringed by 70 shops and with all of Venice's Jewish commerce compressed into this one spot. Today there are only about 500 Jews in all of Venice—and only a few dozen live in the actual ghetto. The square is still surrounded by the six-story "skyscrapers" that once made this a densely packed neighborhood.

Today the square, with its three cistern wells, is quiet. The Jewish people you may see here are likely tourists. Look for the large Jewish senior center/community center (Casa Israelitica di Riposo), flanked by two different Holocaust memorials by the Lithuanian artist Arbit Blatas. The barbed wire and bronze plaques remind us that it was on this spot that the Nazis rounded up 200 Jews for deportation (only 8 returned). The Locanda del Ghetto at #2893 is

Jews in Venice's Ghetto

In medieval times, Jews were grudgingly allowed to do business in Venice, but they weren't permitted to live there until 1385 (subject to strict laws and special taxes). Anti-Semitic forces tried to oust them from the city, but in 1516, the doge compromised by restricting Jews to a special (undesirable) neighborhood. It was located on an easy-to-isolate island near the former foundry *(geto)*—in time the word "ghetto" caught on across Europe as a term for any segregated neighborhood.

The population swelled with immigrants from elsewhere in Europe, reaching 5,000 in the 1600s, the Golden Age of Venice's Jews. Restricted within their tiny neighborhood (the Gheto Novo, or "New Ghetto"), they expanded upward, building six-story "skyscrapers" that still stand today. The community's five synagogues were built atop the high-rise tenements. (As space was very tight and you couldn't live above a house of worship, this was the most practical use of precious land.) Only two synagogues are still active. You can spot them (with their five windows) from the square, but to visit them you have to book a tour through the Jewish Museum.

Relations with the non-Jewish community were complex: While Jewish moneylenders were treated harshly, Jewish merchants were more valued and treated with more respect. The island's two bridges were locked at night, when only Jewish doctors—coming to the aid of Venetians—were allowed to come and go. Eventually the ghetto community was given more land and spread to adjacent blocks.

In 1797, Napoleon opened the ghetto gates and ended its isolation. Complete emancipation for Venice's Jews came with the founding of the Italian republic in the 1860s.

the city's only kosher hotel.

The **Jewish Museum** (Museo Ebraico) at #2902b, a worthwhile stop, has just three rooms. Exhibits include silver menorahs, cloth covers for Torah scrolls, and a concise bilingual exhibit on the Venetian Jewish community up through 1797 (€3, June-Sept Sun-Fri 10:00-19:00, Oct-May Sun-Fri 10:00-17:30, closed Sat and Jewish holidays, bookstore, small café, Campo de Gheto Novo, tel. 041-715-359, www.museoebraico.it). You can see three of the ghetto's five **synagogues** with the 45-minute English tour (€8.50, tours run hourly on the half-hour June-Sept Sun-Fri 10:30-17:30, Oct-May Sun-Fri 10:30-16:30, no tours Sat and Jewish holidays). Group sizes are limited (the 11:30 and 12:30 tours are the most popular), so show up 20 minutes early to be sure you get in.

Backtrack across the bridge that you came in on, and look on the left for the **information point** run by the Jewish community, at

#1222, where Anat Shriki answers questions about ghetto history in fluent English (Mon 9:30-13:30, Tue-Thu 9:30-15:30, Fri 9:30-14:30, closed Sat-Sun, on Calle del Gheto Vechio, no phone, com .ebra@ve.191.it).

Return to the square and exit through Sotoportego del Gheto Novo for the best view of the "fortress ghetto," with tall tenement buildings rising from the canal and an easy-to-lock-up little bridge and gateway.

Venice's Jewish cemetery is on the Lido. For information about cemetery tours, contact the Jewish Museum.

Calatrava Bridge (a.k.a. Ponte della Costituzione)—This controversial bridge, officially called "Constitution Bridge," is just upstream and around the bend from the train station. Only the fourth bridge to cross the Grand Canal, it carries foot traffic between the train station and Piazzale Roma. A modern structure of glass, steel, and stone, the bridge finally opened in 2008 after delays, cost overruns, and questions about its stability.

The bridge was designed by Spanish architect Santiago Calatrava, whose other projects include a museum in his hometown of Valencia, Spain; the twisting torso skyscraper in Malmö, Sweden; and the Olympic Sports complex in Athens, Greece.

The bridge draws snorts from Venetians. With an original price tag of €4 million, the cost rose to around €11 million. The modern design of the bridge is also a sore point for a city with such rich medieval and Renaissance architecture. And, to add practical insult to aesthetic injury, critics say the heavy bridge is crushing the centuries-old foundations at either end, threatening nearby buildings.

Interestingly, Calatrava's modern structure harkens back to the past, employing the same low-arch design of many older Venetian bridges. Pedestrians walk over similar shallow stair steps, and the bridge uses local Istrian stone.

Ca' d'Oro—This "House of Gold" palace, fronting the Grand Canal, is quintessential Venetian Gothic (Gothic seasoned with Byzantine and Islamic accents—see "Ca' d'Oro" on page 66). Inside, the permanent collection includes a few big names in Renaissance painting—Ghirlandaio, Signorelli, and Mantegna; a glimpse at a lush courtyard; and a grand view of the Grand Canal.

Cost and Hours: €6, slow and dry audioguide-€4, Mon 8:15-14:00, Tue-Sun 8:15-19:15, last entry 30 minutes before closing, free peek through hole in door of courtyard, vaporetto: Ca' d'Oro, on Calle Ca' d'Oro at #3932, tel. 041-520-0345, www.cadoro.org.

Castello District

▲**Scuola Dalmata di San Giorgio**—This little-visited "school" (which means "meeting place") features an exquisite wood-paneled chapel decorated with the world's best collection of paintings by Vittorio Carpaccio (1465-1526).

The Scuola, a reminder that cosmopolitan Venice was once Europe's melting-pot, was one of a hundred such community centers for various ethnic, religious, and economic groups, supported by the government partly to keep an eye on foreigners. It was here that the Dalmatians (from the southern coast of present-day Croatia) worshipped in their own way, held neighborhood meetings, and preserved their culture.

Cost and Hours: €4, Mon 14:45-18:00, Tue-Sat 9:15-13:00 & 14:45-18:00, Sun 9:15-13:00, on Calle dei Furlani at #3259a, tel. 041-522-8828.

Getting There: The Scuola is located midway between St. Mark's Square and the Arsenale. Go north from Campo San Provolo (by Church of San Zaccaria), following the street as it changes names from L'Osmarin to St. George to Greci. At the second bridge, turn left on Fondamenta dei Furlani.

◐ Self-Guided Tour: The chapel on the ground floor is one of the best-preserved Renaissance interiors in Venice. Ringing the room is the cycle of paintings that Carpaccio was hired to paint (1502-1507). Pick up the English explanation from the ticket booth.

The scenes tell the story of St. George (the Dalmatians' patron saint), who slew a dragon and metaphorically conquered paganism. Carpaccio cuts right to the climax. In the first panel on the far left, George meets the dragon on the barren plain, charges forward, and jams his spear through the dragon's skull, to the relief of the damsel in distress (in red). George gets there just in time—notice half a damsel on the ground. This painting is one of Carpaccio's masterpieces. He places George and the dragon directly facing each other. Meanwhile, the center of the composition—where George meets dragon—is also the "vanishing point" that draws your eye to the distant horizon. Very clever.

The story of St. George continues in the next panel, as George leads the bedraggled dragon (spear still in his head) before the thankful, wealthy pagan king and queen. Next, they kneel before George (now in red, far right) as he holds a pan of water, baptizing them.

The rest of the panels (about St. Jerome and St. Tryphone) are also by Carpaccio. In the last panel on the right, St. Augustine pauses while writing. He hears something. The dog hears it, too. It's the encouraging voice of St. Jerome, echoing mysteriously through the spacious room. Carpaccio sweated small details like the scattered books and the shadow cast by the statue of Christ.

In the adjoining room, see the cross and censers (incense burners) used by the community in religious processions. Upstairs, there's another paneled room with more depictions of St. George (but not by Carpaccio).

Santa Elena—For a pleasant peek into a completely non-touristy, residential side of Venice, walk or catch vaporetto #1 from St. Mark's Square to the neighborhood of Santa Elena (at the fish's tail). This 100-year-old suburb lives as if there were no tourism. You'll find a kid-friendly park, a few lazy restaurants, and beautiful sunsets over San Marco.

La Biennale—Every odd year (next in 2013), Venice hosts a world's fair of contemporary art in buildings and pavilions scattered over the Giardini park and the Arsenale. The festival is an excuse for temporary art exhibitions, concerts, and other cultural events around the city (see "Holidays and Festivals" in the appendix, roughly Feb-Nov, take vaporetto #1 or #2 to Giardini-Biennale stop, www.labiennale.org).

Venice's Lagoon

With more time, venture to some nearby islands in Venice's lagoon. While still somewhat touristy, they offer an escape from the crowds, a chance to get out on a boat, and some enjoyable diversions for fans of glassmaking and lace.

The islands are listed in order of proximity to Venice, from nearest to farthest. For more information, ✪ see the Venice's Lagoon Tour chapter.

San Michele (a.k.a. Cimitero)—This island is the final resting place of Venetians and a few foreign VIPs, from poet Ezra Pound to composer Igor Stravinsky. Many visitors find this island (expectedly) pretty dead.

Murano—Famous for its glassmaking, this island is home to several glass factories and the **Glass Museum** (Museo Vetrario), which traces the history of this delicate art (€6.50, covered by Museum Pass—see page 25, daily April-Oct 10:00-18:00, Nov-March 10:00-17:00, tel. 041-739-586, www.museicivi civeneziani.it).

Burano—This island's claim to fame is lacemaking, and (along with countless lace shops) it offers a delightful pastel village alternative to big, bustling Venice. Its **Lace Museum** (Museo del Merletto di Burano) is newly renovated (€5.50, covered by Museum Pass—see page 25; Tue-Sun April-Oct 10:00-18:00, Nov-March Wed-Mon 10:00-17:00, closed Mon year-round, last entry 30 minutes before closing, tel. 041-730-034, www.museiciviciveneziani.it).

Torcello—This sparsely populated island features what's claimed to be Venice's oldest church. With impressive mosaics, a climbable bell tower, and a modest museum of Roman sculpture and medieval sculpture and manuscripts, the church is worth a wander (tickets for each sight cost €3-5 or €12 for all sights plus an audioguide; most sights open daily March-Oct 10:30-18:00, Nov-Feb 10:00-16:30, museum closed Mon; museum tel. 041-730-761, church/bell tower tel. 041-730-119).

GRAND CANAL CRUISE

Canal Grande

Take a joyride and introduce yourself to Venice by boat. Cruise the Canal Grande all the way to San Marco, starting at the train station (Ferrovia) or the bus station (Piazzale Roma).

If it's your first trip down the Grand Canal, you might want to stow this book and just take it all in—Venice is a barrage on the senses that hardly needs narration. But these notes give the cruise a little meaning and help orient you to this great city.

This tour is designed to be done on the slow boat #1 (which takes about 45 minutes). The express boat #2 travels the same route, but it skips many stops and takes only 25 minutes, making it hard to sightsee. Also, some #2 boats terminate at Rialto; confirm that you're on a boat that goes all the way to San Marco.

To help you enjoy the visual parade of canal wonders, I've organized this tour by boat stop. I'll point out both what you can see from the current stop, and what to look forward to as you cruise to the next stop. If you download my free audio tour, you won't even have to look at the book (see "Audio Tour" on the next page).

Orientation

Length of This Tour: Allow 45 minutes (25 minutes for an express version on vaporetto #2).

Cost: €6.50 for a 60-minute vaporetto ticket (or covered by a pass). For more on riding the vaporetto, see page 31.

When to Go: Boats run every 10 minutes. Enjoy the best light and the fewest crowds by riding late in the day. Avoid the morning rush hour (8:00-10:00), when local workers and tourists commute into town (from Ferrovia to San Marco—in the same direction as this tour). In the evening, the crowds head the opposite way, and boats to San Marco are less crowded.

Sunset bathes the buildings in gold; after dark, chandeliers light up building interiors.

Getting There: This tour starts at the Ferrovia vaporetto stop (at Santa Lucia train station). It also works if you board upstream from Ferrovia at Piazzale Roma (where airport buses and the People Mover monorail from Tronchetto arrive), a short walk from Ferrovia over the Calatrava Bridge. Just start the tour when your vaporetto reaches Ferrovia.

Tips: You're more likely to find an empty seat if you catch the vaporetto at Piazzale Roma.

Stops to Consider: You can break up the tour by hopping on and off at various sights described in greater depth elsewhere in this book (but remember, a single-fare vaporetto ticket is good for just 60 minutes; passes let you hop on and off all day).

These are all worth considering as hop-off spots: San Marcuola (near the Jewish Ghetto), Mercato Rialto (fish market and famous bridge), Ca' Rezzonico (Museum of 18th-Century Venice), Accademia (art museum and the nearby Guggenheim Collection), and Salute (huge and interesting church).

Information: Some city maps (on sale at postcard racks) have a handy Grand Canal map on the back.

Audio Tour: You can download a free audio version of this tour for your mobile device via www.ricksteves.com/audioeurope, iTunes, or the Rick Steves Audio Europe smartphone app.

Sightseeing Tips: As you board the vaporetto, make a beeline for an open-air seat in the front of the boat, which has the best seats for this tour. From the front, you can easily look left, right, and forward. If you find yourself stuck on the side or in the cabin, do your best. Avoid sitting in the back, only because you'll miss the wonderful forward views.

Some readers do this cruise twice—once in either direction—because it's hard to see it all while trying to read along aboard a moving boat.

Starring: Palaces, markets, boats, bridges—Venice.

The Tour Begins

While you wait for your boat, here's some background on Venice's "Main Street."

At more than two miles long, nearly 150 feet wide, and nearly 15 feet deep, the Grand Canal is the city's largest canal, lined with its most impressive palaces. It's the remnant of a river that once spilled from the mainland into the Adriatic. The sediment it carried formed barrier islands that cut Venice off from the sea, forming a lagoon.

Grand Canal

To Jewish Ghetto

To Jewish Ghetto

STRADA

GUGLIE BRIDGE

Canale de Cannaregio

SAN GEREMIA

PALAZZO CORRER CONTARINI

SAN MARCUOLA

PALAZZO GRITTI

CASINÒ
PALAZZO VENDRAMIN CALERGI

SANTA LUCIA TRAIN STATION (FERROVIA)

SCALZI

LISTA DI SPAGNA

PALAZZO FLANGINI

Grand

Canal

❷

❸

PALAZZO CALBO-CROTTA

Grand

PALAZZO MARCELLO

PALAZZO GIOVANELLI

TURKISH "FONDACO" EXCHANGE

SCALZI BRIDGE

❶

PAL. GRITTI

PALAZZO DONA BALBI

SAN ZAN DEGOLA

PALAZZO CA' TRON

SANTA CROCE

SAN SIMEONE PICCOLO

SAN

CALATRAVA BRIDGE

PIAZZALE ROMA
& PEOPLE MOVER TO STAZIONE MARITTIMA & TRONCHETTO

FRARI

PALAZZO CAPPELLO-LAYARD

Vaporetto Stops

❶ Ferrovia
❷ Riva de Biasio
❸ San Marcuola
❹ San Stae
❺ Ca' d'Oro
❻ Mercato Rialto
❼ Rialto
❽ San Silvestro
❾ Sant'Angelo
❿ San Tomà
⓫ Ca' Rezzonico
⓬ Accademia
⓭ Santa Maria del Giglio
⓮ Salute
⓯ San Marco
⓰ San Zaccaria

SAN TOMÀ

PALAZZO GIUSTINIANI

PALAZZO BARBARIGO

❾

PALAZZO BALBI

❿

PALAZZO MOCENIGO

FIRE STATION

CA' FOSCARI

PALAZZO VECCHIA

PALAZZO GIUSTINIAN

PALAZZO MORO LIN

PALAZZO GRASSI

CA' REZZONICO

⓫

PALAZZO MALIPIERO-CAPPELLO

PALAZZO LOREDAN

PALAZZO FALIER

PALAZZO CONTARINI DEGLI SCRIGNI

PALAZZO GIUSTINIAN LOLIN

PALAZZO QUERINI

⓬

ACCADEMIA BRIDGE & GALLERY

PALAZZO BARBARO

PALAZZO BARBARIGO

FONDAMENTA ZATTERE AL PONTE LONGO

Giudecca Canal

DORSODURO

To Zattere

GRAND CANAL CRUISE

Venice was built on the marshy islands of the former delta, sitting on wood pilings driven nearly 15 feet into the clay (alder was the preferred wood). About 25 miles of canals drain the city, dumping like streams into the Grand Canal. Technically, Venice has only three canals: Grand, Giudecca, and Cannaregio. The 45 small waterways that dump into the Grand Canal are referred to as rivers (e.g., Rio Novo).

Venice is a city of palaces, dating from the days when the city was the world's richest. The most lavish palaces formed a grand

chorus line along the Grand Canal. Once frescoed in reds and blues, with black-and-white borders and gold-leaf trim, they made Venice a city of dazzling color. This cruise is the only way to truly appreciate the palaces, approaching them at water level, where their main entrances were located. Today, strict laws prohibit any changes in these buildings, so while landowners gnash their teeth, we can enjoy Europe's best-preserved medieval city—slowly rotting. Many of the grand buildings are now vacant. Others harbor chandeliered elegance above mossy, empty (often flooded) ground floors.

❶ Ferrovia

The **Santa Lucia train station,** one of the few modern buildings in town, was built in 1954. It's been the gateway into Venice since 1860, when the first station was built. "F.S." stands for "Ferrovie dello Stato," the Italian state railway system.

More than 20,000 people a day commute in from the mainland, making this the busiest part of Venice during rush hour. The **Calatrava Bridge,**

spanning the Grand Canal between the train station and Piazzale Roma upstream, was built in 2008 to alleviate some of the congestion and make the commute easier (for more about the bridge, see page 56).

Opposite the train station, atop the green dome of **San Simeon Piccolo** church, St. Simeon waves *ciao* to whoever enters or leaves the "old" city. The pink church with the white Carrara-marble facade, just beyond the train station, is the **Church of the Scalzi** (Church of the Barefoot, named after the shoeless Carmelite monks), where the last doge (Venetian ruler) rests. It looks relatively new because it was partially rebuilt after being bombed in 1915 by Austrians aiming (poorly) at the train station.

❷ Riva de Biasio

Venice's main thoroughfare is busy with all kinds of **boats:** taxis, police boats, garbage boats, ambulances, construction cranes, and even brown-and-white UPS boats. Somehow they all manage to share the canal in relative peace.

About 25 yards past the Riva de Biasio stop, you'll look left down the broad **Cannaregio Canal** to see what was the **Jewish Ghetto** (see page 53). The twin, palepink, six-story "skyscrapers"—the tallest buildings you'll see at this end of the canal—are reminders of how densely populated the world's original ghetto was. Set aside as the local Jewish quarter in 1516, this area became extremely crowded. This urban island developed into one of the most closely knit business and cultural quarters of all the Jewish communities in Italy, and gave us our word "ghetto" (from *geto*, the copper foundry located here).

❸ San Marcuola

At this stop, facing a tiny square just ahead, stands the unfinished church of San Marcuola, one of only five churches fronting the Grand Canal. Centuries ago, this canal was a commercial drag

of expensive real estate in high demand by wealthy merchants. About 20 yards ahead on the right stands the stately gray **Turkish "Fondaco" Exchange,** one of the oldest houses in Venice. Its horseshoe arches and roofline of triangles and dingleballs are reminders of its Byzantine heritage. Turkish traders in turbans docked here, unloaded their goods into the warehouse on the bottom story, then went upstairs for a home-style meal and a place to sleep. Venice in the 1500s was very cosmopolitan, welcoming every religion and ethnicity, so long as they carried cash. (Today the building contains the city's Museum of Natural History—and Venice's only dinosaur skeleton.)

Just 100 yards ahead on the left, Venice's **Casinò** is housed in the palace where German composer Richard *(The Ring)* Wagner died in 1883. See his distinct, strong-jawed profile in the white plaque on the brick wall. In the 1700s, Venice was Europe's Vegas, with casinos and prostitutes everywhere. Casinòs ("little houses") have long provided Italians with a handy escape from daily life. Today they're run by the state to keep Mafia influence at bay. Notice the fancy front porch, rolling out the red carpet for high rollers arriving by taxi or hotel boat.

❹ San Stae

The San Stae Church sports a delightful Baroque facade. Opposite the San Stae stop, look for the peeling plaster that once made up **frescoes** (scant remains on the lower floors). Imagine the facades of the Grand Canal at their finest. As colorful as the city is today, it's still only a faded, sepia-toned remnant of a long-gone era, a time of lavishly decorated, brilliantly colored palaces.

Just ahead, jutting out a bit on the right, is the ornate white facade of **Ca' Pesaro.** *"Ca'"* is short for *casa* (house). Because only the house of the doge (Venetian ruler) could be called a palace *(palazzo)*, all other Venetian palaces are technically *"Ca'."*

In this city of masks, notice how the rich marble facades along the Grand Canal mask what are generally just simple, no-nonsense brick buildings. Most merchants enjoyed showing off. However, being smart businessmen, they only decorated the side of the buildings that would be seen and appreciated. But look back as you pass Ca' Pesaro (which houses the International Gallery of Modern Art—see page 51). It's the only building you'll see with a fine side facade. Ahead, on the left, with its glorious triple-decker medieval arcade (just before the next stop) is Ca' d'Oro.

❺ Ca' d'Oro

The lacy **Ca' d'Oro** (House of Gold) is the best example of Venetian Gothic architecture on the canal. Its three stories offer different variations on balcony design, topped with a spiny white roofline. Venetian Gothic mixes traditional Gothic (pointed arches and round medallions stamped with a four-leaf clover) with Byzantine styles (tall, narrow arches atop thin columns), filled in with Islamic frills. Like all the palaces, this was originally painted and gilded to make it even more glorious than it is now. Today the Ca' d'Oro is an art gallery (see page 56).

Look at the Venetian chorus line of palaces in front of the boat doing an architectural cancan. On the right is the arcade of the covered **fish market,** with the open-air **produce market** just beyond. It bustles in the

morning but is quiet the rest of the day. This is a great scene to wander through—even though European Union hygiene standards have made it cleaner but less colorful than it once was. Find the *traghetto* gondola ferrying shoppers—standing like Washington crossing the Delaware—back and forth.

There are eight *traghetto* crossings along the Grand Canal, each one marked by a classy low-key green-and-black sign. Make a point to use them. At €0.50 a ride, they are one of the best deals in Venice.

❻ Mercato Rialto

This stop was opened in 2007 to serve the busy market (boats only stop here between 8:00 and 20:00). The long and officious-looking

building at this stop is the Venice courthouse. Straight ahead in the distance, rising above the huge post office, is the tip of the Campanile (bell tower), crowned by its golden angel at St. Mark's Square, where this tour will end. The former post office (100 yards directly ahead, on left side, soon to be a shopping center) used to be the German Exchange, the trading center for German metal merchants in the early 1500s.

You'll cruise by some trendy and beautifully situated wine bars on the right, but look ahead as you round the corner and see the impressive Rialto Bridge come into view.

A major landmark of Venice, the **Rialto Bridge** is lined with shops and tourists. Constructed in 1588, it's the third bridge built on this spot. Until the 1850s, this was the only bridge crossing the

Grand Canal. With a span of 160 feet and foundations stretching 650 feet on either side, the Rialto was an impressive engineering feat in its day. Earlier Rialto Bridges could open to let big ships in, but not this one. When this new bridge was completed, much of the Grand Canal was closed to shipping and became a canal of palaces.

When gondoliers pass under the fat arch of the Rialto Bridge, they take full advantage of its acoustics: *"Volare, oh, oh..."*

❼ Rialto

Rialto, a separate town in the early days of Venice, has always been the commercial district, while San Marco was the religious and governmental center. Today, a winding street called the Mercerie connects the two, providing travelers with human traffic jams and a mesmerizing gauntlet of shopping temptations. This is the only stretch of the historic Grand Canal with landings upon which you can walk. They unloaded the city's basic necessities here: oil, wine, charcoal, iron. Today, the quay is lined with tourist-trap restaurants.

Venice's sleek, black, graceful **gondolas** are a symbol of the city (for more on gondolas, see page 298). With about 500 gondoliers joyriding amid the churning *vaporetti,* there's a lot of congestion on the Grand Canal. Pay attention—this is where most of the gondola and vaporetto accidents take place. While the Rialto is the highlight of many gondola rides, gondoliers understandably prefer the quieter small canals. Watch your vaporetto driver curse the better-paid gondoliers.

Ahead 100 yards on the left, two gray-colored **palaces** stand side by side (the City Hall and the mayor's office). Their horseshoe-shaped, arched windows are similar and their stories are the same height, lining up to create the effect of one long balcony.

❽ San Silvestro

We now enter a long stretch of important **merchants' palaces,** each with proud and different facades. Because ships couldn't navigate beyond the Rialto Bridge, the biggest palaces—with the major shipping needs—line this last stretch of the navigable Grand Canal.

Palaces like these were multi-functional: ground floor for the warehouse, offices and show-rooms upstairs, and the living quarters above the offices on the "noble floors" (with big windows designed to allow in maximum light). Servants lived and worked on the top floors (with the smallest

windows). For fire-safety reasons, the kitchens were also located on the top floors. Peek into the noble floors to catch a glimpse of their still-glorious chandeliers of Murano glass.

❾ Sant'Angelo

Notice how many buildings have a foundation of waterproof white stone *(pietra d'Istria)* upon which the bricks sit high and dry. Many

canal-level floors are abandoned as the rising water level takes its toll.

The **posts**—historically painted gaily with the equivalent of family coats of arms—don't rot underwater. But the wood at the waterline, where it's exposed to oxygen, does. On the smallest canals, little blue gondola signs indicate that these docks are for gondolas only (no taxis or motor boats).

❿ San Tomà

Fifty yards ahead, on the right side (with twin obelisks on the rooftop) stands **Palazzo Balbi,** the palace of an early-17th-century captain general of the sea. These Venetian equivalents of five-star admirals were honored with twin obelisks decorating their pal-aces. This palace, like so many in the city, flies three flags: Italy (green-white-red), the European Union (blue with ring of stars), and Venice (a lion on a field of red and gold). Today it houses the administrative headquarters of the regional government.

Just past the admiral's palace, look immediately to the right, down a side canal. On the right side of that canal, before the bridge, see the traffic light and the **fire station** (with four arches hiding fireboats parked and ready to go).

The impressive **Ca' Foscari,** with a classic Venetian facade (on the corner, across from the fire station), dominates the bend in the canal. This is the main building of the University of Venice, which has about 25,000 students. Notice the elegant lamp on the corner.

The grand, heavy, white **Ca' Rezzonico,** just before the Ca' Rezzonico stop, houses the Museum of 18th-Century Venice (✪ described in the Ca' Rezzonico Tour chapter).

Across the canal is the cleaner and leaner **Palazzo Grassi,** the last major palace built on the canal, erected in the late 1700s. It was purchased by a French tycoon and now displays a contemporary art collection.

⓫ Ca' Rezzonico

Up ahead, the Accademia Bridge leads over the Grand Canal to the **Accademia Gallery** (right side), filled with the best Venetian paintings (✪ described in the Accademia Tour chapter). The bridge was put up in 1934 as a temporary structure. Locals liked it, so it stayed.

⓬ Accademia

From here, look through the graceful bridge and way ahead to enjoy a classic view of **La Salute Church,** topped by a crown-shaped dome supported by scrolls (✪ described in the La Salute

Church Tour chapter). This Church of Saint Mary of Good Health was built to thank God for delivering Venetians from the devastating plague of 1630 (which had killed about a third of the city's population).

The low, white building among greenery (100 yards ahead, on the right, between the Accademia Bridge and the church) is the **Peggy Guggenheim Collection.** The American heiress "retired" here, sprucing up a palace that had been abandoned in mid-construction. Peggy willed the city her fine collection of modern art (✪ described in the Peggy Guggenheim Collection Tour chapter).

As you approach the next stop, notice on the right how the fine line of higgledy-piggledy palaces evokes old-time Venice.

Two doors past the Guggenheim, Palazzo Dario has a great set of characteristic **funnel-shaped chimneys.** These forced embers through a loop-the-loop channel until they were dead—required in the days when stone palaces were surrounded by humble, wooden buildings, and a live spark could make a merchant's workforce homeless. Notice this early Renaissance building's flat-feeling facade with "pasted-on" Renaissance motifs. Three doors later is the **Salviati building** (with the fine mosaics), which was once a glassworks.

⓭ Santa Maria del Giglio

Back on the left stands the fancy Gritti Palace hotel. Hemingway and Woody Allen both stayed here (but not together).

Take a deep whiff of Venice. What's all this nonsense about stinky canals? All I smell is my shirt. By the way, how's your captain? Smooth dockings? To get to know him, stand up in the bow and block his view.

GRAND CANAL CRUISE

⓮ Salute

The huge La Salute Church towers overhead as if squirted from a can of Catholic Reddi-wip. Like Venice itself, the church rests

upon pilings. To build the foundation for the city, more than a million trees were piled together, reaching beneath the mud to the solid clay. Much of the surrounding countryside was deforested by Venice. Trees were exported and consumed locally to fuel the furnaces of Venice's booming glass industry, to build Europe's biggest merchant marine, and to prop up this city in the mud.

As the Grand Canal opens up into the lagoon, the last building on the right with the golden ball is the 17th-century **Customs House,** which now houses the Punta della Dogana Museum of Contemporary Art (listed on page 50). Its two bronze Atlases hold a statue of Fortune riding the ball. Arriving ships stopped here to pay their tolls.

⓯ San Marco

Up ahead on the left, the green pointed tip of the Campanile marks **St. Mark's Square,** the political and religious center of Venice...and the final destination of this tour. You could get off at the San Marco stop and go straight to St. Mark's Square. But I'm staying on the boat for one more stop, just past St. Mark's Square (it's a quick walk back).

Survey the lagoon. Opposite St. Mark's Square, across the water, the ghostly white church with the pointy bell tower is **San Giorgio Maggiore,** with great views of Venice (✪ see the San Giorgio Maggiore Tour chapter). Next to it is the residential island Giudecca, stretching from close to San Giorgio Maggiore past the Venice youth hostel (with a nice view, directly across) to the Hilton Hotel (good nighttime view, far right end of island).

Still on board? If you are, as we leave the San Marco stop, prepare for a drive-by view of St. Mark's Square. First comes the bold white facade of the old mint (where Venice's golden ducat, the "dollar" of the Venetian Republic, was made) and the library facade. Then the twin columns, topped by St. Theodore and St. Mark, who've welcomed visitors since the 15th century. Between the columns, catch a glimpse of two giant figures atop the **Clock Tower**—they've been whacking their clappers every hour since 1499. The domes of **St. Mark's Basilica** are soon eclipsed by the lacy facade of the **Doge's Palace.** Next you'll see the **Bridge of Sighs** (currently under scaffolding), and then the grand harborside promenade—the **Riva.**

Follow the Riva with your eye, past elegant hotels to the green area in the distance. This is the largest of Venice's few **parks,** which hosts the Biennale art show every odd year (next in 2013). Much farther in the distance is the **Lido,** the island with Venice's beach. Its sand and casinos are tempting, but its car traffic disrupts the medieval charm of Venice.

⓰ San Zaccaria

OK, you're at your last stop. Quick—muscle your way off this boat! (If you don't, you'll eventually end up at the Lido.)

At San Zaccaria, you're right in the thick of the action. A number of other *vaporetti* depart from here (see page 32). Otherwise, it's a short walk back along the Riva to St. Mark's Square. Ahoy!

ST. MARK'S SQUARE TOUR

Piazza San Marco

Venice was once Europe's richest city, and Piazza San Marco was its center. As middleman in the trade between Asia and Europe, wealthy Venice profited from both sides. In 1450, Venice had 180,000 citizens (far more than London) and a gross "national" product that exceeded that of entire countries.

The rich Venetians taught the rest of Europe about the good life—silks, spices, and jewels from the East, crafts from northern Europe, good food and wine, fine architecture, music, theater, and laughter. Venice was a vibrant city full of painted palaces, glittering canals, and impressed visitors. Five centuries after its power began to decline, Venice still has all of these, with the added charm of romantic decay. In this tour, we'll spend an hour in the heart of this Old World superpower.

Orientation

Getting There: Signs all over town point to *San Marco*—meaning both the square and the basilica—located where the Grand Canal spills out into the lagoon. Vaporetto stops: San Marco or San Zaccaria.

Campanile: If you ascend the bell tower, it'll cost you €8 (daily Easter-June and Oct 9:00-19:00, July-Sept 9:00-21:00; Nov-Easter 9:30-15:45 except closed from Christmas to mid-Jan; tel. 041-522-4064, www.basilicasanmarco.it).

Clock Tower: To see the interior, you need to reserve a spot on a tour (tours offered Mon-Wed mornings and Thu-Sun afternoons—see page 39 for specifics).

Information: There are two TIs near St. Mark's Square. One is in the southwest corner of the square; the other is along the waterfront at the San Marco-Vallaresso vaporetto stop.

Audio Tour: You can download a free audio version of this tour for your mobile device via www.ricksteves.com/audioeurope, iTunes, or the Rick Steves Audio Europe smartphone app.

Services: Handy public WCs (€1.50) are behind the Correr Museum and also at the waterfront park, Giardinetti Reali (near the TI and San Marco—Vallaresso vaporetto stop).

Cuisine Art: Cafés with live music provide an engaging soundtrack for St. Mark's Square (see "Cafés on St. Mark's Square" sidebar, later). The Correr Museum (at the end of the square opposite the basilica) has a quiet coffee shop overlooking the crowded square. For a list of restaurants in the area, see page 282.

Necessary Eyesores: Expect scaffolding and advertising billboards to cover parts of the square and its monuments when you visit. The Campanile's foundation is being fortified, an effort that will take years. The nearby Bridge of Sighs is also covered with scaffolding during restoration.

Cardinal Points: The square is aligned (roughly) east-west. So, facing the basilica, north is to your left.

Starring: Byzantine domes, Gothic arches, Renaissance arches... and the wonderful, musical space they enclose.

The Tour Begins

• *For an overview of this grand square and the buildings that surround it, view it from the west end of the square (away from St. Mark's Basilica).*

The Piazza

St. Mark's Basilica dominates the square with its Byzantine-style onion domes and glowing mosaics. Mark Twain said it looked like "a vast warty bug taking a meditative walk." (I say it looks like tiara-wearing ladybugs copulating.) To the right of the basilica is its 300-foot-tall Campanile. Between the basilica and the Campanile, you can catch a glimpse of the pale-pink Doge's Palace. Lining the square are the former govern-

ment offices *(procuratie)* that administered the Venetian empire's vast network of trading outposts, which stretched all the way to Turkey.

The square is big, but it feels intimate with its cafés and dueling orchestras. By day, it's great for people-watching and pigeon-chasing. By night, under lantern light, it transports you to another century, complete with its own romantic soundtrack.

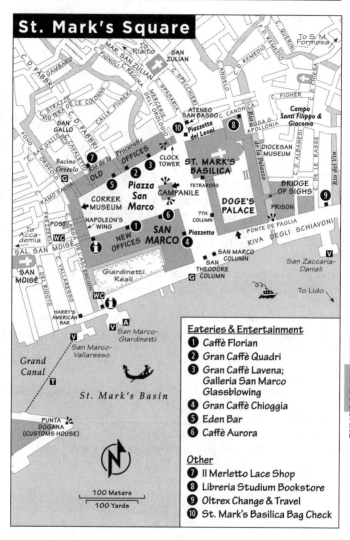

St. Mark's Square

Eateries & Entertainment
1. Caffè Florian
2. Gran Caffè Quadri
3. Gran Caffè Lavena; Galleria San Marco Glassblowing
4. Gran Caffè Chioggia
5. Eden Bar
6. Caffè Aurora

Other
7. Il Merletto Lace Shop
8. Libreria Studium Bookstore
9. Oltrex Change & Travel
10. St. Mark's Basilica Bag Check

100 Meters
100 Yards

The piazza draws Indians in saris, English nobles in blue blazers, and Nebraskans in shorts. Napoleon called the piazza "the most beautiful drawing room in Europe." Napoleon himself added to the intimacy by building the final wing, opposite the basilica, that encloses the square.

For architecture buffs, here are three centuries of styles, bam, side by side, *uno-due-tre,* for easy comparison:

1. On the left side (as you face the basilica) are the "Old" offices, built in about 1500 in solid, column-and-arch Renaissance style.

2. The "New" offices (on the right), in a High Renaissance style from a century later (c. 1600), are a little heavier and more ornate. This wing mixes arches, the three orders of columns from bottom to top—Doric, Ionic, and Corinthian—and statues in the Baroque style.

3. Napoleon's wing, at the opposite end from the basilica, is Neoclassical (c. 1800)—a return to simpler, more austere classical columns and arches. Napoleon's architects tried to make his wing bridge the styles of the other two. But it turned out a little too high for one side and not high enough for the other. Nice try.

Imagine this square full of water, with gondolas floating where people now sip cappuccinos. That happens every so often at very high tides *(acqua alta)*, a reminder that Venice and the sea are intertwined. (Now that one is sinking and the other is rising, they are more intertwined than ever.)

Venice became Europe's richest city from its trade with northern Europeans, Ottoman Muslims, and Byzantine Christians. Here in St. Mark's Square, the exact center of this East-West axis, we see both the luxury and the mix of Eastern and Western influences.

Watch out for pigeon speckle. The pigeons are not indigenous to Venice (they were imported by the Habsburgs) nor loved by residents. In fact, Venetians love seagulls because they eat pigeons. In 2008, Venice outlawed the feeding of pigeons, so their days may be numbered. There are now fewer pigeons, but they're still there. Vermin are a problem on this small island, where it's said that each Venetian has two pigeons and four rats. (The rats stay hidden, except when high tides flood their homes.)

• *The TI is nearby, in the corner of Napoleon's wing. It's wise to confirm your sightseeing plans here and pick up the latest list of opening hours. Behind you (southwest of the piazza), you'll find the public WC (€1.50) and a post office with a helpful stamps-only line (usually closes at 14:00).*

Now approach the basilica. If it's hot and you're tired, grab a shady spot at the foot of the Campanile.

St. Mark's Basilica—Exterior

The facade is a crazy mix of East and West. There are round, Roman-style arches over the doorways, golden Byzantine mosaics, a roofline ringed with pointed French Gothic pinnacles, and Muslim-shaped onion domes (wood, covered with lead) on the roof.

The brick-structure building is blanketed in marble that came from everywhere—columns from Alexandria, capitals from Sicily, and carvings from Constantinople. The columns flanking the doorways show the facade's variety—purple, green, gray, white, yellow, some speckled, some striped horizontally, some vertically, some fluted—all topped with a variety of different capitals.

What's amazing isn't so much the variety as the fact that the whole thing comes together in a bizarre sort of harmony. St. Mark's remains simply the most interesting church in Europe, a church that (paraphrasing Goethe) "can only be compared with itself."

For more on the basilica, inside and out, see the ✪ St. Mark's Basilica Tour chapter.

• *Facing the basilica, turn 90 degrees to the left to see...*

The Clock Tower (Torre dell'Orologio)

Two bronze "Moors" (African Muslims) stand atop the Clock Tower (built originally to be giants, they only gained their ethnicity when the metal darkened over the centuries). At the top of each hour they swing their giant clappers. The clock dial shows the 24 hours, the signs of the zodiac, and, in the blue center, the phases of the moon. Above the dial is the world's first digital clock, which changes every five minutes. The Clock Tower retains some of its original coloring of blue and gold, a reminder that, in centuries past, this city glowed with bright color.

An alert winged lion, the symbol of St. Mark and the city, looks down on the crowded square. He opens a book that reads *"Pax Tibi Marce,"* or "Peace to you, Mark." As legend goes, these were the comforting words that an angel spoke to the stressed evangelist, assuring him he would find serenity during a stormy night that the saint spent here on the island. Eventually, St. Mark's body found its final resting place inside the basilica, and now his winged-lion symbol is everywhere. (Find four in 20 seconds. Go.)

Venice's many lions express the city's various mood swings through history—triumphant after a naval victory, sad when a

Cafés on St. Mark's Square

Cafés line the square. Those with live music feature similar food, prices, and a three- to five-piece combo playing a selection of classical and pop hits, from Brahms to "Bésame Mucho." If you sit outside and get just a drink, expect to pay €12-20, including a €6 cover charge when the orchestra is playing (no cover charge otherwise). A coffee—your cheapest option—costs about €6 if you sit at an outside table, plus the €6 cover charge when the music plays, bringing it to €12 total (even at the venerable Caffè Florian). It's perfectly acceptable to nurse a cappuccino for an hour—you're paying for the music with the cover charge.

Caffè Florian (on the right as you face the church—see map earlier in this chapter) is the most famous Venetian café and one of the first places in Europe to serve coffee (daily April-Oct 10:00-24:00, Nov-March 10:00-21:00). It's been a popular spot for a discreet rendezvous in Venice since 1720. The orchestra here plays a more classical repertoire than at the other cafés. The outside tables are the main action, but do walk inside through the richly decorated, old-time rooms where Casanova, Lord Byron, Charles Dickens, and Woody Allen have all paid too much for a drink (reasonable prices at bar in back).

Gran Caffè Quadri, opposite the Florian, has an equally illustrious history of famous clientele, including the writers Stendhal and Dumas, and composer Richard Wagner. **Gran Caffè Lavena,** near the Clock Tower, is newer and less storied.

Gran Caffè Chioggia, on the Piazzetta facing the Doge's Palace, charges slightly less, with one or two musicians, usually a pianist, playing cocktail jazz.

The following less-expensive options don't have live music, but you can enjoy overhearing music from nearby cafés: **Eden Bar,** next to Gran Caffè Quadri, is touristy, but that doesn't matter when you're enjoying your hot dog and Coke while sitting out on the piazza. **Caffè Aurora,** in the shadow of the Campanile, features nearly all the ambience of the orchestra cafés at half the price.

favorite son has died, hollow-eyed after a plague, and smiling when the soccer team wins. The pair of lions squatting between the Clock Tower and basilica have probably been photographed being ridden by every Venetian child born since the dawn of cameras.

The Campanile

The original Campanile (cam-pah-NEE-lay), or bell tower, was a lighthouse and a marvel of 10th-century architecture until the 20th century (1902), when it toppled into the center of the piazza. It had groaned ominously the night before, sending people scurrying from the cafés. The next morning...crash! The golden angel on top landed right at the basilica's front door, standing up.

The Campanile was rebuilt 10 years later complete with its golden archangel Gabriel, who always faces the breeze. You can ride a lift to the top for the best view of Venice. It's crowded at peak times, but well worth it.

In 2012, you may see construction work around the Campanile's base. Hoping to prevent a repeat of the 1902 collapse, they've wrapped the underground foundations with a titanium girdle to shore up a crack that appeared in 1939.

Because St. Mark's Square is the first place in town to start flooding, there are tide gauges at the outside base of the Campanile (near the exit, facing St. Mark's Square) that show the current sea level *(livello marea)*. Find the stone plaque (near the exit door) that commemorates the high-water 77-inch level from the disastrous floods of 1966. In December of 2008, Venice suffered another terrible high tide, cresting at 61 inches.

If the tide is mild (around 20 inches), the water merely seeps up through the drains. But when there's a strong tide (around 40 inches), it looks like someone's turned on a faucet down below. The water bubbles upward and flows like a river to the lowest points in the square, which can be covered with a few inches of water in an hour or so. When the water level rises one meter above mean sea level, a warning siren sounds, and it repeats if a serious flood is imminent.

Many doorways have three-foot-high wooden or metal barriers to block the high water *(acqua alta)*, but the seawater still seeps in through floors and drains, rendering the barriers nearly

Escape from St. Mark's Square

Crowds getting to you? Here are some relatively quiet areas near St. Mark's Square.

Correr Museum: Sip a cappuccino in the café of this uncrowded history museum in a building that overlooks St. Mark's Square (enter at the far end of the piazza). ✪ See the Correr Museum Tour chapter.

Giardinetti Reali: The small park is along the waterfront, west of the Piazzetta (facing the water, turn right—it's next to the TI and the only place for a legal picnic).

San Giorgio Maggiore: This is the fairy-tale island you see from the Piazzetta (catch vaporetto #2 from the San Zaccaria-M.V.E. stop, past the Bridge of Sighs). ✪ See the San Giorgio Maggiore Tour chapter.

Il Merletto: This lace shop is in a small, decommissioned chapel near the northwest corner of St. Mark's Square (daily 10:00-17:00, go through Sotoportego del Cavalletto and across the little bridge to #95-96, tel. 041-520-8406). Ask for the sheet in English explaining the history of Venetian lace.

La Salute Church: This cool church in a quiet neighborhood is a short €2 hop on vaporetto #1 from the San Marco-Vallaresso stop, or ride the nearby *traghetto*. ✪ See the La Salute Church Tour chapter.

Caffè Florian: The plush interior of this luxurious 18th-century café, located on St. Mark's Square, is generally quiet and nearly empty. A coffee here can be a wonderful break (see "Cafés on St. Mark's Square," earlier).

useless. (To learn the reasons for the flooding, see the sidebar on page 36.)

You might see stacked wooden benches in the square; during floods, the benches are placed end-to-end to create elevated sidewalks. If you think the square is crowded now, when it's flooded it turns into total gridlock, as all the people normally sharing the whole square jostle for space on the narrow wooden walkways.

In 2006, the pavement around St. Mark's Square was taken up, and the entire height of the square was raised by adding a layer of sand, and then replacing the stones. If the columns along the ground floor of the Doge's Palace look stubby, it's because this process has been carried out many times over the centuries.

• *The small square between the basilica and the water is...*

The Piazzetta

This "Little Square" is framed by the Doge's Palace on the left, the library on the right, and the waterfront of the lagoon. In former

days, the Piazzetta was closed to the public for a few hours a day so that government officials and bigwigs could gather in the sun to strike shady deals.

The pale-pink Doge's Palace is the epitome of the style known as Venetian Gothic. Columns support traditional, pointed Gothic arches, but with a Venetian flair—they're curved to a point, ornamented with a trefoil (three-leaf clover), and topped with a round medallion of a quatrefoil (four-leaf clover). The pattern is

found on buildings all over Venice and on the formerly Venetian-controlled Croatian coast, but nowhere else in the world (except Las Vegas).

The two large 12th-century columns near the water were looted from Constantinople. Mark's winged lion sits on top of one. The lion's body (nearly 15 feet long) predates the wings and is more than 2,000 years old. The other column holds St. Theodore (battling a crocodile), the former patron saint who was replaced by Mark. I guess stabbing crocs in the back isn't classy enough for an upwardly mobile world power. Criminals were executed by being hung from these columns in the hopes that the public could learn its lessons vicariously.

Venice was the "Bride of the Sea" because she depended on sea trading for her livelihood. This "marriage" was celebrated annually by the people on Ascension Day. The doge, in full regalia, boarded a ritual boat (his Air Force One equivalent) here at the edge of the

ST. MARK'S SQUARE

Venetian Gothic

$$\bigwedge + \bigcap + \bigcap + \clubsuit =$$

Piazzetta and sailed out into the lagoon. There a vow was made, and he dropped a jeweled ring into the water to seal the marriage.

In the distance, on an island across the lagoon, is one of the grandest views in the city, of the Church of San Giorgio Maggiore. With its four tall columns as the entryway, the church, designed by the late-Renaissance architect Andrea Palladio, influenced future government and bank buildings around the world.

Speaking of architects, I will: Sansovino. Around 1530, Jacopo Sansovino designed the library (here in the Piazzetta) and the delicate Loggetta at the base of the Campanile (pictured on page 79; it was destroyed by the collapse of the tower in 1902 and was pieced back together as much as possible).

The Tetrarchs and the Doge's Palace's Seventh Column

Where the basilica meets the Doge's Palace is the traditional entrance to the palace, decorated with four small Roman statues—

the Tetrarchs. No one knows for sure who they are, but I like the legend that says they're the scared leaders of a divided Rome during its fall, holding their swords and each other as all hell breaks loose around them. Whatever the legend, these statues— made of precious purple porphyry stone— are symbols of power. They were looted from Constantinople and then placed here proudly as spoils of war. How old are they? They've guarded the palace entrance since the city first rose from the mud.

The Doge's Palace's seventh column (the seventh from the water) tells a story of love, romance, and tragedy in its carved capital: 1) In the first scene (the carving facing the Piazzetta), a woman on a balcony is wooed by her lover, who says, "Babe, I want *you!*" 2) She responds, "Why, little ol' *me?*" 3) They get married. 4) Kiss. 5) Hit the sack—pretty racy for 14th-century art. 6) Nine months later, guess what? 7) The baby takes its first steps. 8) And as was all too common in the 1300s...the child dies.

The pillars along the Doge's Palace look short—a result of the square being built up over the centuries. It's happening again today. The stones are taken up, sand is added, and the stones are replaced, buying a little more time as the sea slowly swallows the city.

• *At the waterfront in the Piazzetta, turn left and walk (east) along the water. At the top of the first bridge, look inland at...*

The Bridge of Sighs

In the Doge's Palace (on your left), the government doled out justice. On your right are the prisons. (Don't let the palatial facade fool you—see the bars on the windows?) Prisoners sentenced in the palace crossed to the prisons by way of the covered bridge in front of you. This was called the Prisons' Bridge until the Romantic poet Lord Byron renamed it in the 19th century. From this bridge, the convicted got their final view of sunny, joyous Venice before entering the black and dank prisons. According to the Romantic legend, they sighed. As you will, too, when you see the scaffolding.

Venice has been a major tourist center for four centuries. Anyone who's ever come here has stood on this very spot, looking at the Bridge of Sighs. Lean on the railing leaned on by everyone from Casanova to Byron to Hemingway.

I stood in Venice, on the Bridge of Sighs,
a palace and a prison on each hand.
I saw, from out the wave, her structures rise,
as from the stroke of the enchanter's wand.
A thousand years their cloudy wings expand
around me, and a dying glory smiles
o'er the far times, when many a subject land
looked to the Winged Lion's marble piles,
where Venice sat in state, throned on her hundred isles!

—from Lord Byron's *Childe Harold's Pilgrimage*

ST. MARK'S BASILICA TOUR

Basilica di San Marco

Among Europe's churches, St. Mark's is peerless. From the outside, it's a riot of domes, columns, and statues, completely unlike the towering Gothic churches of northern Europe or the heavy Baroque of much of the rest of Italy. Inside, the decor of mosaics, colored marbles, and oriental treasures is rarely seen elsewhere. The Christian symbolism is unfamiliar to Western eyes, done in the style of Byzantine icons and even Islamic designs. Older than most of Europe's churches, it feels like a remnant of a lost world.

This is your best chance in Italy (outside of Ravenna) to glimpse a forgotten and somewhat mysterious part of the human story—Byzantium.

Orientation

Cost: Though entering the church is free, three separate, optional sights inside the church require paid admission: the Treasury (€3, includes audioguide—free for the asking), Golden Altarpiece (€2), and San Marco Museum—the sight most worth its entry fee (€4, enter museum up stairs from atrium either before or after you tour the church, skip the €3.50 audioguide).

Hours: The church is open Mon-Sat 9:45-17:00, Sun 14:00-17:00 (Sun until 16:00 Nov-March); the Treasury and Golden Altarpiece close 15 minutes earlier. The San Marco Museum is open daily 9:45-16:45.

Lines: There's almost always a long line to get into St. Mark's. Once inside, it's usually crowded, and you just have to shuffle through on a one-way system. It's best to read this chapter before you go...or while standing in line. Those checking a bag can skip to the front of the line—see "Bag Check" on the next page.

Dress Code: Modest dress (no bare knees or bare shoulders) is strictly enforced, even for kids. Shorts are OK if they cover the knees. To cover bare shoulders, women may be able to buy a shawl *(coprispale)* at the atrium gift shop.

Getting There: Signs throughout Venice point to *San Marco,* meaning both the square and the church. Vaporetto stops: San Marco or San Zaccaria.

Information: Guidebooks are sold at the bookstand in the basilica's atrium. Tel. 041-270-8311, www.basilicasanmarco.it.

Tours: Free, hour-long English **tours** (heavy on the mosaics' religious symbolism) are generally offered Mon-Sat at 11:00; meet in the atrium. But the schedule varies, so see the schedule board in the atrium. You can download a free **audio version** of the tour in this book for your mobile device via www.rick steves.com/audioeurope, iTunes, or the Rick Steves Audio Europe smartphone app.

Length of This Tour: Allow one hour.

Bag Check (and Skipping the Line): Small purses and shoulder-slung bags may be allowed inside the church, but larger bags and backpacks are not. Check them for free for up to one hour at the nearby church called Ateneo San Basso, 30 yards to the left of the basilica, down narrow Calle San Basso (see map on page 87 for location; open daily 9:30-17:00).

Those with a bag to check actually get to skip the line, along with their companions (up to three or so). Leave your bag at Ateneo San Basso and pick up your claim tag. Take your tag to the basilica's tourist entrance. Keep to the left of the railing where the line forms and show your tag to the gatekeeper. He'll let you in, ahead of the line. After touring the church, come back and pick up your bag. (Note: Ateneo San Basso will not let you check small bags that would be allowed inside.)

Services: A free WC is inside the San Marco Museum. Public WCs (€1.50) are nearby (one behind the Correr Museum, another at Giardinetti Reali park).

Theft Alert: St. Mark's Basilica is the most dangerous place in Venice for pickpocketing—inside, it's always a crowded jostle.

Mass: Experience the church in its uncrowded glory at any Mass outside of visiting hours (e.g., 8:00 or 18:45; see website above for full schedule). Enter through the door around the left side of the basilica.

Photography: Although forbidden inside the church, it is allowed on the balcony of the San Marco Museum, which has great views overlooking the square.

Cuisine Art: No food is allowed inside the church. For suggestions nearby, see page 282.

Starring: St. Mark, Byzantium, mosaics, and ancient bronze horses.

The Tour Begins

Start outside in the square, far enough back to take in the whole facade. Then zero in on the details. As you tour the interior, do your best to follow this tour. At busy times, your actual itinerary and pace may be determined by the sheer flow of the masses.

❶ Exterior—Mosaic of Mark's Relics

St. Mark's Basilica is a treasure chest of booty that was looted during Venice's glory days. That's most appropriate for a church built on the stolen bones of a saint.

The **mosaic over the far left door** shows the theft that put Venice on the pilgrimage map. Two men (in the center, with crooked staffs) enter the church bearing a coffin with the body of St. Mark, who looks somewhat grumpy from the long voyage.

St. Mark was the author of one of the Gospels, the four Bible books telling the story of Jesus' life (Matthew, Mark, Luke, and John). Seven centuries after his death, his holy body was in Muslim-occupied Alexandria, Egypt. In 828 A.D., two visiting merchants of Venice "rescued" the body from the "infidels," hid it in a pork barrel (which was unclean to Muslims), and spirited it away to Venice.

The merchants presented the body—not to a pope or bishop—but to the doge (with white ermine collar, on the right) and his wife, the dogaressa (with entourage, on the left), giving instant status to Venice's budding secular state. They built a church here over Mark's bones and made him the patron saint of the city. You'll see his symbol, the winged lion, all over Venice.

The original church burned down in 976 A.D.. Today's structure was begun in 1063. The mosaic, from 1260, shows that the church hasn't changed much since then—you can see the onion domes and famous bronze horses on the balcony.

The St. Mark's you see today, mostly from the 11th century, was modeled after the 6th-century Hagia Sophia in Constantinople.

St. Mark's Basilica

1. Exterior – Mosaic of Mark's Relics
2. Atrium – Mosaic of Noah's Ark & the Great Flood
3. Nave – Mosaics & Greek-Cross Floor Plan
4. Pentecost Mosaic
5. Central Dome – Ascension Mosaic
6. Rood Screen
7. Doge's Pulpit
8. Tree of Jesse Mosaic
9. Last Supper Mosaic
10. Crucifixion Mosaic
11. Nicopeia Icon
12. Rifle on Pillar
13. Discovery of Mark Mosaic
14. Treasury
15. Golden Altarpiece
16. Stairs up to Loggia: San Marco Museum & Bronze Horses

St. Mark's...Cathedral, Church, or Basilica?

All three are correct. The church is also a cathedral, because it's the home church of the local bishop. It's a basilica, because

it's the home of a patriarch and because the meaning of "basilica" evolved into an honorary title conferred on select churches by the pope. Coincidentally, it's also a basilica in the architectural sense. Its floor plan (if you ignore the transepts) has a central nave

with flanking side aisles, a layout patterned after the ancient Roman public buildings called "basilicas." The transepts turn the basilica plan into a cross—in this case, a Greek cross, as it has four equal arms.

Venice needed roots. By building a retro church, the city could imply that it had been around for longer than it actually had been. (Throughout European history, upstarts loved to fake deep roots this way. Germany embraced mystic, medieval lore as it emerged as a modern nation in the 19th century, England cooked up the King Arthur legend, and so on.)

In subsequent centuries, the church was encrusted with materials looted from buildings throughout the Venetian empire. Their prize booty was the four bronze horses that adorn the balcony, stolen from Constantinople during the Fourth Crusade (these are copies, as the originals are housed inside the church museum). The architectural style of St. Mark's has been called "Early Ransack."

• *Enter the atrium (entrance hall) of the basilica, through a sixth-century, bronze-paneled Byzantine door.*

Immediately after being admitted by the dress-code guard, look up and to the right into an archway decorated with fine mosaics.

❷ Atrium—
Mosaic of Noah's Ark and the Great Flood

St. Mark's famous mosaics, with their picture symbols, were easily understood in medieval times, even by illiterate masses. Today's literate masses have trouble reading them, so let's practice on these, some of the oldest (13th century), finest, and most accessible mosaics in the church.

Noah and sons are sawing logs to build a boat. Venetians—who were great ship builders—related to the Ark. At its peak, Venice's Arsenale warship-building plant employed several thousand.

Below that are three scenes of Noah putting all species of animals into the Ark, two by two. (Who's at the head of the line? Lions.) Another scene shows

the Flood in full force, drowning the wicked. Noah sends out a dove twice to see whether there's any dry land where he can dock. He finds it, leaves the Ark with a gorgeous rain-bow overhead, and offers a sacrifice of thanks to God. Easy, huh?

• *Now that our medieval literacy rate has risen, rejoin the slow flow of people. Notice the entrance to the San Marco Museum (Loggia dei Cavalli), which you can visit later. Now climb seven steps, pass through the doorway, and enter the nave. Loiter somewhere just inside the door (crowd flow permitting) and let your eyes adjust.*

❸ The Nave— Mosaics and Greek-Cross Floor Plan

The initial effect is dark and unimpressive (unless they've got the floodlights on). But as your pupils slowly unclench, you'll notice

that the entire upper part is decorated in mosaic—4,750 square yards (imagine paving a football field with contact lenses). These golden mosaics are in the Byzantine style, though many were designed by artists from the Italian Renaissance and later. The often-overlooked lower walls are covered with green-, yellow-, purple-, and rose-colored marble slabs, cut to expose the grain, and laid out in geometric patterns. Even the floor is mosaic, with mostly geometrical designs. It rolls like the sea. Venice is sinking and shifting, creating these cresting waves of stone.

The church is laid out with four equal arms, topped with domes, radiating out from the center to form a Greek cross (+).

Christ as Pantocrator

Most Eastern Orthodox churches have at least one mosaic or painting of Christ in a standard pose—as "Pantocrator," a Greek word meaning "Ruler of All." St. Mark's features several Pantocrators, including the central dome, over the altar, and over the entrance door. The image, so familiar to Orthodox Christians, is a bit foreign to Protestants, Catholics, and secularists.

As King of the Universe, Christ sits (usually on a throne) facing directly out, with penetrating eyes. He wears a halo divided with a cross, worn only by the Trinity. In his left hand is a Bible, while his right hand blesses, with the fingers forming the Greek letters chi and rho, the first two letters of "Christos." The thumb touches the fingers, symbolizing how Christ unites both his divinity and his humanity. On either side of Christ's head are the Greek letters "IC XC," short for "IesuC XristoC."

Those familiar with Eastern Orthodox churches will find familiar elements in St. Mark's: a central floor plan, domes, mosaics, and iconic images of Mary and Christ as Pantocrator—ruler of all things. As your eyes adjust, the mosaics start to give off a "mystical, golden luminosity," the atmosphere of the Byzantine heaven. The air itself seems almost visible, like a cloud of incense. It's a subtle effect, one that grows on you as the filtered light changes. There are more beautiful, bigger, more overwhelming, and even holier churches, but none is as stately.

• *Find the chandelier near the entrance doorway (in the shape of a Greek cross cathedral space station), and run your eyes up the support chain to the dome above.*

❹ Pentecost Mosaic

In a golden heaven, the dove of the Holy Spirit shoots out a pinwheel of spiritual lasers, igniting tongues of fire on the heads of the 12 apostles below, giving them the ability to speak other languages without a Rick Steves phrase book. You'd think they'd be amazed, but their

Mosaics

St. Mark's mosaics are designs or pictures made with small cubes of colored stone or glass pressed into wet plaster. Ancient Romans paved floors, walls, and ceilings with them. When Rome "fell," the art form died out in the West but was carried on by Byzantine craftsmen. They perfected the gold background effect by baking gold leaf into tiny cubes of glass called *tesserae* (tiles). The surfaces of the tiles are pur-

posely cut unevenly to capture light and give off a shimmering effect. The reflecting gold mosaics helped to light thick-walled, small-windowed, lantern-lit Byzantine churches, creating a golden glow that symbolized the divine light of heaven.

St. Mark's mosaics tell the entire Christian history from end to beginning. Entering the church, you're greeted with scenes from the end of the world (Apocalypse) and the Pentecost. As you approach the altar, you walk backward in time to the source, experiencing Jesus' Passion and Crucifixion, his miraculous life, and continuing back to his birth and Old Testament predecessors. Over the altar at the far end of the church (and over the entrance door at the near end) are images of Christ—the beginning and the end, the Alpha and Omega of the Christian universe.

expressions are as solemn as...icons. One of the oldest mosaics in the church (c. 1125), it has distinct "Byzantine" features: a gold background and apostles with halos, solemn faces, almond eyes, delicate blessing hands, and rumpled robes, all facing forward.

This is art from a society still touchy about the Bible's commandment against making "graven images" of holy things. Byzantium had recently emerged from two centuries of Iconoclasm, in which statues and paintings were broken and burned as sinful "false gods." The Byzantine style emphasizes otherworldliness rather than literal human detail. The poet W. B. Yeats stood here and described what he saw: "O sages standing in God's holy fire as in the gold mosaic of a wall, come from the holy fire...and be the singing-masters of my soul."

• *Shuffle along with the crowds up to the central dome.*

❺ Central Dome—Ascension Mosaic

Gape upward to the very heart of the church. Christ—having lived his miraculous life and having been crucified for man's sins—ascends into the starry sky on a rainbow. He raises his right hand

Byzantium

The Byzantine Empire was the eastern half of the ancient Roman Empire that *didn't* "fall" in A.D. 476. It remained Christian, Greek-speaking, and enlightened for another thousand years.

In A.D. 330, Constantine, the first Christian emperor, moved the Roman Empire's capital to the newly expanded city of Byzantium, which he humbly renamed Constantinople (modern Istanbul). With him went Rome's best and brightest. When the city of Rome decayed and fell, plunging Western Europe into its "Dark Ages," Constantinople lived on as the greatest city in Europe.

Venice had strong ties with Byzantium from its earliest days. In the sixth century, Byzantine Emperor Justinian invaded northern Italy, briefly reuniting East and West, and making Ravenna his regional capital. In 800, Venetians asked the emperor in Constantinople to protect them from Charlemagne's marauding Franks.

Soon Venetian merchants were granted trading rights to Byzantine ports in the Adriatic and eastern Mediterranean. They traded raw materials from Western Europe for luxury goods from the East.

When Muslim Ottoman Turks threatened the Christian Byzantine Empire, the Venetians joined the Crusades, the series of military expeditions that were designed to "save" Jerusalem and Constantinople. Venetians grew rich renting ships to the Crusaders in exchange for money, favors, and booty.

During the Fourth Crusade (1202-1204), which went horribly awry, the Crusaders—led by the Venetian doge Dandolo—sacked

and blesses the universe. This isn't the dead, crucified, mortal Jesus featured in most churches, but a powerful, resurrected god, the ruler of all.

Christ's blessing radiates, rippling down to the ring of white-robed apostles below. They stand amid the trees of the Mount of Olives, waving good-bye as Christ ascends. Mary is with them, wearing blue with golden Greek crosses on each shoulder and looking ready to play patty-cake. From these saints, goodness descends, creating the Virtues that ring the base of the dome between the windows. In Byzantine churches, the window-lit dome represented heaven, while the dark church below represented earth—a microcosm of the hierarchical universe.

Beneath the dome at the four corners, the four Gospel writers ("Matev," "Marc," "Luca," and "Ioh") thoughtfully scribble down the heavenly events. This wisdom flows down like water from the symbolic Four Rivers below them, spreading through the church's four equal arms (the "four corners" of the world), and baptizing the congregation with God's love. The church building is a series

Constantinople, a fellow Christian city. This was, perhaps, the lowest point in Christian history, at least until the advent of TV evangelism. The Venetians carried home the bronze horses, the Pala d'Oro enamels, the Treasury's treasures, the Nicopeia icon, and much of the marble that now covers the (brick) church.

Venice rose while the Byzantine Empire faded. Then both civilizations nose-dived when Constantinople finally fell to the Ottomans in 1453.

Today, we find hints of the Byzantine Empire in the Eastern Orthodox Church, in mosaics and icons, and in the looted treasures shipped back to Venice.

of perfect circles within perfect squares—the cosmic order—with Christ in the center solemnly blessing us. God's in his heaven, saints are on earth, and all's right with the world.

Under the Ascension Dome— The Church as Theater

Look around at the church's furniture and imagine a service here. The ❻ **rood screen,** topped with 14 saints, separates the congrega-

tion from the high altar, heightening the "mystery" of the Mass. The ❼ **pulpit on the right** was reserved for the doge, who led prayers and made important announcements. Mosaics were visual aids for the priest, telling the whole story of Jesus. It starts with his ancestors perched in the ❽ **Tree of Jesse** (in the north transept, to the left as you face the altar). The story continues through Jesus' life, to the ❾ **Last Supper** (in the arch leading to the south transept, see photo previous page), and culminates in the ❿ **Crucifixion** (in the west arch).

The Crucifixion mosaic features a stick-figure Christ, emphasizing the symbolic solemnity of the moment, not its Mel Gibson-style gruesomeness. In fact, there aren't very many crucifixes at all in the church, giving it an Eastern Orthodox flavor. While Western Christianity focuses on the death of Jesus, to Orthodox believers, Christ's death is just the tragic Act I. Other scenes in the arch show the rest of the story, Christ's triumphant Resurrection and post-death miracles, leading to the climax, his Ascension (in the central dome).

The Venetian church service is a theatrical multimedia spectacle, combining words (prayers, biblical passages, Latin and Greek phrases), music (chants, a choir, organ, horns, strings), costumes and props (priests' robes, golden reliquaries, candles, incense), set design (the mosaics, rood screen, Golden Altarpiece), and even stage direction (processionals through the crowd, priests' motions, standing, sitting, kneeling, crossing yourself). The symmetrical church is itself part of the set design. The Greek-cross floor plan symbolizes perfection, rather than the more common Latin cross of the crucifixion (emphasizing man's sinfulness). Coincidentally or not, the first modern opera—also a multimedia theatrical experience—was written by St. Mark's *maestro di cappella,* Claudio Monteverdi (1567-1643).

North Transept

In the north transept (the arm of the church to the left of the altar), today's Venetians pray to a painted wooden icon of Mary and baby Jesus known as ⓫ **Nicopeia,** or "Our Lady of Victory" (on the east wall of the north transept, it's a small painting crusted over with a big stone canopy). Supposedly painted by the evangelist Luke, it was once enameled with bright paint and precious stones, and Mary was adorned with a crown and necklace of gold and jewels (now on display in the Treasury). This Madonna has helped Venice persevere through plagues, wars, and crucial soccer games. When Mary answers a prayer, grateful Venetians give her offerings, like the old ⓬ **rifle** that hangs next to a Madonna-and-child on a pillar (as you approach the north transept). A wife prayed to the Madonna for her husband's safe return from war with Austria in 1848. When he came home alive, she gave his rifle to the Virgin in thanks.

• *In the south transept (to the right of main altar), find the dim mosaic high up on the west wall.*

⓭ Discovery of Mark Mosaic

Not a biblical scene, this mosaic depicts the miraculous event that capped the construction of the present church.

It's 1094, the church is nearly complete (see the domes shown in cutaway fashion), and they're all set to re-inter Mark's bones under the new altar. There's just one problem: During the decades of construction, they forgot where they'd stored his body!

So (in the left half of the mosaic), all of Venice gathers inside the church to bow down and pray for help finding the bones. The doge (from the Latin *dux*, meaning leader) leads them. Soon after (the right half), the patriarch (far right) is inspired to look inside a hollow column where he finds the relics. Everyone turns and applauds, including the womenfolk (left side of scene), who stream in from the upper-floor galleries. The relics were soon placed under the altar in a ceremony that inaugurated the current structure.

The south transept also features horseshoe arches atop slender columns, giving the transept the exotic flavor of a Muslim mosque. The door under the rose window leads directly from the Doge's Palace. On important occasions, the doge entered the church through here, ascended the steps of his pulpit, and addressed the people.

St. Mark's Three Museums

Inside the church are three sights, each requiring a separate admission. None is a must-see, but they provide the easiest way (outside of Istanbul or Ravenna) to soak up Byzantine ambience—and admission to the San Marco Museum (the best of the bunch) gives you access to great views over the inside of the church, as well as to St. Mark's Square outside.

⓮ Treasury (Tesoro)

• *The tiny Treasury is in the south transept. The admission fee includes an audioguide (when available)—ask for it. The collection is crammed into two small rooms.*

You'll see Byzantine chalices, silver reliquaries, monstrous monstrances (for displaying the Communion wafer), and icons done in gold, silver, enamels, gems, and semiprecious stones. Some pieces represent the fruit of labor by different civilizations over a thousand-year period. For example, an ancient rock-crystal chalice made by the Romans might be decorated centuries later with

The Legend (Mixed with a Little Truth) of Mark and Venice

Mark (died c. A.D. 68) was a Jewish-born Christian, and he might have actually met Jesus. (The Bible mentions a "Mark" and a "John Mark" who may have been him.) He traveled with fellow convert Paul, eventually settling in Alexandria as the city's first Christian bishop. On a trip to Rome, Peter—Jesus' right-hand man—asked him to write down the events of Jesus' life. This became the Gospel of Mark.

During his travels, Mark stopped in the lagoon (in Aquileia on the north coast of the Adriatic), where he dreamed of a Latin-speaking angel who said, *"Pax tibi Marce, evangelista meus"* ("Peace to you, Mark, my evangelist"), promising him rest after death. Back in Alexandria, Mark was attacked by an anti-Christian mob. They tied him with ropes and dragged his body through the streets until he died.

Eight centuries later, his body lay in an Alexandrian church that was about to be vandalized by Muslim fanatics. Two Venetian traders on a business trip saved the relics from desecration by hiding them in a basket of pork—a meat considered unclean by Muslims—and quickly setting sail. The perilous voyage home was only completed after many more miracles. The doge received the body, and in 828 they built the first church of St. Mark's to house it. During construction of the current church (1094), Mark's relics were temporarily lost, and it took another miracle to find them, hidden inside a column. Today, Venetians celebrate Mark on the traditional date of his martyrdom, April 25.

The events of Mark's life are portrayed vividly in many mosaics throughout the basilica. Unfortunately, most of them are either off-limits to tourists or in the dim reaches of the church. Enjoy them by buying a St. Mark's guidebook with photos.

ST. MARK'S BASILICA

Byzantine enamels, and then finished still later with gold filigree by Venetian goldsmiths. This is marvelous handiwork, but all the more marvelous for having been done when Western Europe was still mired in mud. Here are some highlights.

• *Enter the main room, to the right. Start with the large glass case in the center of the room.*

Main Room: This display case holds the most precious Byzantine objects (mostly war booty brought here during the

Fourth Crusade). The hanging lamp with the protruding fish features 4th-century Roman rock crystal framed in 11th-century Byzantine metalwork. Just behind it, a black bucket, carved with scenes of satyrs chasing nymphs, epitomizes the pagan world that was fading as Christianity triumphed. Also in the case are blue-and-gold lapis lazuli icons of the Crucifixion and of the Archangel Michael, featuring a Byzantine specialty—enamel work (more on that craft at the Golden Altarpiece). See various chalices (cups used for the bread and wine during Mass) made of onyx, agate, and rock crystal, and an incense burner shaped like a domed church.

• *Along the walls, find the following displays (working counterclockwise around the room).*

The first three glass cases have bowls and urns made of glass or rock crystal, gold and silver, and precious stones, and laced with elaborate filigree (twisted wires). The styles blend elements from the three medieval cultures that cross-pollinated in the Eastern Mediterranean: Venetian, Byzantine, and Islamic. Next comes the Urn of Artaxerxes I (middle of the right wall), an Egyptian-made object that once held the ashes of the great Persian king who ruled 2,500 years ago (r. 465-425 B.C.). The next cases hold religious paraphernalia used for High Mass—chalices, reliquaries, candlesticks, bishops' robes, and a 600-year-old crosier (ceremonial shepherd staff) still used today by the chief priest on holy days.

Next is the Ciborio di Anastasia (far left corner), a small marble canopy that once arched over the blessed communion wafer during Mass. The object may be a gift from "Anastasia," the name carved on it in Greek. She was a lady-in-waiting in the court of the emperor Justinian (483-565). Christian legend has it that she was so beautiful that Justinian (a married man) pursued her amorously, so she had to dress like a monk and flee to a desert monastery.

Moving to the next wall, you'll see two large golden panels that once fronted an altar; flanking the panels are two golden candlesticks. What detail! The smiling angels at the top, the literary lion, the man with the weight on his shoulders, the row of queens... all the way down to the roots. Continuing counterclockwise, see a photo of a Madonna adorned with jewels, gold, and enamel. If you like this, it's just a taste of what the Pala d'Oro offers.

Next to the Madonna, notice the granite column that extends below current floor level—you can see how the floor has risen as things have settled in the last 1,000 years.

Relics/Sanctuary Room: Straight ahead, the glass case over the glowing alabaster altar contains elaborate gold-and-glass reliquaries holding relics of Jesus' Passion—his torture and execution. The reliquary showing Christ being whipped (from 1125) holds a stone from the column he was tied to. You may scoff, but of Europe's many "Pieces of the True Cross" and "Crown of Thorns"

ST. MARK'S BASILICA

relics, these have at least some claim of authenticity. Legend has it that Christ's possessions were gathered up in the fourth century by Constantine's mother and taken to Constantinople. During the Crusade heist of 1204, Venetians brought them here. They've been paraded through the city every Good Friday for 800 years.

Back by the room's entrance is a glass reliquary with the bones of Doge Orseolo (r. 976-978), who built the church that preceded the current structure. Another contains the bones of St. George, legendary dragon slayer.

⑮ Golden Altarpiece (Pala d'Oro)

• *The Golden Altarpiece is located behind the main altar.*

Under the stone canopy sits the high altar. Inside the altar is an urn (not visible) with the mortal remains of Mark, the Gospel writer. (Look through the grate of the altar to read *Corpus Divi Marci Evangelistae*, or "Body of the Evangelist Mark.") He rests in peace, as an angel had promised him. Shh.

As you shuffle along, notice the marble canopy's support columns carved with New Testament scenes in the 13th century. (On the right-hand pillar closest to the altarpiece, fourth row from the bottom: Is that a genie escaping from a bottle while someone tries to stuff him back in?)

The Golden Altarpiece is a stunning golden wall made of 250 blue-backed enamels with religious scenes, all set in a gold frame and studded with 15 hefty rubies, 300 emeralds, 1,500 pearls, and assorted sapphires, amethysts, and topaz. The Byzantine-made enamels (c. 1100) were part of the Venetians' plunder of 1204, subsequently pieced together by Byzantine craftsmen specifically for St. Mark's high altar. It's a bit much to take in all at once, but get up close and find several details you might recognize:

In the center, Jesus as Ruler of the Cosmos sits on a golden throne, with a halo of pearls and jewels. Like a good Byzantine Pantocrator, he dutifully faces forward and gives his blessing while stealing a glance offstage at Mark ("Marcus") and the other saints.

Along the bottom row, Old Testament prophets show off the books of the Bible they've written. With halos, solemn faces, and elaborately creased robes, they epitomize the Byzantine icon style.

Follow Mark's story in the panels along the sides. In the bottom left panel, Mark meets Peter (seated) at the gates of Rome. It was Peter (legend has it) who gave Mark the eyewitness account of Jesus' life that Mark wrote down in his Gospel. Mark's story ends in the bottom right panel with the two Venetian merchants returning by ship, carrying his coffin here to be laid to rest.

Byzantium excelled in the art of *cloisonné* enameling. A piece of gold leaf is stamped with a design, then filled in with pools of enamel paint, which are baked on. Look at a single saint to see the detail work: The gold background around the saint is the gold-leaf medallion that gets stamped. The golden folds in the robe are the raised edges of the impression. The different colors of the robe are different-colored paints in the recessed areas, each color baked on in a separate firing. Some saints even have pearl crowns or jewel collars pinned on. This kind of craftsmanship—and the social infrastructure that could afford it—made Byzantium seem like an enchanted world during Europe's dim Middle Ages.

After you've looked at some individual scenes, back up as far as this small room will let you and just let yourself be dazzled by the whole picture—this "mosaic" of Byzantine greatness. This magnificent altarpiece sits on a swivel (notice the mechanism at its base) and is swung around on festival Sundays so the entire congregation can enjoy it.

⑯ San Marco Museum (Museo di San Marco)— Mosaics, Bronze Horses, View of the Piazza, and More

• *The staircase up to the museum is in the atrium near the main entrance. The sign says* Loggia dei Cavalli, Museo. *Ascend the steps, buy your ticket, and enter. You'll see several models of the church at various stages of its history. From there, you'll spill out by the museum's three highlights: view of the interior (right), view of the square (out the door to the left), and bronze horses (directly ahead). Belly up to the stone balustrade to survey the interior.*

View of Church Interior

Scan the church, with its 8,000 square meters of mosaics, then take a closer look at the Pentecost Mosaic (first dome above you, described earlier). The unique design at the very top signifies the Trinity: throne (God), Gospels (Christ), and dove (Holy Spirit). The couples below the ring of apostles are the people of the world (I can find Asia, Judaea, and Cappadocia), who, despite their different languages, still understood the Spirit's message.

If you were a woman in medieval Venice, you'd enjoy this same close-up view, because in the Middle Ages, women climbed the same stairs you just did and found a spot along the balconies at your feet. The balcony was for women, the nave for men, and the altar for the priests. Back then the rood screen (the fence with the 15 figures on it) separated the priest from the public, and he officiated with his back to the people.

Appreciate the patterns of the mosaic floor—one of the finest in Italy—that covers the floor like a Persian carpet.

• *From here, the museum loops you to the far (altar) end of the church, then back to the bronze horses. Along the way, you'll see...*

Mosaic Fragments

These mosaics once hung in the church, but when they became damaged or aesthetically old-fashioned, they were replaced by new and more fashionable mosaics. These few fragments avoided the garbage can. You'll see mosaics from the church's earliest days (and most "Byzantine" style, c. 1070) to more recent times (1700s, realistic Renaissance detail). Many are accompanied by small photos that show where the fragment used to fit into a larger scene.

The mosaics—made from small cubes of stone or colored glass pressed into wet clay—were assembled on the ground, then cemented onto the walls. Artists draw the pattern on paper, lay it on the wet clay, and slowly cut the paper away as they replace it with cubes. The first mosaic on your left as you enter shows a reproduction of a paper "cast" of a mosaic.

• *Continuing on, you'll see other artwork and catch glimpses of the interior of the church from the north transept. Here you get a close-up view of the Tree of Jesse mosaic, showing Jesus' distant ancestor at the root and his mom at the top. Continue on to the Sala dei Banchetti (WCs near the room's entrance).*

Sala dei Banchetti

This large, ornate room—once the doge's banquet hall—is filled with religious objects, tapestries and carpets that once adorned the church, Burano lace vestments, illuminated music manuscripts, a doge's throne, and much more.

Try reading some music. The manuscripts date from the 16th century—before the age of treble and bass clefs. You'll see a C clef along the left margin of each staff (which could slide along the staff to locate middle C). From this, you could chant notes in proper relationship to each other, following the rhythm indicated.

In the center of the hall stands the most prestigious artwork here, the Pala Feriale, by Paolo Veneziano (1345). On ordinary workdays, these 14 scenes painted on wood covered the basilica's golden Pala d'Oro. The top row is seven saints (including crucified Christ). Below are seven episodes in Mark's life. In the first panel, Mark kneels before a red-robed Saint Peter and receives his calling. Next, he arrives in Alexandria and makes his first convert. Then Jesus appears to Mark. Mark is beaten to death and dragged through the streets. The panel of the sailboat tells the story of the Venetian merchants' trip home with Mark's relics. A storm at sea billows their sails, ripples the flag, churns the waves, and scares the

ST. MARK'S BASILICA

crew as the ship heads toward the rocks. But then Mark himself appears miraculously at the stern and calms the storm, bringing the ship (and his own body) safely to Venice. Paolo proudly signed his name (along the bottom) and the names of his two assistants, his sons Luca and Giovanni. In the next panel, Mark's long-lost body is rediscovered hidden in a column. Finally, worshippers gather at Mark's tomb by the altar of the basilica.

• *Now double back toward the museum entrance, through displays of stone fragments from the church, finally arriving at...*

The Bronze Horses (La Quadriga)

Stepping lively in pairs and with smiles on their faces, they exude energy and exuberance. Art historians don't know how old they are—they could be from ancient Greece (fourth century B.C.) or ancient Rome during its Fall (fourth century A.D.). Professor Carbon Fourteen says they're from around 175 B.C. Originally, the horses pulled a chariot *Ben-Hur* style. These bronze statues were not hammered and bent into shape by metalsmiths, but were cast from clay molds by using the lost-wax technique. The bronze is high quality, with 97 percent copper. Originally gilded, they still have some streaks of gold. Long gone are the ruby pupils that gave the horses the original case of "red eye."

Megalomaniacs through the ages have coveted these horses not only for their artistic value, but because they symbolize Apollo, the Greco-Roman god of the sun...and of secular power. The doge spoke to his people standing between the horses when they graced the balcony atop the church's facade (where the copies—which you'll see next—stand today).

Their expressive faces seem to say, "Oh boy, Wilbur, have we done some travelin'." Legend says they were made in the time of Alexander the Great, then taken by Nero to Rome. Constantine took them to his new capital in Constantinople to adorn the chariot racecourse. The Venetians then stole them from their fellow Christians during the looting of noble Constantinople (in 1204) and brought them to St. Mark's.

What goes around comes around, and Napoleon came around and took the horses when he conquered Venice in 1797. They stood atop a triumphal arch in Paris until Napoleon's empire was "blown-aparte" and they were returned to their "rightful" home.

The horses were again removed from their spot when they were attacked by their most dangerous enemy yet—modern man.

The threat of oxidation from pollution sent them galloping for cover inside the church.

• *The visit ends outside on the balcony overlooking St. Mark's Square.*

The Loggia and View of St. Mark's Square

You'll be drawn repeatedly to the viewpoint of the square, but remember to look at the facade to see how cleverly all the looted architectural elements blend together. Ramble among the statues of water-bearing slaves that serve as drain spouts. The horses are modern copies (note the 1978 date on the hoof of the horse to the right).

Be a doge, and stand between the bronze horses overlooking St. Mark's Square. Under the gilded lion of St. Mark, in front of the four great Evangelists (who once stood atop the columns), and flanked—like Apollo—by the four glorious horses, he inspired the Venetians in the square below to do great things.

Admire the mesmerizing, commanding view of the center of this city, which so long ago was Europe's only superpower, and today is just a small town with a big history—one that's filled with tourists.

DOGE'S PALACE TOUR

Palazzo Ducale

Venice is a city of beautiful facades—palaces, churches, carnival masks—that can cover darker interiors of intrigue and decay. The Doge's Palace, with its frilly pink exterior, hides the fact that the "Most Serene Republic" (as Venice called itself—"serene" meaning stable) was far from serene in its heyday.

The Doge's Palace housed the fascinating government of this rich and powerful empire. It also served as the home for the Venetian ruler known as the doge (pronounced "dohzh"), or duke. For four centuries (about 1150-1550), this was the most powerful half-acre in Europe. The rest of Europe marveled at the way Venice could govern itself without a dominant king, bishop, or tyrant. The doges wanted their palace to reflect the wealth and secular values of the Republic, impressing visitors and serving as a reminder that the Venetians were Number One in Europe.

Orientation

Cost: €14 combo-ticket (€13 Nov-March) includes the Correr Museum; from April through October, the combo-ticket includes your choice of a third city-run museum. The palace is also covered by the Museum Pass (€18). For specifics, see "Sightseeing Passes for Venice" on page 25.

Hours: Daily April-Oct 8:30-18:30, Nov-March 8:00-17:30, last entry one hour before closing.

Crowd Control: To avoid the long peak-season line at the Doge's Palace, you have several options (the first is best).

    • Buy your combo-ticket at the Correr Museum or at one of the less-crowded, included city-run museums. Then go straight to the Doge's Palace turnstile, skirting along to the right of the long ticket-buying line and entering at the

Doge's Palace

To Rialto

C. CANONICA

RUG. S. APOLLONIA

To San Zaccaria

MERCERIE

Piazzetta dei Leoni

50 Meters

50 Yards

CLOCK TOWER

ST. MARK'S BASILICA

Rio de Palazzo

Piazza San Marco

TETRARCHS

PORTA DELLA CARTA (EXIT)

STAIRWAY OF GIANTS

BRIDGE OF SIGHS

CAMPANILE

Courtyard

DOGE'S PALACE

NEW PRISON

NEW OFFICES

Piazzetta

PONTE DELLA PAGLIA

RIVA DEGLI SCHIAVONI

SAN MARCO COLUMN

ENTRY

TOUR BEGINS

ST. THEODORE COLUMN

St. Mark's Basin

VAPORETTO STOP

V

To Vaporetto, & WC

"prepaid tickets" entrance.

• Buy your ticket online—at least 48 hours in advance—on the museum website (www.museiciviciveneziani.it).

• In peak season, visit the palace at about 17:00, when the line diminishes (but note that this doesn't work from November through March, when the museum closes at 17:30 rather than 18:30).

• Book a guided Secret Itineraries Tour (see "Tours," below).

Getting There: The palace is next to St. Mark's Basilica, on the lagoon waterfront, and just off St. Mark's Square. Vaporetto stops: San Marco or San Zaccaria.

Information: There are some English descriptions, and guide-books are on sale in the bookshop. Tel. 041-271-5911, www.museiciviciveneziani.it.

Tours: The fine **Secret Itineraries Tour** follows the doge's footsteps through rooms not included in the general admission price. Though the tour skips the palace's main hall, you're welcome to visit the hall afterward on your own. Two or three 1.25-hour English-language tours run each morning. Reserve ahead, as tours fill up as much as a month in advance in peak season—although you can try just showing up at the information desk (€18, includes Doge's Palace admission but not Correr Museum; discounted to €12 if you have a combo-ticket or a Museum Pass; to reserve from the US dial 011-39-041-4273-0892, within Italy call 848-082-000, or reserve online at www.museicivicineveneziani.it).

The **audioguide** tour is dry but informative (€5, €8/2 people, 1.5 hours, need ID or credit card for deposit). Pick it up after you pass through the turnstile after the ticket counter.

Length of This Tour: Allow 1.5 hours.

Services: Some WCs are in the courtyard; more are halfway up the stairs to the balcony level. An elevator (off the courtyard) is available for those who have difficulty climbing stairs. Any bag bigger than a large purse must be checked (free) in the courtyard.

Photography: Not allowed.

Cuisine Art: A sandwich-and-salad café is in the palace courtyard (€4 *panini*, €9 salads, €2.50 cappuccino). Nearby are expensive cafés on St. Mark's Square, and good sandwich bars on Calle delle Rasse (two blocks behind the palace—see page 283).

Starring: Big rooms bare of furnishings but crammed with history, Tintoretto masterpieces, and the doges.

The Tour Begins

Exterior

"The Wedding Cake," "The Tablecloth," or "The Pink House" is also sometimes known as the Doge's Palace. The style is called

Venetian Gothic—a fusion of Italian Gothic with a delicate Islamic flair. The columns originally had bases on the bottoms, but these were covered over as the columns sank, and the square was built up over the centuries. If you compare this lacy, top-heavy structure with the massive fortress palaces of Florence, you realize the wisdom of building a city in the middle of the sea—you have no natural enemies except gravity. This unfortified palace in a city with no city wall was the doge's way of saying, "I am an elected and loved ruler. I do not fear my own people."

The palace was originally built in the 800s, but most of what we see came after 1300, as it was expanded to meet the needs of the empire. Each doge wanted to leave his mark on history with a new wing, but so much of the city's money was spent on the palace that finally a law was passed levying an enormous fine on anyone who even mentioned any new building. That worked for a while, until one brave (and wealthy) doge proposed a new wing, paid his fine...and started building again.

• *Enter the Doge's Palace from along the waterfront. After you pass through the turnstile, ignore the signs and cross the courtyard to stand at the foot of the grand staircase topped by two statues.*

The Courtyard and the Stairway of Giants (Scala dei Giganti)

Imagine yourself as a foreign dignitary on business to meet the doge. In the courtyard, you look up a grand staircase topped

with two nearly nude statues of, I think, Moses and Paul Newman (more likely, Neptune and Mars, representing Venice's prowess at sea and at war). The doge and his aides would be waiting for you at the top, between the two statues and beneath the winged lion. No matter who you were—king, pope, or emperor—you'd have to hoof it up. The powerful doge would descend the stairs for no one.

Many doges were crowned here, between the two statues. The doge was something like an elected king—which makes sense only in the dictatorial republic that was Venice. Technically, he was just a noble selected by other nobles to carry out their laws and decisions. Many doges tried to extend their powers and rule more as divine-right kings. Many others just put on their funny hats and accepted their role as figurehead and ceremonial ribbon-cutter. Most were geezers, elected in their 70s and committed to preserving Venetian traditions.

The palace is attached to the church, symbolically welding church and state. Both buildings have ugly brick behind a painted-lady veneer of marble. In this tour, we'll see the similarly harsh inner workings of an outwardly serene, polished republic.

The courtyard is a hodgepodge of architectural styles, as the palace was refurbished over the centuries. There are classical statues in Renaissance niches, shaded by Baroque awnings, topped by Flamboyant Gothic spires, and crusted with the Byzantine onion domes of St. Mark's Basilica.

DOGE'S PALACE

• *Cross back to near the entrance and follow the signs up the tourists' staircase to the first-floor balcony (loggia), where you can look back down on the courtyard (but not the backside of Paul Newman). From this point on, it's hard to get lost (though I've managed). It's a one-way system, so just follow the arrows.*

Midway along the balcony, you'll find a face in the wall, the...

Mouth of Truth

This fierce-looking androgyne opens his/her mouth, ready to swallow a piece of paper, hungry for gossip. Letterboxes like this (some with lions' heads) were scattered throughout the palace. Originally, anyone who had a complaint or suspicion about anyone else could accuse him anonymously *(denontie secrete)* by simply dropping a slip of paper in the mouth. This set the blades of justice turning inside the palace.

• *Toward Paul Newman is the entrance to the...*

Golden Staircase (Scala d'Oro)

The palace was architectural propaganda, designed to impress visitors. This 24-karat gilded-ceiling staircase was something for them to write home about. As you ascend the stairs, look back at the floor below and marvel at its 3-D pattern.

• *Start up the first few steps of the Golden Staircase. Midway up, at the first landing, turn right, which takes you up into the...*

Doge's Apartments (Appartamento del Doge)

The dozen or so rooms on the first floor are where the doge actually lived. The blue-and-gold-hued Sala dei Scarlatti (Room 5) is typical of the palace's interior decoration: gold-coffered ceiling, big stone fireplace, velvety walls with paintings, and a spackled floor. There's very little original furniture, as doges were expected to bring their own. Despite his high office, the doge had to obey several rules that bound him to the city. He couldn't leave the palace unescorted, he couldn't open official mail in private, and he and his family had to leave their own home and live in the Doge's Palace.

Paintings by Titian, Veronese, and Tintoretto

The doge had only the top Venetian painters decorate his palace. While the palace was once rich in Titians, fires in the late 1500s destroyed nearly all the work by the greatest Venetian master. As the palace was hastily reconstructed, the Titians were replaced with works by Veronese and Tintoretto. (Most of these canvases were painted in workshops, and quickly patched in to fill empty spaces.)

Veronese used the best pigments available—from precious stones, sapphires, and emeralds—and his colors have survived vividly. These Veronese paintings are by his hand and are fine examples of his genius. Tintoretto, on the other hand, didn't really have his heart in these commissions, and the pieces here were done by his workshop.

The paintings of the Doge's Palace are a study of old Venice, with fine views of the old city and its inhabitants. The extravagant women's gowns in the paintings by Veronese show off a major local industry—textiles. While the paintings are not generally of masterpiece quality, they're historically interesting. They prove that in the old days, Venice had no pigeons.

The large Room 6, the Sala dello Scudo (Shield Hall), is full of maps and globes. The maps trace the eye-opening trip across Asia—from Italy to Greece to Palestine, Arabia, and "Irac"—of local boy Marco Polo (c. 1254-1325). Finally, he arrived at the other side of the world. This last map (at the far end of the room) is shown "upside-down," with south on top, giving a glimpse of the Venetian worldview circa 1550. It depicts China, Taiwan (Formosa), and Japan (Giapan), while America is a nearby island with California and lots of Terre Incognite.

In Room 7, the Sala Grimani, are several paintings of the lion of St. Mark, including the famous one by Vittore Carpaccio of a smiling lion (on the long wall). The lion holds open a book with these words, *"Pax Tibi Marce..."* ("Peace to you, Mark"), which according to legend were spoken by an angel welcoming St. Mark to Venice. In the background is the Doge's Palace and the Campanile.

When you reach Room 10, the Sala dei Filosofi (Philosophers' Hall), pop up the humble stairway and look back at a Titian quickie, painted in just three days. This fresco of St. Christopher carrying the Christ child across the lagoon was made for a doge who believed that if you looked at St. Christopher, you wouldn't die that day.

• *After browsing the dozen or so private rooms of the Doge's Apartments, continue up the Golden Staircase to the third floor, which was the "public" part of the palace. The first room at the top of the stairs is the...*

Square Room (Atrio Quadrato)

The ceiling painting, ***Justice Presenting the Sword and Scales to Doge Girolamo Priuli***, is by Tintoretto. (Stand at the top of the painting for the full 3-D effect.) It's a late-Renaissance masterpiece. So what? As you'll soon see, this palace is wallpapered with Titians, Tintorettos, and Veroneses. Many have the same theme you see here: a doge, in his ermine cape, gold-brocaded robe, and funny one-horned hat with earflaps, kneeling in the presence of saints, gods, or mythological figures.

• *Enter the next room.*

Room of the Four Doors (Sala delle Quattro Porte)

This was the central clearinghouse for all the goings-on in the palace. Visitors presented themselves here and were directed to their destination—the courts, councils, or the doge himself.

The room was designed by Andrea Palladio, the architect who did the impressive Church of San Giorgio Maggiore, across the Grand Canal from St. Mark's Square. On the intricate stucco ceiling, notice the feet of the women dangling down below the edge (above the windows), extending the illusion.

On the wall next to the door you entered is a painting by (ho-hum) Titian, showing a **doge kneeling** with great piety before a woman embodying Faith holding the Cross of Jesus. Notice old Venice in the misty distance under the cross. This is one of many paintings you'll see of doges in uncharacteristically humble poses—paid for, of course, by the doges themselves.

Executive & Legislative Rooms

```
                         ROOM 11    ROOM 12

                         COLLEGIO   SENATE
                          HALL       HALL
   Courtyard                         ❾
                            ❻      ❽
                ❼
                ❺    ❹
 (Not to scale)                    ROOM OF
                                   THE 4 DOORS   ❸
                                        ❷
                         SQUARE
                ❶        ROOM
                      GOLDEN    HALL
                     STAIRCASE  OF THE
                               COUNCIL OF 10
```

❶ TINTORETTO – Justice Presenting the Sword and Scales
❷ TITIAN – Doge Kneeling
❸ TIEPOLO – Venice Receiving Neptune
❹ VERONESE – The Rape of Europa
❺ TINTORETTO – Bacchus and Ariadne
❻ VERONESE – Discussion
❼ VERONESE – Mars and Neptune with Campanile and Lion
❽ TINTORETTO – Triumph of Venice
❾ Clocks

G. B. Tiepolo's well-known *Venice Receiving Neptune* is now displayed on an easel, but it was originally hung on the wall above the windows where they've put a copy (you'll get closer to the painting as you progress through the museum). The painting shows Venice as a woman—Venice is always a woman to artists—reclining in

luxury, dressed in the ermine cape and pearl necklace of a doge's wife (dogaressa). Crude Neptune, enthralled by the First Lady's beauty, arrives bearing a seashell bulging with gold ducats. A bored Venice points and says, "Put it over there with the other stuff."

• *Enter the small room with the big fireplace and several paintings.*

Ante-Collegio Hall (Sala dell'Anticollegio)

It took a big title or bribe to get in to see the doge. Once accepted for a visit, you would wait here before you entered, combing your hair, adjusting your robe, popping a breath mint, and preparing the gifts you'd brought. While you cooled your heels and warmed your hands at the elaborate fireplace, you might look at some of the paintings—among the finest in the palace, worthy of any museum in the world.

The Rape of Europa (on the wall opposite the fireplace), by Paolo Veronese, most likely shocked many small-town visitors with its risqué subject matter. Here Zeus, the king of the Greek gods,

DOGE'S PALACE

appears in the form of a bull with a foot fetish, seducing a beautiful earthling, while cupids spin playfully overhead. The Venetian Renaissance looked back to pagan Greek and Roman art, a big change from the saints and crucifixions of the Middle Ages. This painting doesn't portray the abduction in a medieval condemnation of sex and violence, but rather as a celebration in cheery pastel colors of the earthy, optimistic spirit of the Renaissance.

Tintoretto's ***Bacchus and Ariadne*** (to the right of the fireplace)

is another colorful display of Venice's sensual tastes. The God of Wine seeks a threesome, offering a ring to the mortal Ariadne, who's being crowned with stars by Venus, who turns slowly in zero gravity. The ring is the center of a spinning wheel of flesh, with the three arms like spokes.

But wait, the doge is ready for us. Let's go in.

• *Enter the next room and approach your imaginary doge.*

Collegio Hall (Sala del Collegio)

Flanked by his cabinet of six advisers—one for each Venetian neighborhood—the doge would sit on the wood-paneled platform at the far end to receive ambassadors, who laid their gifts at his feet and pleaded their countries' cases. All official ceremonies, such as the ratification of treaties, were held here.

At other times, it was the "Oval Office" where the doge and his cabinet (the executive branch) met privately to discuss proposals to give to the legislature, pull files from the cabinets (along the right wall) regarding business with Byzantium, or rehearse a meeting with the pope. The wooden benches around the sides (where they sat) are original. The clock on the wall is a backward-running 24-hour clock with Roman numerals and a sword for hands.

The ceiling is 24-karat gold, with paintings by Veronese. These are not frescoes (painting on wet plaster), like those in the Sistine Chapel, but actual canvases painted in Veronese's studio and then placed on the ceiling. Within years, Venice's humidity would have melted frescoes like mascara.

The T-shaped painting of the woman with the spider web (on the ceiling, opposite the big window) represents the Venetian symbol of **Discussion.** You can imagine the webs of truth and lies woven in this room by the doge's scheming advisers.

In **Mars and Neptune with Campanile and Lion** (the ceiling painting near the entrance), Veronese presents four symbols of the Republic's strength—military, sea trade, city, and government (plus a cherub about to be circumcised by the Campanile).

• *Enter the large Senate Hall.*

Senate Hall (Sala del Senato)

While the doge presided from the stage, senators mounted the podium (middle of the wall with windows) to address their 120 colleagues. The legislators, chaired by the doge, debated and passed laws in this room.

Venice prided itself on its self-rule (independent of popes, kings, and tyrants), with most power placed in the hands of these annually elected men. Which branch of government really ruled? All of them. It was an elaborate system of checks and balances to make sure no one rocked the boat, no one got too powerful, and the ship of state sailed smoothly ahead.

Tintoretto's large **Triumph of Venice** on the ceiling (central painting, best viewed from the top) shows the city in all its glory. Lady Venice is up in heaven with the Greek gods, while barbaric lesser nations swirl up to give her gifts and tribute. Do you get the feeling the Venetian aristocracy was proud of its city?

On the wall are two large clocks, one of which has the signs of the zodiac and phases of the moon. And there's one final oddity in this room, in case you hadn't noticed it yet. In one of the wall paintings (above the entry door), there's actually a doge...not kneeling.

• *Exiting the Senate Hall, you pass again through the Room of the Four Doors, then around the corner into a hall with a semicircular platform at the far end.*

Hall of the Council of Ten (Sala del Consiglio dei Dieci)

By the 1400s, Venice had a worldwide reputation for swift, harsh, and secret justice. The dreaded Council of Ten—10 judges, plus the doge and his six advisers—met here to dole out punishment to traitors, murderers, and "morals" violators. (Note the 17 wood

Judicial Rooms

① Secret Door to Prisons
② VERONESE – Copy of Jupiter Descending
③ Stairs up to Armory Museum
④ Armory Museum (on Mezzanine)
⑤ Stairs down to Hall of the Grand Council

Not to scale

ROOM OF THE 4 DOORS
GOLDEN STAIRCASE
HALL OF THE COUNCIL OF 10
SALA DELLA BUSSOLA
Courtyard
BARRIER
ARMORY MUSEUM

panels where they presided.)

Slowly, they developed into a CIA-type unit with their own force of police officers, guards, spies, informers, and even assassins. They had their own budget and were accountable to no one, soon making them the de facto ruling body of the "Republic." It seemed no one was safe from the spying eye of the "Terrible Ten." You could be accused anonymously (by a letter dropped into a Mouth of Truth), swept off the streets, tried, judged, and thrown into the dark dungeons in the palace for the rest of your life without so much as a Miranda warning.

It was in this room that the Council decided who lived or died, and who was decapitated, tortured, or merely thrown in jail. The small, hard-to-find **door** leading off the platform (the fifth panel to the right of center) leads through secret passages to the prisons and torture chambers.

The large, central, oval ceiling painting by Veronese (a copy of the original stolen by Napoleon and still in the Louvre) shows *Jupiter Descending from Heaven to Strike Down the Vices,* redundantly informing the accused that justice in Venice was swift and harsh. To the left of that, Juno showers Lady Venice with coins, crowns, and peace.

Though the dreaded Council of Ten was eventually disbanded, today their descendants enforce the dress code at St. Mark's Basilica.

• *Pass through the next room, turn right and head up the stairs to the Armory Museum.*

Armory Museum (L'Armeria)

The aesthetic of killing is beyond me, but I must admit I've never seen a better collection of halberds, falchions, ranseurs, targes, morions, and brigandines in my life. The weapons in these three

DOGE'S PALACE

rooms make you realize the important role the military played in keeping the East-West trade lines open.

Room 1: In the glass case on the right, you'll see the suit of armor worn by the great Venetian mercenary general, Gattamelata (far right, on horseback), as well as "baby's first armor" (how soon they grow up!). A full suit of armor could weigh 66 pounds. Before gunpowder, crossbows (look up) were made still more lethal by turning a crank on the end to draw the bow with extra force.

Room 2: In the thick of battle, even horses needed helmets. The hefty broadswords were brandished two-handed by the strongest and bravest soldiers who waded into enemy lines. Suspended from the ceiling is a large triangular banner captured from the Ottoman Turks at the Battle of Lepanto (1571).

Room 3: At the far (left) end of the room is a very, very early (17th-century) attempt at a 20-barrel machine gun. On the walls and weapons, the "C-X" insignia means that this was the private stash of the "Council of Ten."

Room 4: In this room, rifles and pistols enter the picture. Don't miss the glass case in the corner, with a tiny crossbow, some torture devices (including an effective-looking thumbscrew), the wooden "devil's box" (a clever item that could fire in four directions at once), and a nasty, two-holed chastity belt. These "iron breeches" were worn by the devoted wife of the Lord of Padua.

• *Exit the Armory Museum (enjoy a closer look at that early machine gun). Go downstairs, turn left, and pass through the long hall with a wood-beam ceiling. Now turn right and open your eyes as wide as you can to see the...*

Hall of the Grand Council (Sala del Maggiore Consiglio)

It took a room this size to contain the grandeur of the Most Serene Republic. This huge room (175 by 80 feet) could accommodate up to 2,600 people at one time. The engineering is remarkable. The ceiling is like the deck of a ship—its hull is the rooftop, creating a huge attic above that.

The doge presided from the raised dais, while the nobles—the backbone of the empire—filled the center and lined the long walls. Nobles were generally wealthy men over 25, but the title had less to do with money than with long bloodlines. In theory, the doge, the Senate, and the Council of Ten were all subordinate to the Grand Council of nobles who elected them.

Hall of the Grand Council

Piazzetta

3

4

SALA
DELLO
SCRUTINIO

HALL
OF THE
GRAND
COUNCIL

Courtyard

2

1

From
Armory Museum

To Prisons &
Bridge of Sighs

1 TINTORETTO – Paradise
2 VERONESE – The
Apotheosis of Venice
3 Doge Falier (blacked out)
4 DOMENICO ROBUSTI –
Siege of Constantinople

Not to scale

On the wall over the doge's throne is Tintoretto's monster-piece, *Paradise*, the largest oil painting in the world. At 570 square

feet, it could be sliced up to wall-paper an apartment with enough left over for placemats.

Christ and Mary are at the top of heaven, surrounded by 500 people. It's rush hour in heaven, and all the good Venetians made it. The painting leaves you feeling that you get to heaven not by being a good Christian, but by being a good Venetian. Tintoretto worked

on this in the last years of his long life. On the day it was finished, his daughter died. He got his brush out again and painted her as saint number 501. She's dead center with the blue skirt, hands clasped, getting sucked up to heaven. (At least that's what an Italian tour guide told me.)

Veronese's *The Apotheosis of Venice* (on the ceiling at the Tintoretto end—view it from the top) is a typically unsubtle work showing Lady Venice being crowned a goddess by an angel.

Ringing the hall are portraits, in chronological order, of the first 76 doges. The one at the far end that's blacked out is the notorious **Doge Marin Falier,** who opposed the will of the Grand Council in 1355. He was tried for treason, beheaded, and airbrushed from history.

Along the entire wall to the right of Paradise, the *Siege of Constantinople* (by Tintoretto's son, Domenico Robusti) shows Venice's greatest military (if not moral) victory, the conquest of the fellow-Christian city of Constantinople during the Fourth Crusade (1204). The mighty walls of Constantinople repelled every attack for nearly a thousand years. But the sneaky Venetians (in the fifth painting) circled around back and attacked where the walls rose straight up from the water's edge. Skillful Venetian oarsmen cozied their galleys right up to the dock, allowing soldiers to scoot along crossbeams attached to the masts and on to the top of the city walls. In the foreground, an archer cranks up his crossbow. The gates are opened, the Byzantine emperor parades out to surrender, and tiny Doge Dandolo says, "Let's go in and steal some bronze horses."

But soon Venice would begin its long slide into historical oblivion. One by one, the Ottomans gobbled up Venice's trading outposts. In the West, the rest of Europe ganged up on Venice to reduce her power. By 1500, Portugal had broken Venice's East-West trade monopoly by finding a sea route to the East around the southern tip of Africa. To top it off, despite winning a famous victory in the bloody Battle of Lepanto in 1571 (depicted in paintings in the adjoining Sala dello Scrutinio), Venice's reputation as a naval power began to suffer; their ships could not compete with Spain's more modern, more effective armada. Over the centuries, Venice remained a glorious city, but not the world power she once was. Finally, in 1797, the French general Napoleon marched into town shouting *"Liberté, Egalité, Fraternité."* The Most Serene Republic was finally conquered, and the last doge was deposed in the name of modern democracy.

Out the windows (if they're open) is a fine view of the domes of the basilica, the palace courtyard below, and Paul Newman.

The adjoining **Sala dello Scrutinio** room overlooks the Piazzetta. From its balcony, a newly elected doge was presented to the people of Venice. A noble would announce, "Here is your doge, if it pleases you." That was fine, until one time when the people weren't pleased. From then on they just said, "Here is your doge."

• *Consider reading about the prisons here in the Grand Council Hall, where there are more benches and fewer rats.*

To reach the prisons, exit the Grand Hall by squeezing through the door to the left of Tintoretto's monsterpiece. Follow signs for Prigioni/ Ponte dei Sospiri, *passing through several rooms. In Room 31, pause at four fascinating paintings by Hieronymus Bosch (once hung in the Hall of the Council of Ten), showing sinners tortured in hell by genetic mutants and* Wizard of Oz *monkeys. In a room adjoining Room 31, you'll find a narrow staircase going down, following signs to the prisons.*

(Don't miss it, or you'll miss the prisons altogether and end up at the bookshop near the exit.) Then cross the covered Bridge of Sighs over the canal to the prisons. Start your visit in the cells to your left.

Prisons

The palace had its own dungeons. In the privacy of his own home, a doge could oversee the sentencing, torturing, and jailing of

political opponents. The most notorious cells were "the wells" in the basement, so-called because they were deep, wet, and cramped.

By the 1500s, the wells were full of political prisoners. New prisons were built across the canal (to the east of the palace) and connected with a covered bridge.

Medieval justice was harsh. The cells consisted of cold stone with heavily barred windows, a wooden plank for a bed, a shelf, and a bucket. (My question: What did they put on the shelf?) You can feel the cold and damp.

Circle the cells. Notice the carvings made by prisoners—from olden days up until 1930—on some of the stone windowsills of the cells, especially in the far corner of the building.

Explore the rest of the prisons. You can descend lower to the cells known as "the wells." Or stay on this floor, where there's a room displaying ceramic shards found in archaeological digs. Adjoining that are more cells, including the farthest cell, where you can see the bored prisoners' compelling and sometimes artistic graffiti.

• *Wherever you roam, you'll end up where you entered. Now re-cross...*

The Bridge of Sighs

According to romantic legend, criminals were tried and sentenced

in the palace, then marched across the canal here to the dark prisons. On this bridge, they got one last look at Venice. They gazed out at the sky, the water, and the beautiful buildings.

• *Cross back over the Bridge of Sighs, pausing (if scaffolding allows) to look through the marble-trellised windows at all of the tourists and the heavenly Church of San Giorgio Maggiore. Heave one last sigh and leave the palace.*

CORRER MUSEUM TOUR

Museo Correr

A doge's hat, gleaming statues by Canova, and paintings by the illustrious Bellini family—for some people, that's a major museum; for others, it's a historical bore. But the Correr Museum has one more thing to offer, and that's a quiet refuge—a place to rise above St. Mark's Square when the piazza is too hot, too rainy, or too overrun with tourists. Besides, the museum is included if you've bought a ticket to the Doge's Palace. Those who enter are rewarded with an easy-to-manage overview of Venice's art and history.

Orientation

Cost: €14 combo-ticket (€13 Nov-March) includes the Doge's Palace; from April through October, this combo-ticket includes your choice of a third city-run museum. The Correr is also covered by the Museum Pass (€18). The two lesser museums inside the Correr are included in any Correr ticket (National Archaeological Museum and the Monumental Rooms of the Marciana National Library—described briefly in this chapter). For specifics, see "Sightseeing Passes for Venice" on page 25.

Tickets to tour the Clock Tower (€12, requires reservation, see page 42), also include admission to the Correr Museum.

Hours: Daily April-Oct 10:00-19:00, Nov-March 10:00-17:00, last entry one hour before closing.

Getting There: The entrance is on St. Mark's Square in Napoleon's wing—the building at the far end of the square, opposite the basilica. Climb the staircase to the first-floor ticket office and bookstore.

Information: English descriptions are provided throughout. Tel. 041-240-5211, www.museiciviciveneziani.it.

Length of This Tour: Allow one hour.

Baggage Check: Free and mandatory for bags bigger than a large purse.

Photography: Not allowed.

Cuisine Art: The museum café has a few tables with a view of St. Mark's Square (€3.50 cappuccino, €6 *panini*, €2 pastries).

Starring: Canova statues, Venetian historical artifacts, the Bellini family, and a Carpaccio.

The Tour Begins

The Correr Museum gives you admission and access to three connected museums—the Correr proper (which we'll see), the National Archaeological Museum, and the Marciana National Library.

The Correr itself is on three long, skinny floors that parallel St. Mark's Square. This tour covers the first two floors: The first floor contains Canova statues and Venetian history; the second floor displays a chronological overview of Venetian paintings.

First Floor

• *Buy your ticket. After entering, you'll likely find yourself in the long, skinny Room 3, the Loggia Napoleonica. From there, turn right into the large Ballroom (Room 2). Note that, because of temporary exhibits, you sometimes enter Room 2 directly from the bookshop, sometimes through Room 3, and sometimes Room 2 is closed altogether.*

Room 2 (Ballroom)
Canova—*Orpheus and Eurydice*
(*Orfeo*, 1775-1776; *Euridice*, 1775)
Orpheus is leading his beloved back from hell when she is tugged from behind by the cloudy darkness. She calls for help. Orpheus

looks back and smacks his forehead in horror...but he can do nothing to help, and he has to hurry on.

In this youthful work, Venice's greatest sculptor, Antonio Canova, already shows elements of his later style: high-polished, slender, beautiful figures; an ensemble arrangement, with more than one figure; open space between the figures that's almost as compelling as the figures themselves;

CORRER MUSEUM

Correr Museum—First Floor

To St. Mark's Basilica

To Marciana Nat'l Library

CAMPANILE

NATIONAL ARCHAEO-LOGICAL MUSEUM

Piazza

TOURISTS

18 | 19

17

ARMORY →

16

STAIRS TO SECOND FLOOR

15

MAPS →

14

San

13 WC

THE SEA →

12

COINS →

11

10

9

8

7

Marco

DOGES →

6

5

PIGEONS

4

CANOVA

CAFÉ

LOGGIA NAPOLEONICA
3   3

ROOM 1

BALLROOM 2

CANOVA

TICKETS

ENTRY UP STAIRS FROM PIAZZA SAN MARCO

Not to scale

and a statue group that's interesting from many angles.

Carved by a teenage Canova, this piece captures the Rococo spirit of Venice in the late 1700s—elegant and beautiful, but tinged with bittersweet loss. Even Canova's later works—which were more sober, minimalist, and emotionally restrained—retained the elegance and romantic sentiment of the last days of the Venetian Republic.

• *Enter the long hallway known as the Loggia Napoleonica, and admire its views over St. Mark's Square.*

Antonio Canova
(1757-1822)

Son of a Venetian stonemason, Canova grew up with a chisel in his hand in a studio along the Grand Canal, precociously mastering the sentimental, elegant Rococo style of the late 1700s. At 23, he went to Rome and beyond, studying ancient

statues at the recently discovered ruins of Pompeii. These archaeological finds inspired a new Renaissance-style revival of the classical style. Canova's pure, understated elegance and "neo"-classical style soon became the rage all over Europe.

Called to Paris, Canova became Napoleon's court sculptor and carved perhaps his best-known work: Napoleon's sister as Venus, reclining on a couch (now in the Borghese Gallery, Rome). Canova combined Rococo sentiment and elegance with the cool, minimal lines of classicism.

Room 3 (Loggia Napoleonica)

Find Canova's pyramid-shaped model of the ***Monument to Titian*** *(Monumento a Tiziano,* 1795*).* Canova intended this design (based on the pyramid of Gaius Cestius in Rome) for a tomb for the painter Titian. But it was used instead for the tomb of an Austrian princess in Vienna as well as for Canova's own memorial in the Frari Church (for more on Titian's and Canova's monuments, see page 152).

• *Continue on into Room 4.*

Room 4
Canova—*Daedalus and Icarus (Dedalo e Icaro,* 1778-1779)
Serious Daedalus straps wax-and-feather wings, which he's just crafted, onto his son's shoulders. The boy is thrilled with the new toy, not knowing what we know—that the wax in the wings will soon melt in the sun and plunge him to his death. Daedalus' middle-aged, sagging skin contrasts with Icarus' supple form. Canova, a stonemason's son, displays the tools of the family trade on the base.

CORRER MUSEUM

Canova was only 20 when Venice's procurator commissioned this work from the hometown prodigy. It was so realistic that it caused a stir—skeptics accused Canova of not really sculpting it, but making it from plaster casts of live humans.

Room 5
Canova—*Cupid and Psyche* (*Amore e Psiche*, c. 1787)

Though not a great painting, this is Canova's 2-D version of a famous scene he set in stone (now in the Louvre). The two lovers spiral around each other in the never-ending circle of desire. The two bodies and Cupid's two wings form an X. But the center of the composition is the empty space that separates their hungry lips.

Canova—*Paris* (*Paride*, 1807)
The guy with black measles is not a marble statue of Paris; it's a plaster of Paris, a life-size model that Canova used in carving the real one in stone. The dots are sculptor's "points," which tell the sculptor how far into the block he should chisel to establish the figure's rough outline.

Other Canovas
The other large statues in the Canova rooms are either lesser works or more plaster *(gesso)* studies for works later executed in marble. You'll also see small clay models in which Canova worked out ideas before chiseling into an expensive block of marble.

• *Enter the world of Venice's doges. On an easel in Room 6, find a doge portrait.*

Room 6: The Doge
Lazzaro Bastiani—*Portrait of Francesco Foscari* (*Ritratto di Francesco Foscari*, c. 1460)
Foscari, dressed in the traditional brocaded robe and cap with cloth earflaps, introduces us to the powerful, regal world of the doges, the "elected princes" who served as ceremonial symbols of the glorious Republic of Venice.

Foscari (1373-1457, buried in the Frari Church) became doge

The Doge's World

While some doges were powerful dictators, and others merely doddering figureheads, all of Venice's rulers were expected to put on a good show at official events. St. Mark's Square was the site of many ceremonial parades. At the head came flag bearers and trumpet players sounding a fanfare. Next came the bigwigs, the archbishop, the bearer of the doge cap, the doge's chair, and finally Il Serenissimo himself, under an umbrella. Noble ladies looked on from the windows above—the very windows of today's Correr Museum.

The process of electing a new doge was as baffling as the American Electoral College: Thirty nobles were chosen by casting lots, then 21 of them were eliminated by lots. The remaining 9 elected 40 nobles, whose number was whittled down to 25 by lots...and so on through several more steps, until, finally, 41 electors—chosen by their peers and by chance—selected the next doge.

when Venice was at its historical peak as a prosperous sea-trading empire, with peaceful ties to eastern Ottomans and mainland Europeans. He has a serene look of total confidence...a look that would slowly melt as he led Venice on a 31-year war of expansion that devastated northern Italy, embroiled Venice in messy European politics, and eventually drained the city's coffers. Meanwhile, the Ottomans captured Constantinople. By the time the Venetian Senate "impeached" Foscari, forcing his resignation, Venice was sapped, soon to be surpassed by the new maritime powers of Spain and Portugal.

In the glass case, find doge memorabilia, including the funny **doge cap** with a single horn at the back, often worn over a cloth cap with earflaps.

• *High on the wall opposite the room's entrance, find the large painting by...*

Andrea Michieli—*Arrival at San Marco of Dogaressa Morosina Grimani (Sbarco a San Marco della Dogaressa Morosina Grimani*, c. 1597)

Although doges were men, several wives were crowned with ceremonial titles. This painting shows coronation ceremonies along the water by the Piazzetta. The lagoon is jammed with boats. Notice the Doge's Palace on the right, the Marciana National Library on the left (designed by Jacopo Sansovino), and the Campanile and Clock Tower in the distance. The *dogaressa* (left of center, in yellow, wearing her doge cap tilted back) arrives to receive the front-door key to the Doge's Palace.

The doge's private boat, the *Bucintoro* (docked at lower left, with red roof), has brought the First Lady and her entourage of red-robed officials, court dwarves, musicians, dancers, and ladies in formal wear. She walks toward the World Theater (on the right, in the water), a floating pavilion used for public ceremonies.

• *The displays in Rooms 7-10 change often. Browse the exhibits, but also appreciate the fact that these rooms were once government offices.*

Rooms 7-10: Government Offices

Some of the rich furnishings in these rooms—pictures of doge processions (often in Room 7), rare books in walnut bookcases (Room 8), a Murano chandelier, wood-beamed ceiling, and portraits of political bigwigs—are reminders that this wing once housed the administrative offices of a wealthy, sophisticated, trade-oriented republic.

• *Move to Room 11 to view Venetian coins. The collection runs chronologically clockwise around the room.*

Room 11: Coins and the Treasury

The Venetian ducat weighed only a bit more than a US penny, but was mostly gold (by decree, 99 percent pure gold, weighing 3.5 grams). First minted around 1280 (find Giovanni Dandolo's *zecchino*, or "sequin," in the first glass case to the right of the door that leads into the next room), it became the strongest currency in all Europe for nearly 700 years, eventually replacing the Florentine florin. In Renaissance times, 100 ducats would be an excellent salary for a year, with a single ducat worth about $1,000. The most common design shows Christ on the "heads" side, standing in an oval of stars. "Tails" features the current doge kneeling before St. Mark and the inscription "sacred money of Venice" *(SM Veneti).*

Also in Room 11, find **Tintoretto's painting** of three red-robed treasury officials who handled ducats in these offices (*St. Justina and the Treasurers*, 1580). The richness of their fur-lined robes suggests the almost religious devotion that officials were expected to have as caretakers of the "sacred money" of Venice.

Room 12: Venice and the Sea

Venice's wealth came from its sea trade. Raw materials from Europe were exchanged for luxury goods from eastern lands controlled by Muslim Ottomans and Byzantine Christians.

Models of Galleys (*Modello di Galera*)

These fast oar- and wind-powered warships rode shotgun for Venice's commercial fleets plying the Mediterranean. With up to 150 men (four per oar, some prisoners, mostly proud professionals) and three horizontal sails, they could cruise from Venice to Constantinople in about a month. In battle, they specialized in turning on a dime to aim cannons, or in quickly building up speed to ram other ships with their formidable prows. Also displayed are large lanterns from a galley's stern.

• *Find two similar paintings depicting...*

The Battle of Lepanto (*Battaglia di Lepanto*, c. 1571)

The two paintings (by unknown Venetian artists) capture the confusion of a famous battle fought off the coast of Greece in 1571

between Muslim Ottomans and a coalition of Christians. This battle ended Ottoman dominance at sea. Sort it out by their flags. The turbaned Ottomans fought under the crescent moon. On the Christian side, Venetians had the winged lion, the pope's troops flew the cross, and Spain was marked with the Habsburg eagle.

The fighting was fierce and hand-to-hand as the combatants boarded each other's ships and cannons blasted away point-blank. Miguel de Cervantes fought in this battle; he lost his hand and had to pen *Don Quixote* one-handed.

The Christians won, sinking 113 enemy ships and killing up to 30,000. It was a major psychological victory, as it was a turning point in the Ottoman threat to Europe.

But for Venice, it marked the end of an era. The city lost 4,000 men and many ships, and never fully recovered its trading empire in Ottoman lands. Moreover, Spain's cannon-laden sailing ships proved to be masters of the waves, making Spain the next true naval power. Venice's shallow-hulled galleys, so swift in the placid Mediterranean, were no match on the high seas.

Room 13: The Arsenale

A 17th-century pen-and-ink plan *(Pianta dell'Arsenale)* by Antonio di Natale shows a bird's-eye view of the shipbuilding center located

near the tail of Venice. This rectangular, artificial harbor was surrounded by workshops where ships could be mass-produced as though on a modern assembly line (but it was the workers who moved). If needed, they could crank out a galley a day. The Arsenale's entrance (lower left of painting) is still guarded today by the two lions.

Room 14: The Map Room (Venezia Forma Urbis)

Old maps show a city relatively unchanged over the centuries,

hemmed in by water. Find your hotel on Jacopo de' Barbari's big black-and-white map from 1500. There's the Arsenale in the fish's tail. There's Piazza San Marco with a church standing where the Correr Museum entrance is today. The Accademia Bridge hadn't been built yet (nor had the modern train station). We'll see more about Barbari's impressive map upstairs.

Rooms 15-18: Armory

You'll find weapons from medieval times to the advent of gunpowder—maces, armor, swords, Ottoman pikes, rifles, cannons, shields, and a teeny-tiny pistol hidden in a book (in a glass case in Room 17).

• *Those interested in visiting the National Archaeological Museum (Greek and Roman statues) and the impressive Marciana National Library can reach them from Rooms 18 and 19 (included with Correr Museum admission). It's a bit of a detour to the library, and some may wish to skip ahead to "Venetian Painting."*

National Archaeological Museum and Marciana National Library

In the archaeological museum, you pass through room after room of ancient statues (mostly copies that aren't that ancient). You eventually reach the library, famous in Renaissance times because Venice was a major center of printing and secular knowledge. The library displays antique globes and manuscripts. On the ceiling are *tondi* (round) paintings of virtues and allegories of the liberal arts, such as mathematics, geometry, and music. The three *tondi* immediately above where you enter are by Paolo Veronese. The walls are richly decorated with portraits of renowned scholars and ancient philosophers who twist and turn in their niches in classical Baroque style. The smaller room at the end of the hall features Roman copies of Greek statuary and a trompe l'oeil ceiling that makes the wood-beam ceiling appear even higher. The painting in the center of the ceiling by Titian shows Lady Wisdom seated in the clouds reading a book and a scroll.

• *Backtrack to Room 14 (WCs nearby), then head upstairs to the second floor, following signs to* La Quadreria—Picture Gallery. *Enter Room 25.*

Second Floor

Venetian Painting

The painting highlights (the Bellinis) are located at the far end of this wing, and you have permission to hurry there. But along the way, trace the development of Venetian painting from golden Byzantine icons to Florentine-inspired 3-D to the natural beauty of Bellini and Carpaccio.

Room 25

Paolo Veneziano—*Six Saints* (*Sei Santi,* 1340s)

Gold-backed saints combine traits from Venice's two stylistic sources: Byzantine (serene, elongated, somber, and iconic, with gold background, like the mosaics in St. Mark's) and the Gothic of mainland Europe (curvy, expressive bodies posed at a three-quarter angle, colorful robes, and individualized faces).

CORRER MUSEUM

Correr Museum —Second Floor

Room 26

Lorenzo Veneziano—*Figures and Episodes of Saints (Figure e Storie di Santi,* second half of 14th century)

Influence from the mainland puts icons in motion, adding drama to the telling of the lives of the saints (here, in the small scenes above the three saints). St. Nicholas grabs the executioner's sword and lifts him right off the ground before he even knows what's happening.

Room 27: Flamboyant Gothic

Architectural fragments of Gothic buildings remind us that Venice's distinctive architecture is Italian Gothic, filtered through Eastern exoticism. You'll see examples, in both paint and stone, of pointed arches decorated with the flame-like curlicues that gave the Flamboyant Gothic style its name.

Room 29: International Gothic

Master of the Jarves Cassoni—*Story of Alatiel (Storie di Alatiel,* first half of 15th century)

As humanism spread, so did art that was not exclusively religious. These scenes, painted on the panels of a chest, depict a story from Boccaccio's bawdy *Decameron.* Done in the elegant, detailed naturalism of the International Gothic style, the painting emphasizes decorative curves—curvy filigree patterns in clothes, curvy boats, curvy sails, curvy waves, curvy horses' rumps—all enjoyed as a pleasing pattern.

Room 31: Ferrarese Painters

Antonio da Crevalcore (?)—*Portrait of a Young Man* (*Ritratto di Gentiluomo,* c. 1475)

The young man in red is not a saint, king, or pope, but an ordinary citizen painted, literally, wart and all. On the window ledge is a strongly foreshortened book. And behind the young man, the curtain opens to reveal a new world—a spacious 3-D vista courtesy of the Tuscan Renaissance.

Room 32

Jacopo de' Barbari—*Perspective View of Venice* (*Veduta Prospettica di Venezia,* 1500)

How little Venice has changed in 500 years! Barbari's large, intricately detailed woodcut of the city put his contemporaries in a unique position—a mile up in the air, looking down on the rooftops. He chronicles nearly every church, alleyway, and gondola. Both the final product and the carved wood block from which it was printed are on display, a tribute to Barbari's painstaking labor.

Room 33: Flemish Artists

Pieter Brueghel II—*Adoration of the Magi* (*Adorazione dei Magi,* 1617-1633)

The detailed, everyday landscapes of Northern masters strongly influenced Venetian artists. Lost in this snowy scene of the secular working world is Baby Jesus in a stable (lower left), worshipped by the Magi. Venetians learned that landscape creates its own mood, and humans don't have to be the center of every painting.

Room 34

Antonello da Messina—*Pietà* (*La Pietà,* c. 1475)

The Sicilian painter Messina wowed Venice with this work when he visited in 1475, bringing a Renaissance style and new painting techniques. After a thousand years of standing rigidly on medieval crucifixes, the body of Christ finally softens into a natural human posture. The scene is set in a realistic, distant landscape.

Remember this work, as I'll refer to it later.

Room 36: The Bellini Family (I Bellini)

One family single-handedly brought Venetian painting into the Renaissance—the Bellinis.

Jacopo Bellini—*Crucifixion* (*La Crocifissione*, c. 1450)

Father Jacopo (c. 1400-1470) had studied in Florence when Donatello and Brunelleschi were pioneering 3-D naturalism.

Daughter Cecilia (not a painter) married the painter Mantegna, whose precise lines and statuesque figures influenced his brothers-in-law.

Gentile Bellini—*Portrait of Doge Mocenigo* (*Ritratto del Doge Mocenigo*, c. 1478-1485)

Elder son Gentile (c. 1429-1507) took over the family business and established a reputation for documenting Venice's rulers and official ceremonies. His straightforward style and attention to detail capture the ordinary essence of this doge.

Giovanni Bellini—*Crucifixion* (*La Crocifissione*, c. 1453-1455)

Younger son Giovanni (c. 1430-1516) became the most famous Bellini, the man who pioneered new techniques and subject matter, trained Titian and Giorgione, and almost single-handedly invented the Venetian High Renaissance.

Compare this early *Crucifixion* (young Giovanni's earliest documented work) with his father's version. Young Giovanni weeds out all the crowded, medieval mourners, leaving only Mary and John. Behind, he paints a spacious (Mantegnesque) landscape, with a lake and mountains in the distance. Our eyes follow the winding road from Christ to the airy horizon, ascending like a soul to heaven.

Giovanni Bellini—*The Dead Christ Supported by Two Angels (Cristo Morto Sorretto da Due Angeli,* 1453-1455)

In another early work, Giovanni explores human anatomy, with exaggerated veins, a heaving diaphragm, and even a hint of pubic hair. Mentally compare this stiff, static work with Antonello da Messina's far more natural *Pietà*, done 20 years later, to see how far Giovanni still had to go. In fact, Giovanni was greatly influenced by Antonello, appreciating the full potential of the new invention of oil-based paint. Armed with this more transparent paint, he could add subtler shades of color and rely less on the sharply outlined forms we see here.

Giovanni Bellini—*Madonna and Child (Madonna col Bambino,* c. 1470-1475)

Though the canvas is a bit wrinkled, its subject is one Giovanni would paint again and again—lovely, forever-young Mary (often shown from the waist up) holding rosy-cheeked Baby Jesus. He portrayed the holiness of mother and child with a natural-looking, pastel-colored, soft-focus beauty.

Room 38

Vittore Carpaccio—*Two Venetian Gentlewomen (Due Dame Veneziane,* c. 1490)

Two well-dressed Venetians look totally bored, despite being surrounded by a wealth of exotic pets and amusements. One lady absentmindedly plays with a dog, while the other stares into space. Romantics imagined them to be kept ladies awaiting lovers, but the recent discovery of the once-missing companion painting tells us they're waiting for their menfolk to return from hunting. If you like Carpaccio, the Scuola Dalmata di San Giorgio (between St. Mark's Square and Arsenale) has the world's best collection; see page 57.

The colorful details and love of luxury are elements that would dominate the Venetian High Renaissance. Fascinating stuff, but my eyes—like theirs—are starting to glaze...

ACCADEMIA TOUR

Galleria dell'Accademia

The Accademia (ack-ah-DAY-mee-ah) is the greatest museum anywhere for Venetian Renaissance art and a good overview of painters whose works you'll see all over town. Venetian art is underrated and, I think, misunderstood. It's nowhere near as famous today as the work of the florescent Florentines, but—with historical slices of Venice, ravishing nudes, and very human Madonnas—it's livelier, more colorful, and simply more fun.

Orientation

Cost: €6.50.

Hours: Mon 8:15-14:00, Tue-Sun 8:15-19:15, last entry 45 minutes before closing.

Avoiding Lines: Visit early or late to miss the crowds (300 people are allowed in at any one time). Better yet, reserve an entry time (€1) at least a day in advance. It's better to do this by phone (tel. 041-520-0345; calls answered Mon-Fri 9:00-18:00, Sat 9:00-14:00, closed Sun) than online, since you can't cancel or change Internet reservations (www.gallerieaccademia.org). Reserved tickets must be picked up 20 minutes in advance.

Getting There: The museum faces the Grand Canal, just over the Accademia Bridge (15-minute walk from St. Mark's Square—follow signs to *Accademia*). Vaporetto stop: Accademia.

Information: Some of the Accademia's rooms have information in English. The bookshop sells guidebooks for €14. Museum tel. 041-522-2247 (no reservations taken at this number), www.gallerieaccademia.org.

Renovation: The museum is nearing the end of a years-long expansion, which will open up the ground floor to visitors. In 2012, some rooms may still be closed for construction, traffic may be rerouted, and some paintings may reside temporarily in other rooms. A few key works may not be on view at all. Expect changes, and be flexible in taking this tour.

Audioguide: The dull audioguide costs €5 (€7/2 people).

Length of This Tour: Allow one hour.

Baggage Check: Purses and handbags are allowed, but large bags must be checked and may be subject to a charge of €0.50.

Photography: Not allowed.

Cuisine Art: Just outside the museum, Ristorante/Pizzeria Accademia Foscarini is a simple pizza joint with a great Grand Canal setting at the base of the Accademia Bridge (closed Tue).

Nearby: While you're in the Accademia neighborhood, consider visiting the ✪ Ca' Rezzonico, ✪ Peggy Guggenheim Collection, and historic ✪ La Salute Church.

Starring: Titian, Veronese, Giorgione, Bellini, and Tintoretto.

The Tour Begins

Venice—Swimming in Luxury

The Venetian love of luxury shines through in Venetian painting. We'll see grand canvases of colorful, spacious settings peopled with happy locals in extravagant clothes having a great time. The museum proceeds chronologically from the Middle Ages to the 1700s. But before we start at the medieval beginning, let's sneak a peek at a work by the greatest Venetian Renaissance master, Titian.

• *Buy your ticket, check your bag, and head upstairs to a large hall filled with gold-leaf altarpieces. Immediately past the turnstile, turn left and enter the small Room 24. But if renovation prevents access to Room 24 here, try visiting it at the end of this tour, when you can approach it from another direction.*

Titian (Tiziano Vecellio)—*Presentation of the Virgin (Presentazione della Vergine, 1534-1538)*

A colorful crowd gathers at the foot of a stone staircase. A dog eats a bagel, a mother handles a squirming baby, an old lady sells eggs, and onlookers lean out the windows. Suddenly the crowd turns and points at something. Your eye follows up the stairs to a larger-than-life high priest in a jeweled robe.

But wait! What's that along the way? In a pale blue dress that sets her apart from all the other colored robes, dwarfed by the enormous staircase and columns, the tiny, shiny figure of the child Mary almost floats up to the astonished priest. She's unnaturally small, easily overlooked at first glance. When we finally notice her, we realize all the more how delicate she is amid the bustling crowd, hard stone, and epic grandeur. Venetians love this painting and call it, appropriately enough, the "Little Mary."

The painting is a parade of colors. Titian (TEESH-un) leads your eyes from the massive buildings to the deep blue sky and mountains in the background to the bright red robe of the man in the crowd to glowing Little Mary. Titian painted the work especially for this room, fitting it neatly around the door on the right. The door on the left was added later, cutting into Titian's masterpiece.

Accademia—Medieval Art

ROOM 2
EARLY RENAISSANCE

ROOM 1

Courtyard

ROOM 24

STAIRS FROM GROUND FLOOR (TICKETS & COATROOM)

Not to scale

❶ TITIAN – *Presentation of the Virgin*

❷ VENEZIANO – *Madonna and Child with Two Donors*

❸ JACOBELLO – *Coronation of the Virgin in Paradise*

This work is typical of Venetian Renaissance art. Here and throughout this museum, you will find: 1) bright, rich color; 2) big canvases; 3) Renaissance architectural backgrounds; 4) slice-of-life scenes of Venice; and 5) 3-D realism. It's a religious scene, yes, but it's really just an excuse to display secular splendor—Renaissance architecture, colorful robes, and human details.

Now that we've gotten a taste of Renaissance Venice at its peak, let's backtrack and see some of Titian's predecessors.

• *Return to Room 1, stopping at a painting (near the turnstile) of Mary and Baby Jesus.*

Medieval Art

Paolo Veneziano—*Madonna and Child with Two Donors* (*Madonna col Bambino e Due Committenti*, c. 1325)

Mary sits in heaven. The child Jesus is a baby in a bubble, a symbol of his "aura" of holiness.

Notice how two-dimensional and unrealistic this painting is. The sizes of the figures reflect their religious importance—Mary is huge, being the mother of Christ as well as the "Holy Mother Church." Jesus is next in size, then the two angels who crown Mary. Finally, in the corner, are two mere mortals kneeling in devotion. The golden halos let us know who's holy and who's not. Medieval Venetian artists, with their close ties to the East, borrowed techniques such as gold-leafing, frontal poses, and "iconic" faces from the religious icons of Byzantium (modern-day Istanbul).

Most of the paintings in Room 1 are altarpieces, intended to sit in the center of a church for the faithful to meditate on during services. Many feature the Virgin Mary being crowned in triumph. Very impressive. But it took Renaissance artists to remove Mary from her golden never-never land, clothe her in human flesh, and bring her down to the real world we inhabit.

• *In the far right corner of the room, you'll find...*

Jacobello del Fiore—*Coronation of the Virgin in Paradise* (*Incoronazione della Vergine in Paradiso*, 1438)

This swarming beehive of saints and angels is an attempt to cram as much religious information as possible into one space. The architectural setting is a clumsy try at three-dimensionality (the railings of the wedding-cake structure are literally glued on). The color-coordinated saints are simply stacked one on top of the other, rather than receding into the distance as they would in real life.

• *Enter Room 2 at the far end of this hall.*

Early Renaissance (1450-1500)

Only a few decades later, artists rediscovered the natural world and ways to capture it on canvas. With this Renaissance, or "rebirth," of the arts and attitudes of ancient Greece and Rome, painters took a giant leap forward. They weeded out the jumble of symbols, fleshed out cardboard characters into real people, and placed them in spacious 3-D settings.

Giovanni Bellini—*Enthroned Madonna with Child,* a.k.a. *San Giobbe Altarpiece* (*Madonna in Trono col Bambino,* c. 1480)

Mary and the Baby Jesus meet with saints beneath an arched half-dome, engaging in a sacred conversation *(sacra conversazione)*. A trio of musician angels jams at her feet. In its original church setting, the painting's pillars and arches matched the real ones around it (there may be a photo reconstruction nearby), as though Bellini had blown a hole in the wall and built another chapel, allowing us mortals to mingle with holies.

Giovanni Bellini (bell-EE-nee) takes only a few figures, places them in this spacious architectural setting, and balances them, half on one side of Mary and half on the other. Left to right, you'll find St. Francis (medieval founder of an order of friars), John the Baptist, Job, St. Dominic (founder of another order of monks),

Accademia—Early Renaissance

1 GIOVANNI BELLINI – Enthroned Madonna with Child

2 MANTEGNA – St. George

3 GIO. BELLINI – Madonna and Child between St. Catherine and Mary Magdalene

4 GIORGIONE – The Tempest

St. Sebastian, and St. Louis.

The painting has a series of descending arches. At the top is a Roman arch. Hanging below that is a triangular canopy. Then comes a pyramid-shaped "arch" formed by the figures themselves, with Mary's head at the peak, echoed below by the pose of the three musicians. Subconsciously, this creates a mood of serenity, order, and balance, not the hubbub of the *Coronation*. Look at St. Sebastian—even arrows can't disturb his serenity.

In Bellini's long career, he painted many altarpieces in the *sacra conversazione* formula: The Virgin and Child surrounded by saints "conversing" informally about holy matters while listening to some tunes. The formula, developed in the 1430s and 1440s by Fra Angelico (1400-1455) and other Florentine artists, became a common Renaissance theme. Compare this painting with other *sacras* by Bellini in the Frari Church (see page 146) and the Church of San Zaccaria (see page 48).

• *Climb the small staircase and pass through Room 3 into the small Room 4. (If Room 4 is closed for renovation, these paintings may be on display in Room 13.)*

Andrea Mantegna—*St. George* (*San Giorgio,* c. 1460)

This Christian dragon slayer is essentially a Greek nude sculpture with armor painted on. He rests his weight on one leg in the same asymmetrical pose *(contrapposto)* as a classical sculpture, Michelangelo's *David,* or an Italian guy on the street corner. The doorway he stands in resembles a niche designed for a classical statue.

Mantegna (mahn-TAYN-yah) was trained in the Tuscan tradition, in which painters were like sculptors, "carving" out figures (like this) with sharp outlines, filling them in with color, and setting them in distant backdrops like the winding road behind George. When Mantegna married Giovanni Bellini's sister, he brought Florentine realism and draftsmanship to his in-laws.

St. George radiates Renaissance optimism—he's alert but relaxed, at rest but ready to spring into action, humble but confident. With the broken lance in his hand and the dragon at his feet, George is the strong Renaissance Man slaying the medieval dragon of superstition and oppression.

• *Find three women and a baby on a black background.*

Giovanni Bellini—*Madonna and Child between St. Catherine and Mary Magdalene (Madonna col Bambino tra Sta. Caterina e Maria Maddalena, c. 1490)*

In contrast to Mantegna's sharp-focus 3-D, this painting features three female heads on a flat plane with a black velvet backdrop.

Their features are soft, hazy, and atmospheric, glowing out of the darkness as though lit by soft candlelight. It's not sculptural line that's important here, but color—warm, golden, glowing flesh tones. The faces emerge from the canvas like cameos.

Bellini painted dozens of Madonna and Childs in his day. (Others are nearby.) This Virgin Mary is pretty, but she's upstaged by the sheer idealized beauty of Mary Magdalene (on the right). Mary Magdalene's hair is down, like the prostitute that legend says she was, yet she has a childlike face, thoughtful and repentant. This is the perfect image of the innocent woman who sinned by loving too much.

Bellini was the teacher of two more Venetian greats, Titian and Giorgione, schooling them in the new medium of oil painting. Mantegna painted *St. George* using tempera paint (pigments dissolved in egg yolk), while Bellini pioneered oils (pigments in vegetable oil)—a more versatile medium. Applying layer upon transparent layer, Bellini painted creamy complexions with soft outlines, bathed in an even light. His gift to the Venetian Renaissance was the "haze" he put over his scenes, giving them an idealized, glowing, serene, and much copied atmosphere. (You can see more of Bellini's work at the Correr Museum, Frari Church, and the Church of San Zaccaria.)

• *Around the partition (in Room 5), you'll find...*

Giorgione (Giorgio da Castelfranco)—*The Tempest* (*La Tempesta*, c. 1505)

It's the calm before the storm. The atmosphere is heavy—luminous but ominous. There's a sense of mystery. Why is the woman nurs-

ing her baby in the middle of the country-side? And the soldier—is he ogling her or protecting her? Will lightning strike? Do they know that the serenity of this beautiful landscape is about to be shattered by an approaching storm?

The mystery is heightened by contrasting elements. The armed soldier contrasts with the naked mother and her baby. The austere, ruined columns contrast with the lusciousness of Nature. And, most impor-

tant, the stillness of the foreground scene is in direct opposition to the threatening storm in the background. The landscape itself is the main subject, creating a mood, regardless of what the painting is "about."

Giorgione (jor-JONE-ay) was as mysterious as his few paintings, yet he left a lasting impression. A student of Bellini, he learned to use haziness to create a melancholy mood of beauty. But nothing beautiful lasts—flowers fade, Mary Magdalenes grow old, and Giorgione died at 33. In *The Tempest*, the fleeting stillness is about to be shattered by the slash of lightning, the true center of the composition.

• *Exit and browse through several rooms. Check out the bookstore, then continue up the five steps to the large Room 10.*

Venetian High Renaissance (1500-1600)— Titian, Veronese, and Tintoretto

Paolo Veronese—*Feast in the House of Levi* (*Convito in Casa di Levi*, 1573)

Parrrrty!! Stand about 10 yards away from this enormous canvas, to where it just fills your field of vision...and hey, you're invited. Venice loves the good life, and the celebration is in full swing. You're in a huge room with a great view of Venice. Everyone's dressed to kill in colorful silk and velvet robes. Conversation roars and the servants bring on the food and drink.

This captures the Venetian attitude (more love, less attitude) as well as the style of Venetian Renaissance painting. Remember: 1) bright colors, 2) big canvases, 3) Renaissance architectural settings, 4) scenes of Venetian life, and 5) 3-D realism. Painters had mastered realism and now gloried in it.

The *Feast in the House of Levi* is, believe it or not, a religious work painted for a convent. The original title was *The Last Supper*. In the center of all the wild goings-on, there's Jesus, flanked by his disciples, sharing a final meal before his crucifixion.

This festive feast captures the optimistic spirit of Renaissance Venice. Life was a good thing and beauty was to be enjoyed. Renaissance men and women saw the divine in the beauties of Nature and glorified God by glorifying man.

Uh-uh, said the Church. In its eyes, the new humanism was the same as the old hedonism. The false spring of the Renaissance froze quickly after the Reformation, when half of Europe left the Catholic Church and became Protestant.

Veronese (vayr-oh-NAY-zay) was hauled before the Inquisition, the Church tribunal that punished heretics. What did he mean by painting such a bawdy Last Supper? With dwarf jesters? And apostles picking their teeth (between the columns, left of center)? And dogs and cats? And a black man, God forbid? And worst of all, some German soldiers—maybe even Protestants!—at the far right?

Veronese argued that it was just artistic license, so they asked to see his—it had expired. But the solution was simple. Rather than change the painting, just fine-tune the title. *Sì, no problema.* Veronese got out his brush, and *The Last Supper* became the *Feast in the House of Levi,* written in Latin on the railing to the left: *"FECIT D. COVI..."*

Titian—*Pietà* (c. 1573)

Jesus has just been executed, and his followers grieve over his body before burying it. Titian painted this to hang over his own tomb.

Titian was the most famous painter of his day—perhaps even more famous than Michelangelo.

Accademia—High Renaissance

ROOM 10

ROOM 11

Not to scale Courtyard From Early Renaissance

1 VERONESE – Feast in the House of Levi
2 TITIAN – Pietà
3 TINTORETTO – The Removal of St. Mark's Body

He excelled in every subject: portraits of dukes, kings, and popes; racy nudes for their bedrooms; solemn altarpieces for churches; and pagan scenes from Greek mythology. He was cultured and witty, a fine musician and businessman—an all-around Renaissance kind of guy.

Titian was old when he painted this. He had seen the rise and decline of the Renaissance and had experienced much sadness in his own life. Unlike Titian's colorful and exuberant "Little Mary," done at the height of the Renaissance, this canvas is dark, the mood more somber.

The dead Christ is framed by a Renaissance arch like the one in Bellini's *Enthroned Madonna,* but here the massive stones overpower the figures, making them look puny and helpless. The lion statues are downright scary. Instead of the clear realism of Renaissance paintings, Titian uses rough, messy brushstrokes, a technique that would be picked up by the Impressionists three centuries later. Titian adds a dramatic compositional element—starting with the lion at lower right, a line of motion sweeps up diagonally along the figures, culminating in the grief-stricken Mary Magdalene, who turns away, flinging her arm and howling out loud.

The kneeling figure of an old, bald man is a self-portrait of the aging Titian, tending to the corpse of Jesus, who symbolizes the once powerful, now dead Renaissance Man. In the lower right, a painting-within-the-painting shows Titian and his son kneeling, asking the Virgin to spare them from the plague of 1576. Unfortunately, first the son, then the father, succumbed.

(For more Titians, see the ✪ Frari Church Tour chapter and the ✪ Doge's Palace Tour chapter.)

• *On the opposite wall, find...*

Tintoretto (Jacopo Robusti)—*The Removal of St. Mark's Body* (*Trafugamento del Corpo di San Marco,* 1562-1566)

The event that put Venice on the map is frozen at its most dramatic moment. Muslim fundamentalists in Alexandria are about to burn St. Mark's body (there's the smoke from the fire in the center), when suddenly a hurricane appears miraculously, sending them running for cover. (See the wisps of baby-angel faces in the storm, blowing on the infidels? Look hard, on the left-hand side.) Meanwhile, Venetian merchants whisk away the body.

Tintoretto makes us part of the action. The square tiles in the courtyard run straight away from us, an extension of our reality, as though we could step right into the scene—or the merchants could carry Mark into ours.

Tintoretto would have made a great black-velvet painter. His colors burn with a metallic sheen, and he does everything possible to make his subject popular with common people.

In fact, Tintoretto was a common man himself, self-taught, who apprenticed only briefly with Titian before striking out on his own. He sold paintings in the marketplace in his youth and insisted on living in the poor part of town, even after he became famous.

Tintorettos abound here, in the next room, and throughout Venice. Look for these characteristics, some of which became standard features of the Mannerist and Baroque art that followed the Renaissance: 1) heightened drama, violent scenes, strong emotions; 2) elongated bodies in twisting poses; 3) strong contrasts between dark and light; 4) bright colors; and 5) diagonal compositions.

(Tintoretto fans will want to see his "Sistine Chapel;" see the ✪ Scuola San Rocco Tour chapter.)

• *Spend some time in this room, the peak of the Venetian Renaissance and the climax of the museum. After browsing, enter Room 11 and find a large, round painting. Stand underneath it for the full effect.*

Elegant Decay (1600-1800)

Giovanni Battista Tiepolo—*Discovery of the True Cross (La Scoperta della Vera Croce, c. 1745)*

Tiepolo blasts open a sunroof and we gaze up into heaven. We (the viewers) stand in the hole where they've just dug up Christ's cross, looking up dresses and nostrils as saints and angels cavort overhead.

Tiepolo was the last of the great colorful, theatrical Venetian painters. He took the colors, the grand settings, and the dra-

Accademia—Elegant Decay

ROOM 11 ROOM 10 HIGH RENAISSANCE

Courtyard

Not to scale

ROOM 20

ROOM 17

To Exit

ROOM 23 TEMPORARY EXHIBITS

1 TIEPOLO – Discovery of the True Cross
2 CANALETTO – Perspective with Portico
3 GUARDI – San Giorgio Maggiore & the Giudecca
4 GENTILE BELLINI – Procession in St. Mark's Square

ACCADEMIA

matic angles of previous Venetian masters and plastered them on the ceilings of Europe's Baroque palaces, such as the Royal Palace in Madrid, Spain; the Residenz in Würzburg, Germany; and the Ca' Rezzonico in Venice (❂ see the Ca' Rezzonico Tour chapter). This piece is from a church ceiling.

Tiepolo's strongly "foreshortened" figures are masterpieces of technical skill, making us feel as if the heavenly vision is taking place right overhead. Think back on those clumsy attempts at three-dimensionality we saw in the medieval room, and realize how far painting has come. The fresco fragments hanging around the corners of this room were salvaged from a church bombed in World War I.

• *In the rooms branching off the long corridor to your left, you'll find works of the later Venetians. As you walk down the corridor, the first left is Room 17.*

Canaletto and Guardi: Views of Venice

By the 1700s, Venice had retired as a world power and become Europe's number-one tourist attraction. Wealthy offspring of the nobility traveled here to soak up its art and culture. They wanted souvenirs, and what better memento than a picture of the city itself?

Guardi and Canaletto painted "postcards" for visitors who lost their hearts to the romance of Venice. The city produced less art as it became art itself. Here are some familiar views of a city that has aged gracefully.

Canaletto (Giovanni Antonio Canal)— *Perspective with Portico* (*Prospettiva con Portico*, 1765)

Canaletto gives us a sharp-focus, wide-lens, camera's-eye perspective on the city. Although this view of a portico looks totally realistic, Canaletto has compressed the whole scene to allow us to see more than the human eye could realistically take in. We see the portico as though we were standing underneath it, yet we also see the entire portico at one glance. The pavement blocks, the lines of columns, and the slanting roof direct our eye to the far end, which looks very far away indeed. Canaletto even paints a coat of arms (at right) at a very odd angle, showing off his mastery of 3-D perspective.

Francesco Guardi—*San Giorgio Maggiore and the Giudecca* (*San Giorgio Maggiore e Giudecca*, c. 1774)

Unlike Canaletto, with his sharp-focus detail, Guardi sweetens Venice up with a haze of messy brushwork. In this familiar view

across the water from St. Mark's Square, he builds a boatman with a few sloppy smudges of paint. Guardi catches the play of light at twilight, the shadows on the buildings, the green of the water and sky, the pink light off the distant buildings, the Venice that exists in the hearts of lovers—an Impressionist work a century ahead of its time.

• *Return to the corridor, turn left at the end, then take another left, and then left again. Are you in Room 20? If so, find...*

Gentile Bellini—*Procession in St. Mark's Square* (*Processione in Piazza San Marco*, 1496)

A fitting end to our tour is a look back at Venice in its heyday.

Painted by Giovanni's big brother, this wide-angle view—more than any human eye could take in at once—reminds us how little Venice has changed over the centuries. There is St. Mark's gleaming gold with mosaics, the four bronze horses, the three flagpoles out front, the old Campanile on the right, and the Doge's Palace. There's the guy selling 10 postcards for a dollar. (But there's no Clock Tower with the two bronze Moors yet, the pavement's different, the church is covered with gold, and there are no café orchestras playing "New York, New York.") Every detail is in perfect focus, regardless of its distance from us, presented for our inspection. Take some time to linger over this and the other views of old Venice in this room. Then get outta here and enjoy the real thing.

• *To exit, backtrack to the main corridor and turn left. There are often temporary exhibits in Room 23, the large former chapel branching off the corridor. Say* ciao *to Titian's "Little Mary" on the way out.*

FRARI CHURCH TOUR

Basilica di Santa Maria Gloriosa dei Frari

For many travelers, this church offers the best art-appreciation experience in Venice, because so much of its great art is in situ—right where it was designed to be seen, rather than hanging in museums. And it's about the only Gothic church you'll tour here. Because Venice's spongy ground could never support a real stone Gothic church (like you'd find in France), the Frari is made of light and flexible brick. The white limestone foundation insulates the building from the wet soil.

The church was built by the Franciscan order, which arrived in Venice around 1230 (the present building was consecrated in 1492). Franciscan men and women were inspired by St. Francis of Assisi (c. 1182-1226), who dedicated himself to a nonmaterialistic lifestyle—part of a reform movement that spread across Europe in the early 1200s. The Roman Church felt distant and corrupt, and there was a hunger for religious teaching that connected with everyday people. While some of these movements were dubbed heretical (like that of the Cathars in southern France), the Franciscans (and Dominicans) eventually earned the Church's blessing.

The spirit of St. Francis of Assisi warms both the church of his "brothers" *(frari)* and the art that decorates it. The Franciscan love of all of creation—Nature and Man—later inspired Renaissance painters to capture the beauty of the physical world and human emotions, showing worshippers the glory of God in human terms.

Orientation

Cost: €3.

Hours: Mon-Sat 9:00-18:00, Sun 13:00-18:00, last entry 30 minutes before closing, no visits during services.

Dress Code: Modest dress is recommended.

Getting There: It's on Campo dei Frari, near the San Tomà vaporetto and *traghetto* stops. From the dock, follow signs to *Scuola Grande di San Rocco*.

Information: Tel. 041-272-8611, www.basilicadeifrari.it.

Audioguides: You can rent an audioguide for €2 (€3/2 people). Or download a free audio version of my tour via www.ricksteves .com/audioeurope, iTunes, or the Rick Steves Audio Europe smartphone app.

Length of This Tour: Allow one hour.

Photography: Prohibited.

Cuisine Art: The church square is ringed with small, simple, reasonably priced cafés.

Concerts: The church occasionally hosts evening concerts (€20, buy ticket at church, no concerts in winter). For concert details, look for fliers, check the website, or call the church at tel. 041-272-8618.

Nearby: For efficient sightseeing, combine your visit with the ✪ Scuola San Rocco, located behind the Frari Church. The ✪ Ca' Rezzonico is a seven-minute walk away: From the back end of the Frari Church, go through alleyway Sotoportego S. Rocco, turn left at the first T intersection, then right at the big white building. If you reach Campo San Barnaba, you've passed it—ask someone, *Dov'è Ca' Rezzonico?"* (doh-VEH kah ret-ZON-ee-koh).

Starring: Titian, Giovanni Bellini, Paolo Veneziano, and Donatello.

The Tour Begins

• *Enter the church and turn right, finding a spot at the far end with a good view down the long nave toward the altar.*

❶ Church Interior and Choir (1250-1443)

The simple, spacious (110-yard-long), well-lit Gothic church— with rough wood crossbeams and a red-and-white color scheme— is truly a remarkable sight in a city otherwise crammed with exotic froufrou. Traditionally, churches in Venice were cross-shaped, but because the Franciscans were an international order, they weren't limited to Venetian tastes. This new T-shaped footprint featured

Frari Church

Not to scale

To Accademia

Campo San Rocco

To Scuola San Rocco

❷ ALTAR

❸

❹

❺ SACRISTY

TRANSEPT

CHAPTER HOUSE

❻

CHOIR

TICKETS

❾

ENTRY

N A V E

Campo dei Frari

❽

❼

To Rialto

❶

TOUR BEGINS

❶ View of Church Interior & Choir

❷ TITIAN – The Assumption of the Virgin

❸ Tomb of Doge Foscari

❹ DONATELLO – Statue of John the Baptist

❺ GIO. BELLINI – Madonna and Child with Saints and Angels

❻ VENEZIANO – Madonna and Child with Doge Francesco Dandolo

❼ Tomb of Titian

❽ Canova Monument

❾ TITIAN – Madonna of Ca' Pesaro

a long, lofty nave—flooded with light and suited to large gatherings—where common people heard sermons.

The wooden choir area in the center of the nave allowed friars to hold smaller, more intimate services. From the early 16th century, as worshippers entered the church and looked down the long nave to the altar, they were greeted by Titian's altarpiece—then, as now, framed by the arch of the choir entrance.

Walk prayerfully toward the Titian, stopping in the finely carved 1480s choir. Notice the fine inlay above the chairs, showing the Renaissance enthusiasm for Florentine-style depth and perspective. Surviving choirs such as this are rare. (In response to Luther's challenge, Counter-Reformation churches discarded the idea of the choirs and altar screens in order to get priests closer to their flocks.)

• *Approach Titian's heavenly vision.*

❷ Titian (Tiziano Vecellio)— *The Assumption of the Virgin* (1516-1518)

Glowing red and gold like a stained-glass window, this altarpiece sets the tone of exuberant beauty found in this church. At the end of her life (though looking 17 here), Mary was miraculously "assumed" into heaven. As cherubs lift her up to meet a Jupiter-like God, the stunned apostles on earth reach up to touch the floating bubble of light.

Look around. The church is littered with chapels and tombs "made possible by the generous financial support" of rich people who donated to the Franciscans for the good of their souls (and usually for tomb-topping statues of themselves, as well). But the Franciscans didn't sell their main altar; instead they hired the new whiz artist, Titian, to create a dramatic altar painting.

Unveiled in 1518, the work scandalized a Venice accustomed to simpler, more subdued church art. The rich colors, twisting poses, and mix of saccharine angels with blue-collar apostles were unheard of. Most striking, this Virgin is fully human, not a stiff icon on a throne. The Franciscans thought this Mary aroused excitement rather than spirituality. They agreed to pay Titian only after the Holy Roman Emperor offered to buy the altar if they refused.

In a burst of youthful innovation, Titian (1488-1576) had rewritten the formula for church art, hinting at changes to come with the Mannerist and Baroque styles. He energized the scene with a complex composition, overlapping a circle (Mary's bubble) and a triangle (draw a line from the apostle reaching up to Mary's face and down the other side) on three horizontal levels (God in heaven, Man on earth, Mary in between). Together, these elements draw our eyes from the swirl of arms and legs to the painting's focus—the radiant face of a triumphant Mary, "assumed body and soul into heaven."

• *Also in the apse (behind the main altar) are marble tombs lining the walls. On the wall to the right of the altar is the...*

❸ Tomb of Doge Foscari (15th Century)

This heavy, ornate tomb marks the peak of Venice's worldly power. Doge Francesco Foscari (1373-1457) assumed control of the city's powerful seafaring empire and then tried to expand it onto the mainland, battling Milan in a 31-year war of attrition that swept through northern Italy. Meanwhile, on the unprotected eastern front, the Ottomans took Constantinople (1453) and scuttled Venice's trade. Venice's long slide into historical oblivion had begun. Financially drained city fathers forced Foscari to resign, turn in his funny hat, and hand over the keys to the Doge's Palace.

• *In the first chapel to the right of the altar, you'll find...*

❹ Donatello—Statue of John the Baptist (1438)

In the center of the altarpiece, the cockeyed prophet of the desert—emaciated from his breakfast of bugs 'n' honey and dressed in animal skins—freezes mid-rant when he spies something in the distance. His jaw goes slack, he twists his face and raises his hand to announce the coming of...the Renaissance.

The Renaissance began in the Florence of the 1400s, where Donatello (1386-1466) created realistic statues with a full range of human emotions. This warts-and-all John the Baptist contrasts greatly with, say, Titian's sweet Mary. Florentine art (including painting) was sculptural, strongly outlined, and harshly realistic, with muted colors. Venetian art was painterly, soft focus, and beautiful, with bright colors.

Florentine expatriates living in Venice commissioned Donatello to make this wooden statue for their local chapel.

• *Enter the sacristy through the door at the far end of the right transept. You'll bump into an elaborate altar crammed with reliquaries. Opposite that (near the entrance door) is a clock, intricately carved from a single piece of wood. At the far end of the room, you'll find...*

❺ Giovanni Bellini—*Madonna and Child with Saints and Angels* (1488)

The Pesaro family, who negotiated an acceptable price and place for their family tomb, funded this delightful chapel dominated by a Bellini masterpiece.

Mary sits on a throne under a half-dome, propping up Baby Jesus (who's just learning to stand), flanked by saints and serenaded by musician angels. Giovanni Bellini (c. 1430-1516), the father of the Venetian Renaissance, painted fake columns and a dome to match the real ones in the gold frame, making the painting seem to be an extension of the room. He completes the illusion with glimpses of open sky in the background. Next, he fills the artificial niches with symmetrically posed, thoughtful saints—left to right, find Saints Nicholas, Peter, Mark, and Sean Connery (Benedict).

Bellini combined the meditative poses of the Venetian Byzantine tradition with Renaissance improvements in modern art. He made the transition from painting with medieval tempera (egg yolk-based) to painting in oil (pigments dissolved in vegetable oil). Oils allowed a subtler treatment of colors because artists could apply them in successive layers. And because darker colors aren't so muddy when painted in oil, they "pop," effectively giving the artist a brighter palette.

Bellini virtually invented the formula (later to be broken by his precocious pupil, Titian) for Venetian altarpieces. This type of holy conversation *(sacra conversazione)* between saints and Mary can also be seen in Venice's Accademia and Church of San Zaccaria.

Renaissance humanism demanded Madonnas and saints that were accessible and human. Bellini delivers, but places them in a physical setting so beautiful that it creates its own mood of serene holiness. The scene is lit from the left, but nothing casts a harsh shadow—Mary and the babe are enveloped in a glowing aura of reflected light from the golden dome. The beauty is in the details, from the writing in the dome, to the red brocade backdrop, to the swirls in the marble steps, to the angels' dimpled legs.

• *In the adjoining room, find a painting in the shape of a Gothic arch.*

❻ Paolo Veneziano—*Madonna and Child with Doge Francesco Dandolo* (c. 1339)

Bellini's Byzantine roots can be traced to Paolo Veneziano (literally, "the Venetian"), the first "name" artist in Venice, who helped shape

the distinctive painting style of his city. In turn, Veneziano was inspired by Byzantine artists who had come to Venice in search of greater freedom of expression. They had chafed under strict societies (Byzantine and, in some locales, Islamic) that frowned on painting figurative images. In Venice, these expats found an eager community of rich patrons who indulged their love of deeper color, sentiment, movement, and decoration. (Venice clung to this style to the point that it eventually lagged behind Western Europe.)

In this altarpiece, Veneziano paints Byzantine icons, then sets them in motion. Baby Jesus turns to greet a kneeling Doge Dandolo, while Mary turns to acknowledge the doge's wife. None other than St. Francis presents "Francis" (Francesco) Dandolo to the Madonna. Both he and St. Elizabeth (on the right) bend at the waist and gesture as naturally as 14th-century icons can.

• *Return to the nave and head toward the far end. Turn around and face the altar. The Tomb of Titian is in the second bay on your right.*

❼ Tomb of Titian (1852)

The enormous carved marble monument is labeled "Titiano Ferdinandus MDCCCLII." The tomb celebrates both the man (the center statue shows Titian with a beard and crown of laurels) and his famous paintings (depicted in the background reliefs).

Titian was the greatest Venetian painter, excelling equally in inspirational altarpieces, realistic portraits, joyous mythological scenes, and erotic female nudes.

He moved to Venice as a child, studied first as a mosaic-maker and then under Giovanni Bellini and Giorgione, before establishing his own bold style, which featured teenage Madonnas (see a relief of *The Assumption of the Virgin* behind Titian). He became wealthy and famous, traveling Europe to paint stately portraits of kings and nobles, and colorful, sexy works for their bedrooms. Titian resisted the temptation of big money that drew so many of his contemporary Venetian artists to Rome. Instead he always returned to his beloved Venice (see winged lion on top)...and favorite Frari Church.

In his old age, Titian painted dark, tragic masterpieces, including the *Pietà* (see relief in upper left) that was intended for his tomb but ended up in the Accademia (see page 140). Nearing 90, he labored to finish the *Pietà* as the plague enveloped Venice. One in four people died, including Titian's son and assistant, Orazio. Heartbroken, Titian died soon afterward, probably of the plague, although his death was officially chalked up to influenza (to keep his body from being burned—a requirement for plague victims). His tomb was built three centuries later to remember and honor this great Venetian.

• *On the opposite side of the nave is the pyramid-shaped...*

❽ Canova Monument (1827)

Antonio Canova (1757-1822, see his portrait above the door) was Venice's greatest sculptor. He created gleaming white, highly polished statues of beautiful Greek gods and goddesses in the Neoclassical style. (See several of his works at the Correr Museum.)

The pyramid shape is timeless, suggesting pharaohs' tombs and the Christian Trinity. Mourners, bent over with grief, shuffle up to pay homage to the master artist. Even the winged lion is choked up.

Follow me here. Canova himself designed this pyramid-shaped tomb, not for his own use, but as the tomb of an artist he greatly admired: Titian. But the Frari picked another design for Titian's tomb, so Canova used the pyramid for an Austrian princess...in Vienna. After his death, Canova's pupils copied the design here to honor their master. In fact, Canova isn't buried here—he lies in southern Italy. But inside the tomb's open door, you can (barely) see an urn, which contains his heart.

• *Head back toward the altar. Halfway up the left wall is...*

❾ Titian—*Madonna of Ca' Pesaro* (1519-1526)

Titian's second altarpiece for the Frari Church displays all his many skills. Following his teacher Bellini, he puts Mary (seated) and baby (standing) on a throne, surrounded by saints having a holy conversation. And, like Bellini, he paints fake columns that echo the church's real ones.

But wait. Mary is off-center, Titian's idealized saints mingle with Venetians sporting five o'clock shadows, and the stairs run diagonally away from us. Mary sits not on a throne, but on a pedestal. Baby Jesus is restless. The precious keys of St. Peter seem to dangle unnoticed. These things upset traditional Renaissance symmetry, but they turn a group of figures into a true scene. St. Peter (center, in blue and gold, with book) looks down at Jacopo Pesaro, who kneels to thank the Virgin for his recent naval victory over the Ottomans (1502). A flag-carrying lieutenant drags in a turbaned captive. Meanwhile, St. Francis talks to Baby Jesus while gesturing down to more members of the Pesaro family. The little guy looking out at us (lower right) is the Pesaro descendant who administered the trust fund to keep prayers coming for his dead uncle.

Titian combines opposites: a soft-focus Madonna with photo-realist portraits, chubby winged angels with a Muslim prisoner, and a Christian cross with a battle flag. In keeping with the spirit of St. Francis' humanism, Titian lets mere mortals mingle with saints. And we're right there with them.

SCUOLA SAN ROCCO TOUR

Scuola Grande di San Rocco

The 50-plus paintings in the Scuola Grande di San Rocco—often called "Tintoretto's Sistine Chapel"—present one man's very personal vision of Christian history. Tintoretto spent the last 20 years of his life working practically for free, driven by the spirit of charity that the Scuola, a Christian organization, promoted. For Tintoretto fans, this is the ultimate. Even for the art-weary, his large, colorful canvases, framed in gold on the walls and ceilings of a grand upper hall, are an impressive sight.

Orientation

Cost: €7. (If you see an evening concert here, you can enjoy the art as a bonus; see page 298.)

Hours: Daily 9:30-17:30, last entry 30 minutes before closing.

Getting There: It's next to the Frari Church (see "Getting There" in previous chapter). Vaporetto: San Tomà. For an easy route on foot from the Rialto Bridge, ✪ take the Rialto to Frari Church Walk, following signs to *Scuola Grande di San Rocco*.

Information: Tel. 041-523-4864, www.scuolagrandesanrocco .it. WCs are on the ground floor; get the key from the ticket clerk.

Audioguide: The chapel's fine audioguide costs €1.

Mirrors: Use the mirrors scattered about the museum's Grand Hall, because much of this art is on the ceiling and a pain in the neck.

Length of This Tour: Allow one hour.

Nearby: Right next door is the Church of San Rocco, featuring still more Tintorettos (free, same hours as the Scuola).

Starring: Tintoretto, Tintoretto, and Tintoretto.

Scuola San Rocco

To Accademia

To Frari

Campo
San Rocco

① TOUR BEGINS ⑮

ENTRY →

**GROUND
FLOOR**

TICKETS &
AUDIOGUIDE
KIOSK

⑯

To
San Rocco
Church

WC

STAIRS UP TO
GREAT HALL

SCUOLA SAN ROCCO

(Not to scale)

⑪   ⑫ ⑬   ⑭

CEILING

⑨   ⑧   ⑩

**GREAT
HALL**

PAINTINGS

(UPSTAIRS)

④

⑤   ③

ALBERGO   ②

⑥   ⑦

STAIRS FROM/TO
GROUND FLOOR

❶ The Annunciation
❷ St. Roch in Glory
❸ Christ Before Pilate
❹ Christ Crowned
   with Thorns
❺ The Way to Calvary
❻ The Crucifixion
❼ Three Apples
❽ The Miracle of the
   Bronze Serpent

❾ Moses Strikes Water
   from the Rocks
❿ The Fall of Manna in the Desert
⓫ The Adoration of
   the Shepherds
⓬ The Resurrection
⓭ Tintoretto's Carved Face
⓮ The Last Supper
⓯ The Flight into Egypt
⓰ The Circumcision

The Tour Begins

The art of the Scuola is contained in three rooms—the Ground Floor Hall (where you enter) and two rooms upstairs, including the Great Upper Floor Hall, with the biggest canvases. Your ticket also admits you to the Scuola's small and skippable treasury (one more flight up).

• *Enter on the ground floor, which is lined with big, colorful Tintoretto canvases. Begin with the first canvas on the left.*

Ground Floor Hall

❶ *The Annunciation*

An angel swoops through the doorway, dragging a trail of naked baby angels with him, to tell a startled Mary she'll give birth to Jesus. This canvas has many of Tintoretto's typical characteristics:

- **The miraculous and the everyday mingle side-by-side.** Glorious angels are in a broken-down house with stacks of lumber and a frayed chair.
- **Bright light and dark shadows.** A bright light strikes the brick column, highlighting Mary's face and the angel's shoulder, but casting dark shadows across the room.
- **Strong 3-D sucks you into the scene.** Tintoretto literally tears down Mary's wall to let us in. The floor tiles recede sharply into the distance, making Mary's room an extension of our real space.
- **Colors that are bright, almost harsh,** with a metallic "black-velvet" sheen, especially when contrasted with the soft-focus haze of Bellini, Giorgione, Veronese, and (sometimes) Titian.
- **Twisting, muscular poses.** The angel turns one way, Mary turns the other, and the baby angels turn every which way.
- **Diagonal composition.** Shadows run diagonally on the floor as Mary leans back diagonally.
- **Rough brushwork.** The sketchy pattern on Mary's ceiling contrasts with the precise photo-realism of the brick column.

And finally, *The Annunciation* exemplifies the general theme of the San Rocco paintings—God intervenes miraculously into our everyday lives in order to save us.

• *We'll return to the ground floor later, but let's get right to the highlights. Climb the staircase (taking time to admire the plague scenes that are not by Tintoretto) and enter the impressive Great Hall.*

Wow! Before we tackle the big canvases in this huge room, let's start where Tintoretto did, in the Albergo Hall—the small room in the left

Jacopo Tintoretto
(1518-1594)

The son of a silk dyer ("Tintoretto" is a nickname meaning "little dyer"), Tintoretto applied a blue-collar work ethic to painting, becoming one of the most prolific artists ever. He trained briefly under Titian, but their egos clashed. He was influenced more by Michelangelo's recently completed *Last Judgment,* with its muscular, twisting, hovering nudes and epic scale.

By age 30, Tintoretto was famous, astounding Venice with the innovative *St. Mark Freeing the Slave* (now in the Accademia). He married, had eight children (three of whom became his assistants), and dedicated himself to work and family, shunning publicity and living his whole life in his old Venice neighborhood.

Twenty years of his life were spent decorating the Scuola di San Rocco. It was a labor of love, showing his religious faith, his compassion for the poor, and his artistic passion.

corner of the Great Hall. On the ceiling of the Albergo Hall is an oval painting of St. Roch, best viewed from the doorway.

Albergo Hall (Sala d'Albergo)— Christ's Passion

❷ *St. Roch in Glory* (1564)

Start at the feet of St. Roch (San Rocco), a French medical student in the 1300s who dedicated his short life to treating plague victims. The Scuola di San Rocco was a kind of Venetian "Elks Club" whose favorite charity was poor plague victims.

This is the first of Tintoretto's 50-plus paintings in the Scuola. It's also the one that got him the job, beating entries by Veronese and others.

Tintoretto amazed the judges by showing the saint from beneath, as though he hovered above in a circle of glory. This Venetian taste for dramatic angles and illusion would later become standard in

Baroque ceilings. Tintoretto trained by dangling wax models from the ceiling and lighting them from odd angles.

• *On the walls are scenes of Christ's trial, torture, and execution. Work counterclockwise around the room, starting by the door with...*

❸ Christ Before Pilate (Ecce Homo)

Jesus has been arrested and brought before the Roman authorities in a cavernous hall. Although he says nothing in his own defense, he stands head and shoulders above the crowd, literally "rising above" the slanders. Tintoretto shines a bright light on his white robe, making Christ radiate innocence.

At Christ's feet, an old, bearded man in white stoops over to record the events on paper—it's Tintoretto himself.

❹ Christ Crowned with Thorns

Jesus was beaten, whipped, then mocked by the soldiers, who dressed him as a king "crowned" with thorns. Seeing the blood-stains on the cloth must have touched the hearts of Scuola members, generating compassion for those who suffer.

❺ The Way to Calvary

Silhouetted against a stormy sky, Jesus and two other prisoners trudge up a steep hill, carrying their own crosses to the execution site. The cycle culminates with...

❻ The Crucifixion

The crucified Christ is the calm center of this huge and chaotic scene that fills the wall. Workers struggle to hoist crosses, mourners swoon, riffraff gamble for Christ's clothes, and soldiers mill about aimlessly. Scarcely anyone pays any attention to the Son of God...except us, because Tintoretto directs our eye there.

All the lines of sight point to Christ at the center: the ladder on the ground, the cross being raised, the cross still on the ground, the horses on the right, and the hillsides that slope in. In a trick of multiple perspectives, the cross being raised seems to suck us in toward the center, while the cross still on the ground seems to cause the figures to be sucked toward us.

Above the chaos stands Christ, high above the horizon, higher than everyone, glowing against the dark sky. Tintoretto lets us appreciate the quiet irony lost on the frenetic participants—that this minor criminal suffering such apparent degradation is, in fact, triumphant.

• *Displayed on an easel to the left of and beneath* The Crucifixion *is a small fragment of...*

❼ *Three Apples*

This fragment, from the frieze around the upper reaches of the Albergo Hall, was discovered folded under the frieze in 1905. Because it was never exposed to light, it still retains Tintoretto's original bright colors. All of his paintings are darker today, despite cleaning, due to the irreversible chemical alteration of the pigments.

• *Now step back out into the Great Upper Hall.*

Great Upper Hall— Understanding What You're Standing Under

Thirty-four enormous oil canvases, set into gold frames on the ceiling and along the walls of this impressive room, tell biblical history from Adam and Eve to the Ascension of Christ. Tintoretto's storytelling style is straightforward, and anyone with knowledge of the Bible can quickly get the gist. Tintoretto's success in the Albergo Hall won him the job of the enormous Great Upper Hall.

The ceiling displays Old Testament scenes; the walls show events from the New Testament. Beyond that, the layout is not chronological but symbolic, linked by common themes. Tintoretto shows how God leads mankind to salvation. Evil enters the world with the Original Sin of *Adam and Eve* (at the Albergo end of room, on the ceiling). From there, man must go through many trials, as the ceiling shows—the struggles of Moses and the Israelites, Jonah, and Abraham. But God is always there to help. In the three largest paintings on the ceiling, God saves man from thirst *(Moses Strikes Water from the Rocks)*, illness *(The Miracle of the Bronze Serpent)*, and hunger *(The Fall of Manna in the Desert)*. Christ's story (along the walls) parallels the struggles of men (on the ceiling). But while the first humans *(Adam and Eve)* succumb to Satan's temptation, Christ does not (see *Christ Tempted by Satan*, on the wall nearby). And ultimately—at the altar—mankind is saved by Christ's sacrifice *(The Passover* overhead on the ceiling, and *The Last Supper* on the wall to the left). The art captures the charitable spirit of the school—just as God has helped those who suffer, so should we.

• *Let's look at a few pieces in depth. Start with the largest painting, in the center of the ceiling. View it from the top (the Albergo end), not directly underneath.*

❽ The Miracle of the Bronze Serpent

The tangle of half-naked bodies (at the bottom of the painting) represents the children of Israel, wrestling with poisonous snakes and writhing in pain. At the top of the pile, a young woman gestures toward Moses (in pink), who points to a pole carrying a bronze serpent sent by God. Those who looked at the statue were miraculously healed. His work all done, God (above in the clouds) high-fives an angel.

This was the first of the Great Hall panels Tintoretto painted in response to a terrible plague that hit Venice in 1576. One in four died. Four hundred a day were buried. (They say that Titian, Tintoretto's colleague, died of heartbreak soon after his son died of the plague.) Like today's Red Cross, the Scuola sprang into action, raising funds, sending doctors, and giving beds to the sick—and aid to their families. Tintoretto saw the dead and dying firsthand. While capturing their suffering, he gave a ray of hope that help is on the way: Turn to the cross, and be saved by your faith.

There are dozens of figures in the painting, shown from every conceivable angle. Tintoretto was well aware of where it would hang and how it would be viewed. Walk around beneath it and see the different angles come alive. The painting becomes a movie, and the children of Israel writhe like snakes.

• *The rectangular panel at the Albergo end of the hall is...*

❾ Moses Strikes Water from the Rocks

Moses (in pink, in the center) hits a rock in the desert with his staff, and it miraculously spouts water, which the thirsty Israelites catch in jars. The water spurts like a ray of light. Moses is a strong, calm center to a spinning wheel of activity.

Tintoretto worked fast, and, if nothing else, his art is exuberant. He trained in fresco painting, which must be finished before the plaster dries. With these paintings, he sketched an outline right onto the canvas, then improvised details as he went.

The sheer magnitude of the San Rocco project is staggering. This canvas alone is 300 square feet—like painting a bathroom with an artist's tiny brush. The whole project, counting the Albergo Hall, Great Upper Hall, and the Ground Floor Hall together, totals some 8,500 square feet—more than enough to cover a typical house, inside and out. (The Sistine Chapel ceiling, by comparison, is 5,700 square feet.)

• *The rectangular panel at the altar end of the hall is...*

❿ The Fall of Manna in the Desert

It's snowing bread, as God feeds the hungry Israelites with a miraculous storm. They stretch a blanket to catch it and gather it

up in baskets. Up in the center of the dark cloud is a radiant, almost transparent God, painted with sketchy brushstrokes to suggest he's an unseen presence.

Tintoretto tells these Bible stories with a literalness that was very popular with the poor, uneducated sick who sought help from the Scuola. He was the Spielberg of his day, with the technical know-how to bring imagination to life, to make the miraculous tangible.

• *You could grow old studying all the art here, so we'll select just a couple of the New Testament paintings on the walls. Start at the Albergo end with...*

⓫ The Adoration of the Shepherds

Christ's glorious life begins in a straw-filled stable with cows, chickens, and peasants who pass plates of food up to the new parents. It's night, with just a few details lit by phosphorescent moonlight: the kneeling shepherd's forehead and leggings, the serving girl's shoulders, the faces of Mary and Joseph...and little baby Jesus, a smudge of light.

Notice the different points of view. Tintoretto clearly has placed us on the lower floor, about eye level with the cow, looking up through the roof beams at the night sky. But we also see Mary and Joseph in the loft above as though they were at eye level. By using multiple perspectives (and ignoring the laws of physics), Tintoretto could portray every detail at its perfect angle.

• *In the middle of the long wall, find...*

⓬ The Resurrection

Angels lift the sepulchre lid, and Jesus springs forth in a blaze of light. The contrast between dark and light is extreme, with great dramatic effect.

• *Head for* The Last Supper, *in the corner to the left of the altar. On the way there, look on the wall for a wood carving of Tintoretto (⓭, third statue from altar, directly opposite entry staircase). The artist holds the tools of his trade. His craggy, wrinkled face peers out from under a black cap and behind a scraggly beard.*

⓮ The Last Supper

A dog, a beggar, and a serving girl dominate the foreground of Christ's final Passover meal with his followers. More servants work

in the background. The disciples themselves are dining in the dark, some with their backs to us, with only a few stray highlights to show us what's going on. Tintoretto emphasizes the human, everyday element of that gathering, in contrast to, say, Leonardo da Vinci's more stately version. And he sets the scene at a diagonal for dramatic effect.

The table stretches across a tiled floor, a commonly used device to create 3-D space. But Tintoretto makes the more distant tiles unnaturally small to exaggerate the distance. Similarly, the table and the people get proportionally smaller and lower until, at the far end of the table, tiny Jesus (with glowing head) is only half the size of the disciple at the near end.

Theatrically, Tintoretto leaves it to us to piece together the familiar narrative. The disciples are asking each other, "Is it I who will betray the Lord?" Jesus, meanwhile, unconcerned, hands out Communion bread.

• *Browse the Great Upper Hall and notice the various easel paintings by other artists. Contrast Titian's placid, evenly lit, aristocratic*

Annunciation *(displayed on an easel by the altar) with the blue-collar Tintoretto version downstairs. After you've gotten your fill of the Great Upper Hall, head back downstairs for Tintoretto's last works.*

Ground Floor Hall—The Life of Mary

⓵ *The Flight into Egypt*

There's Mary, Joseph, and the baby, but they're dwarfed by palm trees. Tintoretto, in his old age, returned to composing a

Venetian specialty—landscapes—after years as champion of the Michelangelesque style of painting beefy, twisting nudes. The leafy greenery, the still water, the supernatural sunset, and the hut whose inhabitants go about their work tell us better than any human action that the holy family has found a safe haven.

⓶ *The Circumcision*

This painting, bringing the circumcision of the Baby Jesus into sharp focus, is the final canvas that Tintoretto did for the Scuola. He collaborated on this work with his son Domenico, who carried on the family business.

In his long and prolific career, Tintoretto saw fame and many high-paying jobs. But at the Scuola, the commission became an obsession. It stands as one man's very personal contribution to the poor, to the Christian faith, and to art.

CA' REZZONICO TOUR

Museum of 18th-Century Venice
(Museo del Settecento Veneziano)

*Endowed by nature with a pleasing physical appearance, a
confirmed gambler, a great talker, far from modest, always
running after pretty women...I was certain to be disliked.
But, as I was always willing to take responsibility for my
actions, I decided I had a right to do anything I pleased.*
—from *The Memoirs of Giacomo Casanova* (1725-1798)

Venice in the 1700s was the playground for Europe's aristocrats,
including the wealthy Rezzonico family, who owned this palace.
Today, the Ca' Rezzonico (ret-ZON-ee-koh) contains furniture,
decoration, and artwork from the period. This grand home on the
Grand Canal is the best place in town to experience the luxurious,
decadent spirit of Venice in the Settecento (the 1700s).

Orientation

Cost: €8, free with Museum Pass or as your bonus museum with
the Doge's Palace/Correr Museum combo-ticket (see page
25).

Hours: Wed-Mon April-Oct 10:00-18:00, Nov-March 10:00-
17:00, closed Tue year-round, last entry one hour before
closing.

Getting There: The museum is located in Dorsoduro at #3136,
on the west bank of the Grand Canal, right where the canal
makes its hairpin turn. Take vaporetto #1 to the Ca' Rezzonico
stop (between Rialto and Accademia). There are a number of
ways to reach the museum on foot. From the Accademia, it's
a 10-minute walk heading right as you leave the bridge; when
you reach Campo San Barnaba, cross the bridge in the far right
corner and turn right immediately on Fondamenta Rezzonico.

From the Rialto Bridge, it's a 20-minute walk heading south-west, seven minutes past the Frari Church (directions on page 147). You can also walk to the San Samuele vaporetto stop (on the east side of the Grand Canal, near the Accademia Bridge) and take the quick San Samuele *traghetto* ride across the canal (daily 8:30-13:30, €0.50).

Information: The Ca' Rezzonico is also known as the Museo del Settecento Veneziano. On the ground floor, you'll find a bookstore and WCs. Tel. 041-241-0100, www.museicivici veneziani.it.

Audioguide: The audioguide costs €4 (€6/2 people) and lasts 1.5 hours.

Length of This Tour: Allow 1.5 hours.

Baggage Check: Required and free for bags larger than a purse.

Photography: Prohibited.

Cuisine Art: The museum's café has simple fare (€4 *panini*). For restaurants near Campo San Barnaba, see page 286.

Starring: A beautiful palace with 18th-century furnishings and paintings by G. B. Tiepolo, Canaletto, and Guardi.

The Tour Begins

Our Ca' Rezzonico tour covers two floors. The first floor has rooms decorated with period furniture and ceiling frescoes by

G. B. Tiepolo. The second floor displays paintings by Canaletto, Guardi, G. D. Tiepolo, Longhi, and others. (The third floor painting gallery—which we won't visit—shows lots of flesh in lots of rooms.)

First, step onto the dock on the Grand Canal and admire Ca' Rezzonico's heavy stone facade. This dock was, of course, the main entrance back in the 1700s. Next, admire the 1700s-era covered gondola in the courtyard. Picture this arriving at the Ca's dock for a party during Carnevale. A charcoal heater inside kept the masked and caped passengers warm, as they sipped Prosecco and chatted in French, enjoying their winter holiday away from home....

First Floor

• *Buy tickets on the ground floor, then ascend the grand staircase to the first floor (where you show your ticket), entering the ballroom.*

Ca' Rezzonico—First Floor

CA' REZZONICO

Room 1: Ballroom

A great place for a wedding reception. At 5,600 square feet, it's the biggest private venue in the city. Stand in the center, and the room

gets even bigger, with a ceiling painting that opens up to the heavens and painted, trompe l'oeil (optical illusion) columns and arches that open onto fake alcoves.

Imagine dancing under candlelit chandeliers to Vivaldi's *Four Seasons*. Servants glide by with drinks and finger foods. The gentlemen wear powdered wigs, silk shirts with lacy sleeves, tight velvet coats and breeches, striped stockings, and shoes with big buckles. They carry snuff-

boxes with dirty pictures inside the lids. The ladies powder their hair, pile it high, and weave in stuff—pictures of their children or locks of a lover's hair. And everyone carries a mask on a stick to change identity in a second.

The chandeliers of gold-covered wood are original. But while most of the furniture we'll see is from the 1700s, it's not from the Rezzonico family collection.

• *Promenade across the floor into the next room.*

Room 2: Nuptial Allegory Room

In fact, there *was* a wedding here—see the happy couple on the ceiling, arriving in a chariot pulled by four white horses and serenaded by angels, cupids, and Virtues. In 1757, Ludovico Rezzonico exchanged vows with Faustina Savorgnan in this room, under the bellies of the horses painted for the occasion by Giovanni Battista ("John the Baptist") Tiepolo. G. B. Tiepolo (1696-1770), the best-known decorator of Europe's palaces, was at the height of his fame and technique. He knocked this off in 12 days. His bright colors, mastery of painting figures from every possible angle, wide knowledge of classical literary subjects, and sheer, unbridled imagination made his frescoes blend seamlessly with ornate Baroque and Rococo furniture.

The Rezzonicos were a family of *nouveaux riches* who bought their way into the exclusive club of Venetian patrician families. The ***Portrait of Clement XIII*** (on easel), pink-cheeked and well-fed, shows the most famous Rezzonico. As pope (elected in 1758), Clement spent his reign defending the Jesuit society from anti-Catholic European nobles. A prayer kneeler (in the tiny adjoining chapel, Room 3) looks heavily used, dating from the sin-and-repent era of Settecento Venice.

Room 4: Pastel Room

Europe's most celebrated painter of portraits in pastels was a Venetian, Rosalba Carriera (1675-1757). Wealthy French and English tourists on holiday wanted a souvenir of Venice, and Carriera obliged, with miniature portraits on ivory rather than the traditional vellum (soft animal skin). She progressed to portraits in pastel, a medium that caught the luminous, pale-skin, white-haired, heavy-makeup look that was considered so desirable. Still, her ***Portrait (Ritratto) of Sister Maria Caterina*** has a warts-and-all realism that doesn't hide the nun's heavy eyebrows, long nose, and forehead vein, which only intensifies the spirituality she radiates.

At age 45, Carriera was invited by tourists whom she'd befriended to visit them in Paris. There she became the toast of the town. Returning triumphantly to Venice, she settled into her home on the Grand Canal and painted until her eyesight failed.

Also in the room is the portrait of Cecilia Guardi Tiepolo: wife of famous painter Giovanni Battista Tiepolo, sister of famous painter Francesco Guardi, and mother of not-very-famous painter Lorenzo Tiepolo, who painted this when he was 21.

Room 5: Tapestry Room

Tapestries, furniture, a mirror, and a door with Asian themes that shows an opium smoker on his own little island paradise (lower panel) give a sense of the Rococo luxury of the wealthy. In a

century dominated by the French court at Versailles, Venice was one of the few cities that could hold its own. The furniture ensemble of gilded wood chairs, tables, and chests hints at the Louis XIV (claw-foot) style, but the pieces were made in a Venetian workshop.

Despite Venice's mask of gaiety, in the 1700s it was a poor, politically bankrupt, dirty city. Garbage floated in the canals, the streets were either unpaved or slippery with slime, and tourists could hardly stand visiting St. Mark's Basilica or the Doge's Palace because of the stench of mildew. But its reputation for decay and sleaze was actually romanticized into a metaphor for adventures into shady morality. With licensed casinos and a reputed "20,000 courtesans" (prostitutes), it was a fun city for foreigners freed from hometown blinders.

Room 6: Throne Room

"Nowhere in Europe are there so many and such splendid fêtes, ceremonies, and public entertainments of all kinds as there are in Venice," wrote a visitor from France. As you check out the view of the Grand Canal, imagine once again that you're attending a party here. You could watch the *Forze d'Ercole* (Force of Hercules) acrobats, who stood in boats and kept building a human pyramid—of up to 50 bodies—until they tumbled laughing into the Grand Canal. At midnight the hosts would dim the mirrored candleholders on the walls, so you could look out on a fireworks display over the water.

Carnevale, Venice's prime party time, stretched from the day after Christmas to Lent. Everyone wore masks. Frenchmen, dressed as turbaned Ottoman Turks, mingled with Turkish traders

Famous 18th-Century Venetians

Canaletto (Giovanni Antonio Canal): Painter of Venice views
Antonio Canova: Neoclassical sculptor
Giacomo Casanova: Gambler, womanizer, revolutionary
Carlo Goldoni: Playwright of realistic comedies
Francesco Guardi: Painter of romantic Enlightened ideas
Giovanni Battista (G. B.) Tiepolo: Painter of Rococo ceilings
Giovanni Domenico (G. D.) Tiepolo: Painter son of famous Tiepolo

dressed as harlequins. Fake Barbary pirates fought playfully with skin-blackened "Moors." And long-nosed Pulcinella clowns were everywhere, reveling in the time when all social classes partied as one because "the mask levels all distinctions."

The **ceiling fresco,** again by Giovanni Battista Tiepolo, certainly trompes my oeil. (It's best viewed from the center.) Tiepolo opens the room's sunroof, allowing angels to descend to earth to pick up the Rezzonico clan's patriarch. The old, bald, bearded fellow is crowned with laurels and begins to rise on a cloud up to the translucent temple of glory. The angels hold Venice's Golden Book, where the names of the city's nobles were listed. In 1687, the Rezzonico family bought their way into the exclusive club. Tiepolo captures the moment just as the gang is exiting out the "hole" in the ceiling. The leg of the lady in blue hangs over the "edge" of the fake oval. Tiepolo creates a zero-gravity universe that must have astounded visitors. Walk in circles under the fresco, and watch the bugling angel spin.

• *Pass through the large next room and into...*

Room 7: Tiepolo Room

The ceiling painting by G. B. Tiepolo depicts Nobility and Virtue as a kind of bare-breasted, Thelma-and-Louise duo defeating Treachery, who tumbles down. The painting—which is on canvas, not a fresco like the others—was moved here from another palazzo.

Portraits around the room are by Tiepolo and his sons, Lorenzo and Giovanni Domenico. The paintings are sober and down-to-earth, demonstrating the artistic range of this exceptional family. Giovanni Battista ("G. B.") was known for his flamboyance, but he passed to his sons his penchant for painting wrinkled, wizened old men in the Rembrandt style. In later years, G. B. had the pleasure of traveling with his sons to distant capitals, meeting royalty, and working on palace ceilings. Giovanni Domenico ("G. D.") contributed some of the minor figures in the Ca' Rezzonico ceilings and went on to a successful artistic career of his own. (We'll see his work upstairs.)

This room was the Rezzonicos' game room, and you can see a card table in the center. The big walnut cabinet along the wall is one of the few original pieces of furniture from the Rezzonicos' collection.

Room 8: Passage
This narrow corridor displays vessels for serving three foreign stimulants that became popular beverages in 1700s Venice—coffee, tea, and hot chocolate.

Room 9: Library
Ca' Rezzonico was the home of the English poet Robert Browning (1812-1889) in his later years. Imagine him here in this study, in a melancholy mood after a long winter, reading a book and thinking of words from a poem of his: "Oh to be in England, now that April's there...." Antonio Corradini's marvelous bust of the *Veiled Woman (Dama Velata/Puritas)* adds to the somber mood.

Room 10: Lazzarini Room
The big, colorful paintings are by Gregorio Lazzarini (1655-1730), Tiepolo's teacher. Tiepolo took Lazzarini's color, motion, and twisted poses and suspended them overhead.

Room 11: Brustolon Room
Andrea Brustolon (1662-1732) carved Baroque fantasies into the custom-made tables, chairs, and vase stand that he crafted in his Venice workshop. In black ebony, reddish boxwood, and brown

Giacomo Casanova
(1725-1798)

I began to lead a life of complete freedom, caring for nothing except what pleased me.
　　　　　　—from *The Memoirs of Giacomo Casanova*

Casanova, a real person who wrote an exaggerated autobiography, typifies the Venice that so entranced the rest of Europe.

In his life, he adopted many personae, worked in a number of professions, and always took the adventurous path.

Casanova was born just across the Grand Canal from the Ca' Rezzonico. The son of an actor, Casanova trained to be a priest, but was expelled for seducing nuns. To Venetians he was first known as a fiery violinist at fancy parties in palaces such as the Ca' Rezzonico. He would later serve time in the Doge's Palace prison, accused of being a magician.

As a professional gambler and charmer, he roamed Europe's capitals seducing noblewomen, dueling with fellow men of honor, and impressing nobles with his knowledge of Greek literature, religion, politics, and the female sex. His memoirs, published after his death, cemented his reputation as a genial but cunning rake, rogue, and rapscallion.

walnut, they overwhelm with the sheer number of figures, yet each carving is a gem worth admiring. The big vase stand is a harmony of different colors: a white vase supported by ebony slaves in chains and a brown boxwood Hercules. The slaves' chains are carved from a single piece of wood—a racist motif, but an impressive artistic feat.

The room's flowery Murano glass chandelier—of pastel pinks, blues, and turquoise—is original.

• *Backtrack to Room 10, then turn right into the large, sparsely decorated room called the...*

Room 12: Portego

That funny little cabin in the room is a sedan chair, a servant-powered taxi for Venice's nobles. Four strong-shouldered men ran poles through the iron brackets on either side, then carried it on their shoulders, while the rich rode in red-velvet luxury above the slimy streets.

• *The staircase to the second floor is here in Room 12, in the middle of the long wall. On the second floor, you emerge into Room 13 and find the two Canaletto paintings on the opposite wall.*

Second Floor

The first floor showed the rooms and furniture of the 1700s. The second-floor paintings depict the people who sat in those chairs.

Room 13: Painting Portego—Canaletto

Rich tourists wanting to remember their stay in Venice sought out

Canaletto (1697-1768) for a "postcard" view. The ***Grand Canal from Palazzo Balbi to Rialto*** (by Giovanni Antonio Canal, called Il Canaletto) captures the view you'd see from the palazzo two doors down. With photographic clarity, Canaletto depicts buildings, boats, and shadows on the water, leading the eye to the tiny, half-hidden Rialto Bridge on the distant horizon.

The ***View of Rio dei Mendicante*** chronicles every chimney, every open shutter, every pair of underwear hanging out to dry.

Canaletto was a young theater-set painter working on Scarlatti

operas in Rome when he decided his true calling was painting reality, not Baroque fantasy. He moved home to Venice, set up his easel outside, and painted scenes like these two, directly from nature. It was considered a very odd thing to do in his day.

Despite the seeming photo-realism and crystal clarity, these wide-angle views are more than any human eye could take in without turning side to side. Canaletto, who meticulously studied the mathematics of perspective, was not above tweaking those rules to compress more of Venice into the frame. In the *Grand Canal from Palazzo Balbi to Rialto,* notice there are shadows along both sides of the canal—physically impossible, but more picturesque. His paintings still have a theater-set look to them, but here, the Venice backdrop is the star.

To meet the demand for postcard scenes of Venice, Canaletto resorted in later years to painting from engravings or following formulas. But these two early works reflect his pure vision to accu-

*(side margin)* CA' REZZONICO

Ca' Rezzonico—Second Floor

STAIRS FROM
FIRST FLOOR

ROOM
14

Not to scale

15

17

13

21   20   19   18

Grand

Canal

rately paint the city he loved.

• *From here, we'll move roughly clockwise around the second floor. Head
for the door behind your right shoulder. Room 14 is actually a maze of
several rooms.*

Room 14: G. D. Tiepolo's Frescoes
from the Villa in Zianigo

The son of G. B. Tiepolo decorated the family villa with frescoes

for his own enjoyment. They're
far more down-to-earth than G.
B.'s high-flying fantasies. **New
World** features butts, as ordinary folk crowd around a building with a peep-show window.
The only faces we see are the
two men in profile—Giovanni
Domenico Tiepolo (far right,
with eyeglass) and his father, G. B. Tiepolo (arms folded)—and
baby brother Lorenzo (center). The **Pulcinella Room** (far right

corner) has several scenes (including
one overhead) of the hook-nosed,
white-clothed, hunchbacked clown
who, at Carnevale time, represented
the lovable country bumpkin. But
here, he and his similarly dressed
companions seem tired, lecherous,
and stupid. The decadent gaiety of
Settecento Venice was at odds with
the *Liberté, Egalité,* and *Fraternité*
erupting in France.

• *Backtrack through the maze of Room*

14, winding your way into a room with a harpsichord, or spinet, cleverly named the...

Room 15: Spinet Room

The 1700s saw the development of new keyboard instruments that would culminate by century's end in the modern piano. This particular specimen has strings that are not hammered (like a piano) but plucked (like a mechanical guitar). The spacing of "white" keys and "black" keys is chromatic like a modern piano. This newly invented "tempered" scale of evenly spaced notes let you play in all keys without retuning.

Room 17: Parlor Room

Francesco Guardi (1712-1793), like Canaletto, supplied foreigners with scenes of Venice. But Guardi uses rougher brushwork that casts a romantic haze over the decaying city.

The Parlor (Il Parlatorio delle Monache di S. Zaccaria) is an interior landscape featuring visiting day at a convent school. The girls, secluded behind grills, chat and have tea with family members, friends, ladies with their pets, and potential suitors. Convents were like finishing schools for aristocratic girls, where they got an education and learned manners before re-entering the world. Note the puppet show (starring spouse-abusing Pulcinella).

Guardi's *Il Ridotto di Palazzo Dandolo* shows partygoers in masks at a Venetian palace licensed for gambling. Casanova and others claimed that these casino houses had back rooms for the private use of patrons and courtesans. The men wear the traditional *bautta*—a three-piece outfit consisting of a face mask, three-cornered hat, and cowl. This getup was actually required by law in certain seedy establishments to ensure that every sinner was equally anonymous. The women wear Lone Ranger masks, and parade a hint of cleavage to potential customers.

• *Continuing along, you'll pass back through the Painting Portego and into...*

Room 18: Longhi Room

There is no better look at 1700s Venice than these genre scenes by Pietro Longhi

(1702-1785), depicting everyday life among the upper classes. See ladies and gentlemen going to the hairdresser or to the dentist, dressed in the finery that was standard in every public situation.

Contrast these straightforward scenes with G. B. Tiepolo's sumptuous ceiling painting of nude gods and goddesses. The Rococo fantasy world of aristocrats was slipping increasingly into the more prosaic era of the bourgeoisie.

• *Pass through several rooms to the far corner.*

Room 21: The Alcove

Casanova daydreamed of fancy boudoirs like this one, complete with a large bed (topped with a Madonna by Rosalba Carriera), a walnut dresser, Neoclassical wallpaper, and silver toiletries. Even the presence of the baby cradle would not have dimmed his ardor.

CA' REZZONICO

PEGGY GUGGENHEIM COLLECTION TOUR

Peggy Guggenheim (1898-1979)—an American-born heiress to the Guggenheim fortune and niece of Solomon Guggenheim (who built New York's modern-art museum of the same name)—made her mark as a friend, lover, and patron of modern artists.

As a gallery owner, she introduced Europe's avant-garde to a skeptical America. As a collector, she gave instant status to modern art that was too radical for serious museums. As a patron, she fed starving artists such as Jackson Pollock. And as a person, she lived larger than life, unconventional and original, with a succession of lovers that enhanced her reputation as a female Casanova.

In 1948, Peggy "retired" to Venice, renovating a small, unfinished palazzo on the Grand Canal. Today it's a museum, decorated much as it was during her lifetime, with one of the best collections anywhere of 20th-century art. It's the only museum I can think of where the owner is buried in the garden.

Orientation

Cost: €12, usually includes temporary exhibits (displayed near the café and museum shop).

Hours: Wed-Mon 10:00-18:00, closed Tue, last entry 15 minutes before closing.

Getting There: The museum, overlooking the Grand Canal, is at Dorsoduro 704, a five-minute walk from the Accademia Bridge (vaporetto: Accademia) or from La Salute Church (vaporetto: Salute). A cool way to cross the Grand Canal is via the S.M. del Giglio *traghetto* (runs 9:00-18:00, see map on page 62) or the Dogana *traghetto* from St. Mark's Square (9:00-14:00, see map on page 75; both *traghetti* €0.50).

Information: The ticket desk and museum shop sell an excellent €5 mini-guidebook. Tel. 041-240-5411, www.guggenheim -venice.it.

Tours: Audioguides cost €7. You can book a 1- to 1.5-hour **guided tour** (€60) by calling the museum. Art interns guarding the works are happy to tell you about particular pieces if you ask.

Length of This Tour: Allow one hour.

Baggage Check: Free and required for anything bigger than a small purse.

Photography: Permitted only in garden and terrace.

Cuisine Art: Pricey café on site (€10-20 dishes). See page 284 in the Eating in Venice chapter for recommendations in the Dorsoduro neighborhood.

Nearby: If you like contemporary art, this is your neighborhood. Browse the art galleries, and visit the Punta della Dogana museum (next to La Salute, see page 50).

Starring: Picasso, Kandinsky, Mondrian, Dalí, Pollock...and Peggy herself.

The Tour Begins

After passing through a garden courtyard sprinkled with statues, you enter the palazzo. There's a wing to the left and a wing to the right, plus a modern annex. The collection is (very) roughly chronological, starting to the left with Cubism and ending to the right with post-World War II artists.

The collection's strength is its Abstract, Surrealist, and Abstract-Surrealist art. The placement of the paintings may change, so use this chapter as an overview, not a painting-by-painting tour. What makes this collection unique is that it hangs here in Peggy's home, much as it did in her lifetime. As you tour, keep an eye out for black-and-white photos of Peggy standing alongside her art, taken in the very same rooms in which the paintings now hang.

• *Walk through Peggy's collection and her life. From the sculpture garden, head into the...*

Entrance Hall: Meet Peggy Guggenheim

Picture Peggy Guggenheim greeting guests here—standing under the **trembling-leaf mobile by Alexander Calder,** flanked by two Picasso paintings, surrounded by her yapping dogs and meowing cats, and wearing her Calder-designed earrings, Mondrian-print dress, and "Catwoman" sunglasses.

During the 1950s and 1960s, this old palazzo on the Grand Canal was a mecca for "Moderns," from composer Igor Stravinsky to actor Marlon Brando, from painter Mark Rothko to writer Truman Capote, from choreographer George Balanchine to Beatle John Lennon and performance artist Yoko Ono. They came to sip cocktails, tour the great art, talk about ideas, and meet the woman who had become a living legend.

Pablo Picasso—*On the Beach* (1937)

Curious, balloon-animal women play with a sailboat while their friend across the water looks on. Of all of Peggy's many paintings, this was her favorite.

By the time Peggy Guggenheim first became serious about modern art (about the time this was painted), Pablo Picasso—the most famous and versatile 20th-century artist—had already been through his Blue, Rose, Fauve, Cubist, Synthetic Cubist, Classical, Abstract, and Surrealist phases, finally arriving at a synthesis of these styles. Peggy had some catching up to do.

• *Enter the first room to the left, and you'll see a dining-room table in the center.*

1900-1920: Cubists in the Dining Room

Peggy's **dining-room table** reminds us that this museum was, indeed, her home for the last 30 years of her life. Most of the furniture is now gone, but the walls are decorated much as they were when she lived here, with paintings and statues by her friends, colleagues, and mentors. Here, she entertained countless artists and celebrities (more name-dropping), from actor Paul Newman to poet Allen Ginsberg, from sculptor Henry Moore to playwright Tennessee Williams, from James Bond creator Ian Fleming to glass sculptor Dale Chihuly.

Most of the art in the dining room dates from Peggy's childhood, when she was raised in the lap of luxury in New York, oblivious to the artistic upheavals going on in Europe.

In 1912, the *Titanic* went down, taking Peggy's playboy tycoon father with it...and leaving his 14-year-old daughter with a small but comfortable trust fund and a man-sized hole in her life.

Approaching adulthood, Peggy rejected her traditional American upbringing. She started hanging out at a radical bookstore, got a nose job (a botched operation, leaving her with a rather bulbous schnozz)...and began planning a trip to Europe.

In 1920, 21-year-old Peggy arrived in Paris, where a revolution in art was taking place.

• *Find the following early 20th-century art (or similar pieces) in the Dining Room and surrounding rooms—the Kitchen, the Living Room, the Entrance Hall, and the Library.*

Pablo Picasso—*The Poet* (1911)

Picasso, a Spaniard living in Paris, shattered the Old World into brown shards ("cubes") and reassembled it in Cubist style. It's a vaguely recognizable portrait of a man from the waist up—tapering to a head at the top, smoking a pipe (?), and cradling the traditional lyre of a poet. While the newfangled motion-picture camera could capture a moving image, Picasso suggests motion with a collage of stills.

Marcel Duchamp—*Nude (Study), Sad Young Man on a Train* (1911-1912)

In a self-portrait, Duchamp poses gracefully with a cane, but the moving train jiggles the image into a blur of brown. Duchamp is best known not for paintings like this, but for his outrageous conceptual pieces: his urinal-as-statue *(Fountain)* and his moustache on the *Mona Lisa* (titled *L.H.O.O.Q.*, which—when spoken aloud in French—is a pun that translates loosely as "she has a hot ass"). In a 2004 poll of British artists, Duchamp's urinal was named the most influential modern artwork of all time.

Umberto Boccioni—
Dynamism of a Speeding Horse + Houses (1915)

This sculpture, assembled from wood, cardboard, and metal, captures the blurred motion of the modern world—accelerated by technology, then shattered by World War I, which would leave nine million Europeans dead and everyone's moral compass spinning. (In fact, this statue was shattered by the destructive force of Boccioni's own kids, who scattered the cardboard "houses" while using it as a rocking horse.)

Constantin Brancusi—*Maiastra* (c. 1912)

For the generation born before air travel, flying was magical. This high-polished bird is the first of many by Brancusi, who dreamed of flight. But this bronze bird just sits there. For centuries, a good sculptor was one who could capture movement in stone. Brancusi reverts to the essential forms of "primitive" African art, in which even the simplest statues radiate mojo.

Marc Chagall—*Rain* (1911)

The rain clouds gather over a farmhouse, the wind blows the trees and people, and everyone prepares for the storm. Quick, put the

horse in the barn, grab an umbrella, take a leak, and round up the goats in the clouds.

Marc Chagall, a Russian living in France, reinvented scenes from his homeland with a romantic, weightless, childlike joy in topsy-turvy Paris.

1920s: Abstraction and Various "-Isms"

In the Roaring Twenties, Peggy spent *her* twenties right in the center of avant-garde craziness: Paris. For the rest of her life, Europe—not America—would be her permanent address.

In Paris, trust-funded Peggy lived the bohemian life. Post-WWI Paris was cheap and, after the bitter war years, ready to party. Days were spent drinking coffee in cafés, talking ideas with the likes of activist Emma Goldman, writer Djuna *(Nightwood)* Barnes, and photographer Man Ray. Nights were spent abusing the drug forbidden in America (alcohol), dancing to jazz music into the wee hours, and talking about Freud and s-e-x.

One night, at the top of the Eiffel Tower, a dashing artist and intellectual nicknamed "The King of Bohemia" popped the question. Peggy and Laurence Vail soon married and had two children, but the partying only slowed somewhat. This thoroughly modern couple dug the wild life and the wild art it produced.

Vassily Kandinsky—*White Cross* (1922)

I see white, I see crosses, but where's the white cross? Oh, there it is on the right, camouflaged among black squares.

Like a jazz musician improvising from a set scale, Kandinsky plays with new patterns of related colors and lines, creating something that's simply beautiful, even if it doesn't "mean" anything. As Kandinsky himself would say, his art was like "visual music—just open your eyes and look."

Piet Mondrian—*Composition with Red* (1938-1939)

Like a blueprint for Modernism, Mondrian's T-square style boils painting down to its basic building blocks—black lines, white canvas, and the three primary colors (red, yellow, and blue) arranged in orderly patterns. This stripped-down canvas even omits yellow and blue.

Mondrian started out painting realistic landscapes of the orderly fields in his native Holland. Increasingly, he simplified things into horizontal and vertical grids, creating rectangles of different proportions. This one has horizontal lines to the left, vertical ones to the right. The horizontals appear to dominate, until we see that they're balanced by the tiny patch of red.

For Mondrian, who was heavily into Eastern mysticism, up vs. down and left vs. right were metaphors for life's ever-shifting dualities: good vs. evil, man vs. woman, fascism vs. communism. The canvas is a bird's-eye view of Mondrian's personal landscape.

1930s: Abstract Surrealists

In 1928, Peggy's marriage to Laurence Vail ended, and she entered into a series of romantic attachments. Though not stunningly

Abstract Art

Abstract art simplifies. A man becomes a stick figure. A squiggle is a wave. A streak of red expresses anger. Arches make you want a cheeseburger. These are universal symbols that everyone from a caveman to a banker understands. Abstract artists capture the essence of reality in a few lines and colors, even things a camera can't—emotions, theoretical concepts, musical rhythms, and spiritual states of mind.

Most 20th- and 21st-century paintings are a mix of the real world ("representation") and the colorful patterns of "abstract" art. An abstract artist purposely "abstracts" only some elements of camera-eye reality to make the resulting canvas more provocative, expressive, or challenging.

attractive, she was easy to be with, and she truly admired artistic men.

In 1937, she began an on-again, off-again (so to speak) sexual relationship with playwright Samuel *(Waiting for Godot)* Beckett. Beckett steered her toward Modern painting and sculpture—things she'd never paid much attention to.

She started hanging out with the French Surrealists, from artist Marcel Duchamp to writer André Breton to filmmaker/artist Jean *(Beauty and the Beast)* Cocteau. Duchamp, in particular, mentored her in modern art, encouraging her to use her money to collect and promote it. Nearing 40, she moved to London and launched a new career.

Yves Tanguy—*The Sun in Its Jewel Case* (1937)

In May 1938, this painting was featured at Guggenheim Jeune, the art gallery Peggy opened in London. Tanguy's painting sums up the turbulent art that shocked a sleepy London during that first season.

Weird, phallic, tissue-and-bone protuberances cast long shadows across a moody, dreamlike landscape—the landscape of the mind. (Peggy said the picture "frightened" her, but added, "I got over my fear...and now I own it.") The figures are Abstract (unrecognizable), and the mood is Surreal, producing the style cleverly dubbed Abstract Surrealism.

Peggy was drawn to Yves Tanguy and had a short but intense affair with the married man. Tanguy, like his art, was wacky and spontaneous, occasionally shocking friends by suddenly catching and gobbling up a spider and washing it down with white wine. The Surrealists saw themselves as spokesmen for Freud's "id," the untamed part of the personality that thinks dirty thoughts when the "ego" goes to sleep.

The Guggenheim Jeune gallery exhibited many of the artists we see in this museum, including Kandinsky, Mondrian, and Calder. Guggenheim Jeune closed as a financial flop after just two years, but its shocking paintings certainly created a buzz in the art world, and as the years passed the gallery's failure gained a rosy glow of success.

1939-1940: Peggy's Shopping Spree in Paris

Peggy moved back to Paris and rented an apartment on the Ile St. Louis. In September, Nazi Germany invaded Poland, sparking World War II. All of France waited...and waited...and waited for the inevitable Nazi attack on Paris.

Meanwhile, Peggy spent her days shopping for masterpieces. Using a list compiled by Duchamp and others, she personally visited artists in their studios—from Brancusi to Dalí to Giacometti—often negotiating directly with them. (Picasso initially turned Peggy down, thinking of her as a gauche, bargain-hunting housewife. When she entered his studio he said, "Madame, you'll find the lingerie department on the second floor.") In a few short months, she bought 37 of the paintings now in the collection, perhaps saving them from a Nazi regime that labeled such art "decadent."

In 1941, with the Nazis occupying Paris and most of Europe, Peggy fled her adopted homeland. With her stash of paintings and a new companion—painter Max Ernst—she sailed from Lisbon to safety in New York.

• *Pass back through the Entrance Hall—where Peggy welcomed celebrity guests, from writer Somerset Maugham to actor Rex Harrison to painter Marc Chagall—and into the east wing. The right entryway leads to a room filled with Surrealist canvases.*

1941-1945: Surrealists Invade New York

Trees become women, women become horses, and day becomes night. Balls dangle, caves melt, and things cast long shadows across film-noir landscapes—Surrealism. The world was moving fast, and Surrealists caught the jumble of images. They scattered seemingly unrelated things on the canvas, leaving us to trace the connections in a kind of connect-the-dots game without numbers.

Peggy spent the war years in America. She married Max Ernst, and their house in New York City became a gathering place for exiled French Surrealists and young American artists.

In 1942, she opened a gallery/museum in New York called Art of This Century that featured, well, essentially the collection we see here in Venice. But patriotic, gung-ho America was not quite ready for the nonconformist, intellectual art of Europe.

Max Ernst—*The Antipope* (c. 1942)

The horse-headed nude in red is a portrait of Peggy—at least, that's what she thought when she saw it. She loved the painting and insisted that Max give it to her as a wedding present, renamed *The Mystic Marriage*.

Others read more into it. Is the horse-headed warrior (at right) Ernst himself? Is he being wooed by one of his art students? Is that Peggy's daughter, Pegeen (center), watching the scene, sadly, from a distance? And is Peggy turning toward her beloved Max, subconsciously suspicious of the young student...who would (in fact) soon steal Max from her? Ernst uses his considerable painting skill to

bring to light a tangle of secret urges, desires, and fears—hidden like the grotesque animal faces in the reef they stand on.

Paul Delvaux— *The Break of Day* (1937)

Full-breasted ladies with roots cast long shadows and awaken to a mysterious dawn. If you're counting boobs, don't forget the one reflected in the nightstand mirror.

René Magritte—*Empire of Light* (1953-1954)

Magritte found that, even under a sunny blue sky, suburbia has its dark side.

Salvador Dalí— *The Birth of Liquid Desires* (1931-1932)

Salvador Dalí could draw exceptionally well. He painted "unreal" scenes with photographic realism, making us believe they could truly happen. This air of mystery—the feeling that anything is possible—is both exciting and unsettling. His men explore the caves of the dream world and morph into something else before our eyes.

Personally, Peggy didn't like Dalí or his work, but she dutifully bought this canvas (through his wife, Gala) to complete her collection.

• *Across the hall is the Guest Bedroom, with a fireplace and works by Pollock.*

1945-1948: The Postwar Years : Pollock in the Guest Bedroom

Certain young American painters—from Mark Rothko to Robert Motherwell to Robert De Niro Sr. (the actor's father)—were strongly influenced by Peggy's collection. Adopting the Abstract style of Kandinsky, they practiced Surrealist spontaneity to "express" themselves in the physical act of putting paint on canvas. The resulting style (duh): Abstract Expressionism.

Jackson Pollock—*Enchanted Forest* (1947)

"Jack the Dripper" attacked America's postwar conformity with a can of paint, dripping and splashing a dense web onto the can-

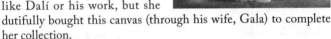

vas. Picture Pollock in his studio, jiving to the hi-fi, bouncing off the walls, throwing paint in a moment of alcohol-fueled enlightenment.

Peggy helped make Pollock a celebrity. She bought his earliest works (which show Abstract-Surrealist roots), exhibited his work at her gallery, and even paid him a monthly stipend to keep experimenting.

By the way, if you haven't yet tried the Venetian specialty *spaghetti al nero di seppia* (spaghetti with squid in its own ink), it looks something like this.

In 1946, Peggy published her memoirs, titled *Out of This Century: The Informal Memoirs of Peggy Guggenheim.* The front cover was designed by Max Ernst, the back by Pollock. Peggy herself was now a celebrity.

• *The room on the other side of the fireplace was Peggy's Bedroom.*

1950s: Peggy in the Bedroom

As America's postwar factories turned swords into kitchen appliances, Peggy longed to return "home" to Europe. The one place that kept calling to her was Venice, ever since she visited here with Laurence Vail in the 1920s. "I decided Venice would be my future home," she wrote. "I felt I would be happy alone there."

In 1947, after a grand finale exhibition by Pollock, she closed the Art of This Century gallery, crated up her collection, and moved to Venice. In 1948, she bought this palazzo and moved in.

This was Peggy's bedroom. She painted it turquoise. She commissioned the **silver headboard by Alexander Calder** for her canopy bed, using its silver frame to hang her collection of earrings, handmade by the likes of Calder and Tanguy. Venetian mirrors hung on the walls, along with a sentimental portrait of herself and her sister as children. Ex-husband Laurence Vail's collage-decorated bottles sat on the nightstand.

In 1951, Peggy met the last great love of her life, an easygoing, blue-collar Italian with absolutely no interest in art. She was 53, Raoul was 30. When Raoul died in 1954 in a car accident, Peggy comforted herself with her pets.

• *The tiny corner room adjoining the bedroom displays paintings by Pegeen.*

Pegeen

Peggy's daughter, Pegeen, inherited some of Laurence Vail's artistic talent, painting childlike scenes of Venice, populated by skinny Barbie dolls with antennae.

The guest bedroom (where the Pollocks are) was a busy place. Pegeen and her brother, Sinbad, visited their mother in Venice, as did Peggy's ex-husbands and their new loves. Other overnight guests ranged from sculptor Alberto Giacometti (who honeymooned here), to author and cultural explorer Paul Bowles, to artist Jean Arp.

• *Cross the hall and go down a few steps into the wing perpendicular to the palazzo, the Mattioli Annex.*

Italians in the Annex

You'll find paintings by well-known Italians **(Modigliani, Boccioni),** as well as the less-famous postwar generation of young Italians who were strongly influenced by Peggy's collection. In 1948, Peggy showed her collection in its own pavilion at the Biennale, Venice's world's fair of art, and it was the hit of the show. Europeans were astounded and a bit dumbfounded, finally seeing the kind of "degenerate" art forbidden during the fascist years, plus the radical new stuff coming out of New York City.

Peggy sponsored young artists, including **Tancredi**—just

one name, back when that was odd—who was given a studio in the palazzo's basement. Tancredi had a relationship with daughter Pegeen, with her mother's blessing. (Pegeen died in 1967 of a barbiturates overdose.)

• *Return to the Entrance Hall, then go out onto the Terrace, overlooking the Grand Canal.*

Exhibitionists on the Terrace

> *You fall in love with the city itself. There is nothing left over in your heart for anyone else.*
>
> —Peggy Guggenheim

The obviously exuberant figure in Marino Marini's equestrian statue, *The Angel of the City* (1948), faces the Grand Canal, spreads

his arms wide, and tosses his head back in sheer joy, with an eternal hard-on for the city of Venice. Every morning, Peggy must have felt a similar exhilaration as she sipped coffee while taking in this unbelievable view.

Marini originally designed his bronze rider with a screw-off penis (which sounds dirtier than it is) that could be removed for prudish guests or by curious ones. Someone stole it for some unknown purpose, so the current organ is permanently welded on.

The palazzo—formally Palazzo Venier dei Leoni—looks modern but is old. Construction began in 1748, but only the ground floor was completed. Legend has it that members of a rival family across the canal squelched plans for the upper stories so their home wouldn't be upstaged. The palazzo remained unfinished until Peggy bought it in 1948 and spruced it up. She added the annex in 1958. The **lions** *(leoni)* of the original palace still guard the waterfront entrance.

Peggy's outlandish and rather foreign presence in Venice—drinking, dressing up outrageously, and sunbathing on her rooftop for all to see—was not immediately embraced by the Venetians. But for artists in the 1950s and 1960s, Peggy's palazzo was *the* place to be, especially when the Biennale brought the jet set. Everyone from actor Alec Guinness, to political satirist Art Buchwald, to gossip columnist Hedda Hopper signed her guest book. Picture Peggy and guests, decked out in evening clothes, hopping into her custom-built gondola (nicknamed *La Barchessa*, after the doge's private boat) to ride slowly down the canal for a martini and a Bellini at Harry's Bar.

GUGGENHEIM COLLECTION

• *Pass back through the Entrance Hall, then outside to the...*

Sculpture Garden

Peggy opened her impressive collection of sculpture to the Venetian public for free. It features first-rate works by all the greats, from Brancusi to Giacometti. After so much art already, you might find the trees—so rare in urban Venice—more interesting.

If, after your visit here, you still don't like modern art, think of what Peggy used to tell puzzled visitors: "Come back again in 50 years."

• *In the southwest corner of the garden (along the brick wall), find...*

Peggy's Grave and Her Dogs' Graves

"Here Lie My Beloved Babies," marks the grave of Peggy's many dogs, her steady companions as she grew old. Note the names of some of these small, long-haired Lhasa Apsos. Along with "Cappuccino" and "Baby," you'll see "Pegeen," after her daughter, and "Sir Herbert," for Herbert Read, the art critic who helped Peggy select her collection.

Peggy's ashes are buried alongside, marked with a simple plaque: "Here Rests Peggy Guggenheim 1898-1979."

Over your right shoulder, the flourishing olive tree is a gift from one of Peggy's old traveling buddies—Yoko Ono.

In the nonconformist 1960s, Peggy's once shocking art and unconventional lifestyle became more acceptable, even commonplace. By the 1970s, she was universally recognized as a major force in early modern art and was finally even honored by the Venetians with a nickname—"The Last Dogaressa" *(L'Ultima Dogaressa)*. When she died in a Padua hospital in 1979, she was mourned by the art world, from composer Virgil Thomson, to choreographer Jerome Robbins, to writer George Plimpton, to composer John Cage, to...

LA SALUTE CHURCH TOUR

Santa Maria della Salute

Where the Grand Canal opens up into the lagoon stands one of Venice's most distinctive landmarks, the church dedicated to Santa Maria della Salute (Our Lady of Health). The architect, Baldassare Longhena—who also did St. Mark's Square's "new" wing and the Ca' Rezzonico—remade Venice in the Baroque style. Crown-shaped La Salute was his crowning achievement, and the last grand Venetian structure built before Venice's decline began.

Orientation

Cost: Free entry to church; €2 to visit the Sacristy.

Hours: Daily 9:00-12:00 & 15:00-17:30, though the Sacristy may have shorter hours.

Getting There: The church is on the Grand Canal, near the point where the canal spills into the lagoon. It's a 10-minute walk from the Accademia Bridge (past the Peggy Guggenheim Collection). By boat, vaporetto #1 delivers you to its doorstep (€2 from San Marco, 5 minutes). The Dogana *traghetto* (runs 9:00-14:00) and S.M. del Giglio *traghetto* (9:00-18:00) both stop nearby (each cost €0.50). If it's November 21, the day of the Festival of the Madonna della Salute, you can walk directly to the church across the Grand Canal on a floating, pontoon-like bridge. There are also extra events and masses in the church on the days leading up to the festival.

Musical Services: Vespers service with organ music Mon-Fri at 15:30, followed by Mass at 16:00. Mass also on Sun at 11:00, followed by organ music at 11:45.

Information: Tel. 041-241-1018, www.seminariovenezia.it.

Length of This Tour: Allow 30 minutes.

Photography: Allowed, but no flash in the church, and no photos at all in the Sacristy.

Starring: Baldassare Longhena's church, minor works by Titian and Giordano, and the Sacristy with major works by Tintoretto and Titian.

The Tour Begins

Exterior

The white stone church has a steep dome that rises above the octagonal structure. It's encrusted with Baroque scrolls, leafy Corinthian columns, and 125 statues, including the lovely ladies lounging over the central doorway. The architect conceived of the church in the shape of a crown.

During the bitter plague of 1630, the Virgin Mary took pity on the city of Venice, miraculously allowing only one in three Venetians (46,000 souls) to die. During this terrible time, Venetians built this church in honor of Our Lady of Health. Her statue tops the lantern, and she's dressed as an admiral, hand on a rudder, welcoming ships to the Grand Canal.

Even today, Mary's intercession is celebrated every November 21, when a floating bridge is erected across the Grand Canal so Venetians can walk from San Marco across the water and right up the seaweed-covered steps to the front door.

At age 32, architect Baldassare Longhena (1598-1682) supported the city's heaviest dome by sinking countless pilings (locals claim over a million) into the sandy soil to provide an adequate foundation. The 12 Baroque scrolls at the base function as buttresses to help support the mammoth dome.

Interior

❶ View from the Entrance

The church has a bright, healthy glow, with white stone (turned gray because of a fungus) illuminated by light filtering through the dome's windows. The nave is circular, surrounded by chapels. In contrast to the ornate Baroque exterior, the inside is simple, with only Corinthian columns and two useless balcony railings up in the dome. The red, white, and yellow marble of the floor adds a cheerful note.

Longhena focuses our immediate attention on the main altar.

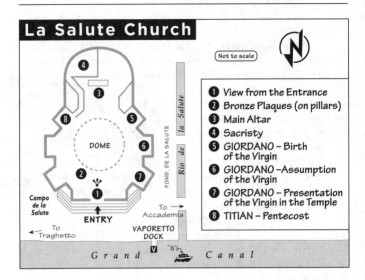

La Salute Church

Not to scale

① View from the Entrance
② Bronze Plaques (on pillars)
③ Main Altar
④ Sacristy
⑤ GIORDANO – Birth of the Virgin
⑥ GIORDANO –Assumption of the Virgin
⑦ GIORDANO – Presentation of the Virgin in the Temple
⑧ TITIAN – Pentecost

DOME

Campo de la Salute

ENTRY

To Traghetto

To Accademia

VAPORETTO DOCK

FOND. DE LA SALUTE

Rio de la Salute

Grand V 🚤 *Canal*

Every other view is blocked by heavy pillars. A master of "theatrical architecture," Longhena only reveals the side chapels one by one, as we walk around and explore. Viewed from the center of the church, the altar and side chapels are framed by arches.

Some of the "marble" is actually brick covered with marble dust. The windows, with clear glass in a honeycomb pattern, bring in maximum light.

• *Look at the pillars near the entrance, opposite the altar, to find the...*

❷ Bronze Plaques

The church is dedicated not just to physical health but to spiritual health as well. The plaques relate that on September 16, 1972, Albino Luciani, the future Pope John Paul I and predecessor of John Paul II, visited here and paid homage to the Virgin of Health (six years later, he fell sick and died after only 30 days in office).

❸ Main Altar

The marble statues on the top of the main altar tell the church's story: The Virgin and Child (center) are approached for help by a kneeling, humble Lady Venice (left). Mary shows compassion and sends an angel baby (right) to drive away Old Lady Plague.

The icon of a black, sad-eyed Madonna with a black baby (12th-century Byzantine) is not meant to be ethnically accurate. Here, a "black" Madonna means an otherworldly one.

• *Find the entrance to the Sacristy, if it's open (entry location varies). It costs €2 to get in, but cheapskates can get a glimpse of the paintings for free by standing outside the entry.*

LA SALUTE CHURCH

❹ Sacristy

Along one wall is Tintoretto's big and colorful *Marriage at Cana* (1551). The receding dinner table leads the eye to Jesus, who is sur-

rounded by the bustle of the wedding feast. On the right, the host (in gray) orders the servant to bring more wine. The apostles at the table portray leading Venetian artists of the day.

On the ceiling are three ultra-dramatic paintings by Titian, with gruesome subjects: *Cain Clubbing Abel, Abraham Sacrificing His Son,* and *David Slaying Goliath* (c. 1543-1544). The panels—featuring stormy clouds, windblown hair, flat tones, and overwrought poses—date from Titian's "Mannerist crisis." After visiting Rome and seeing the work of Michelangelo in the Sistine Chapel, Titian abandoned his standard, sweet, and tested style to paint epic, statuesque, and dramatic works in the Mannerist style. To appreciate his range of styles, contrast the ceiling panels with the painting over the altar, Titian's stately *St. Mark Enthroned with Saints* (c. 1511).

• *Back in the circular nave, there are six side chapels—three to the left, three to the right. Start near the main altar, on the right side (to your right as you face the altar).*

Side Chapel Paintings

Luca Giordano (1632-1705) celebrates the Virgin in three paintings with similar compositions—heaven and angels above, dark earth below.

Giordano, a prolific artist from Naples, was known as "Luca fa presto" (Fast Luke) for the speed (some would say sloppiness) with which he dashed off his paintings.

• *In the chapel to the right of the altar is...*

❺ Giordano—*Birth of the Virgin* (1674)

Little baby Mary in her mom's arms seems like nothing special. But God the Father looks down from above and sends the dove of the Holy Spirit.

• *In the middle chapel, look for...*

❻ Giordano—*Assumption of the Virgin* (1667)

Mary, at the end of her life, is being taken gloriously, by winged babies, up from the dark earth to the golden light of heaven. The apostles cringe in amazement. A later artist thought his statue was better and planted it right in our way.

• *In the chapel closest to the entrance, see...*

❼ Giordano—*Presentation of the Virgin in the Temple* (early 1670s)

Notice how the painting fits the surrounding architecture. It's great to enjoy art in situ. The child Mary (in blue, with wispy halo) ascends a staircase that goes diagonally "into" the canvas. Giordano places us viewers at the foot of the stairs. The lady in the lower left asks her kids, "Why can't you be more like her?!"

• *From here, look directly across to the other side of the nave at Titian's* Pentecost, *in the chapel closest to the main altar. The painting looks its best from this distance and angle.*

❽ Titian (Tiziano Vecellio)—*Pentecost* (1546)

The dove of the Holy Spirit sends spiritual rays that fan out to the apostles below, giving them tongues of fire above their heads. They

gyrate in amazement, each one in a different direction. Using floor tiles and ceiling panels, Titian has created the 3-D illusion of a barrel-arched chapel, with the dove coming right into the church through a fake window. But the painting was not designed for this location and, up close, the whole fake niche looks...fake.

SAN GIORGIO MAGGIORE TOUR

San Giorgio Maggiore is the dreamy church-topped island you see across the lagoon from St. Mark's Square. It's just a five-minute vaporetto ride away. Even if you're not interested in Palladio's influential architecture, Tintoretto's famous *Last Supper,* or the stunning bell-tower views of Venice and the lagoon, it's worth a trip just to escape from tourist-mobbed St. Mark's Square.

Orientation

Cost: Admission to the church is free. It costs €3 to go up the bell tower. Bring €0.50 coins to light the artwork.

Hours: Church open May-Sept Mon-Sat 9:30-12:30 & 14:30-18:00, Sun 8:30-11:00 & 14:30-18:00; Oct-April until 16:30. The elevator up the bell tower runs from 30 minutes after the church opens to 30 minutes before it closes.

Avoiding Crowds: The church is never crowded, but the bell tower and elevator can be. Come early or late to have it to yourself.

Getting There: The only way to reach the church is by taking a five-minute ride on vaporetto #2, which leaves near St. Mark's Square from the San Zaccaria-M.V.E. stop, located east of the Bridge of Sighs by the equestrian statue (€3, 6/hour, ticket valid for 1 hour, direction: Tronchetto, stop: San Giorgio). To get back to St. Mark's Square, take the #2 headed the opposite way (direction: San Marco).

Mass: Mass is held Sun at 11:00. The church is closed to sightseers during Sunday Mass. To attend Mass, held in the Conclave, ring the bell at the door to the right of the main entrance.

Length of This Tour: Allow one hour, more with a trip to the café.

Services: A WC is at the base of the elevator, inside the church.

Cuisine Art: A fine little harborside café, rarely used by tourists, is about 150 yards around the left of the church. Its terrace is peaceful—except at lunchtime, when it's mobbed by librarians (€7 pastas, salads, daily 10:00-20:00, off-season 11:00-15:00).

The Rest of the Island: You can walk along the left side of the church to the café, and see pleasure boats in the marina, but that's it. If you want to see inside the monastery complex (now the home of Fondazione Cini, a nonprofit foundation dedicated to restoring the island), inquire about weekend tours at tel. 041-524-0119 or www.cini.it.

Starring: Palladio, Tintoretto, and views of Venice.

The Tour Begins

Exterior

The facade looks like a Greek temple, a style well-known today because of its architect, Andrea Palladio (1508-1580). Palladio's hugely influential treatise on architecture inspired centuries of architects in England and America with its expert application of Greco-Roman styles. Countless villas, palaces, and churches look like this. They are "Palladian."

Palladio's ingenious facade overlaps two temple fronts. Four tall columns, topped by a triangular pediment resembling a Greek porch, mark the entryway to the tall, central nave. This is superimposed over the facade of the lower side aisles. Behind the facade rises a dome topped with a statue of St. George (the Christian slayer of medieval dragons) holding a flag. The whole complex is completed by the bell tower, which echoes the Campanile in St. Mark's Square across the water.

This church feels so striking because it just doesn't fit with old-school Venice. Palladio makes no concession to the Byzantine legacy of Venice that you see across the water at the Doge's Palace.
• *Walk into the interior of the church.*

❶ View down the Nave, then up the Nave

The interior matches the outer facade, with a high nave flanked by lower side aisles. The walls are white (Palladio's favorite color); the windows have clear, rather than stained, glass; and the well-lit church has a clarity, orderliness, and mathematical perfection that exudes the classical world. In keeping with Palladio's

SAN GIORGIO MAGGIORE

San Giorgio Maggiore

CAFÉ

WC

To Bell Tower & ⑪

CHOIR ⑨

Not to scale

② ④ ③
ALTAR
⑩

DOME

⑧   ⑦

N
A
V
E

⑥
⑤

①

⑫

ENTRY

VAPORETTO #2 DOCK

St. Mark's Basin

To San Zaccaria-M.V.E. (Doge's Palace)

To Vallosso (Giudecca)

① View down the Nave
② Main Altar & Choir
③ TINTORETTO – Last Supper
④ TINTORETTO – Manna from Heaven
⑤ BASSANO – Nativity and Adoration of the Shepherds
⑥ BRUNELLESCHI – Crucifix
⑦ DOMENICO TINTORETTO – St. Benedict and Other Saints

⑧ DOMENICO TINTORETTO – The Stoning of St. Stephen
⑨ Choir
⑩ Statue of an Angel
⑪ To View from the Bell Tower
⑫ Conclave Entrance (Sunday Mass)

SAN GIORGIO MAGGIORE

classical sensitivity, all decor is in harmony (compared to the relative chaos of, say, the Frari Church). Oh, the stout, stony symmetry and mathematical purity—with light spilling in from the canal—it's enough to give a Renaissance architect a... never mind.

❷ Main Altar and Choir

The altar is topped with a bronze globe of the world. The monks

who once lived on this island congregated in the choir area behind the main altar. The choir is designed with acoustics in mind, and the barrel-vault ceiling is backed up with a woofer-shaped apse—all to amplify the Gregorian chants that still fill this church on occasion. (Suddenly I feel a cough coming on...my, the echoes.)

• *On the wall to the right of the altar is...*

❸ Tintoretto—*Last Supper*, 1592-1594

This is the last of several versions of the Last Supper by Tintoretto (1518-1594) that decorate Venice, each one different and inven-

tive (compare it with the Scuola San Rocco version, pictured on page 162). Here, the table stretches diagonally away from us on a tiled floor. The convincing perspective effect is theatrical, engaging the viewer. The scene is

crowded—servants and cats mingle with wispy angels. A blazing lamp, radiating supernatural light, illuminates the otherwise dark interior. At the far left, a beggar is fed, illustrating Christ's concern for the poor. The devilish guy on the right rejects a basket of communion wafers while eyeing a more hedonistic banquet. Your eyes go straight to a well-lit Christ, serving his faithful with both hands—wholeheartedly.

San Giorgio was the church for a Benedictine monastery, an order that stressed a simple lifestyle and concern for the poor. They hired Tintoretto (a common-man's painter) and worked closely with him to hone the message that all are welcome—saints, servants, beggars, sinners—into the Christian faith. The monks appreciated Tintoretto's jumble of the spiritual with the mundane, proclaiming that God works miraculously with us on an everyday level.

This canvas works together theologically with the other canvas flanking the altar.

• *On the wall to the left of the altar is...*

❹ Tintoretto—*Manna from Heaven,* 1591-1592

This painting illustrates the Benedictine motto: Work and pray. Here we see the sunny morning after the storm, when God rained bread down on the hungry Israelites. Some work, others relax prayerfully, and others gather the heavenly meal in baskets, basking in the glow of the miracle. The message: Work and pray, and God will take care of you.

❺-❿ More Art Inside the Church

As long as you're here, check out a few more works. They're minor pieces in art-drenched Venice, but they'd be stars in any American museum.

Back near the entrance, in the first chapel on the right, is Jacopo Bassano's ❺ *Nativity and Adoration of the Shepherds,* where a radiant Baby Jesus lights the dim canvas. In the next chapel is a carved ❻ *Crucifix* by Florentine dome-builder Filippo Brunelleschi.

In the transepts are two works by Jacopo Tintoretto's son, Domenico. In the right transept, the static ❼ *St. Benedict and Other Saints* shows the early monk (to left, in black, bald and bearded) along with Pope Gregory (who wrote about him) having a heavenly vision. ❽ *The Stoning of St. Stephen* (left transept) shows that Domenico had his father's raw talent, but not his flair for dramatic compositions that recede into the distance.

Behind the altar, the ❾ **choir** features 82 stalls elaborately carved in walnut. Here, monks stood and sang, carrying on the prayers, chants, and traditions of the

SAN GIORGIO MAGGIORE

Benedictine order, whose relationship with the island stretched back to A.D. 982 (the monastery closed in 1807).

On your way to the bell tower, you'll pass the original ❿ **statue of an angel** that once stood atop the tower (a copy stands there today). Made in the 18th century of laminated wood covered in lead, it was destroyed by lightning in 1993. Restorers have done their best to piece it back together.

• *You'll find the lift to the top of the bell tower in the far left corner of the church.*

⓫ View from the Bell Tower

The bell tower has no grill (unlike the Campanile at St. Mark's, which has one to keep suicidal people from jumping) and gives a grand view in all directions. Start by looking at the city (to the north), and go clockwise:

Facing North (toward the city): This is the famous view of Venice's skyline, dominated by St. Mark's Campanile. The big, long, brick church farther inland is Santi Giovanni e Paolo. Farther

to the right (east) is the barely visible basin of the Arsenale, the former shipyard, which in its medieval heyday bragged that it was capable of producing a ship a day. Farther still is the green parkland where the Venice Biennale, an international art exhibition, is held every odd-numbered year (next up in 2013). North of Venice, in the hazy distance, you can glimpse several islands. Tiny San Michele (with cypress trees) is the city's cemetery—from here, the island looks connected to Venice. Murano, the next closest, appears to be an extension of the forested cemetery. Burano is to the distant right, with its leaning bell tower. And Torcello (trust me) is just beyond Burano.

Facing East and South: Look out at the lagoon, which leads to the open Adriatic. This tower was once used to spot approaching enemy boats. The lagoon is too shallow for serious shipping; posts mark the channels dredged to let boats pass through. There's a strict speed limit: 5 knots per hour (kph) on the small canals, 7 kph on the Grand Canal, and 11 kph around the perimeter of the island city.

The long, narrow island of Lido in the distance is six miles long and only a half-mile wide (with cars and ferry service to the mainland). The green dome on the island marks the Lido's town center, home to modern hotels and beaches. The Lido serves as

View from San Giorgio Maggiore

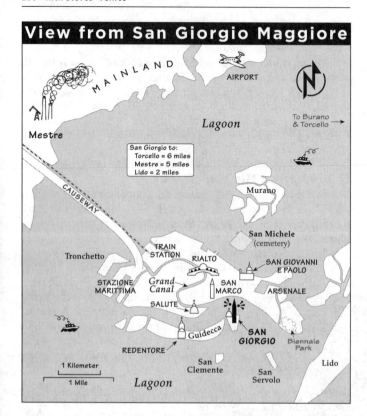

San Giorgio to:
Torcello = 6 miles
Mestre = 5 miles
Lido = 2 miles

a natural breakwater against the wind and waves of the Adriatic Sea, helping create the placid waters of the Venetian lagoon. At the right end of the Lido (visible from here, but not obvious) is the narrow opening to the Adriatic, where the proposed, long-delayed, underwater flood barriers are to be built. Designed to block the *acqua alta* flooding, the multibillion-dollar Moses Project involves the construction of a series of hinged

barriers that will rise up to block high tides threatening the lagoon.

Once a year, the mayor of Venice sails to the opening of the Adriatic to celebrate the ritual marriage of Venice and the sea—the same ritual performed centuries ago by the doges in their gold-leaf boat.

Between the Lido and San Giorgio are several smaller islands, which have been home over the centuries to monasteries and hospitals. The plain, rectangular white building on San Servolo, the little island just before the Lido, was an 18th-century hospital for the insane that now houses a university.

At your feet are the green gardens and the cloisters of the former abbey of San Giorgio (restoration of the grounds by Fondazione Cini is ongoing).

Facing West: Below is the church, with its dome topped by a green St. George carrying a flag (or is his arm still missing?). You

can see the back sides of the white statues atop Palladio's facade. Stretching to the left is the island of Giudecca, which is oh-so-close to the island you're on, but must be reached by a short swim or vaporetto #2. The Giudecca, which has always been isolated from the rest of the city, was a popular place to build villas in Venice's heyday. The island's separation also made it a perfect place for exiles such as Michelangelo, who found refuge and peace here between commissions. Today, except for a few churches, a youth hostel, and a couple of luxury hotels, the Giudecca is home to locals going about their quiet lives, oblivious to the tourism that dominates the rest of Venice. You can see the swimming pool of the jet-setty Ciprani Hotel, the domes of other Palladian churches (the only sights on this otherwise residential island), and, at the far end, the Molino Stucky, an old, industrial flour mill that reopened in 2007 as the Hilton Hotel.

Directly across from you is the grand dome of La Salute Church. At the head of the Grand Canal stands the golden globe of the old Customs House, now the Punta della Dogana contemporary art museum. And in the far distance, through the smog, are the burning smokestacks and cranes of lovely Mestre, on the mainland.

Looking Up: The bells chime the hours, and ring especially loudly at noon. You're warned.

VENICE'S LAGOON TOUR

San Michele, Murano, Burano, and Torcello

Interesting islands hide out in Venice's lagoon, a calm section of the Adriatic protected from wind and waves by the natural break-water of the Lido. The brackish marsh—a mix of fresh water and silt from the mainland's rivers, plus the tide-driven saltwater of the Adriatic—is set among a maze of sandbars. The lagoon is big (212 square miles) and so shallow that you could walk across most of it without getting your hair wet. Centuries ago, the shallow water and treacherous sandbars made the Isle of Venice safe from attack by land or sea. Venice is the only great medieval city that never needed a wall.

Cradled by the lagoon, north of the city, are four islands eas-ily laced together in a half-day trip, a nice escape from the hubbub of Venice. Murano is known for glass, Burano for lace and pho-togenic pastel houses, and tranquil Torcello for its church. San Michele is the cemetery island, the last stop for its residents, but the first stop for the vaporetto from Venice. The lagoon is home to many more islands, but these four are the most worthwhile for visitors.

We'll sail first from Venice to Murano (stopping at San Michele on the way), and then to Burano, from where we'll make a side-trip to Torcello before returning to Venice.

Orientation

Transportation: We'll travel by vaporetto, but there are other options (see sidebar in this chapter). Since single vaporetto tickets (€6.50) expire after one hour, using a vaporetto pass for this lagoon excursion makes more sense (e.g., a 12-hour pass for €16; see page 33 for more on vaporetto tickets).

Venice's Lagoon

To Trieste,
Ljubljana
& Salzburg

A-4

To
Belluno
& Cortina

A-27

E-70
A-4

A-57

A-57

See detail map Torcello

To Padua,
Vicenza,
Verona &
Milan

Mestre

Marco
Polo

Burano
Murano

San Michele

Lido de
Jesolo

Lagoon

Marghera

A-4 E-70 Mira

Stra

Venice

Mal-
contenta

Lido

Brenta Canal

Punta
Sabbioni

Porta de Lido

To
Padua

Lagoon

Malamocco

Adriatic
Sea

To
Padua

Alberoni

Porta de Malamocco

309

516

Pellestrina

Chioggia

Porta de Chioggia

104

Sottomarina

To
Ravenna 309

5 Kilometers

5 Miles

Sightseeing Costs: Murano's Glass Museum costs €6.50, Burano's Lace Museum is €5.50, and all of Torcello's sights together cost €12, including the audioguide (€3-5 for individual sights). The Museum Pass covers the glass and lace museums; you can also choose to use the Doge's Palace/Correr Museum combo-ticket here (see page 25).

When to Go: If you want to visit all of the lagoon sights, keep in mind that Burano's Lace Museum is closed Tuesdays, and Torcello's church museum is closed Mondays.

Information: Pick up a free map of the lagoon and its islands from any TI.

Length of This Tour: Since it takes a minimum of three hours round-trip from St. Mark's to Torcello, allow at least five hours to see all four islands. For an hour-by-hour itinerary, see page 21. Of course, you can shorten this tour by visiting just Murano (and the cemetery if you wish), or just Burano (and Torcello if you'd like).

Starring: World-famous Venetian glass and lace, the mosaics of the oldest Venetian church, and the quieter side of Venice.

Where to Start

You can start from St. Mark's Square, from the train station or bus station, or from the Fondamente Nove vaporetto stop (15 minutes' walk from Rialto). Wherever you start, your first goal is to locate a vaporetto heading to the Colonna stop on the island of Murano (listed on signs and schedules as Murano-Colonna).

From the Rialto and Campo Santa Maria Formosa: Walk 15 minutes to the Fondamente Nove vaporetto stop on the north shore of Venice (the "back" of the fish). Lines #4.1 and #4.2 converge here before heading out to Murano. Catch either one (every 10 minutes).

From Fondamente Nove the boats cross to San Michele (whose stop is called Cimitero) in six minutes, then continue another three minutes to Murano-Colonna.

From St. Mark's Square: Find the San Zaccaria-Jolanda dock, just past the Bridge of Sighs. Catch vaporetto #4.1, which leaves every 20 minutes. It travels around the "tail" of fish-shaped Venice, making several stops before reaching Murano-Colonna after 40 minutes.

From the Train Station or Bus Station: Catch vaporetto #4.2, which leaves every 20 minutes and takes 35-40 minutes to reach Murano-Colonna. (You can also take the express #3 vaporetto, which goes directly to Murano-Colonna twice an hour, but then you'll have to skip the cemetery.)

The Route

Here's our plan: On the way to Murano, we'll make a quick visit to the cemetery (Cimitero stop). We'll arrive at Murano-Colonna, but leave Murano from a different stop (Murano-Faro). At Murano-Faro, we'll board vaporetto #12 for the 30-minute trip to Burano. From Burano, we'll side-trip to Torcello on vaporetto #9 (5-minute trip each way). From Burano, we'll return to Venice on vaporetto #12, arriving either at Fondamente Nove (quicker, 40 minutes) or the San Zaccaria-Pietà stop near St. Mark's Square (more scenic, 70 minutes).

The Tour Begins

• *After leaving Fondamente Nove, the next stop of the #4.1 and #4.2 vaporetto lines is Cimitero. Hop off here for a short visit to...*

San Michele

The cemetery island's location—directly across the water from the emergency room of Venice's San Giovanni e Paolo hospital—is just a coincidence. The stopover is easy, since boats come every 10 minutes. If you even half-enjoy wandering through old cemeteries,

Pound in Italy

How did an Idaho boy end up in a Venetian cemetery? Poet Ezra Pound (1885-1972), who spent much of his life in Europe, settled in Italy in the 1920s, becoming infatuated with Mussolini's Modernist outlook...and his politics. By the early 1940s, Pound was a leading pro-Fascist propagandist, for which he was indicted for treason by the US once the war was over. He was spared execution by successfully (though controversially) pleading insanity, and eventually returned to Italy.

Nevertheless, Pound's most lasting legacy is his poetry. Scholars consider him one of the form's most influential Modernist voices. While Pound's own masterwork was the series of poems called *The Cantos,* his greatest literary contribution was arguably his heavy-handed editing of his friend T. S. Eliot's *The Waste Land.*

This excerpt of one of Pound's *Cantos* was inspired by Venice—a city of stone reflected in the water during a boat ride at night.

From ***Canto XVII***

A boat came,
One man holding her sail,
Guiding her with oar caught over gunwale, saying:
"There, in the forest of marble,
The stone trees—out of water—
the arbours of stone...
the gilt beams flare of an evening..."

And the waters richer than glass...
Dye-pots in the torch-light...
The flash of wave under prows...
Stone trees, white and rose-white in the darkness...
Drift under hulls in the night.
"In the gloom the gold
Gathers the light about it."

you'll dig this one—it's full of flowers, trees, and birdsong, and

has an intriguing chapel (cemetery open daily April-Sept 7:30-18:00, Oct-March 7:30-16:30; reception to the left as you enter, free WC to the right, no picnicking).

The island, which is dedicated to St. Michael and holds a Renaissance church, became Venice's cemetery in 1806 when

San Michele
① Cemetery

Murano
② Fondamenta
   dei Vetrai

③ Church of San Pietro Martire
④ Residential Murano: Ramo da Mula
⑤ Glass Museum
⑥ Santa Maria e San Donato Church

Lagoon Tour

1 Kilometer
1 Mile

Lagoon

10-MIN WALK

CHURCH COMPLEX

Torcello

LINE T 5 MIN

Mazzorbo

Burano

See Burano detail map below

LINE LN

To Sant'Erasmo and Lido

Burano detail

To Torcello

Mazzorbo

LINE T

LINE LN

To Sant'Erasmo and Lido

To Murano

SAN MAURO

MACELLO

COMARE

F. S. MAURO

VIA B. GALUPPI

C. PITTORA

Burano

Sant' Erasmo

FONDAMENTA DELLA GIUDECCA

FISH MARKET

WC

VIGNA

POST

F. TERAMOYA

Piazza Galuppi

Lagoon

FONDAMENTA DEL PIZZO

F. T. PIZZO Park

San Martino Church & Leaning Bell Tower

100 Meters
100 Yards

Burano
7 Bell Tower
8 Merletti d'Arte dalla Lidia Lace Shop
9 Lace Museum
10 Trattoria al Gatto Nero

Torcello
11 Locanda Cipriani Hotel
12 Santa Maria Assunta Church

Eating near Fondamente Nove
13 Ristorante Algiubagio

VENICE'S LAGOON

Napoleon decreed that it was unhygienic to bury bodies within a city. As a result, Venice's coffins were shipped out to San Michele, and since then, Venetians have been buried here. You'll find the dearly departed (often with their photos) sorted into sections of priests *(preti)*, nuns *(suore)*, monks *(frati)*, children *(bambini)*, civilian victims of war, soldiers, military sailors *(marinai)*, and so on.

Foreign Romantics and artists who made Venice their adopted hometown have also chosen this spot as their final resting place. To find the graves of the most famous foreigners, go basically straight ahead from the entrance to the far end, following the maps and signs. In the Evangelico (Protestant) section lies Idaho-born poet Ezra Pound (from the Evangelico gate, he's in the near left quarter of the section—look for a small stone in a large plot).

Ten yards beyond Pound's grave, find Nobel laureate and one-time US Poet Laureate Joseph Brodsky (1940-1996), who was expelled from Soviet Russia, lived the rest of his life in America,

and asked to be buried here in Venice.

In the "Greco" (Orthodox) section, find Russian-born Modernist composer Igor Stravinsky (far right corner, alongside his wife) and the Russian dancer/choreographer Diaghalev (the canopied tomb along the far wall).

• *Return to the dock and catch any #4.1 or #4.2 vaporetto heading toward the right (boats leave every 10 minutes). While you're waiting, look for the blue funeral boat with a rack on wheels for the coffin. It's usually moored next to the vaporetto.*

It's a three-minute crossing to the Murano-Colonna stop. As you approach the island of Murano, you'll see its ghostly lighthouse (faro) off to the right. In centuries past, the faro guided boats from the open sea into town. Near the lighthouse is the stop where you'll leave Murano for the island of Burano.

Murano

Murano is famous for its glass factories. A 1292 law restricted glass production (and its dangerous furnaces) to the isle of Murano to prevent fires on the main island... and to protect the secrets of Venetian glassmaking. Originally, glassmakers made mosaic tiles, later branching out to produce the ornate vases, beaded necklaces, glass sculptures, and wine decanters you'll see here today.

While Murano seems dominated by glassworks and the glass shops that line its main canal, there's more to the island than glass. If you take time to wander, you'll find impressive churches, restaurants, and untouristed residential areas.

From the Colonna vaporetto stop, skip the glass shops in front of you, walk to the right, and wander up the street along the canal, **Fondamenta dei Vetrai** (Glassmakers' Embankment). The Faro district of Murano, on the other side of the canal, is packed with factories *(fabriche)* and their furnaces *(fornaci)*. The brick buildings give Murano a 19th-century, Industrial Age look and feel. At #14 is the entry to the island's small indoor **shopping mall,** with a free WC and a Despar supermarket on the upper floor (Mon-Sat 8:00-19:30, closed Sun).

You'll pass dozens of glass shops along the canal. A cut above is the venerable **Venini** shop, at #47, which shows off the ultimate in modern Venetian glass design (Mon-Sat 9:30-17:30, closed Sun).

Continue up Fondamenta dei Vetrai until you see a tower on your right and a church on your left. The **tower** was built as a fire lookout in this city of furnaces. The **Church of San Pietro Martire** (Mon-Sat 9:00-12:00 & 15:00-18:00, Sun 12:00-17:00,

www.sandonatomurano.it) features Giovanni Bellini's solid-color *Virgin Enthroned with Mark and a Kneeling Doge* (right wall of the nave in the center). This votive painting—showing a doge being introduced to the Virgin Mary by St. Mark—was the doge's way of thanking Mary for his position of power. The doge wears a luxurious ermine cloak (a symbol of royalty) and a ducal crown hat. The sacristy/museum has ornately carved caryatids (human pillars, c. 1660) with expressive faces and arms posed every which way (€1.50 admission; find the stairway from the courtyard by walking past the front of the church with the canal at your back—if it's not open, find a staff member and ask). The carved panels between the caryatids depict scenes from the life of John the Baptist, culminating in his beheading in the far corner. In the next rooms, see ceremonial religious objects and statues, then check out the photos (midway up the steps) of these objects being used in modern-day Venetian parades. Upstairs are piles of relics in glass cases.

For a slice of **residential Murano,** circle counterclockwise around the back of the church and down the street called Ramo da Mula. In this old shell, there's a new vibrancy, as tourist-swamped Venice's high rents and real-estate prices drive locals to the outlying islands. Behind the glass shops, Murano is a workaday community of 6,000 residents. It has real neighborhoods, with moms shopping at markets, schools filled with noisy children, bikes in the front yards, and benches warmed by Venetian old-timers.

Back on the embankment, continue beyond the church to the larger Grand Canal of Murano. Cross the big, green metal bridge and head right 150 yards to the **Glass Museum** (following signs for *Museo Vetrario;* you'll pass a smaller Co-op supermarket and the Murano-Museo vaporetto stop, then bend left). While the display is musty and antiquated, it's well-described in English. The first room, on the lower level, shows ancient glass and glassmaking techniques in order to illustrate how Venice has carried on making the same colors and using the same techniques from its earlier days. Upstairs, on one floor, the museum displays the very best of 500 years of Venetian glassmaking (€6.50, covered by sightseeing passes, daily April-Oct 10:00-18:00, Nov-March 10:00-17:00, last entry 30 minutes before closing, Fondamenta Giustinian 8, tel. 041-739-586, www.museiciviciveneziani.it). If you're really interested in glassmaking, join the museum's twice-weekly **Glass in Action tour.** You get a 45-minute guided tour in English of the museum, followed by a 30-minute glassmaking demonstration and film at Scuola del Vetro Abate Zanette, the nearby glassmakers' training institute (€15 includes museum admission; guided tour Tue and Thu at 12:00 and 14:30, demonstration follows at 14:00 and 16:00; reserve at tel. 041-4273-0892, toll-free within Italy 848-082-000, or by e-mail to info@fmcvenezia.it).

One hundred yards farther along the canal is **Santa Maria e San Donato Church,** the architectural highlight of Murano (free, erratic opening hours, www.sandonatomurano.it). Before entering, note the fine Byzantine Romanesque exterior—especially the stonework of its apse, facing the canal. The interior takes you back to the 12th century. Built when St. Mark's Basilica was under construction, the highlights are its inlaid stone floor and the gorgeous mosaic above the altar. It features Mary as God's mother, gliding in from heaven on her carpet, blessing the faithful with two open

Guided Tours to Murano

I recommend the self-guided tour in this chapter. But if you'd like to test your ability to resist a smooth-talking Italian glass salesman, or if you'd like to join a group for your trip out to Murano, consider these two options.

By Speedboat Tour: The easiest—and priciest—way to see Murano, Burano, and Torcello is to pay about €20 for a rushed and touristy 3- to 5-hour speedboat tour. They leave twice a day in summer from the San Marco-Giardinetti dock; look and listen for guides calling out for potential passengers (April-Oct usually at 9:30 and 14:30, Nov-March at 14:00 only, tel. 041-240-1711). The tours are speedy indeed—live guides race through the commentary in up to five languages—and boats stop for roughly 40 minutes at each island. The stops are for glassblowing and lacemaking demonstrations followed by sales spiels, leaving no time left to explore on your own.

A Free Ride with a Sales Pitch: You can also get to Murano for free on a speedboat. Tourists are practically

kidnapped from St. Mark's Square by the aggressive sales reps who approach them and ferry them out to the island (35-minute ride). Your only obligation is to sit through a fairly interesting 20-minute glassmaking demonstration and sales pitch. After that, there's no obligation to actually buy, and then you're on your own. (In fact, they don't promise you a trip back to Venice.)

During the demonstration, the glassblower typically sticks a rod with raw glass on the end into a furnace, melts the glass, and expands it by blowing through the hollow rod. Then he shapes it with tongs into a vase, a glass, or a piece of art. This is followed by an almost comically high-pressure sales pitch in the showroom. (The spiel is brief, and there really is no obligation to buy anything.) If you do buy something, see page 294 for tips on having a purchase shipped home.

If you just want to see a glassblower in action, you don't need to go out to Murano—visit Galleria San Marco, at #139 on St. Mark's Square (see Shopping in Venice chapter).

hands. Her three stars symbolize her virginity: before, during, and after giving birth to Jesus.

A WWI monument lies at the base of the church's bell tower, and next to that, the Snack Bar Da Ice serves good salads and sandwiches.

When you're ready to leave Murano, find your way back to the green metal bridge and cross back toward San Pietro Martire. Near the church, cross the narrow canal to Fondamenta Daniele Manin. Before the next bridge, turn left on the street called Bressagio, which takes you toward the white-stone lighthouse *(faro)* and its Murano-Faro vaporetto dock.

To your right are some of Murano's actual glass factories and their showrooms. At #25, the Ai Dogi factory's showroom has an open kiln area where you can watch a glassblower at work during the summer only (April-Sept Mon-Fri roughly 11:00-16:00, no activity on weekends or off-season).

• *To continue our tour, walk over to the Murano–Faro vaporetto stop and catch the #12 vaporetto to* **Burano** *(2/hour, 30 minutes). If you'd prefer to head straight back to Venice, take either the #3 vaporetto (for the train station and bus station) or the #4.2 (for Fondamente Nove and St. Mark's Square).*

Burano

Burano has three vaporetto docks side-by-side (*vaporetti* in and out, and the shuttle to Torcello). Upon arrival, note departure times—most boats leave twice an hour.

Famous for its lace and picturesque pastel houses, Burano is a sleepy island with a sleepy community (pop. 2,700)—village Venice without the glitz. Its colorfully painted homes look like Venice before the plaster peeled off. Each adjoining townhouse is painted its own color. While Venice is a showy city of merchants, Burano is a humble town of fishermen. Though the island's main drag is mobbed with tourists by day, at night it's quiet. Laundry hangs over alleyways, and sunshades (typical of the area) cover the doors of residents' homes. The church's bell tower leans at a five-degree angle...the same as Pisa's.

This town's history is ancient, explained in part by its name. "Burano" comes from the Venetian word for "breeze"—and a breeze meant survival on the lagoon. It kept away the malaria-carrying mosquitoes that made other places (like Torcello) less habitable.

Boating in Venice

Italian law stipulates that a luxury tax is levied on all boats—except in Venice, where they're considered a necessity.

Venetians go everywhere by boat. Calling a taxi? A boat comes. Going to the hospital to have a baby? Just hop on the vaporetto. Garbage day? You put your bag on the canal edge, and a garbage boat mashes it and takes it away.

Many residents own a boat, though it's not always practical for everyday activities. If you want to cruise to the grocery store, you first have to check the tide table to make sure your boat can fit beneath certain bridges. And parking is always a huge problem everywhere—either you know a friend nearby with a grandfathered parking space, or your partner has to "circle the block" while you shop.

Locals rely more on the public *vaporetti* and *traghetti*. While tourists pay plenty for these boats, Venetians ride cheap and easy. An all-year pass costs less than €1 a day.

Gondolas are strictly for tourists these days, but in earlier times, these flat-bottomed boats were the only way to negotiate the tricky, shallow lagoon. The oarsman had to stand up in the back of the boat to see oncoming sandbars. Today, boats ply confidently between the shifting sandbanks of the lagoon, thanks to thoroughfares defined by modern pilings.

While many Venetians own a car for driving on the isle of Lido or the mainland, they admit, "We're not very much beloved on the road."

The island can be covered in a five-minute stroll. From the vaporetto dock, follow the crowds into the center. Turn left at the canal. A bridge leads to Piazza Galuppi, and just beyond that—near the far tip of this little island—is Burano's famous leaning church **bell tower.** The church has a fine, restored Tiepolo painting of the Crucifixion.

The main drag from the vaporetto stop into town is packed with tourists and lined with shops, some of which sell Burano's locally produced white wine. Wander to the far side of the island, and the mood shifts. Explore to the right of the leaning tower for a peaceful yet intensely pastel, small-town lagoon world. Benches lining a little promenade at the water's edge make another pretty picnic spot.

Most tourists visit Burano for its lace, and they're not disappointed. Lace is cheaper in Burano than in Venice, and serious shoppers should comparison-shop in Venice before visiting Burano. Of the many lace shops, I like **Merletti d'Arte dalla Lidia** for its fine private museum (in the rear of the shop and upstairs). Paola, who speaks English, gives visitors a warm welcome as she shows off the masterpieces of lace from all over Europe. Ask her for a magnifying glass to marvel at the intricate knots, and be sure to go upstairs (daily 9:30-18:00, just off the big square opposite the leaning tower at Via Baldassarre Galuppi 215, tel. 041-730-052, www.dallalidia.com).

Lace fans enjoy the **Lace Museum** (Museo del Merletto di Burano), which reopened in 2011 after an extensive renovation (€5.50, covered by passes—see page 25, April-Oct Tue-Sun 10:00-18:00, Nov-March Tue-Sun 10:00-16:00, closed Mon year-round, last entry 30 minutes before closing, some English descriptions, tel. 041-730-034, www.museicivicineziani.it).

For a picnic, the park next to Burano's only vaporetto dock is hard to beat. And you'll find plenty of touristy eateries on Burano, all enthusiastic about their fish. While you have plenty of options for a quick bite, if you want to dine, consider **Trattoria al Gatto Nero.** They serve good traditional dishes outside overlooking the peaceful canal, or in the dressy interior (€15 pastas, €20 *secondi*, closed Mon, crisp service, 3-minute walk from the ferry dock and from the thriving main tourist drag at Fondamenta de la Giudecca 88, tel. 041-730-120).

• *To reach our tour's next stop,* **Torcello,** *take the shuttle boat (Line T) that runs on the hour and the half-hour back and forth (five-minute trip). (If you want to skip Torcello and head right back to* **Venice,** *see the very end of this chapter.)*

Torcello

This is the birthplace of Venice, where the first mainland refugees settled, escaping the barbarian hordes. Yet today, it's the least-developed island (pop. 20) in its most natural state, marshy and shrub-covered. There's little for tourists to see except the church (a 10-minute walk from the dock), which claims to be the oldest in Venice and has impressive mosaics.

From the vaporetto dock, walk through a salty landscape and think of the original inhabitants. Romanized farmers came here, escaping the Germanic barbarians who started streaming through the mainland in the fifth century. By the 11th century, the teeny island had 11 churches. But one look around tells you that this place was inhospitable—the farming was poor, there was no fresh water, and mosquitoes and malaria were big problems. Even though residents diverted the flow of mainland rivers, the lagoon silted up around them anyway, and the island was slowly abandoned.

Approaching the church, you'll pass by the remote yet fancy **Locanda Cipriani Hotel** next door. With just five rooms, it's hosted Thomas Mann, Queen Elizabeth II, and Princess Diana. The hotel has a delightful garden that's (kind of) open to the public.

The **Santa Maria Assunta Church** complex consists of four sights: the church itself, the bell tower (behind the church, climb a

ramped stairway for great lagoon views), a sacristy, and a small museum (facing the church, in two separate buildings) that displays Roman sculpture and medieval sculpture and manuscripts. Tickets for each sight cost €3-5, or €12 for all sights, including an audioguide (most open daily March-Oct 10:30-18:00, Nov-Feb 10:00-16:30, museum closed Mon, last entry 30-60 minutes before closing, museum tel. 041-730-761, church/bell tower tel. 041-730-119). There's a pay WC between the museum's two buildings.

The ruins in front of the church used to be a baptistery from the ninth century; in those days, you couldn't enter a church until you were baptized.

Inside the church, the brick walls and wood-beam ceiling are classic Venetian building materials—that is, flexible—to accommodate the ever-shifting sands underneath. The altar has the relics of St. Heliodorus (d. 390), a local-born bishop who was the travel partner of the famed St. Jerome on a trip to the Holy Land. The columns of the rood screen (separating the altar area from the congregation) were obviously scavenged from elsewhere—note the variety of capitals. You can see a bit of the church's original black-and-white mosaic floor (ninth century) under a small glassed-over section on the right side of the nave. In the 12th century, flooding forced them to rebuild 12 inches higher. The apse mosaic (over the altar) shows Mary and baby Jesus above and the 12 apostles below.

In the right apse, with its sumptuous vault, find Christ Pantocrator, ruler of all, flanked by archangels Michael and Gabriel. On the ceiling, Christ is represented by the sacrificial lamb.

The mosaic on the back wall is famous. Six horizontal bands depict the Last Judgment (and other scenes). From top to bottom, see:

1. The Crucifixion.

2. A striding Christ pulling a soul out from Limbo while stepping on a devil.

3. Christ, in an almond-shaped bubble, as the Creator, flanked by souls in Paradise. From the bottom of the bubble pours a river of fire, which runs down the wall to hell.

4. Angels preparing the Throne of Judgment—empty except for a book. Note Adam and Eve kneeling below.

5 and 6. Archangel Michael (over the door) weighing souls on a scale, while mischievous devils try to tip the scales in their favor.

On the right are the fires of hell, where sinners—many of them turbaned Muslims—are tormented by black-skinned demons. A crude display of the seven deadly sins appears at the lower right: pride (crowned heads in flames), lust (bodies in flames), gluttony (guys eating even their fingers), envy (skulls with worms eating out their coveting eyes), greed (fancy earrings), laziness (useless hands and cut-off feet), and anger (a man waist-deep in cold water to cool down).

• *Avoid the eighth deadly sin—missing your vaporetto—by allowing at least 10 minutes to get from the church back to the boat dock. Boats generally depart at :15 and :45 past the hour. To get back to Venice, return to Burano (5 minutes), and from there, catch the #12 vaporetto line back to Venice. You can catch the #12 in either direction—clockwise or counterclockwise around the lagoon. The clockwise #12 boat sails from Burano once an hour to St. Mark's Square (landing at the San Zaccaria-Pietà dock). It's often a big double-decker boat, and goes via Punta Sabbioni on the island of Sant'Erasmo and the Lido—by taking it you get a fine lagoon cruise experience.*

The counterclockwise #12 line leaves more frequently (twice an hour at :26 and :56) and, technically, gets you back to Venice faster (45 minutes from Burano to Fondamente Nove via Murano-Faro). This is good if your hotel or other final destination is near Fondamente Nove (the "back" of the fish). But if you need to get to St. Mark's, you'll have to change at Fondamente Nove to the #42 vaporetto to San Zaccaria (30 minutes)—in which case, you'll get back faster by taking the clockwise lagoon-cruise #12 boat.

ST. MARK'S TO RIALTO WALK

Two rights and a left (simple!) can get you from St. Mark's Square to the Rialto Bridge via a completely different route from the one most tourists take. Along the way, take in some lesser sights in the area west of St. Mark's Square. You finish where many fish do—at the market.

Orientation

Length of This Walk: Allow one hour for a leisurely walk (30 minutes with no stops).

San Moisè Church: Free, Mon-Sat 9:30-12:30, Sun Mass only at 11:00, tel. 041-296-0630.

La Fenice Opera House: Typically open daily 9:30-13:30, but schedule varies depending on rehearsal and performance schedules (dry 45-minute audioguide-€8, box office phone answered daily 9:00-18:00, tel. 041-2424, www.teatrola fenice.it).

Scala Contarini del Bovolo: Likely closed for renovation but viewable for free any time from the outside. Once it reopens, it's likely to cost a few euros to climb (possibly daily 10:00-18:00, closed weekends in winter).

Rialto Market: The souvenir stalls are open daily; the produce market is closed on Sunday and Monday; and the fish market is closed on Sunday. The market is lively only in the morning.

Overview

There are actually three easy routes from St. Mark's Square to Rialto:

1. Along the crowded Mercerie (a.k.a. the "Marzarie"; follow the tourists underneath the Clock Tower).

...shot on Calle dei Fabbri (exit St. Mark's Square ...n Caffè Quadri).

...ly longer but more interesting route described in this chapter.

The Walk Begins

Start at St. Mark's Square

• *From the square, walk to the waterfront and turn right. You're walking on recently raised Venice—in 2006, the stones were taken up and six inches of extra sand put down, to minimize flooding. Continue along the water toward the white TI pavilion.*

Along the waterfront, you'll see the various boats that ply Venice's waters. The gondolas here are often more expensive than elsewhere. Classic wooden motorboats operating as water taxis are pricey (about €60 from here to the train station), but they are a classy splurge if you split the fare with others. Hotel shuttle boats bring guests here from distant, $700-a-night hotels.

Run the gauntlet of souvenir stands to the entrance to the Giardinetti Reali (Royal Gardens). The grounds offer some precious greenery in a city built of stone on mud. Nearby are €1.50 WCs, a TI in a cute 18th-century former coffeehouse pavilion, and public pay phones where you can call home just to tell everyone where you are right now. From atop the bridge by the TI, look across the mouth of the Grand Canal to view the big dome of La Salute Church, and the guy balancing a bronze ball on one foot on top of the old Customs House, which is now a contemporary art museum (the Punta della Dogana, described on page 50).

• *Twelve steps down and 20 yards ahead on the right is...*

❶ Harry's American Bar

Hemingway put this bar on the map by making it his hangout in the late 1940s. If Brad and Angelina are in town, this is where they'll be. If they're not, you'll see plenty of dressed-up Americans looking around for celebrities. The discreet (and overpriced) restaurant upstairs is where the glitterati hang out. The street-level bar is for gawkers. If you wear something a bit fancy (or artsy bohemian), you can pull up a stool at the tiny bar by the entrance and pay too much for a Bellini (Prosecco and peach juice), which was invented right here.

• *Head inland down Calle Vallaresso, one of Venice's most exclu-*

St. Mark's to Rialto Walk

1. Harry's American Bar
2. San Moisè Church
3. Matteo lo Greco Studio
4. La Fenice Opera House
5. Ponte de la Verona
6. Daniele Manin Statue
7. Scala Contarini del Bovolo
8. Teatro Goldoni
9. View of Rialto Bridge

sive streets, past fancy boutiques such as Pucci, Gucci, and Roberto Cavalli. At the T intersection, turn left and head west on Salizada San Moisè (which becomes Calle Larga XXII Marzo). You'll pass the fine Mondadori Bookstore, then continue to the first bridge and a square dominated by the fancy façade of a church. Climb the bridge, and against a soundtrack of tourists negotiating with hustling gondoliers, look back at the ornate...

❷ San Moisè Church

This is the parish church for St Mark's; because of tourist crowds at the basilica, this is where the community actually worships. While it's one of Venice's oldest churches, dating from the 10th century (note the old tower on the right), its busy facade is 17th-century Baroque. This was an age when big shots who funded such projects expected to see their faces featured (see the bust of Mr. Fini in the center). Moses *(Moisè)* caps the facade.

Inside, the altarpiece depicts Mount Sinai, with Moses (kneeling) receiving the two tablets with the Ten Commandments. The alcove to the left of the altar has Tintoretto's 16th-century *Christ Washing the Disciples' Feet.*

The ugly modern building on the right marks the former Venice headquarters of the Nazis during World War II. Its fascist facade still gives locals the Mussolini-creeps. Now a five-star hotel, it's one of the few modern buildings in town.

• *Continue past the bridge, down Calle Larga XXII Marzo, a big street that seems too wide and large for Venice. It was created during the 19th century by filling in a canal. You can make out the outline of the sidewalks that once flanked the now-gone canal. Pass by the Vivaldi look-alikes selling concert tickets and immigrants illegally selling knockoffs of Prada bags.*

Halfway down the street, turn right on tiny Calle del Sartor da Veste. Go straight, crossing a bridge, and passing the studio of sculptor **Matteo lo Greco** *(❸ on map), whose plump people in bronze celebrate life with a lighter-than-air joy. Then, at the next square, you'll find...*

❹ La Fenice Opera House (Gran Teatro alla Fenice)

Venice's famed opera house, built in 1792 (read the MDCCXCII on the facade), was reduced to a hollowed-out shell by a disastrous fire in 1996. After a vigorous restoration campaign, "The Phoenix"— true to its name—has risen again from the ashes. La Fenice resumed opera productions in 2004, opening with *La Traviata.* The theater is usually open daily to the public (for information, see listing at the beginning of this chapter).

Venice is one of the cradles of the art form known as opera. An opera is a sung play and a multimedia event, blending music, words, story, costume, and set design. Some of the great operas were first performed here in this luxurious setting. Verdi's *Rigoletto* (1851) and *La Traviata* (1853) were actually commissioned by La Fenice. The man who put words to some of Mozart's opera tunes was a Venetian, Lorenzo da Ponte, who drew inspiration from the city's libertine ways and joie de vivre. In recent years, La Fenice's musical standing was overshadowed by its reputation as a place for the wealthy to parade in furs and jewels.

• *Continue north along the same street (though its name is now Calle de la Verona), to a small bridge over a quiet canal.*

❺ Ponte de la Verona

Pause atop this bridge, where reflections can make you wonder which end is up. Looking above you, see bridges of stone propping

up leaning buildings, and there's a view of the "Leaning Tower" of San Stefano.

People actually live in Venice. Notice their rooftop gardens, their laundry, their plumbing, electricity lines snaking into their apartments, and the rusted iron bars and bolts that hold their crumbling homes together. On one building, find centuries-old relief carvings—a bearded face and a panel of an eagle with its prey.

While many Venetians own (and love) their own boats, parking watercraft is a huge problem. Getting a spot is tough, and

when you finally find one, it's very expensive and rarely near your apartment. (For more on boating in Venice, see page 213.) People once swam freely in the canals. Find the sign that reads *Divieto di Nuoto* ("swimming not allowed").

• *Continue north. At the T intersection, turn right on Calle de la Mandola. You'll cross over a bridge into a spacious square dominated by a statue and an out-of-place modern building.*

❻ Campo Manin

The centerpiece of the square is **a statue of Daniele Manin** (1804-1857), Venice's fiery leader in the battle for freedom from Austria and eventually a united Italy (the Risorgimento). The statue faces the red house Manin lived in. Chafing under Austrian rule, the Venetians rose up in 1848. The Austrians laid siege to the city (1849) and bombarded it into surrender. Manin was banished and spent his final years in Paris, still proudly drumming up

support for modern Italy. In a rare honor, he's buried in St. Mark's Basilica.
• *Scala Contarini del Bovolo is a block south of here, with yellow signs pointing the way. Facing the Manin statue, turn right and exit the square down an alley. Follow yellow signs to the left, then immediately to the right, into a courtyard with one of Venice's hidden treasures...*

❼ Scala Contarini del Bovolo

The Scala is a cylindrical brick tower with five floors of spiral staircases faced with white marble banisters (probably closed for renovation during your visit).

Built in 1499, it was the external staircase of a palace (external stairs saved interior space for rooms). Architecture buffs admire the successful blend of Gothic, Byzantine, and Renaissance styles.

If the tower is open, you can pay a small fee to wind your way up the "snail shell" (*bovolo* in the local dialect). It's 113 steps to the top, where you're rewarded with views of the Venetian skyline.
• *Unwind and return to the Manin statue. Continue east, circling around the big Cassa di Risparmio bank, marveling at its Modernist ugliness. At Campo San Luca, turn left (north) on Calle del Forno. Note the 24-hour pharmacy vending machine that dispenses shower gel, Band-Aids, bug repellant, toothbrushes, toothpaste, condoms, and other after-hours necessities. Heading north, glance 20 yards down the street to the right at the flag-bedecked...*

❽ Teatro Goldoni

Though this theater looks modern, it dates from the 1500s, when Venice was at the forefront of secular entertainment. Many of Carlo Goldoni's (1707-1793) groundbreaking comedies got their first performances here, and the theater was renamed in his honor. It's still a working theater of mainly Italian productions.
• *Continue north on Calle del Forno. You're very close to the Grand Canal. Keep going north, jogging to the right at the small square (Corte del Teatro), then left down a teeny-tiny alleyway. Pop! You emerge on the Grand Canal, about 150 yards downstream from the...*

❾ Rialto Bridge

Of Venice's more than 400 bridges, only four cross the Grand Canal. Rialto was the first among these four.

The original Rialto Bridge, dating from 1180, was a platform supported by boats tied together. It linked the political side (Palazzo Ducale) of Venice with the economic center (Rialto). Rialto, which takes its name from *riva alto* (high bank), was one of the earliest Venetian settlements. When Venice was Europe's economic superpower, this was where bankers, brokers, and merchants conducted their daily business.

Rialto Bridge II was a 13th-century wooden drawbridge. It was replaced in 1588 by the current structure, with its bold single arch (spanning 160 feet) and arcades on top designed to strengthen the stone span. Its immense foundations stretch 650 feet on either side. Heavy buildings were then built atop the foundations to hold everything in place. The Rialto remained the only bridge crossing the Grand Canal until 1854.

Reliefs of the Venetian Republic's main mascots, St. Mark and St. Theodore, crown the arch. Barges and *vaporetti* run the busy waterways below, and merchants vie for tourists' attention on top.

The Rialto has long been a symbol of Venice. Aristocratic inhabitants built magnificent palaces just to be near it. The poetic Lord Byron swam to it all the way from Lido Island. And thousands of marriage proposals have been sealed right here, with a kiss, as the moon floated over *La Serenissima*.

• *From here, you can return to St. Mark's Square, or walk over the bridge into the fish market—following my Rialto to Frari Church Walk (next chapter).*

RIALTO TO FRARI CHURCH WALK

Cross the Rialto Bridge, and dive headlong into Venice's thriving market area. The area west of the Grand Canal is less touristy—a place where "real" Venetians live. This 20-minute walk is the most direct route from the Rialto Bridge to the Frari Church and Scuola San Rocco. This chapter is less a collection of sights than it is a tour of the Rialto market area, followed by a convenient, easy-to-follow route through the San Polo area. After exploring the lively produce and stinky fish markets, you'll see pubs and squares that are at least a bit off the tourist path.

Orientation

Length of This Walk: Allow about a leisurely hour.

When to Go: The markets are lively only in the morning. The produce market is closed on Monday, and both markets (produce and fish) are closed on Sunday.

Church of San Polo: €3, Mon-Sat 10:00-17:00, closed Sun, last entry 15 minutes before closing.

Tragicomica Mask Shop: Daily 10:00-19:00, at Calle dei Nomboli 2800, tel. 041-721-102, www.tragicomica.it.

Eateries: Many pubs and restaurants in the Rialto area are recommended in the Eating in Venice chapter.

Overview

- Head west from the Rialto Bridge one long block, and explore the colorful Rialto produce market and nearby fish market.
- When you're ready to move on, head down Ruga Vechia San Giovanni. Walk southwest along the Ruga (paralleling the Grand Canal) about a quarter-mile to spacious Campo San Polo.

- From Campo San Polo, continue southwest another 200 yards, then jog left, then right, where you'll see *Scuola Grande di San Rocco* signs pointing you to the Scuola San Rocco and the Frari Church next door.

The Walk Begins

• *From the top of the Rialto Bridge, walk down the bridge (heading away from the St. Mark's side) and about 50 yards onward until you see an old square on your right. Go to its fountain.*

❶ Campo San Giacomo

This square, named for the church that faces it (both also known as "San Giacometto"), looks today much like it did in the 16th century.

The buildings lining the square are High Renaissance, mostly built after a 1514 fire devastated this area. Find the MDXX date on the arcade: It was built in 1520. Only the church predates that fire. The square is designed to collect rainwater and store it in a cistern that once fed this fountain (for more on this system, see page 36).

Back when the Rialto Bridge was a drawbridge (until the 1590s), big ships would dock alongside this historic market. Imagine the commotion as ships tied up to load and unload their spices, oil, wine, and jewels. The line of buildings between Campo San Giacomo and the canal was once a strip of banks. It's still called Bancogiro, which means the place where letters of credit were endorsed. Back when carrying cash meant carrying gold and silver—heavy and dangerous—letters of credit were a godsend. Behind today's trashy jewelry stands are real jewelry shops. In fact, the street across from the market has been called "Street of Jewelers" for more than 500 years.

Opposite the church, a granite hunchback supports steps leading to a column. Until the 1550s, when a financial crisis knocked it for an economic loop, Venice was Europe's trading capital. You could call this neighborhood the "Wall Street" of medieval Europe. In those days, this column was the closest thing they had to a *Wall Street Journal*. Someone climbed the stair each noon

Rialto to Frari Church Walk

and stood on the column to read aloud the daily news from the doge: which ships had docked, which foreign ambassadors were in town, the price of pepper, and so on.

Behind the hunchback, the lane Calle de la Sicurtà is named for the maritime insurance companies that once did business here.

The church facade is one of the oldest in town. Back before clocks had minute hands (like the one on this church), its porch was a shelter for the poor. The spirit of St. James the Minor, for whom the church is named, watched over the business community, encouraging honesty in

RIALTO TO FRARI CHURCH

❶ Campo San Giacomo
❷ Produce Market
❸ Fish Market
❹ The Ruga
❺ Campo San Polo
❻ Church of San Polo
❼ Tragicomica Mask Shop

a time when banking regulations were nonexistent.

Walk along the canal side of the church. The large white building behind the church was and still is the city's fiscal administration building. Walk left, out to the canal, and look back at the structure. Notice how it tilts out (probably because the bridge's huge foundation is compressing the mud beneath it).

Now walk along the canal to a little canalside dead-end that's as close as you can get to the Rialto Bridge. Take in the great view of the bridge. The former post office (directly across from you) was originally the German merchants' hall (see the seal). It's about to be reincarnated as a Benetton-owned shopping center.

You're standing under a former prison. Study the iron grills over the windows. Notice the interlocking pipes with alternating joints—you couldn't cut just one and escape.

• *From the prison, walk back along the canal, through the triple archway, cross the square, and enter the square named Casaria (for the historic cheese market). Today, this is Venice's...*

❷ Produce Market (Erberia)

Colorful stalls offer fresh fruit and vegetables, some quite exotic. Nothing is grown on the island of Venice, so everything is shipped in daily from the mainland. The

Mercato Rialto vaporetto stop is a convenient place for boats to unload their wares, here in the heart of fish-shaped Venice. At #205, the shop called Macelleria Equina sells horse and donkey *(asino)* meat. Continue along the canal, exploring all the produce stalls.

• *Follow your nose straight ahead (passing six alleyways on your left) until you see* Mercato del Pesce *on the brick wall of the open-air arcade that houses the...*

❸ Fish Market (Pescaria)

This market is especially vibrant and colorful in the morning. The open-air stalls have the catch of the day—Venice's culinary spe-

cialty. Find eels, scallops, crustaceans with five-inch antennae, and squid destined for tonight's risotto soaking in their own ink. This is the Venice that has existed for centuries: Workers toss boxes of fish from delivery boats while shoppers step from the

traghetto (gondola shuttle) into the action. It's a good peek at workaday Venice. Shoppers are exacting and expect to know if the fish is fresh or frozen, farmed or wild. Local fish are small and considered particularly tasty because of the high concentration of salt at this end of the Adriatic. Any salmon you see are farmed, mostly from northern Europe. It's not unusual to pay €30 per kilo (about 2.2 pounds) for the best fish.

Locate a square white Istrian stone on a wall between two arches. It lists the minimum length permitted for a fish to be sold. Sardines must be seven centimeters; *peocio* (mussels) must be three centimeters. (Below that, someone has added a penis joke: *El Mio 3.7 cm*—"Mine's two inches.")

Now turn left and walk away from the water to the end of the fish market. You're on Campo de la Becarie (Butchers' Square). Within 40 yards of here (find Calle de le Do Spade) are several of my favorite local bars serving the Venetian version of tapas, *cicchetti*. If it's lunchtime, consider dropping by one or more of these for a progressive feast: Cantina Do Mori, Bar all'Arco, Ostaria ai Storti, and Cantina Do Spade (for descriptions, see pages 279 and 280).

And, if the market has you ready for a fishy nibble, drop by the hole-in-the-wall Pesce Pronto for tasty fish hors d'oeuvres (#319, on Calle de le Becarie o Panataria; see listing on page 280).

When you're ready, follow Ruga dei Spezieri (Spicers' Road) back toward Rialto. Along the way, pop into Antica Drogheria Mascari at #580, which hides a vast enoteca holding 600 different Italian wines arranged by region, plus spices and lots of gifty edibles.

• *At the end of Ruga dei Spezieri, you'll see a sign for* Ruga Vechia San Giovanni. *Turn right along it.*

❹ The Ruga

This busy street is lined with shops that get progressively less touristy and more practical. As you walk, you'll see fewer trinkets and more clothes, bread, shoes, watches, shampoo, and underwear.

• *The Ruga changes names as you go. Just keep heading basically straight (little jogs are OK). When in doubt, follow signs pointing to* Ferrovia *(train station). You'll cross one bridge, then shortly after come to...*

❺ Campo San Polo

One of the largest squares in Venice, Campo San Polo is shaped like an amphitheater, with its church tucked away in the corner (just ahead of you). Antica Birraria la Corte, a fine and family-friendly pizzeria/ristorante, is located at the far side (see listing on page 282). The square's amphitheater shape was determined by a curved canal at the base of the buildings. Today, the former canal is now a *rio terà*—a street made of landfill. A few rare trees grace the square, as do rare benches occupied by grateful locals. In the summer, bleachers and a screen are erected for open-air movies, a true *Cinema Paradiso* experience.

• *On the square is the...*

❻ Church of San Polo (S. Paolo Apostolo)

This church, one of the oldest in Venice, dates from the ninth century (€3, English description at ticket desk). The wooden, boat-shaped ceiling recalls the earliest basilicas built after Rome's fall. While the church is skippable for many, art enthusiasts visit to see Tintoretto's *Last Supper,* Giovanni Battista Tiepolo's *Virgin Appearing to St. John of Nepomuk* and his son Domenico's *Stations of the Cross,* and Veronese's *Betrothal of the Virgin with Angels.*

• *From the Church of San Polo, continue about 200 yards (following Ferrovia signs). You'll cross a bridge, jog left when you have to, then right, onto Calle dei Nomboli. On the right at #2800, directly across the alley from the Casa Goldoni museum, you'll see the...*

❼ Tragicomica Mask Shop

One of Venice's best mask stores, Tragicomica is also a workshop that offers a glimpse into the process of mask-making. Venice's

masks have always been a central feature of the celebration of Carnevale—the local pre-Lent, Mardi Gras-like blowout. (The translation of Carnevale is "good-bye to meat," referring to the lean days of Lent.) You'll see Walter and Alessandra hard at work.

Many masks are patterned after standard characters of the theater style known as commedia dell'arte: the famous trickster Harlequin, the beautiful and cunning Columbina, the country bump-kin Pulcinella (who later evolved into the wife-beating Punch of marionette shows), and the solemn, long-nosed Doctor *(dottore).*

• *Continuing along, cross the bridge and veer right. You'll soon see pur-ple signs directing you to Scuola Grande di San Rocco. Follow these until you bump into the back end of the Frari Church, with Scuola San Rocco next door.*

    ✪ See the Frari Church Tour chapter; also see the ✪ Scuola San Rocco Tour chapter.

ST. MARK'S TO SAN ZACCARIA WALK

San Zaccaria, one of the oldest churches in Venice, is just a few minutes on foot from St. Mark's Square. The church features a Bellini altarpiece and a submerged crypt that might be the oldest place in Venice. This short walk gets you away from (some of) the bustle of St. Mark's, includes a stroll along the waterfront, and brings you right back to where you started.

Orientation

Length of This Walk: Allow about an hour for a leisurely walk (though the actual distance is short).

Church of San Zaccaria: Free, Mon-Sat 10:00-12:00 & 16:00-18:00, Sun 16:00-18:00 only. Mass is held Mon-Sat at 18:30, and Sun at 10:00 and 12:00. Admission to the crypt costs €1. A €0.50 coin illuminates Bellini's altarpiece.

The Walk Begins

❶ Start at St. Mark's—Piazzetta dei Leoni

Facing St. Mark's Basilica, start in the small square to the left of the church (Piazzetta dei Leoni), with the 18th-century stone lions that kids love to sit on. The white building at the east end of the square houses the offices of Venice's "patriarch," the special title given to the local bishop (see the yellow-and-white Vatican flag). In the 1950s, this is where the future Pope John XXIII presided as

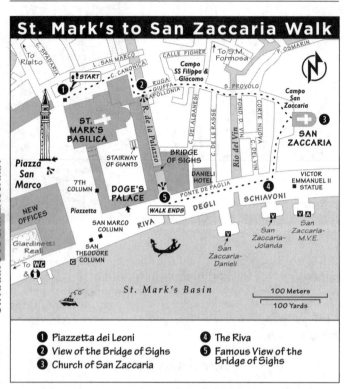

St. Mark's to San Zaccaria Walk

1 Piazzetta dei Leoni
2 View of the Bridge of Sighs
3 Church of San Zaccaria
4 The Riva
5 Famous View of the Bridge of Sighs

Venice's patriarch and cardinal. The popular, warm-hearted cardinal went on to become the "Sixties Pope," who oversaw major reforms in the Catholic Church. You'll see a plaque dedicated to "Papa Giovanni XXIII" on the building to the left of the basilica.
• *Head east along Calle de la Canonica, circling behind the basilica. You'll reach a bridge with a...*

❷ View of the Bridge of Sighs

This lesser-known view of the Bridge of Sighs (probably behind scaffolding when you visit) also lets you see the tourists who are ogling it, with cameras cocked.

On the near side of the bridge is a common sight in neighborhood Venice: a street-side altarpiece and donation box. As the street signs tell you, the bridge you're on marks the boundary between two traditional neighborhoods, the *sestiere* (district) of San Marco and that of Castello. Throughout this walk, you'll pass relics of a fast-fading era: newspaper stands, public telephones, and a 24-hour cigarette vending machine.

• *Continue east. You'll cross another bridge with a view of a "Modern Bridge of Sighs," which connects two wings of the exclusive Danieli Hotel. Continue east another 50 yards, through the gate of what was once a cloistered Benedictine convent, until you run into the...*

❸ Church of San Zaccaria

Back in the ninth century, when Venice was just a collection of wooden houses and before there was a St. Mark's Basilica, a

stone church and convent stood here. This is where the doges worshipped, public spectacles occurred, and sacred relics were kept. Today's structure dates mostly from the 15th century.

The tall facade by Mauro Codussi (who also did the Clock Tower in St. Mark's Square) and others is early Renaissance. The "vertical" effect produced by the four support pillars that rise up to an arched crown is tempered by the horizontal, many layered stories and curved shoulders.

In the northwest corner of Campo San Zaccaria (near where you entered) is a plaque from 1620 listing all the things that were prohibited "in this square" *(in questo campo),* including games, obscenities, dishonesty, and robbery, all "under grave penalty" *(sotto gravis pene).*

• *Enter the church. The second chapel on the right holds the...*

Body of Zachariah (S. Zaccaria)

Of the two bodies in the chapel, the upper one in the glass case

(supported by stone angels) is the reputed body of Zachariah, the father of John the Baptist. Back when mortal remains were venerated and thought to bring miracles to the faithful, Venice was proud to own the bones of St. Zachariah ("San Zaccaria," also known as Zacharias).

• *The church is virtually wallpapered with art. On the opposite side of the nave (second chapel on the left), you'll find...*

Giovanni Bellini—*Madonna and Child with Saints* (1505)

Mary and the baby, under a pavilion, are surrounded by various saints interacting in a so-called *sacra conversazione* (holy conversation), which in this painting is more like a quiet meditation. The saints' mood is melancholy, with lidded eyes and downturned faces. A violinist angel plays a sad solo at Mary's feet.

This is one of the last of Bellini's paintings in the *sacra conversazione* formula, the newer type of altarpiece that liberated the Virgin, Child, and saints from the separate cells of the older triptych style. Compare this to his other variations on this theme in the Accademia (see page 132) and Frari Church (see page 146). The life-size saints stand in an imaginary extension of the church—the pavilion's columns match those of the real church. We see a glimpse of trees and a cloudy sky beyond. Bellini establishes a 3-D effect using floor tiles. The four saints pose symmetrically, and there's a harmony in the big blocks of richly colored robes—blue, green, red, white, and yellow. A cool white light envelops the whole scene, casting no dark shadows.

The ever innovative Bellini was productive until the end of his long life—he painted this masterpiece at age 75. The German artist Albrecht Dürer said of him: "He is very old, and still he is the best painter of them all."

• *On the right-hand side of the nave is the entrance (€1 entry fee) to...*

The Crypt

Before you descend into the crypt, the first room (Chapel of Sant'Atanasio) contains **Tintoretto's** *Birth of John the Baptist* (c. 1560s, on the altar), which tells the back story of Zachariah. In the background, old Zachariah's wife, Elizabeth, props herself up in bed while nurses hold and coo over her newborn son, little John the Baptist. The birth was a miracle, as she was past childbearing age. On the far right, Zachariah—the star of this church—witnesses the heavens opening up, bringing this miracle to earth.

The five **gold thrones** (displayed in this room or one of the next rooms) were once seats for doges. Every Easter, the current doge would walk from St. Mark's Square to this religious center and thank the nuns of San Zaccaria for giving the land for the square.

The small next room contains religious objects as well as an engraving of the doge parading into Campo San Zaccaria.

Next comes the Chapel of San Tarasio, dominated by an impressive (but likely scaffolded) 15th-century prickly gold altarpiece by Antonio Vivarini. The predella (seven small scenes beneath the altarpiece) may be by Paolo Veneziano, the 14th-century grandfather of Venetian painting. Look down through glass in the floor to see the 12th-century mosaic floor from the original church. In fact, these rooms were parts of the earlier churches.

Finally, go downstairs to the **crypt**—the foundation of a church built in the 10th century. The crypt is low and the water table high, so the room is often flooded, submerging the bases of the columns. It's a weird experience, calling up echoes of the Dark Ages.

• Emerge from the Church of San Zaccaria into the small campo. *Before leaving the* campo, *check out the small art gallery (free), the pink Carabinieri police station (a former convent), and the thirst-quenching water fountain. Now, turn left and head south—past that cigarette machine—until you pop out at the waterfront.*

❹ The Riva

The waterfront promenade known as the "Riva" provides a great view of the Church of San Giorgio Maggiore. To get there, catch vaporetto #2 from the San Zaccaria-M.V.E. stop nearby. (For more on the handy *vaporetti* departing from San Zaccaria, see page 32.)

The big equestrian monument depicts Victor Emmanuel II, who helped lead Italy to unification and became the country's first king in 1861. Beyond that (over the bridge) is the four-columned La Pietà Church, where Antonio Vivaldi once directed the music. A bit beyond that (not visible from here) is the Arsenale.

The Riva is lined with many of Venice's most famous luxury hotels. For a peek at the *most* famous and luxurious, turn right, cross over one bridge, and nip into the **Danieli Hotel.** Tuck in your shirt, stand tall and aristocratic, and (with all the confidence of a guest) be swept by the revolving door into the sumptuous interior of what was once the Gothic Palazzo Dandolo. As you check out the Danieli's restaurant menu (that's why you're there, isn't it?), admire the lobby, the old-style chandeliers, water-taxi drive-up entrance, and the occasional celebrity. Since 1820, the Danieli has been Venice's most exclusive hotel. Exquisite as all this is, it still gets flooded routinely in the winter.

• Facing the water, turn right and head west toward St. Mark's Square. The commotion atop a little bridge marks the...

❺ Famous View of the Bridge of Sighs

The Bridge of Sighs will likely be covered by scaffolding for several years for renovation. From this historic bridge (according to

romantic legend), prisoners took one last look at Venice before entering the dark and dank prisons. And sighed. Lord Byron picked up on the legend in the early 1800s and gave the bridge its famous nickname, making this sad little span a big stop on the Grand Tour. Look high up on your left—while that rogue Casanova wrote of the bridge in his memoirs, he was actually imprisoned here in the Doge's Palace. Nowadays the bridge is a human traffic jam of gawking tourists and clever pickpockets during the day, though it's breathtakingly romantic in the lonely late-night hours.

• From here, you can take one last look at the lagoon, then ponder the billboards on the Bridge of Sighs and the sweaty crowds of St. Mark's Square...and sigh.

SLEEPING IN VENICE

For hassle-free efficiency and the sheer magic of being close to the action, I favor hotels that are handy to sightseeing activities.

I've listed rooms in four neighborhoods: St. Mark's bustle, the Rialto action, the quiet Dorsoduro area behind the Accademia art museum, and near the train station (handy for train travelers, but far from the action). I also mention several apartment rentals, big fancy hotels, cheap dorms, and places on the mainland.

A major feature of this book is its extensive listing of good-value rooms. I like places that are clean, small enough to have a hands-on owner and stable staff, central yet not in the tourist flood zone, relatively quiet at night (except for the song of gondoliers), reasonably priced, friendly, run with a respect for Venetian traditions, and not listed in other guidebooks. (In Venice, for me, six out of these eight criteria means it's a keeper.) I'm more impressed by a handy location and a fun-loving philosophy than flat-screen TVs and shoeshine machines.

Outside of holidays and weekends, it's possible to visit Venice without booking ahead, but it's smart, simple, and less stressful to have a reservation in place. Book a room as soon as you know when you'll be in town. Contact the hotel directly, not through any tourist information room-finding service (they can't give opinions on quality).

If you arrive on an early flight or an overnight train, your room probably won't be ready first thing in the morning. You should be able to drop your bag safely at the hotel and dive right into sightseeing.

Note that hotel websites are particularly valuable for Venice, because they often include detailed directions that can help you (and your bags) get to your rooms with a minimum of wrong turns in this navigationally challenging city.

Rates and Deals

Over the past decade, Venice has seen the opening of several big new hotels, countless little boutique hotels, and the conversion of many private homes to short-term rental apartments. Capacity jumped from 13,000 rooms in 2000 to 23,000 rooms in 2010. Now the city is overbuilt for hotels. Demand is soft and, therefore, so are the prices.

These days, it seems no Venetian hotel expects to actually get its published "rack rate." While I wish I could promise a set price or a discount for readers of this book, it's a pricing free-for-all; most hotels have tossed straight pricing out the window. Hoteliers are willing and eager to make a deal. I'd suggest emailing several hotels to ask for their best price. Comparison-shop and make your choice.

I've described my recommended accommodations using a Sleep Code; see the sidebar. Prices listed are for one-night stays in peak season (April, May, June, Sept, and Oct), include breakfast, and assume you're booking directly (not through a TI or online hotel-booking engine). Prices can climb even higher during a few festivals. Almost all places drop prices from November through March (except during Carnevale—Feb 11-21 in 2012—and Christmas) and in July and August. A €180 double can cost €80-90 in winter. Off-season, don't pay the rates I list.

In general, prices can soften if you do any of the following: offer to pay cash, stay at least three nights, or mention this book. You can also try asking for a cheaper room or a discount, or offer to skip breakfast. To save money during a relatively slow time, consider arriving without a reservation and dropping in at the last minute. Big, fancy hotels put empty rooms on an aggressive push list, offering great prices.

As you look over the listings, you'll notice that some accommodations promise special prices to my readers who book direct (without using a room-finding service or hotel-booking website, which take a commission). To get these rates, you must mention this book when you reserve, and then show the book upon arrival. Some readers with ebooks have reported difficulty getting a Rick Steves discount. If this happens to you, please show this to the hotelier: Rick Steves discounts apply to readers with ebooks as well as printed books.

Many hotels in Venice list rooms on www.venere.com, especially for last-minute vacancies (two to three weeks before the date). Before you bite, check to see if rates are lower than the prices in this book.

For tips on making reservations, see page 240.

Travel Review Websites: TripAdvisor (www.tripadvisor.com) and similar review websites are popular tools for finding hotels,

Sleep Code

(€1 = about $1.40, country code: 39)

Price Rankings

To help you easily sort through these listings, I've divided the accommodations into three categories based on the price for a standard double room with bath during high season:

$$$ Higher Priced—Most rooms €180 or more.

$$ Moderately Priced—Most rooms between €130-180.

$ Lower Priced—Most rooms €130 or less.

I always rate hostels as $, whether or not they have double rooms, because they have the cheapest beds in town. Prices can change without notice; verify the hotel's current rates online or by email. For other updates, see www.ricksteves.com/update.

Abbreviations

To give you maximum information in a minimum of space, I use the following code to describe the accommodations. Prices listed are per room, not per person. When a price range is given for a type of room (such as double rooms listing for €100-150), it means the price fluctuates with the season, size of room, or length of stay; expect to pay the upper end for peak-season stays.

S = Single room (or price for one person in a double).

D = Double or Twin room. "Double beds" are often two twins sheeted together, and are usually big enough for nonromantic couples.

T = Triple (generally a double bed with a single).

Q = Quad (usually a double bed and 2 small singles; adding an extra child's bed to a T is usually cheaper).

b = Private bathroom with toilet and shower or tub.

s = Private shower or tub only (the toilet is down the hall).

According to this code, a couple staying at a "Db-€140" hotel would pay a total of €140 (about $200) for a double room with a private bathroom. Unless otherwise noted, breakfast is included, hotel staff speak basic English, and credit cards are accepted.

If I mention "Internet access," there's a public terminal in the lobby for guests to use. If I use the terms "Wi-Fi" or "cable Internet," you can access it in your room, but only if you have your own laptop or other Wi-Fi device.

SLEEPING IN VENICE

Making Reservations

Given the quality of the accommodations I've found for this book, I'd recommend that you reserve your rooms in advance, particularly if you'll be traveling during peak season. Book several weeks ahead, or as soon as you've pinned down your travel dates. Note that some national holidays jam things up and merit your making reservations far in advance (see "Holidays and Festivals" on page 406).

Phoning: To call Italy from the US or Canada, dial 011-39 and then the local number. (The 011 is our international access code, and 39 is Italy's country code.) If you're calling Italy from another European country, dial 00-39-local number. (The 00 is Europe's international access code.) To call a Venice hotel from anywhere in Italy (including Venice), simply dial the local number. Land lines start with 0, mobile lines start with 3. For more tips on calling, see page 378.

Requesting a Reservation: To make a reservation, contact hotels directly by email, phone, or fax. Email is the clearest and most economical way to make a reservation. Or you can go straight to the hotel website; many have secure online reservation forms and can instantly inform you of availability and any special deals. But be sure you use the hotel's official site and not a booking agency's site—otherwise you may pay higher rates than you should. Most recommended hotels are accustomed to guests who speak only English.

The hotelier wants to know these key pieces of information (also included in the sample request form in the appendix):

- number and type of rooms
- number of nights
- date of arrival
- date of departure
- any special needs (e.g., bathroom in the room or down the hall, twin beds vs. double bed, air-conditioning, quiet, view, ground floor, etc.)

When you request a room, use the European style for writing dates: day/month/year. For example, for a two-night stay in July, I would request "1 double room for 2 nights, arrive 16/07/12, depart 18/07/12." Consider carefully how long you'll stay; don't just assume you can tack on extra days once you arrive. Make sure you mention any discounts offered—for Rick Steves readers or otherwise—when you make the reservation.

Confirming a Reservation: If the hotel's response tells you its room availability and rates, it's not a confirmation. You must tell them that you want that room at the given rate. Most hoteliers will request your credit-card number to hold the room. While you can email your credit-card information (I do), it's safer to share that confidential info via phone call, fax, split between two emails, or via a secure online reservation form (if the hotel has one on its website).

Canceling a Reservation: If you must cancel your reservation, it's courteous to do so with as much advance notice as possible. Simply make a quick phone call or send an email. Family-run hotels lose money if they turn away customers while holding a room for someone who doesn't show up. Understandably, many hoteliers bill no-shows for one night.

Cancellation policies can be strict: For example, you might lose a deposit if you cancel within two weeks of your reserved stay, or you might be billed for the entire visit if you leave early. Internet deals may require prepayment, with no refunds for cancellations. Ask about cancellation policies before you book.

If canceling via email, request confirmation that your cancellation was received to avoid being accidentally billed.

Reconfirming Your Reservation: Always call to reconfirm your room reservation a few days in advance from the road. (Don't have a TI call for you; they may take a commission.) Smaller hotels appreciate knowing your estimated time of arrival. If you'll be arriving late (after 17:00), alert your hotelier. On the small chance that a hotel loses track of your reservation, bring along a hard copy of their emailed or faxed confirmation.

Reserving Rooms as You Travel: You can make reservations as you travel, calling hotels a few days to a week before your arrival. If everything's full, don't despair. Call a day or two in advance and fill in a cancellation. If you'd rather travel without any reservations at all, you'll have greater success snaring rooms if you arrive at your destination early in the day. When you anticipate crowds (weekends are worst), call hotels at about 9:00 or 10:00 on the day you plan to arrive, when the hotel clerk knows who'll be checking out and just which rooms will be available. If you encounter a language barrier, ask the fluent receptionist at your current hotel to call for you.

but have drawbacks. To write a review, people need only an email address—making it easy to hide their true identity. If a hotel is well reviewed in a guidebook or two, and also gets good ratings on TripAdvisor, it's probably a safe bet—but I wouldn't stay at a hotel based solely on a TripAdvisor recommendation.

Types of Accommodations

Hotels

The double rooms in Venice listed in this book will range from about €90 (very simple, toilet and shower down the hall) to €450 (plush Grand Canal views and maximum plumbing), with most clustered around €130-180 (with private bathrooms).

Solo travelers find that the cost of a *camera singola* (single room) is often only 25 percent less than a *camera doppia* (double room). Three or four people can economize by requesting one big room. (If a Db is €110, a Qb would be about €150.) Most listed hotels have rooms for anywhere from one to five people. If there's room for an extra cot, they'll cram it in for you (charging you around €25). English works in all but the cheapest places.

Nearly all places offer private bathrooms. Generally rooms with a bath or shower also have a toilet and a bidet (which Italians use for quick sponge baths). The cord that dangles over the tub or shower is not a clothesline. You pull it when you've fallen and can't get up.

Double beds are called *matrimoniale,* even though hotels aren't interested in your marital status. Twins are *due letti singoli.* Even if a single or triple room isn't listed, ask—they can accommodate you.

When you check in, usually the receptionist will ask for your passport and may want to keep it for a couple of hours. Italian hotels are legally required to register each guest with the local police. Relax. Americans are notorious for making this chore more difficult than it needs to be.

Assume that breakfast is included in the prices I've listed, unless otherwise noted. If breakfast is included but optional, you may want to skip it. While convenient, it's usually expensive—€5-8 for a simple continental buffet with ham, cheese, yogurt, and unlimited *caffè latte.* A picnic in your room followed by a coffee at the corner café can be lots cheaper.

More pillows and blankets are usually in the closet or available on request. In Italy, towels and linens aren't always replaced every day. Hang your towel up to dry. Budget hotels often use "waffle" or very thin, tablecloth-type towels that take less water and electricity to launder.

Most hotel rooms have a TV and phone, and some kind of Internet access (usually Wi-Fi) is the norm—if not in all rooms,

---

Chill Out

All but the cheapest hotels have air-conditioning. Because Europeans are generally careful with energy use, you'll find government-enforced limits on air-conditioning and heating. There's a one-month period each spring and fall when neither is allowed. Air-conditioning is worth seeking out in summer (though it may be on only at certain times of the day), and is rarely available from fall through spring.

Most hotel rooms with air conditioners come with a control stick (like a TV remote) that generally has the same symbols and features: fan icon (click to toggle through wind power, from light to gale); louver icon (choose steady airflow or waves); snowflake and sunshine icons (cold air or heat, depending on season); clock ("O" setting: run x hours before turning off; "I" setting: wait x hours to start); and the temperature control (20-21 degrees Celsius is comfortable).

then at least at reception. Simpler places rarely have phones in the room. Pricier hotels usually come with a small stocked mini-fridge called a *frigo bar* (FREE-goh bar; pay for what you use).

Hoteliers can be a great help and source of advice. Most know Venice well, and can assist you with everything from public transit and airport connections to finding a good restaurant, the nearest launderette, or an Internet café.

Even at the best places, mechanical breakdowns occur: Air-conditioning malfunctions, sinks leak, hot water turns cold, and toilets gurgle and smell. Report your concerns clearly and calmly at the front desk. For more complicated problems, don't expect instant results.

If you suspect night noise will be a problem, ask for a quiet room in the back or on an upper floor. To guard against theft in your room, keep valuables out of sight. Some rooms come with a safe, and other hotels have safes at the front desk. Use them if you're concerned.

Checkout can pose problems if surprise charges pop up on your bill. If you settle up your bill the night before you leave, you'll have time to discuss and address any points of contention (before 19:00, when the night shift usually arrives).

Above all, keep a positive attitude. Remember, you're on vacation. If your hotel is a disappointment, spend more time out enjoying the city you came to see.

Hotels Beyond This Book: If you're traveling beyond my recommended destinations, you'll find accommodations where you need them. Any town with tourists has a TI that books rooms or can give you a list and point you in the right direction. In the absence of a TI, ask people on the street or in cafés or restaurants for help.

Apartments

Many Venetians rent out their apartments, which can be a great value for families or multiple couples traveling together. Rentals are generally by the week, with prices starting around €100 per day. A bigger place for a family of four to five rents for around €200 per day. Apartments typically offer a couple of bedrooms, a sitting area, and a teensy *cucinetta* (kitchenette), usually stocked with dishes and flatware. After you check in, you're basically on your own. While you won't have a doorman to carry your bags or a maid to clean your room each day, you will get an inside peek at a Venetian home, and you can save lots of money—especially if you take advantage of the cooking facilities—with no loss of comfort.

Several of these recommended hotels, all listed later in this chapter, rent apartments (with small kitchens) on the side. **$$$ Hotel Campiello,** east of St. Mark's Square, has three modern, upscale, and quiet family apartments for up to six people, just steps away from their hotel. **$$ Pensione Guerrato,** west of the Rialto Bridge, has apartments for four to eight people. **$$ Locanda la Corte,** east of the Rialto Bridge, has two quads for up to eight (in hotel, no kitchen). **$ Alloggi Henry,** located close to the train station, can accommodate up to nine in their apartment.

Hostels

You'll pay about €25 per bed to stay at a hostel. Travelers of any age are welcome if they don't mind dorm-style accommodations and meeting other travelers. Most hostels offer kitchen facilities, Internet access, Wi-Fi, and laundry (generally self-service). **Independent hostels** tend to be easygoing, colorful, and informal (no membership required); see www.hostelz.com, www.hostels europe.com, www.hostels.com, and www.hostelworld.com. **Official hostels** are part of Hostelling International and adhere to various rules (such as a 17:00 check-in, lockout during the day, a curfew at night); they require that you either have a membership card or pay extra per night (www.hihostels.com).

Accommodations

Hotels in Venice can be tricky to locate. While I've tried to give clear directions, you'll do best by following the arrival instructions provided on your hotel's website. Most sites have a good map; if yours does, print it out. Or search by "civic number" (I've included these in my listings) at www.venicexplorer.net; it's better than other map websites, which often choke on Venetian addresses.

Remember that Venice has six districts: San Marco, Castello, Cannaregio, San Polo, Santa Croce, and Dorsoduro. I've listed the district for each hotel below.

Near St. Mark's Square

To get here from the train station or Piazzale Roma bus station, ride the vaporetto to San Zaccaria—either the slow #1 or the fast #2 (from the Tronchetto parking lot, it's #2 only). Consider using your ride to follow my tour of the Grand Canal (◐ see Grand Canal Cruise chapter); to make sure you arrive via the Grand Canal, confirm that your boat goes "*via Rialto*."

Nearby Laundries: Lavanderia Gabriella offers full service a few streets north of St. Mark's Square (€15/load includes wash, dry, and fold; drop off Mon-Fri 8:00-12:30, closed Sat-Sun; pick up 2 hours later or next working day; with your back to the door of San Zulian Church, go over Ponte dei Ferali, take first right down Calle dei Armeni, then first left on Rio Terà de le Colonne to #985; tel. 041-522-1758, Elisabetta).

Effe Erre, a modern self-service *lavanderia,* is near the recommended Hotel al Piave on Ruga Giuffa at #4826 (€14/load, daily 6:30-23:00, mobile 349-058-3881, Massimo).

East of St. Mark's Square

Located near the Bridge of Sighs, just off the Riva degli Schiavoni waterfront promenade, these places rub drainpipes with Venice's most palatial five-star hotels.

$$$ Hotel Campiello, lacy and bright, was once part of a 19th-century convent. Ideally located 50 yards off the waterfront, on a tiny square, its 16 rooms offer a tranquil, friendly refuge for travelers who appreciate comfort and professional service (Sb-€130, Db-€180, 10 percent discount with cash and this book if you reserve direct and pay on arrival, air-con, elevator, free Wi-Fi; from the San Zaccaria vaporetto stop, take Calle del Vin, between pink Hotel Danieli and Hotel Savoia e Jolanda, to Castello 4647; tel. 041-520-5764, fax 041-520-5798, www.hcampiello.it, campiello@hcampiello.it; family-run for four generations, currently by Thomas, Monica, Nicoletta, and Marco). They also rent three modern family apartments, under rustic timbers just steps away (up to €380/night).

$$$ Hotel Fontana is a nice family-run place with 15 rooms near a school, two bridges behind St. Mark's Square. Their annex across the street has much lower ceilings and slightly lower prices (Sb-€120, Db-€180, family rooms, 10 percent cash discount, quieter rooms on garden side, 2 rooms have terraces for €20 extra, air-con, elevator, free Internet access, pay Wi-Fi by reception, on Campo San Provolo at Castello 4701, tel. 041-522-0579, fax

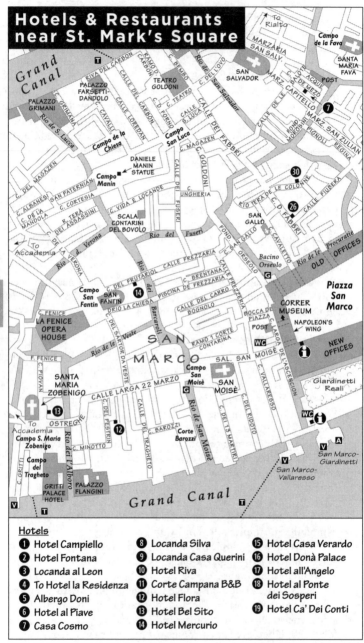

Hotels & Restaurants near St. Mark's Square

Hotels

1. Hotel Campiello
2. Hotel Fontana
3. Locanda al Leon
4. To Hotel la Residenza
5. Albergo Doni
6. Hotel al Piave
7. Casa Cosmo
8. Locanda Silva
9. Locanda Casa Querini
10. Hotel Riva
11. Corte Campana B&B
12. Hotel Flora
13. Hotel Bel Sito
14. Hotel Mercurio
15. Hotel Casa Verardo
16. Hotel Donà Palace
17. Hotel all'Angelo
18. Hotel al Ponte dei Sosperi
19. Hotel Ca' Dei Conti

Eateries & Services

- **20** Ristorante alla Conchiglia
- **21** Trattoria da Giorgio ai Greci
- **22** Ristorante Antica Sacrestia
- **23** Birreria Forst Café
- **24** Bar Verde
- **25** Ristorante alla Basilica
- **26** Rizzo Café
- **27** Gran Caffè Lavena (Gelato)
- **28** Todaro Gelateria
- **29** Coop Supermarket
- **30** Lavanderia Gabriella
- **31** Lavanderia Effe Erre

SLEEPING IN VENICE

041-523-1040, www.hotelfontana.it, info@hotelfontana.it, cousins Diego and Gabriele). From the San Zaccaria vaporetto dock, take Calle de le Rasse—to the left of pink Hotel Danieli—then turn right at the end, and continue to the first square.

$$ Locanda al Leon rents 14 decent, reasonably priced rooms just off Campo Santi Filippo e Giacomo (Db-€145-155, Tb-€180, Qb-€230, these prices with cash and this book, air-con, free Internet access and Wi-Fi, Campo Santi Filippo e Giacomo, Castello 4270, tel. 041-277-0393, fax 041-521-0348, www.hotelal leon.com, leon@hotelalleon.com, Giuliano and Marcella). From the San Zaccaria vaporetto stop, take Calle dei Albanesi (two streets left of pink Hotel Danieli) to its far end.

$$ Hotel la Residenza is a grand old palace facing a peaceful square. It has 15 great rooms on three levels and a huge, luxurious lounge with a piano. This is a great value for romantics—you'll feel like you're in the Doge's Palace after hours. Hang out in the living room and you become royalty (Sb-€100, Db-€165-200, air-con, free Wi-Fi, on Campo Bandiera e Moro at Castello 3608, tel. 041-528-5315, fax 041-523-8859, www.venicelaresidenza.com, info @venicelaresidenza.com, Giovanni). From the Bridge of Sighs, walk east along Riva degli Schiavoni, cross three bridges, and take the first left up Calle del Dose to Campo Bandiera e Moro.

$ Albergo Doni is dark and quiet—a bit of a time-warp—with 13 well-worn, once-classy rooms up a creaky stairway. It's run by a likable smart aleck named Gina, her niece Tessa, and her nephew, an Italian stallion named Nikos (D-€95, Db-€120, T-€125, Tb-€160, reserve with credit card but pay in cash, ceiling fans, three Db rooms have air-con, free Wi-Fi by reception, avoid their overflow apartment, on Fondamenta del Vin at Castello 4656, tel. & fax 041-522-4267, www.albergodoni.it, albergodoni @hotmail.it). From the San Zaccaria vaporetto stop, cross one bridge to the right and take the first left (marked Calle del Vin), then turn left at the little square named Ramo del Vin, jog left, and find the hotel ahead on Fondamenta del Vin.

North of St. Mark's Square
$$ Hotel al Piave, with 28 fine, air-conditioned rooms above a bright and classy lobby, is fresh, modern, and comfortable. You'll enjoy the neighborhood and always get a cheery welcome (Db-€150, Tb-€200; family suites-€280 for 4, €300 for 5, or €320 for 6; cash discount, free Wi-Fi, on Ruga Giuffa at Castello 4838/40, tel. 041-528-5174, fax 041-523-8512, www.hotelalpiave .com, info@hotelalpiave.com, Mirella, Paolo, Ilaria, and Federico speak English). From the San Zaccaria vaporetto stop, take the street to the right of the Bridge of Sighs to Campo Santi Filippo e Giacomo, and continue on Calle drio la Chiesa. Cross the bridge,

continue straight, then turn left onto Ruga Giuffa until you find the hotel on your left at #4838.

$$ Casa Cosmo is a humble little five-room place run by Davide, Caterina, and their parents. While it comes with minimal services and no public spaces (aside from a tiny rooftop terrace), it's air-conditioned, very central, somewhat inexpensive, and quiet (Db-€140-150, Tb-€160-170, Qb-€180-190, 10 percent discount with this book if you reserve direct and pay cash, breakfast in your room—or €5/person less without breakfast, free Wi-Fi, lots of stairs, on Calle de Mezo at San Marco 4976, tel. 041-296-0710, fax 041-862-3439, www.casacosmo.com, info@casacosmo.com). From the Rialto vaporetto stop, head inland on Larga Mazzini (which becomes the Mercerie). Turn right at the Bata shoe shop, then immediately left onto tiny Calle de Mezo to #4976.

$$ Locanda Silva is a big, basic, beautifully located hotel with a functional style, renting 23 decent old-school rooms (S-€70, Sb-€80, D-€90-100, Db-€135, Tb-€160, Qb-€180, request 10 percent Rick Steves discount, another 10 percent off if you stay at least 2 nights, closed Jan, air-con, pay Wi-Fi, on Fondamenta del Remedio at Castello 4423, tel. 041-522-7643, fax 041-528-6817, www.locandasilva.it, info@locandasilva.it, Sandra and Massimo). From St. Mark's Square, go around the left side of the basilica, turn left by the Studium bookstore, take the second right down Calle del Remedio, then turn left at the canal on Fondamenta del Remedio.

$$ Locanda Casa Querini rents six bright, high-ceilinged rooms on a quiet square tucked away behind St. Mark's. You can enjoy your breakfast or a sunny picnic/happy hour sitting at their tables right on the sleepy little square (Db-€150, third person-€20-25, one cheaper small double, ask for cash discount, air-con, pay Wi-Fi, halfway between San Zaccaria vaporetto stop and Campo Santa Maria Formosa at Castello 4388 on Campo San Zaninovo/Giovanni Novo, tel. 041-241-1294, fax 041-523-6188, www.locandaquerini.com, casaquerini@hotmail.com, Patrizia and Silvia). From the San Zaccaria vaporetto stop, take the street to the right of the Bridge of Sighs to Campo Santi Filippo e Giacomo, continue on Calle drio la Chiesa, take the second left, and curl around to the left into the little square, Campo San Zaninovo/Giovanni Novo.

$ Hotel Riva, with gleaming marble hallways, big exposed beams, fine antique furnishings, and lots of stairs, is romantically situated on a canal along the gondola serenade route. You could actually dunk your breakfast rolls in the canal (but don't). Ten of the 30 rooms come with air-conditioning for no extra charge—request one when you reserve. Or, if you prefer a view and lots of light but no air-conditioning, you can ask Sandro to hold a corner *(angolo)* room for you (Sb-€90, D-€100, Db-€120-140, Tb-€170-190, higher prices are for corner rooms, reserve with credit card but pay with cash only, on Ponte de l'Anzolo at Castello 5310, tel. 041-522-7034, fax 041-528-5551, www.hotelriva.it, info@hotelriva .it, Daniella). Facing St. Mark's Basilica, walk behind it on the left along Calle de la Canonica, take the first left (at blue *Pauly & C* mosaic in street), continue straight, go over the bridge, and angle right to the hotel at Ponte de l'Anzolo.

$ Corte Campana B&B, run by enthusiastic and helpful Riccardo, rents three quiet and characteristic rooms just behind St. Mark's Square. One room has a private bath down the hall (Db-€125, Tb-€165, Qb-€190, prices are soft, cash only, 2-night minimum, at least €10/night less for stays of 4 nights, air-con, free Internet access, pay Wi-Fi, on Calle del Remedio at Castello 4410, tel. & fax 041-523-3603, mobile 389-272-6500, www.corte campana.com, info@cortecampana.com). Print out complete directions, including photos of all the street signs, from Riccardo's website.

West of St. Mark's Square

$$$ Hotel Flora sits buried in a sea of fancy designer boutiques and elegant hotels almost on the Grand Canal. It's formal, with uniformed staff and grand public spaces, yet the 43 rooms have a homey warmth and the garden oasis is a sanctuary for foot-weary guests (generally Db-€260, check website for special discounts or email Sr. Romanelli for 10 percent Rick Steves discount off stan- dard prices, air-con, elevator, free Wi-Fi and Internet access, San Marco 2283a, tel. 041-520-5844, fax 041-522-8217, www.hotelflora .it, info@hotelflora.it). It's at the end of Calle dei Bergamaschi, one of several skinny lanes just off Calle Larga XXII Marzo.

$$$ Hotel Bel Sito offers pleasing yet well-worn Old World character, 34 rooms, generous public spaces, a peaceful courtyard, and a picturesque location—facing a church on a small square between St. Mark's Square and the Accademia (Sb-€110, Db-€185, air-con, free Wi-Fi, elevator; catch vaporetto #1 to Santa Maria del Giglio stop, take street inland to square, hotel is at far end to your right on Campo Santa Maria Zobenigo/del Giglio at San Marco 2517; tel. 041-522-3365, fax 041-520-4083, www.hotelbelsito venezia.it, info@hotelbelsito.info, manager Rossella).

$$ Hotel Mercurio offers 25 peaceful, comfortable, and recently renovated rooms near La Fenice Opera House. Some rooms offer canal views (Sb-€130, Db-€170, Tb-€200, Qb-€230-250, €10 less with cash, air-con, pay Wi-Fi, on Calle del Fruttariol at San Marco 1848, tel. 041-522-0947, fax 041-241-1079, www .hotelmercurio.com, info@hotelmercurio.com, Monica, Vittorio,

Flexible Floors

All over town, from palaces to cheap, old hotels, you'll find speckled floors *(pavimento alla Veneziana)*. While they might

look like cheap linoleum, these are historic—protected by the government and a pain for Venetian landlords to maintain. As Venice was built, it needed flexible flooring to absorb the inevitable settling of the buildings. Through an expensive and laborious process, several layers of material were built up and finished with a broken marble top that was shaved and polished to what you see today. While patterns were sometimes designed into the flooring, it's often just a speckled hodgepodge. Keep an eye open for this. Once a year, the floor is rubbed with natural oil to maintain its flexibility, and craftspeople still give landlords fits when repairs are needed.

and Natale). From the San Marco-Vallaresso vaporetto stop, follow Calle Vallaresso to Calle Frezzaria, turn right, and follow it over a bridge as it becomes Calle del Frutariol. The hotel is on the left just before La Fenice Opera House.

Near the Rialto Bridge
Vaporetto #2 brings you to the Rialto quickly from the train station, the Piazzale Roma bus station, and the parking-lot island of Tronchetto. You can also take the slower vaporetto #1 (but not from Tronchetto).

West of the Rialto Bridge
$ Pensione Guerrato, above the colorful Rialto produce market and just two minutes from the Rialto Bridge, is run by friendly, creative, and hardworking Roberto and Piero. Their 800-year-old building—with 24 spacious, air-conditioned, and charming rooms—is simple, airy, and wonderfully characteristic (D-€90, Db-€130, Tb-€150, Qb-€170, Quint/b-€185, these prices with this book and cash, check website for special discounts, Rick Steves readers can ask for €5/night discount below Web specials, free Wi-Fi, on Calle drio la Scimia at San Polo 240a, tel. & fax 041-528-5927, www.pensioneguerrato.it, pensione.guerrato@gmail.com, Monica and Rosanna). From the train station, take vaporetto #1 to the Mercato Rialto stop (comes before the "Rialto" stop), exit the boat to your right, and follow the waterfront. Calle drio la

Eateries & Nightlife

8 Trattoria da Bepi

9 Vini da Gigio

10 Trattoria Ca' d'Oro

11 Osteria al Bomba

12 Osteria "Alla Botte"

13 Osteria di Santa Marina

14 Rosticceria San Bartolomeo

15 Osteria al Portego

16 Osteria alle Testiere & Cip Ciap Pizza

17 Osteria al Mascaron

18 Peter Pan Kebabs

19 Cantina Do Mori

20 Bar all'Arco & Ostaria ai Storti

21 Cantina Do Spade

22 Pesce Pronto

Hotels & Restaurants near the Rialto Bridge

To Vaporetto Dock

Lagoon

Hotels
1. Pensione Guerrato
2. Hotel al Ponte Antico
3. Locanda la Corte
4. Casa Pisani Canal Hotel
5. To Alloggi Barbaria
6. Hotel Giorgione
7. Foresteria della Chiesa Valdese

100 Meters
100 Yards

FONDAMENTE NOVE

L'Acqua Dolce

C. VENIER

C. DEL FORNO

6

C. PROVERBI

PRETI

SANTI APOSTOLI

Campo de la Cason

C. MAL

SAN CANZIAN

CANNAREGIO

Rio dei Santi Apostoli

Campo San Canzian

Rio TERA

SAN CANZIAN

C. WIDMANN

Campo Santa Maria Nova

28

Rio de la Panada

CALLE DE LA TESTA

Rio dei Mendicanti

FONDAMENTA DEI MENDICANTI

HOSPITAL

Campo Corner

MAZANEN

SALIZADA BAGATIN

BOLDU

MIRACOLI

SANTA MARIA DEI MIRACOLI

CALLE LARGA GALLINA

Campo Santi Giovanni & Paolo

COLLEONI STATUE

SANTI GIOVANNI & PAOLO (SAN ZANIPOLO)

Rio de San Gio Grisostomo

SAN GRISOSTOMO

SAN GIOVANNI GRISOSTOMO

C. CASTELI

C. DE LA ERBE

4

ASEO

COIN DEP'T STORE

C. SCALETA

FRUTARIOL

C. PIOMBO

Campo Santa Marina

Rio de Santa Marina

3

SALIZADA S. ZANIPOLO

C. BRESSANA

MADONA

To

5

OSPEDALETO

SLEEPING IN VENICE

33

Campo S. Bartolomeo

12

BISSA

PONTE S. ANTONIO

14

Rio de la Fava

15

13

C. CARMINATI

LARGA

MARCELLO

Rio del Piombo

CASTELLO

18

FELZI

C. LONGA S. MARIA FORMOSA

17

C. DEL ORBI

7

C. DE L'AQUILA NERA

SAN LIO

SALIZADA SAN LIO

C. DE LA NAVE

C. FAVA

Rio d. Pestrin

FOND. DEI PRETI

Campo Santa Maria Formosa

35

C. DEL STAGNER

S. STAGNER

Campo de la Fava

SANTA MARIA FAVA

K. MALVASIA

C. SAN ANTONIO

DEL PARADISO

VENIERA

36

MONDO NOVO

16

30

SANTA MARIA FORMOSA

Rio de S. M. Formosa

RUGA GIUFFA

POST

S. SALV.

C. ACQUE

C. DE MEO

CAPITELLO

S. ZUL.

MARZ.

To San Marco

SAN MARCO

C. DE LE BANDE

C. DIETRO MAGAZEN

CALLE QUERINI

F. D. REMEDIO

C. MEZO

To San Marco

34

---

23. Bancogiro Bar
24. Al Mercà
25. Antica Ostaria Ruga Rialto
26. Osteria al Diavolo e l'Acquasanta
27. Trattoria Pizzeria al Nono Risorto
28. Osteria da Alberto
29. Grom Gelateria
30. Coop Supermarket
31. Billa Supermarket
32. Small Deli
33. Bácaro Jazz Venezia Wine Bar
34. Planet Restaurant
35. Devil's Forest Pub
36. Inishark Pub

Scimia (not simply Scimia, the block before) is on the left—you'll see the hotel sign. My tour groups book this place for 50 nights each year. Sorry. The Guerrato also rents family apartments in the old center (great for groups of 4-8) for around €55 per person.

East of the Rialto Bridge

$$$ **Hotel al Ponte Antico** is exquisite, professional, and small. With nine plush rooms, a velvety royal living/breakfast room, and its own dock for water taxi arrivals, it's perfect for a romantic anniversary. Because its wonderful terrace overlooks the Grand Canal, Rialto Bridge, and market action, its non-canal-view rooms may be a better value (Db-€310, superior Db-€390, deluxe canal-front Db-€470, air-con, free Wi-Fi and Internet access; 100 yards from Rialto Bridge, find Campo San Bartolomeo, exit square on the statue's back side, cross bridge, pass Coin department store on right, then turn left down the dark and empty Calle del Aseo to Cannaregio 5768; tel. 041-241-1944, fax 041-241-1828, www.alponte antico.com, info@alponteantico.com).

$ **Locanda la Corte** is perfumed with elegance without being snooty. Its 19 attractive, high-ceilinged, wood-beamed rooms—Venetian-style, done in earthy pastels—circle a small, quiet courtyard (Sb-€100, standard Db-€150, superior Db-€170, 10 percent discount with cash, ask for Rick Steves discount, suites and family rooms available, air-con, free Wi-Fi and Internet access, on Calle Bressana at Castello 6317, tel. 041-241-1300, fax 041-241-5982, www.locandalacorte.it, info@locandalacorte.it, Marco, Raffaela, and Tommy the cat). Take vaporetto #5.2 from the train station to Fondamente Nove, exit the boat to your left, follow the waterfront, and turn right after the second bridge to reach Santi Giovanni e Paolo. Facing the Rosa Salva bar, take the street to the left (Calle Bressana); the hotel is a short block away at #6317, before the bridge.

$ **Casa Pisani Canal Hotel** is a sweet little place renting five rooms (Db-€110-130, huge Db suite overlooking canal-€240, air-con, free Wi-Fi and Internet access, on Calle de le Erbe at Cannaregio 6105, tel. 041-724-1030, fax 041-724-1039, www .casapisanicanal.it, info@casapisanicanal.it, Tortorella family). It's close to Campo Santi Giovanni e Paolo, and reachable either from Fondamente Nove or Rialto; see their website for directions.

$ **Alloggi Barbaria** rents eight backpacker-type rooms on one floor around a bright but institutional-feeling common area. Beyond Campo Santi Giovanni e Paolo, this Ikea-style place is a long walk from the action, in a residential neighborhood, and only a step above a youth hostel (Db-€90-100, third or fourth person-€25 each, pay cash for best price, family deals, limited breakfast, air-con, free Wi-Fi, on Calle de le Capucine at Castello 6573, tel. 041-522-2750, fax 041-277-5540, www.alloggibarbaria.it, info @alloggibarbaria.it, Giorgio and Fausto). Take vaporetto #5.2 from the train or bus stations to Ospedale stop, turn left as you get off the boat, then right down Calle de le Capucine.

Near the Accademia Bridge

As you step over the Accademia Bridge, the commotion of touristy Venice is replaced by a sleepy village laced with canals. This quiet area, next to the best painting gallery in town, is a 15-minute walk from the Rialto or St. Mark's Square.

The fast vaporetto #2 connects the Accademia Bridge with the train station (15 minutes), Piazzale Roma bus stop (20 minutes), Tronchetto parking lot (25 minutes), and St. Mark's Square (5 minutes). For hotels south of the Accademia Bridge, vaporetto #5.1 to Zattere (or the Alilaguna speedboat from the airport to Zattere) is a good option.

South of the Accademia Bridge

$$$ Pensione Accademia fills the 17th-century Villa Maravege like a Bellini painting. Its 27 rooms are comfortable, elegant, and air-conditioned. You'll feel aristocratic gliding through its grand public spaces and lounging in its wistful, breezy gardens (Sb-€140, standard Db-€239, bigger "superior" Db-€289, Qb-€335, ask for discount when you book, pay Wi-Fi; on Fondamenta Bollani at Dorsoduro 1058; facing Accademia art museum, go right, cross the bridge, go right to where the small canal hits the big one; tel. 041-521-0188, fax 041-523-9152, www.pensioneaccademia.it, info @pensioneaccademia.it).

$$$ Hotel Agli Alboretti is a cozy, family-run, 23-room place in a quiet neighborhood a block behind the Accademia art museum. With red carpeting and wood-beamed ceilings, it feels classy (Sb-€120, Db-€210, Tb-€240, Qb-€260, air-con, elevator, free Wi-Fi, 100 yards from the Accademia vaporetto stop on Rio Terà A. Foscarini at Dorsoduro 884, tel. 041-523-0058, fax 041-521-0158, www.aglialboretti.com, info@aglialboretti.com, Anna).

$$$ Hotel Belle Arti has a grand entry and a formal, stern staff. With the ambience of a modern American hotel, its 64 rooms feel out of place in musty Old World Venice (Sb-€150, Db-€240, Tb-€270, air-con, elevator, pay Wi-Fi in lobby; 100 yards behind Accademia art museum: facing museum, jog left, then right, down Rio Terà A. Foscarini to Dorsoduro 912a; tel. 041-522-6230, fax 041-528-0043, www.hotelbellearti.com, info@hotelbellearti.com).

$$ Pensione la Calcina, the home of English writer John Ruskin in 1876, maintains a 19th-century formality. It comes with all three-star comforts in a professional yet intimate package. Its 32 rosy, perfumed rooms are squeaky clean, with nice wood

Hotels

1. Pensione Accademia
2. Hotel Agli Alboretti
3. Hotel Belle Arti
4. Pensione la Calcina
5. Casa Rezzonico
6. Hotel Galleria
7. Don Orione Religious Guest House
8. Ca' San Trovaso
9. Casa di Sara
10. Foresteria Levi
11. Novecento Hotel
12. Locanda Art Déco
13. Albergo San Samuele

Hotels & Restaurants near Accademia Bridge

SLEEPING IN VENICE

Eateries & Nightlife

14 Ristorante/Pizzeria Accademia Foscarini

15 Enoteca Cantine del Vino Già Schiavi

16 Terrazza del Casin dei Nobili

17 Casin dei Nobili

18 Pane Vino e San Daniele

19 Enoteca e Trattoria la Bitta

20 Venice Jazz Club

21 Pizza al Volo

22 El Chioschetto alle Zattere

23 Piccolo Mondo el Souk

24 Grom Gelateria

25 To Billa Supermarket

26 Small Deli

furniture, hardwood floors, and a peaceful canalside setting facing Giudecca Island (Sb-€140, Sb with view-€150, Db-€150-240, Db with view-€290-310, Qb-€280, air-con, free Wi-Fi and Internet access, rooftop terrace, buffet breakfast outdoors on platform over lagoon, near Zattere vaporetto stop at south end of Rio de San Vio at Dorsoduro 780, tel. 041-520-6466, fax 041-522-7045, www .lacalcina.com, info@lacalcina.com). Guests get discounted meals at their La Piscina restaurant.

$$ Casa Rezzonico is a silent getaway far from the madding crowds. Its private garden terrace has perhaps the lushest grass in Italy, and its seven spacious, very Venetian rooms have garden/canal views (Sb-€130, Db-€160, Tb-€190, Qb-€220, ask for discount when you book, air-con, free Wi-Fi, on Fondamenta Gherardini at Dorsoduro 2813, tel. 041-277-0653, fax 041-277-5435, www .casarezzonico.it, info@casarezzonico.it). Take vaporetto #1 to Ca' Rezzonico, head up Calle del Traghetto, cross Campo San Barnaba to the canal, and continue on Fondamenta Gherardini to #2813.

$$ Hotel Galleria has nine tight, velvety rooms, most with views of the Grand Canal. Some rooms are quite narrow. It's run with a family feel by Luciano and Stefano (S-€85, D-€125, skinny Grand Canal view Db-€155, palatial Grand Canal view Db-€185, includes breakfast in room, ceiling fans, free Wi-Fi, 30 yards from Accademia art museum, next to recommended Foscarini pizzeria at Dorsoduro 878a, tel. 041-523-2489, fax 041-520-4172, www .hotelgalleria.it, info@hotelgalleria.it).

$$ Don Orione Religious Guest House is a big cultural center dedicated to the work of a local man who became a saint in modern times. Filling an old monastery, it feels institutional, like a modern retreat center—clean, peaceful, and strictly run, with 74 rooms. It's beautifully located, comfortable, and a fine value (Sb-€88, Db-€144, Tb-€187, Qb-€224, profits go to mission work in the developing world, groups welcome, air-con, elevator, pay Wi-Fi, on Rio Terà A. Foscarini, Dorsoduro 909a, tel. 041-522-4077, fax 041-528-6214, www.donorione-venezia.it, info@don orione-venezia.it). From the Zattere vaporetto stop, turn right, then turn left. It's just after the church at #909a.

$ Ca' San Trovaso rents seven simple rooms split between the main building and a nearby annex. The location is peaceful, on a small canal (Sb-€90, Db-€115, Db with bigger canal view and air-con-€130, Tb-€145, these prices with cash—includes breakfast in your room, air-con in most rooms, free cable Internet, no common space except small roof terrace, off Fondamenta de le Romite at Dorsoduro 1350/51, tel. 041-277-1146, mobile 339-445-8821, fax 041-277-7190, www.casantrovaso.com, info@casantrovaso.com, Mark and his son Alessandro). From the Zattere vaporetto stop, exit left, and cross a bridge. Turn right at tiny Calle Trevisan, cross another bridge, cross the adjacent bridge, take an immediate right, and then the first left. Nearby, Mark's wife Cristina runs **Casa di Sara,** a brightly colored B&B with four quiet rooms, a tiny roof terrace, and the same prices (mobile 345-070-8547, www.casa disara.com, info@casadisara.com).

North of the Accademia Bridge

$$$ Foresteria Levi, run by a foundation that promotes research on Venetian music, offers 35 quiet, institutional yet comfortable and spacious rooms (Sb-€100, Db-€190, Tb-€210, Qb-€240, ask for Rick Steves discount—10-20 percent in high season, 20-50 percent in low season; fans, elevator, free Wi-Fi, laundry, on Calle Giustinian at San Marco 2893, tel. 041-786-711, fax 041-786-766, www.foresterialevi.it, info@foresterialevi.it). It's 80 yards from the Accademia Bridge on the St. Mark's side. Leaving the bridge (opposite the Accademia vaporetto stop), take an immediate left, cross the Ponte Giustinian bridge, and go down Calle Giustinian straight to the Fondazione Levi building. Buzz the *Foresteria* door to the right.

$$$ Novecento Hotel rents nine plush rooms on three floors. This boutique hotel is decorated circa-1900 throughout, with a big lounge and an elegant living room (Db-€240-260, air-con, lots of stairs, free Wi-Fi; on Calle del Dose, off Campo San Maurizio at San Marco 2683; tel. 041-241-3765, fax 041-521-2145, www.nove cento.biz, info@novecento.biz).

$$ Locanda Art Déco is a charming little place, though there's not much Art Deco to be seen. A wrought-iron staircase leads from the inviting lobby to six small but thoughtfully deco-rated rooms on three floors (Db-€140-160, nicer Db-€170-200, Tb-€200-230, 3-night minimum on weekends, 5 percent cash dis-count, air-con, free Wi-Fi, lots of stairs; on Calle de le Botteghe, just north of the Accademia Bridge off Campo San Stefano, at San Marco 2966; tel. 041-277-0558, fax 041-270-2891, www.locanda artdeco.com, info@locandaartdeco.com). They also rent loft apartments.

$ Albergo San Samuele is a backpacker place: dumpy but in a great locale. It rents 12 basic rooms in a crumbling old palace near Campo San Stefano. Sleep here only if their price is far less than other listings (S-€70, D-€90, Db-€110, extra bed-€30, no break-fast, free Wi-Fi and Internet access, on Salizada San Samuele at San Marco 3358, tel. 041-520-5165, fax 041-522-8045, www.albergo sansamuele.it, info@albergosansamuele.it).

Near the Train Station

I don't recommend the train station area. It's crawling with noisy, disoriented tourists with too much baggage and people whose life's

SLEEPING IN VENICE

Hotels near the Train Station

1 Hotel Abbazia
2 Locanda Herion
3 Albergo Marin & Launderette
4 The Chef's Wife B&B
5 Hotel S. Lucia
6 Alloggi Henry
7 Brek Cafeteria

Road to Mestre & Mainland

Lagoon

Road to Mestre & Mainland

To Tronchetto

FOND. DE

CALLE DELLA MISERICORDIA

RAMO DEI SCALZI

C. PRIULI DEI CAVALLETTI

SANTA LUCIA TRAIN STATION (FERROVIA)

SCALZI

Ferrovia W

Ferrovia Scalzi

SCALZI BRIDGE

WC

Ferrovia

SAN SIMEONE PICCOLO

NOVA DE S.

FOND. DE SAN SIMEONE PICCOLO

CAMP. DE LE CHIOVERETE

C. DEI BERGAMASCHI

To Stazione Marittima & Tronchetto

RAMPA SAN BASILIO

PONTE DELLA SANTA CHIARA

Canale de Santa Chiara

PEOPLE MOVER

Canale de Santa Liberta

COOP SUPER-MARKET

Piazzale Roma

CALATRAVA BRIDGE

FOND. DE LA CROCE

F. DEI TOLENTINI

F. DEL FORNO

CASE NOVE

CAMPO D. LA

PARKING GARAGE

RIO TERA SAN ANDREA

Piazzale Roma

BUS STATION

Giardino Papadopoli

Rio Novo

F. PAPADOPOLI

F. CONDULMER

C. DE CA'AMAI

Canale de Santa Maria Maggiore

SANTA   CROCE

Campiello de Lana

SAN NICOLO DA TOLENTINO

F. MINOTTO

F. D. GAFFARO

FONDAMENTA DE S. PONTE

C. D.S. BIAGIA GALLO

C. BASEGO

Rio de la Cazziola

F. DEL RIO NUOVO

100 Meters
100 Yards

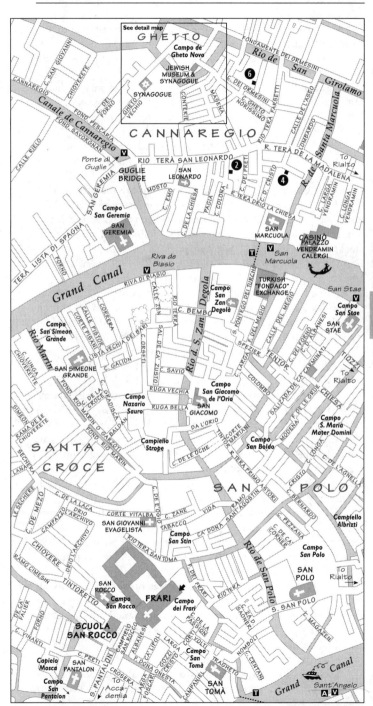

SLEEPING IN VENICE

calling is to scam visitors out of their money. It's so easy just to hop a vaporetto upon arrival and sleep in the Venice of your dreams. Still, some like to park their bags near the station, and if so, these places stand out.

Nearby Laundry: Orange, the nearest self-service laundry, is across the Grand Canal from the station (€14/load, daily 7:30-22:30, follow directions to recommended Albergo Marin, on Ramo de le Chioverete at Santa Croce 665b).

$$$ Hotel Abbazia, in the dreary hotel zone near the train station, fills a former abbey with both history and class. The refectory makes a grand living room for guests, a garden fills the old courtyard, and the halls leading to 50 rooms are monkishly wide (Db-€180, larger Db-€210—choose Venetian or modern style, ask for 10 percent Rick Steves discount when you book direct, aircon, free Wi-Fi, no elevator but plenty of stairs, fun-loving staff, 2 blocks from the station on the very quiet Calle Priuli dei Cavaletti, Cannaregio 68, tel. 041-717-333, fax 041-717-949, www.abbazia hotel.com, info@abbaziahotel.com).

$ Locanda Herion rents 17 basic rooms for a decent price (Db-€120, 10 percent discount with cash, air-con, pay Wi-Fi, on Campiello Augusto Picutti at Cannaregio 1697a, tel. 041-275-9426, fax 041-275-6647, www.locandaherion.com, info@locandaherion .com). Exiting the train station, turn left to follow Rio Terà Lista de Spagna. Cross the Ponte de Guglie bridge and turn right at the yellow *San Marcuola traghetto* sign to find the hotel.

$ Albergo Marin and its staff offer 19 good-value, quiet rooms handy to the train station (Sb-€110, D-€90, Db-€120, Tb-€150, 5 percent cash discount, fans on request, free Wi-Fi in public spaces, on Ramo de le Chioverete at Santa Croce 670b, tel. 041-718-022, fax 041-721-485, www.albergomarin.it, info@albergomarin.it, Giacomo). From the station, cross the stone bridge over the Grand Canal and go right along the embankment. Take the first left, then the first right, then right again to #670b.

$ The Chef's Wife B&B is run by American Stacy Gibboni. The "chef" is her Italian husband, who runs the La Colombina restaurant next door. Together they rent one sprawling and very cozy 2-bedroom apartment (with electric kettle and fridge but no kitchen) for two to four people (Db-€100, Tb/Qb-€150, ask for Rick Steves rate, 2-night minimum, simple breakfast; huge living room has piano, board games, and DVD player; no air-con, free Wi-Fi, adjacent to Stacy's art studio, on Campiello del Pegoloto at Cannaregio 1801, no phone calls, www.thechefswife.eu, stacys guesthouse@hotmail.it). It's near the San Marcuola vaporetto stop—see Stacy's website for directions.

$ Hotel S. Lucia, 150 yards from the train station, is oddly modern and sterile, with bright and spacious rooms and tight showers. Its 15 rooms are simple and clean. Guests enjoy their sunny garden area out front (S-€60, D-€80, Db-€105, Tb-€130, 5 percent cash discount, breakfast-€5, air-con, pay Wi-Fi, on Calle de la Misericordia at Cannaregio 358, tel. 041-715-180, fax 041-710-610, www.hotelslucia.com, info@hotelslucia.com, Gianni and Alessandra). Exit the station, head left, then take the second left onto Calle de la Misericordia. The hotel is 100 yards ahead on the right.

$ **Alloggi Henry,** a family-owned hotel, rents 15 simple and flowery rooms in a quiet residential neighborhood near the Jewish Ghetto. It's a 10-minute walk from the train station (D-€80, Db-€100, Tb-€130, Qb-€160, prices good with cash and this book through 2012, 10 percent discount if you stay at least 3 nights, no breakfast, air-con, free Wi-Fi, on Calle Ormesini at Cannaregio 1506e, tel. 041-523-6675, fax 041-715-680, www.alloggihenry.com, info@alloggihenry.com, Manola and Henry). From the station, follow Lista de Spagna, San Leonardo, and Farsetti. Turn left on Calle Ormesini, then turn right into tiny Campiello Briani. They also rent a three-room apartment that sleeps up to nine.

Big, Fancy Hotels that Discount Shamelessly

Here are several big, plush, four-star places with greedy, sky-high rack rates (around Db-€300) that often have great discounts (as low as Db-€120) for drop-ins, off-season travelers, or online booking through their websites. All are on the map on page 246, except for Hotel Giorgione. If you want sliding-glass-door, uniformed-receptionist kind of comfort and formality in the old center, these are worth considering: $$$ **Hotel Giorgione** (big, garish, shiny, near Rialto Bridge, www.hotelgiorgione.com, see map on page 252); $$$ **Hotel Casa Verardo** (elegant and quietly parked on a canal behind St. Mark's, more stately, www.casaverardo.it); $$$ **Hotel Donà Palace** (sitting like Las Vegas in the touristy zone a few blocks behind St. Mark's Basilica, works with neighbors $$$ **Hotel all'Angelo** and $$$ **Hotel al Ponte dei Sosperi** to rent 100 overpriced but often discounted rooms, all on Calle Larga San Marco, www.donapalace.it); and $$$ **Hotel Ca' Dei Conti** (five minutes northeast of St. Mark's Square, palatial and perfectly located but €500 rooms are worth it only when deeply discounted, www.cadeiconti.com).

Cheap Dormitory Accommodations

$ **Foresteria della Chiesa Valdese,** run by the Methodist Church, has a mixture of dorms (6-9 beds) and private rooms (2-5 beds) with bath, close to both St. Mark's Square and the Rialto Bridge. This chilly, run-down yet charming old place has elegant ceiling paintings. They take reservations for the rooms, but only accept walk-ins for the dorms (dorm bed-€31, Db-€92-102, Tb-€111-117, Qb-€144-152, 5b-€170, price depends on view and amenities, €5/person less for stays of 2 nights or more; includes breakfast, sheets, towels, and lockers; must check in and out when office is open—8:30-20:00, no air-con, elevator, on Fondamenta Cavagnis at Castello 5170, tel. 041-528-6797, fax 041-241-6238, www.foresteria venezia.it, info@foresteriavenezia.it). From Campo Santa Maria Formosa, walk past Bar all'Orologio to the end of Calle Longa and cross the bridge—it's the second door, see map page 252.

$ **Venice's youth hostel,** on Giudecca Island with 260 beds and grand views across the Bay of San Marco, is a godsend for backpackers shell-shocked by Venetian prices. It's an old-school hostel—big rooms stacked with bunk beds (€25 beds with sheets and breakfast in 8- to 20-bed dorms, cheaper for hostel members, lockers, towels-€5, pay Wi-Fi, room lock-out 10:30-13:30, office open 24 hours, Fondamenta Zitelle 86, tel. 041-523-8211, fax 041-523-5689, www.ostellovenezia.it, info@ostellovenezia.it). Take vaporetto #4.1 from the bus or train stations (from the Tronchetto parking lot, take vaporetto #2) to the Zitelle stop, then walk right along the embankment to #86.

On the Mainland

While I prefer to stay in the heart of the action, these two places combine fine prices with easy bus links into Venice and are particularly good options for those who need to park a car.

$ **Villa Dolcetti** is a 1635 building with six comfortable rooms in a suburb of Venice. Art lovers Diego and Tatiana provide a buffet breakfast, free parking, and lots of sightseeing advice (Db-€75, superior Db-€85, Tb-€90-110, these prices for Rick Steves readers booking direct, air-con, free Internet access and Wi-Fi, tel. 041-563-1077, fax 041-563-1139, www.villadolcetti.com, info@villa dolcetti.com). It's in the town of Oriago di Mira, at Via Venezia 85. Steps away is a bus stop on the Venice-Padua line that connects you to Venice's Piazzale Roma (2/hour, 25 minutes).

$ **Villa Mocenigo Agriturismo,** about 10 miles from Marco Polo Airport, is a working, family-run farm in a peaceful rural location between Venice and Padua. Its 10 rooms are furnished with antiques, and regional specialties are served for dinner (Sb-€40-55, Db-€60-74, extra bed-€20-25, dinner with wine about €20 per person, air-con, free parking, Via Viasana 59 in Mirano-Venezia, tel. & fax 041-433-246, mobile 335-547-4728, www.villamocenigo .com, info@villamocenigo.com). Email them for directions by car or bus. Buses to Venice leave directly from the villa (3/hour, 45 minutes).

EATING IN VENICE

The Italians are masters at the art of fine living. That means eating...long and well. Lengthy, multicourse lunches and dinners and
endless hours sitting in outdoor cafés are the norm. Americans eat
on their way to an evening event and complain if the check is slow
in coming. For Italians, dining is an end in itself, and only rude
waiters rush you. When you want the bill, mime-scribble on your
raised palm or ask for it: *"Il conto?"* You may have to ask for it more
than once. To save time, you could ask for the check when you
receive the last item you order.

Even those of us who liked dorm food will find that the cafés,
cuisine, and wines become a highlight of our Italian adventure.
Trust me: This is sightseeing for your palate, and even if the rest of
you is sleeping in cheap hotels, your taste buds will relish an occasional first-class splurge. You can eat well without going broke.
But be careful: You're just as likely to blow a small fortune on a
disappointing meal as you are to dine wonderfully for €25.

Restaurants

Looking for an "untouristy restaurant" in Venice is like looking
for the same thing at Disneyland. Venice restaurants exist to feed
tourists. Still, some cater to groups and sloppy big spenders, while
others respect their clientele—both locals and travelers. Avoid
the places with big signs boasting, "We speak English and accept
credit cards." High-rent restaurants parked on famous squares or
canals must pass on their costs, and they generally serve tourists
bad food at high prices. The natives eat better at low-rent holes-
in-the-wall, which need to be good to be known. While Venetians
still eat out and have their favorites, a restaurateur once confided
in me that no restaurant in Venice can be truly untouristy: They all
want and need the tourist euro.

Eating with the Seasons

Italian cooks love to serve you fresh produce and seafood at its tastiest. If you must have porcini mushrooms outside of fall, they'll be frozen. Each region in Italy has its specialties, which you'll see displayed in open-air markets. To get a plate of the freshest veggies at a fine restaurant, request *"Un piatto di verdure della stagione, per favore."*

Here are a few examples of what's fresh when:

April-May:	Squid, green beans, asparagus, artichokes, and zucchini flowers
April-May, Sept-Oct:	Black truffles
May-June:	Asparagus, zucchini, cantaloupe, and strawberries
May-Aug:	Eggplant
Oct-Nov:	Mushrooms, white truffles, and chestnuts
Nov-Feb:	Radicchio
Fresh year-round:	Clams, meats

Before you sit down, look at a menu to see what extra charges a restaurant tacks on. As elsewhere in Italy, many (but not all) restaurants in Venice add a cover charge *(coperto)* of €1.50-3.50 per person to your bill. Sometimes this is phrased as "bread and cover" *(pane e coperto)*. It's not negotiable, even if you don't eat the bread. Restaurants with a service charge (usually around 12 percent) are in the minority. Places with both a cover *and* a service charge are best avoided—that's a clue that a restaurant could be overpriced and touristy. There's never any need to tip.

You can save a lot by getting fixed-priced meals, which are frequently exempt from cover and service charges. However, the cheapest ones tend to be bland and heavy, pairing a very basic pasta with reheated schnitzel and roast meats (usually around €15-20, often called *menù turistico*, or sometimes, usually falsely, *menù del giorno*—menu of the day). It's worth paying more for an inventive fixed-price meal that shows off the chef's creativity. While fixed-price meals can be easy and convenient, galloping gourmets order à la carte with the help of a menu translator. (The *Rick Steves' Italian Phrase Book & Dictionary* has a menu decoder with enough phrases for intermediate eaters.) When going to an especially good restaurant with an approachable staff, my favorite strategy is to simply say, "Make me happy" (in this case, it's just fine to set a price limit).

Tipping

In Italy, the service charge *(servizio)* is usually built into your bill's grand total in one of two ways. If the menu states *servizio incluso* (or nothing at all), the listed prices already include service. If the menu states *servizio non incluso,* or *servizio* with a specific percentage, a fixed percentage (usually 10-15 percent of the total) will be added as a line item to the bottom of the bill. In either case, the total you pay already includes a basic tip. Italians don't tip beyond this, but if you're pleased with the service, you can round up the bill by a euro or two. If you pay your bill with a credit card, it's best to tip in cash—leave it on the table or hand it directly to your server. If you order your food at a counter, don't tip.

A full meal consists of an appetizer (antipasto, €4-6), a first course *(primo piatto,* pasta, rice, or soup, €5-12), and a second course *(secondo piatto,* expensive meat and fish dishes, €10-20). Vegetables *(contorni, verdure)* may come with the *secondo* or cost extra (€4-6) as a side dish. But only the truly famished eat all of this. The euros can add up in a hurry. Light and budget eaters get a *primo piatto* each and share an antipasto.

Note that seafood and steak may be sold by weight (priced by the kilo—1,000 grams, or just over two pounds; or by the *etto*—

100 grams). The letters "s.q." means according to quantity. Fish is usually served whole with the head and tail; you can't just get half a fish or a filet unless it already comes prepared as just a filet *(filetto,* sometimes *trancio*—slice, as in tuna or swordfish). However, you can ask your waiter to select a smaller fish for you. Sometimes, especially for steak, restaurants require a minimum order of four or five *etti*. Beware, or be shell-shocked by €50 entrées. Make sure you're really clear on the price before ordering.

Some special dishes come in large quantities meant for two people; the shorthand way of showing this on a menu is "x2" (meaning "times two"), and the price listed generally indicates the cost per person.

Cheap Meals

The keys to eating affordably in Venice are pizza, bars/cafés, cafeterias, and picnics. *Panini* and *tramezzini* (sandwiches, described on page 272) are sold fast and cheap at bars everywhere and can stave off midmorning hunger. There's a great "sandwich row" of cheap cafés near St. Mark's Square (see page 283). For speed, value, and ambience, you can get a filling plate of typically Venetian appetizers at nearly any bar. For quick, fun eating, I like small, stand-up mini-meals at *cicchetti* **bars** best (many are recommended in this chapter).

Pizzerias

Pizza, readily available, is cheap if you avoid the most crowded areas. A pizza at a sit-down place will run about €8-10, plus drinks and cover. If you prefer takeout, try one of the hole-in-the-wall shops that bake huge, round family-size pizzas (about 20 inches across) for €11 and "normal" ones (12 inches) for €6. You can also buy by the slice; at the base of the Rialto Bridge (by the vaporetto stop on the St. Mark's side), family-size pizzas are cut into eight slices which sell for €4 each. At shops around Campo Santa Maria Formosa or Campo San Barnaba, pizzas are cut into six slices which cost €2 each. (Do the math.)

Key pizza vocabulary: *capricciosa* (generally ham, mushrooms, olives, and artichokes), *funghi* (mushrooms), *marinara* (tomato sauce, oregano, garlic, no cheese), *quattro formaggi* (four different cheeses), and *quattro stagioni* (different toppings on each of the pizza's four quarters, for those who can't choose just one menu item). If you ask for pepperoni on your pizza, you'll get *peperoni* (green or red peppers, not sausage); request *diavola* instead (the closest thing in Italy to American pepperoni). Kids like the simple *margherita* (cheese with tomato sauce).

Bars/Cafés

Italian "bars" are not taverns, but cafés. These neighborhood hangouts serve coffee, mini-pizzas, sandwiches, and drinks from the cooler. Many dish up plates of fried cheese and vegetables from under the glass counter, ready to reheat. This budget choice is the Italian equivalent of English pub grub. Unique to Venice, *cicchetti* bars specialize in finger foods and appetizers that can combine to make a quick and tasty meal. See "The Stand-Up Progressive Venetian Pub-Crawl Dinner" sidebar later in this chapter.

For quick meals, bars usually have trays of cheap, ready-made sandwiches (*panini* or *tramezzini*)—some are delightful grilled. (Others are lots of mayo between crustless slices of Wonder Bread.) To save time for sightseeing and room for dinner, consider a ham-and-cheese *panino* at a bar (called *toast*, have it grilled twice if you want it really hot) for lunch.

To get food "for the road," say, *"Da portar via"* (or *"da portar canale"*...for the canal). Many bars are small—if you can't find a table, you'll need to stand up. Most charge extra for table service.

All bars have a WC *(toilette, bagno)* in the back, and customers (and the discreet public) may use it.

Bars serve great drinks—hot, cold, sweet, caffeinated, or alcoholic. Chilled bottled water, still *(naturale)* or carbonated *(frizzante)*, is sold cheap to go.

Coffee: Take some time to learn Italian coffee lingo—the names and the rituals are a little different from those at your hometown java joint. If you ask for *"un caffè,"* you'll get espresso. If you ask for a latte, you'll get just that—a glass of hot milk. Starbucks-style mochas aren't on the menu at all.

Cappuccino is served to locals before noon and to tourists at any time of day. (To an Italian, cappuccino is a breakfast drink and a travesty after anything with tomatoes.) Italians like their coffee only warm—to get it hot, request *"Molto caldo"* (MOHL-toh KAHL-doh; very hot) or *"Più caldo, per favore"* (pew KAHL-doh, pehr fah-VOH-ray; hotter, please).

Experiment with a few of the options:
- *Cappuccino:* Espresso with foamed milk on top
- *Caffè latte:* Tall glass with espresso and hot milk mixed, no foam
- *Caffè hag:* Instant decaf (you can order decaffeinated versions of any coffee drink—ask for it *decaffeinato;* day-kah-fay-ee-NAH-toh)
- *Macchiato* (mah-kee-AH-toh): Espresso with only a little milk (*macchiato* means "marked" or "stained")
- *Latte macchiato:* Hot milk with a shot of espresso
- *Caffè americano:* Espresso diluted with water
- *Caffè freddo:* Sweet and iced espresso
- *Cappuccino freddo:* Iced cappuccino
- *Caffè corretto:* Espresso with a shot of liqueur, usually grappa or Sambuca, but amaretto is also good

Other Hot Drinks: *Cioccolato* is hot chocolate. *Tè* is hot tea. *Tè freddo* (iced tea) is usually from a can—sweetened and flavored with lemon or peach.

Juice: *Spremuta* means freshly squeezed as far as *succo* (fruit juice) is concerned (order *una spremuta*); it's usually orange juice, and in February through April it's almost always made from blood oranges. (Note: *Spumante* means sparkling wine.)

Beer: Beer on tap is *alla spina*. Get it *piccola* (33 cl, 11 oz), *media* (50 cl, about a pint), or *grande* (a liter, about 2 pints). Italians drink mainly lager beers. You'll find local brews (Peroni or Moretti) and imports such as Heineken as well. A *lattina* is a can and a *bottiglia* (boh-TEEL-yah) is a bottle.

Wine: To order a glass (*bicchiere;* bee-kee-AY-ree) of red *(rosso)* or white *(bianco)* wine, say, *"Un bicchiere di vino rosso/bianco."* House wine *(vino della casa)* comes in a carafe: quarter-liter (8.5 oz, *un* *quarto*), half-liter pitcher (17 oz, *un mezzo*), or one-liter pitcher (34 oz, *un litro*). An *ombra* is the smallest glass. For a brief guide to Italian wines, see page 274.

Prices: You'll notice a two-tiered pricing system. It's cheapest to drink a cup of coffee while standing at the bar; you'll pay more for that same cup to sit at an indoor table, and often still more at an outdoor table. Many places have a *listino prezzi* (price list) with two columns—*al bar* and *al tavolo*—posted somewhere by the bar or cash register. If you're on a budget, don't sit without first checking out the financial consequences. Ask, "Same price if I sit or stand?" by saying, *"Costa uguale al tavolo o al banco?"* (KOH-stah oo-GWAH-lay ahl TAH-voh-loh oh ahl BAHN-koh?) A cup of coffee at any bar generally costs only a euro if you stand.

Picnics

Picnicking saves lots of euros and is a great way to sample regional specialties. The only legal place to picnic in public in Venice is Giardinetti Reali, the waterfront park near St. Mark's Square. Eating anywhere outdoors, you may be besieged by pigeons. A picnic in your room can be a better bet.

Venice has an outdoor market and several supermarkets (see below). Every neighborhood has an *alimentari*, a one-stop corner grocery store with deli meats and cheeses (most will slice and stuff your sandwich for you if you buy the ingredients there).

Juice-lovers can get a liter of O.J. for the price of a Coke or coffee. Look for "100% *succo*" (juice) on the label or be surprised by something diluted and sugary sweet. Hang onto the half-liter plastic mineral-water bottles (sold everywhere for about €1). Buy juice in cheap liter boxes, drink some, and store the extra in your water bottle. You'll also save money by buying water in big bottles (a third of the price of small bottles—even cheaper in supermarkets) to keep in your hotel room and use to refill your smaller, more portable bottle. (I drink the tap water—*acqua del rubinetto*.)

Picnics can be adventures in high cuisine. Be daring. Try the fresh mozzarella, presto pesto, shriveled olives, marinated eggplant or artichokes, sun-dried tomatoes, and any UFOs the locals are excited about. Shopkeepers are happy to sell small quantities of produce. Rather than pick your own produce, it is customary to let the merchant choose the produce for you. Say, *"Per oggi"* (pehr

EATING IN VENICE

OH-jee, "for today"), and he or she will grab you something ready to eat, weigh it, and make the sale. If you suspect you're being over-charged, know the cost per kilo and study the weighing procedure as if you're doing the arithmetic.

A typical picnic for two might be fresh rolls, 100 grams of meat (about a quarter pound, called *un etto* in Italy), 100 grams of cheese, two tomatoes, three carrots, two apples, yogurt, and a liter box of juice. Total cost—about €10.

Outdoor Market near the Rialto: The **fruit and vegetable mar-ket** that sprawls for a few blocks just past the Rialto Bridge is a fun place to assemble a picnic (best Mon-Sat 8:00-13:00, closed Sun). The adjacent **fish market** is wonderfully slimy (closed Sun-Mon). Side lanes in this area are speckled with fine little hole-in-the-wall munchie bars, bakeries, and cheese shops.

Neighborhood Deli near the Rialto: One tiny **alimentari** just around the corner from the Rialto market sells an intriguing (and spicy!) concoction of cheese, Kalamata olives, sun-dried tomatoes, olive oil, and hot peppers that they call *intruglio*. It goes great with a fresh roll (€2.50-3). To get there from the market, walk to the end of Ruga dei Orefici, turn left onto Ruga Vechia San Giovanni, and then right under Sotoportego dei Do Mori. It's just on your left at #414; see map on page 253 (Mon-Sat 9:00-20:00, Sun 11:00-19:00).

Neighborhood Deli near the Accademia Bridge: A small deli hides along the main route between the Accademia and St. Mark's Square (at #2512, on the zigzag bridge near the Church of Santa Maria Zobenigo/del Giglio, see map on page 257).

Produce Stand near St. Mark's Square: To find the produce stand near the square, face St. Mark's Basilica, then walk along its left side, heading east down Calle de la Canonica. Cross the bridge and turn left at Campo Santi Filippo e Giacomo.

Supermarket near St. Mark's Square: A handy (but often mobbed) **Coop** supermarket is between St. Mark's and Campo Santa Maria Formosa, on the corner of Salizada San Lio and Calle del Mondo Novo at #5817. It has a great selection of picnic supplies, including packaged salads for less than €2 (daily 8:30-20:00).

Other Supermarkets: The largest supermarket in town is the **Coop** at Piazzale Roma, next to the vaporetto stop at #504-507 (daily 8:30-20:00). It's an easy walk from the train station, as is the **Billa** supermarket on Campo San Felice (at #3660, along the Strada Nova between the train station and Rialto area, Mon-Sat 8:30-20:00, Sun 9:00-20:00). Another **Billa** supermarket is conve-nient for those staying in Dorsoduro: It's at #1492, at the far west of the Zattere embankment, by the San Basilio vaporetto stop and the cruise-ship docks (Mon-Sat 8:00-20:00, Sun 9:00-19:00).

Venetian Cuisine

Even more so than the rest of Italy, Venetian cuisine relies heavily on fish, shellfish, risotto, and polenta. Along with the usual pizza and pasta fare, here are some typical foods you'll encounter.

Bar Snacks

Venetians often eat a snack—*cicchetti* or *panini*—while standing at a bar. (Remember, you'll usually pay more if you sit, rather than stand.)

Cicchetti: Generic name for various small finger foods served in some pubs—like appetizers or tapas, Venetian-style. Designed as a quick meal for working people, the selection and ambience are best on workdays (Mon-Sat lunch and early dinner). See "The Stand-Up Progressive Venetian Pub-Crawl Dinner," later.

Panini: Sandwiches made with rustic bread, filled with meat, vegetables, and cheese, served cold or toasted—*riscaldato* (ree-skahl-DAH-toh). You can eat your sandwich at the bar or take it with you.

Tramezzini: Crustless, white bread sandwiches served cold and stuffed with a variety of fillings (e.g., egg, tuna, or shrimp), mixed with a mayonnaise dressing. The selection is best in the morning and skimpy by afternoon.

Appetizers *(Antipasti)*

Antipasto di mare: A marinated mix of fish and shellfish served chilled.

Asiago cheese: The Veneto region's specialty, a cow's-milk cheese that's either *mezzano*—young, firm, and creamy; or *stravecchio*—aged, pungent, and granular.

Sarde in saor: Sardines marinated with onions.

Rice *(Riso)*, Pasta, and Polenta

Risotto: Short-grain rice, simmered in broth and often flavored with fish and seafood. For example, *risotto nero* is risotto made with squid and its ink, and *risotto ai porcini* contains porcini mushrooms.

Risi e bisi: Rice and peas.

Pasta e fagioli: Bean and pasta soup.

Bigoli in salsa: A long, fat, whole-wheat noodle (one of the few traditional pastas) with anchovy sauce.

Polenta: Cornmeal boiled into a mush and served soft or cut into firm slabs and grilled. Polenta is a standard accompaniment with cod *(baccalà)*, or calf liver and onions *(fegato alla veneziana)*.

Seafood *(Frutti di Mare)*

Some sea creatures found in the Adriatic are slightly different from their American cousins. Generally, Venetian fish are smaller than American salmon and trout (think sardines and anchovies). The shellfish are more exotic. The most common fish on Venetian plates—such as sea bass, bream, salmon, and turbot—are farmed, not wild. The weirder the animal (eel, octopus, frogfish), the more local it is.

Remember that seafood can be sold by weight rather than a set price (if you see "100 g" or *"l'etto"* by a too-good-to-be-true price on the menu, that's the cost per 100 grams—about a quarter pound). As noted earlier, the abbreviation "s.q." means according to quantity (you pay for the weight of the particular piece).

Baccalà: Dried Atlantic salt cod that's rehydrated and served with polenta, or chopped up and mixed with mayonnaise as a topping for *cicchetti* (appetizers).

Branzino: Sea bass, grilled and served whole (with head and tail).

Calamari: Squid, usually cut into rings and either deep-fried or marinated.

Cozze: Mussels, often steamed in an herb broth with tomato.

Gamberi: The generic name for shrimp. *Gamberetti* are small shrimp, and *gamberoni* are large shrimp. (Language tip: *-etti* signifies little, and *-oni* indicates big.)

Moleche col pien: Fried soft-shell crabs.

Orata: Sea bream, a common European game fish that is now widely farmed.

Pesce fritto misto: Assorted deep-fried seafood (often calamari and prawns).

Pesce spada: Swordfish.

Rombo: Turbot, a flatfish similar to flounder.

Rospo: Frogfish, a small marine fish.

Salmone: Salmon, farm-raised in northern Europe and shipped in.

Seppia: Cuttlefish, a squid-like creature that sprays black ink when threatened. *Seppia al nero* is the squid in its own ink, often served over spaghetti. It's sweet and tender when grilled—either *grigliata* or *alla griglia* (without its ink).

Sogliola: Sole, served poached or oven-roasted.

Italian Labels and Lingo

The ancient Greeks who colonized Italy more than 2,000 years ago called it *"Oenotria"*—land of the grape. Little has changed over the centuries. Ideal conditions for grapes (warm climate, well-draining soil, and an abundance of hillsides) make the Italian peninsula a paradise for grape-growers, winemakers, and wine drinkers. Italy makes and consumes more wine per capita than any other country.

In almost every part of Italy you'll find wine varieties designed to go with the regional cuisine. Choosing a wine can be intimidating, but the Italian government tries to help you choose something decent, even if you're clueless. In general, wines are designated by one of four categories:

Vino da Tavola (table wine) is the lowest grade. It's inexpensive, but Italy's wines are so good that, for many people, a basic *vino da tavola* is just fine with a meal. Many restaurants, even modest ones, take pride in their house wine *("vino della casa")*, bottling their own or working with wineries.

Denominazione di Origine Controllata (DOC), a cut above table wine, is usually cheap, but can be surprisingly good. You'll see DOC wines all over Italy. In Tuscany, for example, many such wines come from the Chianti region, located between Florence and Siena.

Denominazione di Origine Controllata e Guarantita (DOCG) is the highest grade, and can be identified by the pink or green label on the neck and the scary price tag on the shelf. They're generally a good bet if you want a quality wine, but you don't know anything else about the winemaker.

Vitello di mare: "Sea veal," like swordfish—firm, pink, mild, and grilled.

Vongole: Small clams steamed with fresh herbs and wine, or served as a first course, such as *spaghetti alle vongole.*

Zuppa di pesce: Seafood stew.

Dessert *(Dolci)*

Tiramisù: Spongy ladyfingers soaked in coffee and Marsala, layered with mascarpone cheese and bitter chocolate. Arguably Venetian in origin, the literal meaning of the word is "pick-me-up."

Venetian cookies: There are numerous varieties, due perhaps to Venice's position in trade (spices) and the Venetians' love of celebrations. Many treats were created for certain feast days

Indicazione Geographica Tipica (IGT) is a broad group of wines that range from basic to some of Italy's best. It includes the "Super Tuscans"—wines that don't follow the strict "recipe" required for DOC or DOCG status, but that give local vintners more opportunity to be creative. Super Tuscans are made from a mix of international grapes (such as Cabernet Sauvignon) grown in Tuscany and aged in small oak barrels for only two years. The result is a lively full-bodied wine that dances all over your head... and is worth the steep price for aficionados.

Visit an *enoteca* (wine bar) and sample these wines side-by-side to figure out what you like—and what suits your pocketbook.

Words to Live By, or...How to Describe Wine in Italian

As you can see from many of the words listed below, adding a vowel to the English word often gets you close to the Italian one. Have some fun, gesture like a local, and you'll have no problems speaking the language of the *enoteca*. *Salute!*

dry	*secco*	SAY-koh
sweet	*dolce*	DOHL-chay
earthy	*terroso*	tay-ROH-zoh
tannic	*tannico*	TAH-nee-koh
young	*giovane*	JOH-vah-nay
mature	*maturo*	mah-TOO-roh
sparkling	*spumante*	spoo-MAHN-tay
fruity	*fruttoso*	froo-TOH-zoh
full-bodied	*corposo*	kor-POH-zoh
elegant	*elegante*	ay-lay-GAHN-tay

and religious holidays. *Pinza,* a sweet made with corn, wheat flour, and raisins (and sometimes figs, almonds, and lemon), is made for Epiphany, January 6. *Fritole* are tiny doughnuts associated with Carnevale (Mardi Gras). *Bussola* rings are made for Easter. Other popular treats are *bisse* (seahorse-shaped cookies) and *croccante* (made with toasted corn and almonds, similar in texture to peanut brittle).

Cocktails

Spritz: The dominant predinner drink *(aperitivo)* among Venetians is the *spritz.* This refreshing *aperitivo* mixes white wine, soda, and ice with a liquor of your choice and is garnished with an olive or skewer of fruit. Most popular with Venetians are *uno spritz con Campari* (bitter—traditionally the man's choice) or con *Aperol* (sweeter, a supposedly feminine choice). Between 18:00 and 20:00, this happy pink drink seems to dominate Venice's watering holes.

Bellini: A cocktail of Prosecco and white-peach puree; invented (and drunk by Hemingway) at the pricey Harry's American Bar (near San Marco-Vallaresso vaporetto stop).

Tiziano: Grape juice and Prosecco.

Sgroppino: A traditional drink of squeezed lemon juice, lemon gelato, and vodka, designed to finish off a meal.

Top Local Wines

Prosecco: Sparkling wine, usually a predinner drink, but can be ordered any time. It's neutral-tasting, making it easy to drink too much.

Soave: Crisp white (great with seafood) from near Verona. *Soave Classico* designates a higher quality.

Valpolicella: Light, dry, fruity red from the hills north of Verona. If you ordered the house wine *(vino della casa),* you're likely drinking Valpolicella.

Bardolino: Also made from Valpolicella grapes, it's a similar wine but grown near Lake Garda.

Amarone: Rich, intense red, with alcohol content at about 16 percent, made from Valpolicella grapes.

Fragolino: A sweet, slightly fizzy dessert wine made from a strawberry-flavored grape.

Grappa: Distilled *vinacce* (grape skins and stems left over from winemaking) make this powerful firewater. A *stravecchio* is an aged grappa, making it somewhat mellower.

Restaurants

While touristy restaurants are the scourge of Venice, the following places are still popular with actual Venetians and respect the tourists who happen in. First trick: Walk away from triple-language menus. Second trick: For freshness, eat fish. Most seafood dishes are the catch-of-the-day. Third trick: Eat later. A place may feel really touristy at 19:00, but if you come back at 21:00 it can be filled with locals. Tourists eat barbarically early, which is fine with the restaurants because they fill tables that would otherwise be used only once in an evening.

Near the Rialto Bridge
North of the Bridge

These restaurants are located beyond Campo Santi Apostoli, along the Strada Nova, the main drag going toward the train station.

Trattoria da Bepi, bright and alpine-paneled, feels like a classic. Ask for the seasonal specialties—the crab dishes are excellent. There's good seating inside and out (€8-10 pastas, €14-18 *secondi*, €1.50 cover, Fri-Wed 12:00-14:30 & 19:00-22:00, closed Thu, half a block off Campo Santi Apostoli on Salizada Pistor at #4550, tel. 041-528-5031, Loris).

Little **Vini da Gigio** has a passion for good food and a traditional Venetian menu (€12-16 pastas, €18-22 *secondi*, no cover, Wed-Sun 12:00-14:30 & 19:00-22:30, closed Mon-Tue, 4 blocks from Ca' d'Oro vaporetto stop on Fondamenta San Felice at #3628a—it's behind the church on Campo San Felice, tel. 041-528-5140).

Trattoria Ca' d'Oro, while a little less accessible and inviting to the tourist, is a venerable favorite with a small, appealing menu and an enthusiastic following. Just to sip wine and enjoy *cicchetti* at the bar is a treat—their *polpette* (tuna and potato meatballs) are famous, and the house wine will set you back just €0.50. It's also fine for a meal (€9-10 pastas, €10-11 *secondi*, €1.50 cover, Fri-Sat and Mon-Wed 11:30-14:30 & 18:30-22:30, Sun 18:30-22:30, closed Thu, reservations recommended, cash only; from the Ca' d'Oro vaporetto dock, walk 100 yards directly away from the canal, cross Strada Nova into an alley called Ramo Ca' d'Oro, and it's straight ahead at #3912; tel. 041-528-5324).

Osteria al Bomba is a *cicchetti* bar with a female touch, thanks to Giovanna. It's unusual (clean, no toothpicks, no cursing) and quite good, with lots of veggies. You can stand and eat at the bar—try a little €3 *crostino* with polenta and cod—or oversee the construction of the house *"antipasto misto di cicchetti"* plate (€15, enough fish and vegetables for two) and choose your wine by the glass from the posted list. A seat at the long table comes with a €2 *coperto* (daily 12:00-15:00 & 18:00-23:00; on Calle de l'Oca; from Campo Santi Apostoli, walk toward the train station, find #4294 on your right and turn down the small alley to #4297 ahead of you; tel. 041-520-5175).

East of the Rialto Bridge

The first four listings are relatively close to the bridge. The rest are near Campo Santa Maria Formosa, one of my favorite community scenes. While the restaurants fronting the square aren't much, several good options for dining lie a short walk away.

Osteria "Alla Botte," despite being located a minute from the Rialto Bridge, is packed with a casual neighborhood clientele in two simple, woody rooms. For a classic Venetian taste, try the €18 all-seafood *antipasto misto* (daily 12:00-15:00 & 19:00-23:00, two short blocks off Campo San Bartolomeo in the corner behind the statue—down Calle de la Bissa at #5482, notice the "day after" photo showing a debris-covered Venice after the notorious 1989

Pink Floyd open-air concert, tel. 041-520-9775, Cristiano).

Osteria di Santa Marina, on the wonderful Campo Marina, serves pricey, near-gourmet cuisine in a dressy dining room. The presentation is impressive, but you feel there's more pretense than love of food. Cheap-eating tricks are frowned on in this elegant, borderline stuffy restaurant (enticing menu with €15 pastas and €25 *secondi*, €3 cover, €75-80 fixed-price meals, Tue-Sat 12:30-14:30 & 19:30-22:00, Mon 19:30-22:00, closed Sun, reserve for dinner, eat indoors or outdoors on pleasant little square, between Rialto Bridge and Campo Santa Maria Formosa on Campo Marina at #5911, tel. 041-528-5239).

Rosticceria San Bartolomeo is a cheap—if confusing—self-service diner, a throwback budget eatery with a likeably surly staff. Take out, grab one of the few tiny tables, or munch at the bar—I'd skip the uninviting upper floor, where you pay higher prices and a €2 cover for table service (good €6-7 pasta, great fried *mozzarella al prosciutto* for €1.50, delightful fruit salad, €1 glasses of wine, prices listed on wall behind counter, no cover or service charge downstairs, daily 9:00-21:30, tel. 041-522-3569). To find it, imagine the statue on Campo San Bartolomeo walking backward 20 yards, turning left, and going under a passageway—now, follow him.

Osteria al Portego is a friendly neighborhood eatery—one of the best in town. Carlo serves good meals and excellent *cicchetti*—best enjoyed early, around 18:00 (from 19:00 to 21:00, tables are reserved for those ordering from the menu; the *cicchetti* are picked over by 21:00). Prices for food and wine are posted clearly on the wall. The *cicchetti* here can make a great meal, but you should also consider sitting down for a dinner from their fine menu. This place can get very busy, so reserve ahead if you want a table (€13 pastas, €0.80 glass of house wine, daily 10:30-15:00 & 18:00-21:30, near Campo Marina at #6015 on Calle Malvasia, tel. 041-522-9038). To find the Osteria, first find Rosticceria San Bartolomeo (listed above), then continue over a bridge to Campo San Lio, turn left, and follow Calle Carminati straight about 50 yards over another bridge; it's straight ahead.

Near Campo Santa Maria Formosa: **Osteria alle Testiere** is my top dining recommendation in Venice. Hugely respected, they are dedicated to quality, serving up creative, artfully presented market-fresh seafood (there's no meat on the menu), homemade pastas, and fine wine in what the chef calls a "Venetian Nouvelle" style. With only 22 seats, it's tight and homey, yet elegant. They have daily specials, 10 wines by the glass, and one agenda: a great dining experience. Luca, the owner/host, is gracious and passionate about his food. This is one place to let loose and trust your host. Reservations are almost always necessary for their three seatings: 12:30, 19:00, and 21:30 (€19 pastas, €25 *secondi*, plan on spending

€50 for dinner, no cover or service charge, closed Sun-Mon; on Calle del Mondo Novo, just off Campo Santa Maria Formosa, at #5801; tel. 041-522-7220).

Osteria al Mascaron is where I've gone for years to watch Gigi, Momi, and their food-loving band of ruffians dish up rustic-yet-sumptuous pastas with steamy seafood to salivating foodies. The pastas seem pricey at €24-32, but they're meant for two (it's OK to ask for single portions). The €16 *antipasto misto* plate—have fun pointing—and two glasses of wine make a terrific light meal, and their seafood pastas make beautiful memories (€2 cover, Mon-Sat 12:00-15:00 & 19:00-23:00, closed Sun, reservations smart Fri-Sat; on Calle Longa Santa Maria Formosa, a block past Campo Santa Maria Formosa, at #5225; tel. 041-522-5995).

Fast and Cheap Eats: The veggie stand on Campo Santa Maria Formosa is a fixture. For *döner kebabs* (€3.50) and pizza to go (€2/slice), head down Calle Longa to **Peter Pan** at #6249 (daily 11:00-24:00). For classier pizza to go, visit **Cip Ciap** (next to Osteria alle Testiere near the bridge, at #5799a).

West of the Rialto Bridge

Most of these places are informal, serving *cicchetti* and/or light meals. The first bars listed are within 200 yards of each other, a few steps behind the Rialto fish market; the rest are farther away from this hive of eateries (see map on page 252). This area is very crowded by day, nearly empty early in the evening, and crowded with young Venetians later.

Most bars are closed 15:00-18:00 (though Cantina Do Mori and Ostaria ai Storti stay open all day), and offer glasses of house wine for under €1, better wine for around €2.50, and *cicchetti* for €1-2. At each place, look for the list of snacks and wine by the glass at the bar or on the wall. If you're ready for dessert, try dipping a Burano biscuit in a glass of strawberry-flavored *fragolino* or another sweet dessert wine.

A strip of five places between Campo San Giacomo and the Grand Canal (such as the recommended Bancogiro Bar and Al Mercà) make a thriving youth *spritz* scene that's worth a look even if you don't eat or drink there.

Cantina Do Mori has been famous with locals (since 1462) and savvy travelers (since 1982) as a convivial place for fine wine. You'll choose from a forest of little edibles on toothpicks and *francobolli* (a spicy selection of 20 tiny, mayo-soaked sandwiches nicknamed "stamps"). Go here to be abused in a fine atmosphere—the frowns are part of the shtick (Mon-Sat 8:30-20:00, closed Sun, stand-up only, arrive early before the *cicchetti* are gone, tel. 041-522-5401). From the Rialto Bridge, walk 200 yards down Ruga dei Orefici, away from St. Mark's Square—then turn left on Ruga

The Stand-Up Progressive Venetian Pub-Crawl Dinner

My favorite Venetian dinner is a pub crawl *(giro d'ombra)*—a tradition unique to Venice, where no cars means easy crawling. (*Giro* means stroll, and *ombra*—slang for a glass of wine—means shade, from the old days when a portable wine bar scooted with the shadow of the Campanile bell tower across St. Mark's Square.)

Venice's residential back streets hide plenty of characteristic bars *(bacari)* with countless trays of interesting toothpick munchies *(cicchetti)* and blackboards listing the wines that are uncorked and served by the glass. This is a great way to mingle and have fun with the Venetians. Bars don't stay open very late, and the *cicchetti* selection is best early, so start your evening by 18:00. Most bars are closed on Sunday. For a stress-free pub crawl, consider taking a tour with the charming Alessandro Schezzini (see page 35).

Cicchetti bars have a social stand-up zone and a cozy gaggle of tables where you can generally sit down with your *cicchetti* or order from a simple menu. In some of the more popular places, the crowds happily spill out into the street. Food generally costs the same price whether you stand or sit.

I've listed plenty of pubs in walk-

Vechia San Giovanni, then right at Sotoportego Do Mori to #429.

Bar all'Arco, a bustling one-room joint that's almost across from Cantina Do Mori at #436, is particularly enjoyable for its tiny open-face sandwiches (closed Sun, tel. 041-520-5666).

Ostaria ai Storti, which has a homey feel, is a fun place to congregate. Check out the photo of the market in 1909, below the bar. Alessandro speaks English and enjoys helping educate travelers while serving *fragolino* (€8 pastas, €12 *secondi*, €1.50 cover, daily 9:00-22:30, Nov-March closes 15:00-18:00, 20 yards from Cantina Do Mori and around the corner on Calle San Matio at #819, tel. 041-523-6861).

Cantina Do Spade is run by Sebastiano, who clearly lists the *cicchetti* and wines of the day (daily 11:00-15:00 & 18:00-21:00, 30 yards down Calle de le Do Spade from Ostaria ai Storti at #860, tel. 041-521-0583).

At **Pesce Pronto,** you can sample fish while watching the market action. Bruno and Umberto serve artful fish hors d'oeuvres, *sfornato con pesce* (a savory, baked pastry), and many other fresh ing order for a quick or extended crawl. If you've crawled enough, most of these bars make a fine one-stop, sit-down dinner.

While you can order a plate, Venetians prefer going one-by-one...sipping their wine and trying this...then give me one of those...and so on. Try deep-fried mozzarella cheese, gorgonzola, calamari, artichoke hearts, and anything ugly on a toothpick. *Crostini* (small toasted bread with something on it) are popular, as are marinated seafood, olives, and prosciutto with melon. Meat and fish (*pesce;* PESH-ay) munchies can be expensive; veggies (*verdure*) are cheap, at about €3 for a meal-sized plate. In many places, there's a set price per food item (e.g., €1.50). To get a plate of assorted appetizers for €8 (or more, depending on how hungry you are), ask for *"Un piatto classico di cicchetti misti da €8"* (oon pee-AH-toh KLAH-see-koh dee cheh-KET-tee MEE-stee dah OH-toh ay-OO-roh). Bread sticks (*grissini*) are free for the asking.

Bar-hopping Venetians enjoy an *aperitivo,* a before-dinner drink. Boldly order a Bellini, a *spritz con Aperol,* or a Prosecco, and draw approving looks from the natives.

Drink the house wines. A small glass of house red or white wine (*ombra rosso* or *ombra bianco*) or a small beer (*birrino*) costs about €1. The house keg wine is cheap—€1 per glass, about €4 per liter. *Vin bon,* Venetian fine wine, may run you from €2 to €6 per little glass. There are usually several fine wines uncorked and available by the glass. A good last drink is *fragolino,* the local sweet wine—*bianco* or *rosso.* It often comes with a little cookie (*biscotti*) for dipping.

fish tidbits—all at a fair price. This fancy hole-in-the-wall is fun for a quick bite—eat standing up or take it to go. From 12:45 to 14:15, they serve €10-12 "express plates" of pasta and other choices (Tue and Sat 9:00-15:00 & 18:00-20:00, Wed-Fri 9:00-15:00 & 19:00-23:30, closed Sun-Mon, facing the fish market on Calle de le Becarie o Panataria at #319, tel. 041-822-0298).

The **Bancogiro Bar** is expensive but good if you like strong cheese and canalside tables (€3.50 cover, €2.50 *cicchetti* at bar, €15 cheese plate, Tue-Sun 12:00-23:00, closed Mon, on Campo San Giacomo at #122, tel. 041-523-2061).

Al Mercà, a few steps away and off the canal, is an even livelier little nook with a happy crowd, where young locals gather to grab drinks and little snacks. The price list is clear, and I've found the crowd to be welcoming to tourists interested in connecting (stand at the bar only—no tables, Mon-Sat 9:30-14:30 & 18:00-21:00, closed Sun, on Campo Cesare Battisti at #213).

Antica Ostaria Ruga Rialto, a.k.a. "the Ruga," is a neighborhood fixture where Giorgio and Marco serve great bar snacks and wine to a devoted clientele. Treats here are their polenta, sardine with onions, and veggies. Bar or table, no problem—they're happy to make you a €3, €6, or €10 mixed plate (daily 11:00-14:30 & 19:00-24:00, easy to find—just past the Chinese restaurant on Ruga Vechia San Giovanni at #695a, tel. 041-521-1243).

Osteria al Diavolo e l'Acquasanta, three blocks west of the Rialto Bridge, serves good—if pricey—Venetian dishes, and makes a handy lunch stop for sightseers. Though they list *cicchetti* and wine by the glass on the wall, I'd come here for a light meal rather than for appetizers (€8-11 pastas, €12-17 *secondi*, 12 percent service charge, Wed-Mon 12:00-14:30 & 19:00-21:30, closed Tue, hiding at #561 on Calle de la Madona—a quiet street just off Ruga Vechia San Giovanni, tel. 041-277-0307).

Antica Birraria la Corte is an everyday eatery on the delightful Campo San Polo, between the Rialto Bridge and the Frari Church. Popular for its €7-10 pizza, calzones, and salads, it fills the far side of this cozy, family-filled square. While the interior is a sprawling beer hall, it's a joy to eat on the square, where metal tables teeter on the cobbles, the wind plays with the paper mats, and children run free (€11-12 pastas, €14-19 *secondi*, €2 cover, daily 12:00-14:30 & 19:00-22:30, Campo San Polo 2168, see map on page 226, tel. 041-275-0570).

Trattoria Pizzeria al Nono Risorto is unpretentious, inexpensive, youthful, and famous for serving good pizza in a nice setting. You'll sit in a gravelly garden under a leafy canopy, surrounded by Italians enjoying huge €8 salads, pastas, and pizzas, and €12-17 grilled meat or fish dishes (Fri-Tue 12:00-14:30 & 19:00-22:30, Thu 19:00-22:30, closed Wed, reservations smart on weekends; from Rialto fish market, get out your map and walk 3 minutes away from the Rialto to Campo San Cassiano—it's just over the bridge on Sotoportego de Siora Bettina at #2338; tel. 041-524-1169).

Near St. Mark's Square
For locations, see the map on page 246.

Dining near St. Mark's Square
The following three places are a few blocks east of St. Mark's Square and offer classy dining experiences. The first two listings are the best canalside dining values I've found in Venice. Both specialize in fish, and have a reasonable-for-the-romantic-setting menu. If you want a canalside seat for dinner, call to reserve it, and honor your reservation; don't go to another restaurant. To reach these from St. Mark's Square, head behind the basilica to Campo San Provolo, then follow Calle Osmarin to the Ponte dei Greci bridge and Fondamenta San Lorenzo. To get to the third, head up

Chiesa from Campo San Provolo.

Ristorante alla Conchiglia has a few lovely tables that line the sleepy canal and a fresh, bright interior. They specialize in turbot, a flatfish similar to flounder. There's a €1.50 cover and 12 percent service charge, which is waived if you order the fixed-price meal (€7-10 pizzas lunch only, big €14 salads, basic €15 fixed-price meal, daily 12:00-22:30, closed Dec and Jan, on Fondamenta San Lorenzo at #4990, tel. 041-528-9095, Franco and son Alessandro).

Trattoria da Giorgio ai Greci, right next door, also has a half-dozen canalside tables. They offer €17 and €21 fixed-price meals with no cover or service charge—the €21 version has more interesting and authentic choices (€1.50 cover and 12 percent service charge for à la carte orders, daily 12:00-22:30, on Fondamenta San Lorenzo at #4988, tel. 041-528-9780, enthusiastically run by Giorgio and sons Davide and chatty Roberto).

Ristorante Antica Sacrestia is a classic restaurant where the owner, Pino, takes a hands-on approach to greeting guests. His staff serve creative €33-50 fixed-price meals and a humdrum €20 *turistico* one. You can also order à la carte; try the delightful €21 antipasto spread. There's no cover or service charge, and my readers are welcome to a free *sgroppino* (lemon vodka after-dinner drink) upon request (€12-16 pastas and pizzas, €17-30 *secondi*, Tue-Sun 11:30-15:00 & 18:00-22:30, closed Mon, immediately behind San Zaninovo/Giovanni Novo Church on Calle de la Sacrestia at #4442, tel. 041-523-0749).

Budget Eateries near St. Mark's Square

Picnicking isn't allowed on St. Mark's Square, but you can legally take your snacks to the nearby Giardinetti Reali, the small park along the waterfront west of the Piazzetta.

"Sandwich Row": On Calle de le Rasse, just steps away from the tourist intensity at St. Mark's Square, is a handy strip I call "Sandwich Row." Lined with sandwich bars, it's the closest place to St. Mark's to get a decent sandwich at an affordable price with a place to sit down (most places open daily 7:00-24:00, €1 extra to sit; from the Bridge of Sighs, head down the Riva and take the second lane on the left). I particularly like **Birreria Forst,** a café which serves a selection of meaty €2.80 sandwiches with tasty sauce on wheat bread, or made-to-order sandwiches for around €3.80 (Sun-Fri 10:00-21:00, closed Sat, air-con, rustic wood tables, Calle de le Rasse at #4540, tel. 041-523-0557) and **Bar Verde,** a more modern sandwich bar with fun people-watching views from its corner tables (big €4 sandwiches, splittable €8 salads, fresh pastries, at the end of Calle de le Rasse at #4526, facing Campo Santi Filippo e Giacomo).

Ristorante alla Basilica, just one street behind St. Mark's

Romantic Canalside Settings

Of course, if you want a meal with a canal view, it generally comes with lower quality or a higher price. But if you're aiming for a canalside memory, these places can be great. I've listed the better-value places below, along with advice for coping with the tourist traps.

Near the Rialto Bridge: Several *cicchetti* bars line the Grand Canal, with front tables just off **Campo San Giacomo** (a.k.a. "Giacometto"), between the market and the Rialto Bridge (described on page 279). You can get good light meals in this area, but these bars don't offer romantic dining per se.

Rialto Bridge Tourist Traps: Venetians are embarrassed by the lousy food and aggressive "service" at the string of joints dominating the best romantic, Grand Canal-fringing real estate in town. Still, if you want to linger over dinner with a view of the most famous bridge and the songs of gondoliers oaring by (and don't mind eating with other tourists), this can be enjoyable. Don't trust the waiter's recommendations for special meals. The budget ideal would be to get a simple pizza or pasta and a drink for €15, and savor the ambience without getting ripped off. But few restaurants will allow you to get off that easy. To avoid a dispute over the bill, ask if there's a minimum charge—before

Basilica, is a church-run, indoor, institutional-feeling place that serves a solid €13 fixed-price lunch (including water) daily from 11:45 to 15:00. It's not self-serve—you'll be seated and can choose a pasta, a *secondi*, and a vegetable side dish off the menu (sometimes a wait, air-con, great bathrooms, on Calle dei Albanesi at #4255, tel. 041-522-0524).

Rizzo, like most Venetian "bars," is an eat-at-the-counter café with sandwiches, pizza, pastries, and other reasonably priced snacks. It stands out for its handy location, north of St. Mark's Square on the main drag of Calle dei Fabbri, and its tiny grocery shelf with yogurt and other quick bites (Mon-Sat 8:00-20:00, closed Sun, on Calle dei Fabbri at #933a, tel. 041-522-3388).

In Dorsoduro

Near the Accademia Bridge

Ristorante/Pizzeria Accademia Foscarini, next to the Accademia Bridge and Galleria, offers decent €10-11 pizzas in a great canalside setting. Their toasted *farciti* sandwich is a local favorite (€6.50 at the table). Though the pizzas may be forgettable, this place is both you sit down (most places have one).

Near the Accademia: Ristorante/Pizzeria Accademia Foscarini, next to the Accademia Bridge, offers decent pizzas overlooking the canal with no cover or service charge (see page previous page).

East of St. Mark's Square: Ristorante alla Conchiglia and **Trattoria da Giorgio ai Greci,** a few blocks behind St. Mark's; both have a few tables next to one of the smaller canals frequented by gondoliers (photo oppo-

site, see page 283).

Overlooking the Giu-decca Canal: Terrazza del Casin dei Nobili, located in Zattere—on the Venice side of the wide Giudecca Canal—gets the warm, romantic evening sun (next page).

On Fondamente Nove with a View of the Open Lagoon: Ristorante Algiubagio offers a good opportunity to eat well while overlooking the lagoon (next page).

On Burano: Trattoria al Gatto Nero sits on a tranquil canal under a tilting bell tower in the pastel townscape of Burano. If you're touring the lagoon and want to enjoy Burano without the crowds, go late and consider a dinner here (see page 214).

EATING IN VENICE

scenic and practical—on each visit to Venice, I grab a pizza lunch here while I ponder the Grand Canal bustle (no cover or service charge, May-Oct Wed-Mon 7:00-22:30, Nov-April until 21:00, closed Tue, on Rio Terà A. Foscarini at #878c, tel. 041-522-7281).

Enoteca Cantine del Vino Già Schiavi is much-loved for its €1 *cicchetti* and €3.50-4 sandwiches (order from list on board).

It's also a good place for a €1-2 glass of wine and appetizers (Mon-Sat 8:00-20:30, closed Sun, 100 yards from Accademia art museum on San Trovaso canal; facing Accademia, take a right and then a forced left at the canal to the second bridge—it's at #992, tel. 041-523-0034). You're wel-come to enjoy your wine and finger food hanging out at the bar, sitting on the bridge out front, or in the nearby square—which actually has grass. This is primarily a wine shop with great prices for bottles to go—and plastic glasses for picnickers.

Terrazza del Casin dei Nobili, located on Zattere (the Venice side of the Giudecca Canal), takes full advantage of the warm, romantic evening sun. They serve finely crafted, regional specialties with creativity at tolerable prices. The canalside seating is breezy and beautiful, but comes with the rumble of *vaporetti* from the nearby stop. The interior is bright and hip (good €9-10 pizzas, €10-13 pastas, €15-25 *secondi*, €2 cover, Fri-Wed 12:00-23:00, closed Thu; from Zattere vaporetto stop, turn left to #924; tel. 041-520-6895, Ruggiero and Eleonora). On Wednesday and Sunday evenings in summer, there's live music nearby on the Zattere promenade—see page 301.

Near Campo San Barnaba

A number of restaurants are near this small square, a short walk from the Accademia. As these are each within a few steps of each other and the energy and atmosphere can vary, I like to survey the options before choosing (although reservations may be necessary later in the evening).

Casin dei Nobili ("Pleasure Palace of Nobles")—related to the Terrazza del Casin dei Nobili, listed above—has a high-energy, informal, modern setting with outdoor seating on a patio. The creative, €18 fixed-price lunch specials are worth it (€13 pastas, €13-25 *secondi,* good pizzas, €10 "fantasy salads," Tue-Sun 12:00-15:00 & 19:00-23:00, closed Mon; on Calle de le Casin, a half-block south of Campo San Barnaba, at #2765; tel. 041-241-1841, Damiano).

Pane Vino e San Daniele is a busy little place that feels real, with the TV on, an enticing blackboard listing the day's specials, and the kitchen action filling its dining room (€7.50 pastas, €10-12 salads and *secondi*, €1 cover, on Calle Longa San Barnaba at #2861, tel. 041-243-9865).

Enoteca e Trattoria la Bitta is dark and woody, with a soft-jazz bistro feel and a small, forgettable back patio. They serve beautifully presented, traditional Venetian food with—proudly—no fish. Their helpful waitstaff and small menu are clearly focused on quality. Reservations are required (€10 pastas, €16-25 *secondi,* €2 cover, dinner only, Mon-Sat 18:30-23:00, closed Sun, cash only, between previous two listings on Calle Longa San Barnaba at #2753a, tel. 041-523-0531).

Elsewhere in Venice

On Fondamente Nove: **Ristorante Algiubagio,** though not cheap, is a good place to eat well overlooking the northern lagoon. The name is a combination of the owners' four names—Alberto, Giulio, Barbara, and Giovanna—who strive to impress visitors with quality, creative Venetian cuisine made using the best ingredients. Reserve a table on the lagoon facing the island of San Michele or in their classy cantina dining room (€16-18 pastas, €24-25 *secondi*, €3.50 cover, €29-42 fixed-price meals, Wed-Mon 12:00-15:00 & 19:00-22:30, closed Tue; on Fondamente Nove, to the left of the vaporetto dock as you face the water, at #5039; tel. 041-523-6084). This is a convenient place to eat if you're taking the vaporetto out to the islands in the lagoon (described in Venice's Lagoon Tour chapter; see map on page 207).

Near Campo Santa Maria Nova: **Osteria da Alberto,** with excellent daily specials, €13 seafood dishes, €9-11 pastas, a good house wine, and a woody and characteristic interior, is one of my standbys. It's smart to reserve at night—I'd request a table in the front (€1.80 cover, Mon-Sat 12:00-14:30 & 18:30-22:30, closed Sun; on Calle Larga Giacinto Gallina, midway between Campo Santi Apostoli and Campo Santi Giovanni e Paolo, next to Ponte de la Panada bridge at #5401—see map on page 252; tel. 041-523-8153, run by Graziano and Giovanni).

Near the Train Station: There are piles of eateries near the station. The **food circus** in the station itself is quite good, with peaceful garden seating out back in summer, big €3-4 sandwiches, and slices of pizza for €2.90. A block away is a small branch of the efficient and economic **Brek,** a popular self-service cafeteria chain (€4-5 pastas, €6-9 *secondi*, daily 11:30-22:00, head left as you leave the station and walk about 50 yards past the bridge along Rio Terà Lista di Spagna to #124—see map on page 260).

Gelato

You'll find good *gelaterie* in every Venetian neighborhood, offering one-scoop cones for about €1.50. Look for the words *artigianale* or

produzione propria, which indicates that a shop makes its own gelato. The popular, inventive, upscale **Grom** ice-cream chain has two branches in Venice, one on Campo San Barnaba at #2761 (beyond the Accademia bridge), and another one at the Strada Nova at #3844, not far from the Rialto (cheapest cone-€2.50, both open Sun-Thu 12:00-22:30, Fri-Sat 12:00-23:30).

On St. Mark's Square, two venerable cafés have *gelato* counters in summer: **Gran Caffè Lavena** (April-Oct daily until 24:00, no gelato Nov-March, first café to left of the Clock Tower, behind the first orchestra, at #134) and **Todaro** (on the corner of the Piazzetta at #5, near the water and just under the column topped by St. Theodore slaying a crocodile).

VENICE WITH CHILDREN

Some of the best fun I've had with my kids has been in Venice. The city doesn't need an amusement park...it is one big fantasy world. It's safe and like nothing else your kids have ever seen. Though there's lots of pavement and few parks or playgrounds, just being there—and free to wander—can be delightful.

If you're bringing the family, consider these tips:

• Don't overdo it. Tackle just one or two key sights each day and mix in a healthy dose of enjoyable activities. A vaporetto ride is a great way to start your visit.

• Follow this book's crowd-beating tips. Kids dislike long lines even more than you do.

• Eat dinner early (19:00 at restaurants), and skip the romantic places. Try self-service cafeterias, out-of-the-way bars (children are welcome), or fast-food restaurants, where kids can move around without bothering others. For pizza, favorite choices for kids include *margherita* (tomato and cheese) and spicy *diavola*, which is the closest thing on the menu to sliced pepperoni sausage (if you ask for *peperoni*, you'll get bell peppers). Picnic lunches and dinners work well. For ready-made picnics, drop by an *alimentari* (deli) or a supermarket. For fast and kid-friendly meals in the center, you'll find a couple of American hamburger joints between the Rialto Bridge and St. Mark's Square, great pizzerias on squares everywhere, and plenty of gelato.

• Give your kid a cheap camera. Venice turns anyone into a photographer.

• Look for family and child discounts. If buying the Doge's Palace/

Correr Museum combo-ticket, ask for the family discount (available to two adults with at least two children up to age 18). A family ticket is also available for the Chorus Pass. The Rolling Venice youth discount pass gives discounts on many sights and transportation for travelers under 30 (see page 26).

• Venice is great for older children and teens, but presents challenges if you're traveling with toddlers or infants. You'll need to keep toddlers safely in hand, as there are rarely any fences or walls between the sidewalk and the water. (The Campo Santa Maria Formosa is the rare place in Venice where you'll find railings.) You won't have much use for strollers—with hundreds of stepped bridges, Venice is a frustrating obstacle course. Try toting your baby in a carrier instead.

• While Venice is short on parks, its many small squares have served as playgrounds for local children for centuries. Let your kids run around while you take a seat at a café or bench.

• Turn the city into a scavenger hunt. Look on buildings for a winged lion, search the shop windows for a mask with a long nose, scour the canal for a fire boat—and extra points for a (yuck) dead pigeon! Wait for the world's first digital clock (on the Clock Tower

in St. Mark's Square) to flip over. Find pickpockets in action at the viewing point for the Bridge of Sighs. Wave at romantics in gondolas from bridges over popular gondola routes.

• In Venice, pick up a copy of *VivaVenice: A Guide to Exploring, Learning, and Having Fun* by Paola Zoffoli. It's full of interesting facts, and it's sold at many bookstores in the city. *Venice for Kids,* by Elisabetta Pasqualin, is a great guidebook for tweens and up, available at many museum bookshops. *A Walk Thru Venice* (purchase locally) is a fun history book for older kids.

• Involve your children in the trip. Let them lead you through the maze of Venice's back streets. Get lost together. If your children are old enough, they can be the tour guides and read this book's self-guided tours. (Standard tip for good guides: a two-scoop gelato.)

• If you're taking the train to another city, check for family discounts; see page 389 for information.

Sights and Activities

Watch the pigeons on St. Mark's Square. (Though feeding them is now against the law, they're still around.) If you yell, the birds will just ignore you, but tossing a sweater into the air kicks off a pigeon evacuation. And anyone of any age enjoys the magic of **St. Mark's Square at night.**

Ride the elevator to the top of the **Campanile** bell tower to enjoy the grand view, and be there as the huge bells whip into ear-shattering action at the top of each hour (see the St. Mark's Square Tour chapter).

Take in a **glassblowing demonstration** at Galleria San Marco (just off St. Mark's Square, see page 294). Part of the **Doge's Palace** tour includes the dark, dank prison and a creative armory.

Ride lots of **boats** (vaporetto, gondola, *traghetto*, or speedboat tours of the lagoon). Sit in the front seat of a vaporetto for my Grand Canal Cruise. See how many kinds of service boats you can spot while on the canal (UPS, police, fire, and so on).

The Rialto **fish market** is as fishy as they get (closed Sun, on the canal two blocks west of Rialto Bridge). Watch the people unload the boats at the market. You can leave by *traghetto* and cross the Grand Canal (*traghetto* dock at market).

Be choosy when taking kids to museums. The venerable and fascinating (to adults) Accademia will probably bore children. But don't skip art entirely. Kids like holding mirrors to see the ceiling paintings at the **Scuola San Rocco.** The **Peggy Guggenheim Collection** has colorful modern art, by Picasso and others, that interests kids.

A **children's park** is near the train station (facing the canal with your back to station, walk down the stairs and a block left past the shops to a small opening in the wall on the left—you'll see the playground inside). The bigger **Giardini park** has swings and playground equipment (on the far end of town—in Venice's "fish tail," near Giardini vaporetto stop). The **Lido** (beach) island sounds more intriguing than it is, though it can be a kid-friendly place to visit or stay, given the beaches and bike-riding possibilities.

If your kids are likely to enjoy a **soccer game,** consider a trip to the stadium located in the Santa Elena district. Venice's team is currently in the fifth-ranked Italian Serie D league (not so good), so the crowds aren't as enthusiastic as usual, but games are fun nonetheless. Matches take place on Sundays from September to June (ask at the TI). Buy a scarf with the team colors—black, orange, and green—and join the fun. Goal!

Make a point to include some **Venetian history.** Taking advantage of the information in this book, explain St. Mark (look for winged lions, page 77), the birth of the city (page 366), how and why the city floods (page 36), and the story of the gondolas (page 298).

SHOPPING IN VENICE

Long a city of aristocrats, luxury goods, and merchants, Venice was built to entice. While no one claims it's great for bargains, it has a shopping charm that makes paying too much strangely enjoyable. Carnevale masks, lace, glass, antique paper products, designer clothing, fancy accessories, and paintings are all popular with tourists visiting Venice. But remember—anything not made locally is brought in by boat—and therefore generally more expensive than elsewhere in Italy. The shops near St. Mark's Square charge the most.

Shops are generally open from 9:00 to 13:00 and from 15:00 to 19:30. In touristy Venice, more shops are open on Sunday than in the rest of the country. If you're buying a substantial amount from nearly any shop, bargain—it's accepted and almost expected. Offer less and offer to pay cash; merchants are very conscious of the bite taken by credit-card companies.

For ordinary clothing and housewares, the best all-purpose department store is the Coin store on the St. Mark's Square side of the Rialto Bridge (Mon-Sat 9:30-19:30, Sun 11:00-19:30; from the bridge, head north toward Ferrovia, the train station).

For information on VAT refunds and customs regulations, see page 14.

Shopping Streets

Here's the best route to kick off your Venetian shopping spree:

St. Mark's Square: Walk the entire colonnaded square past pricey jewelry, glass, lace, and clothing stores. A half-block detour out the far end leads to several high-fashion shops along Calle Vallaresso.

Mercerie: This is the main street between St. Mark's Square (also labeled as "Marzarie," leave the square from under the Clock

Mask Making

In the 1700s, when Venice was Europe's party town, masks were popular—sometimes even mandatory—to preserve the anonymity of visiting nobles doing things forbidden back home. At Carnevale (the weeks-long Mardi Gras leading up to Lent), everyone wore masks. The most popular were based on characters from the lowbrow comedic theater called commedia dell'arte. We all know Harlequin (simple, Lone Ranger-type masks), but there were also long-nosed masks for the hypocritical plague doctor, pretty Columbina masks, and so on.

Masks are made with the simple technique of papier-mâché. You make a mold of clay, smear it with Vaseline (to make it easy to remove the finished mask), then create the mask by draping layers of paper and glue atop the clay mold.

You'll see mask shops all over town. Just behind St. Mark's Square, on a quiet canal just inland from the Church of San Zaccaria (on Fondamente de l'Osmarin), is a corner with two fascinating mask and costume shops. The **Ca' del Sol** mask and costume shop (two showrooms connected by a little bridge) and **Atelier Marega** are both worth a look. After you cross the bridge to the second Ca' del Sol shop, head to the next door farther on to the wood-carving shop of **Paolo Brandolisio** (Mon-Fri 9:30-13:00 & 15:30-19:00, tel. 041-522-4155, http://paolobrandolisio.altervista.org). You can pop in to watch Paolo carving traditional oars and *forcola* (the oarlock of the gondola, a symbol of Venetian life and a popular art piece). To check out Paolo virtually, search for "forcole e remi" on YouTube to watch videos of him working.

Out near the Frari Church, the **"Tragicomica" Mask Shop** is highly respected and likely to have artisans at work (daily 10:00-19:00, 200 yards past Church of San Polo on Calle dei Nomboli at #2800, tel. 041-721-102, www.tragicomica.it).

Tower) and the Rialto, noted for its high rent, high prices, fancy windows, and designer labels. Then, go over the...

Rialto Bridge: The streets at either side are a cancan of shopping temptations. Continue down the street to...

Ruga Vechia San Giovanni (a.k.a. Ruga): Away from the intensity of the tourist center, you'll enter the San Polo neighborhood (west side of Rialto Bridge) with plenty of inviting shops, but fewer crowds and better prices.

Elsewhere in Venice: Art-lovers browse the **art galleries** between the Accademia and the Peggy Guggenheim Collection.

Venetian Glass

Popular Venetian glass is available in many forms: vases, tea sets, decanters, glasses, jewelry, lamps, mod sculptures (such as solid-

glass aquariums), and on and on. Shops will ship it home for you, but you're likely to pay as much or more for the shipping as you are for the item(s), and you may have to pay duty on larger purchases. Make sure the shop insures their merchandise *(assicurazione)*, or you're out of luck if it breaks. If your item arrives broken and it has been insured, take a photo of the pieces, send it to the shop, and they'll replace it for free. For a cheap, packable souvenir, consider the glass-bead necklaces sold at vendors' stalls throughout Venice.

Some visitors feel that because they're in Venice, they ought to grab the opportunity to buy glass. Remember that you can buy fine glass back home, too (Venice stopped forbidding its glassblowers from leaving the republic a few centuries ago), under less time pressure.

If you'd like to watch a quick glassblowing demonstration, try **Galleria San Marco,** a tour-group staple on St. Mark's Square at #139, which offers great demos every few minutes. They let individual travelers flashing this book sneak in with tour groups to see the show (and sales pitch). And, if you buy anything, show this book and they'll take 20 percent off the listed price. The gallery faces the square behind the orchestra nearest to the church; come to the door at #139, go through the shop and climb the stairs (daily 9:00-18:00, tel. 041-271-8671, fax 041-271-8679, info@galleriasan marco.it, manager Marino Busetto).

If you're serious about glass, visit the island of **Murano,** its glass museum, and many shops (see page 208). You'll find greater variety on Murano, but prices are usually the same as in Venice.

Souvenir Ideas

The most popular souvenirs and gifts are Murano glass (described above), Burano lace (fun lace umbrellas for little girls), Carnevale masks (fine shops and artisans all over town), art reproductions (posters, postcards, and books), prints of Venetian scenes, traditional stationery (pens and marbled paper products of all kinds), calendars with Venetian scenes, silk ties, scarves, and plenty of goofy knickknacks (Titian mousepads, gondolier T-shirts, and little plastic gondola condom holders).

Along Venice's many shopping streets, you'll notice fly-by-night street vendors selling knockoffs of famous-maker handbags

(Louis Vuitton, Gucci, etc.). These vendors are willing to bargain. But buyer beware: If you're caught purchasing fakes, you could get hit with a fine. Legitimate manufacturers are raising a stink about these street merchants, and the government is trying to rid the city of them. Authorities frustrated in their attempts to actually arrest the merchants have made it illegal to buy counterfeit items. Their hope: The threat of a huge fine will scare potential customers away—so unlicensed merchants will be driven out of business and off the streets.

NIGHTLIFE IN VENICE

You must experience Venice after dark. The city is quiet at night, as tour groups stay in the cheaper hotels of Mestre on the mainland, and the masses of day-trippers return to their beach resorts and cruise ships.

Do what you must to reserve energy for evening: Take a nap, or skip a few sights during the day. When the sun goes down, a cool breeze blows in from the lagoon, the lanterns come on, the peeling plaster glows in the moonlight, and Venice resumes its position as Europe's most romantic city.

Though Venice comes alive after dark, it does not party into the wee hours. By 22:00, restaurants are winding down; by 23:00, many bars are closing; and by midnight, the city is shut tight. Evenings are made for wandering—even Venice's dark and distant back lanes are considered safe after nightfall. Enjoy the orchestras on St. Mark's Square. Experience Vivaldi's *Four Seasons* in a candlelit 17th-century church. Pop into small bars for an appetizer and a drink. Lick gelato. As during the day, it's the city itself that is the star. But Venice under a cloak of darkness has an extra dose of magic and mystery—the ambience that has attracted visitors since the days of Casanova.

Sightseeing

You can stretch your sightseeing day at the Accademia (Tue-Sun until 19:15), Correr Museum (April-Oct daily until 19:00), Punta della Dogana (Wed-Mon until 19:00), and the Campanile (the bell tower on St. Mark's Square, daily Easter-June and Oct until 19:00, July-Sept until 21:00, closes at 15:45 in the off-season). The self-guided walks in this book are most enjoyable in the evening.

Gondola Rides

Gondolas cost lots more after 19:00, but are also more romantic and relaxing under the moon. A rip-off for some, this is a traditional must for romantics. Gondoliers charge €80 for a 40-minute ride during the day, €100 from 19:00 on. These prices are standard, and listed in the TI's *Shows & Events* brochure, as well as on the gondoliers' association website (www.gondolavenezia.it). To add *musica* (a singer and an accordionist), you'll need to arrange it in advance, and it'll cost an additional €110 before 19:00, or €130 after 19:00. You can divide the cost—and the romance—among up to six people per boat, but you'll need to save two seats for the musicians if you choose to be serenaded. Only two seats (the ones in back) are next to each other.

Because you might get a narration plus conversation with your gondolier, talk with several and choose one you like who speaks English well. To avoid misunderstandings, establish the price and duration of the trip before boarding, enjoy your ride, and pay only when you're finished. I don't recommend haggling, but if you want to try, you might find softer prices during the day. Most gondoliers honor the official prices, but a few might try to scam you out of some extra euros.

Pick a gondola station in an area you'd enjoy paddling in. I often go to the Bacino Orseolo gondoliers just off the northwest corner of St. Mark's Square (go through Sotoportego de l'Arco Celeste), but there are stations all over the more frequented parts of Venice. On cold, dark winter evenings, you will have trouble finding a gondolier; try at Hotel Bauer, on Campo San Moisè, or ask your hotelier for help.

If you've hired musicians and want to hear a Venetian song *(un canto Veneziano)*, try requesting *"Venezia La Luna e Tu."* Asking to hear *"O Sole Mio"* (which comes from Naples) is like asking a lounge singer in Cleveland to sing "The Eyes of Texas."

Glide through nighttime Venice with your head on someone's shoulder. Follow the moon as it sails past otherwise unseen buildings. Silhouettes gaze down from bridges while window glitter spills onto the black water. You're anonymous in the city of masks, as the rhythmic thrust of your striped-shirted gondolier turns old crows into songbirds. This is extremely relaxing (and, I think,

Gondolas

Two hundred years ago, there were 10,000 gondolas in Venice. Although the aristocracy preferred horses to boats through the early Middle Ages, begin-ning in the 14th century, when horses were outlawed from the streets of Venice, the noble class embraced gondolas as a respectable form of transportation.

The boats became *the* way to get around the lagoon's islands. To navigate over the countless shifting sandbars, the boats were flat (no keel or rudder) and the captains stood up to see.

Today, there are only 500 gondolas, used only by tourists. The boats are prettier now, but they work the same way they always have. Single oars are used both to propel and to steer the boats, which are built curved a bit on one side so that an oar thrusting from that side sends the gondola in a straight line.

These sleek yet ornate boats typically are about 35 feet long and 5 feet wide, and weigh about 1,100 pounds. They travel about three miles an hour (same as walking) and take the same energy to row as it does to walk. They're always painted black (six coats)—the result of a 17th-century law a doge enacted to eliminate competition between nobles for the fanciest rig. But each has unique upholstery, trim, and detailing, such as the squiggly shaped, carved-wood oarlock *(forcula)* and metal "hood ornament" *(ferro)*. The six horizontal lines and curved

worth the extra cost to experience at night). Women, beware... while gondoliers can be extremely charming, local women say that anyone who falls for one of these Romeos "has slices of ham over her eyes."

For cheap gondola thrills during the day, stick to the €0.50 one-minute ferry ride on a Grand Canal *traghetto*. At night, *vaporetti* are nearly empty, and it's a great time to cruise the Grand Canal on the slow boat #1. Or hang out on a bridge along the gondola route and wave at romantics.

St. Mark's Square

For tourists, St. Mark's Square is the highlight, with lantern light and live music echoing from the cafés. Just being here after dark is a thrill, as **dueling café orchestras** entertain (see sidebar on page 78). Every night, enthusiastic musicians play the same songs, creating the same irresistible magic. Hang out for free behind the top of the *ferro* represent Venice's six *sestieri* (districts) and the doge's funny cap. All in all, it takes about two months to build a gondola.

The boats run about €35,000-50,000, depending on your options (air-con, cup holders, etc.). Every 40 days, the boat's hull must be treated with a new coat of varnish to protect against a lagoon-dwelling creature that eats into wood. A gondola lasts about 15 years, after which it can be refinished (once) to last another 10 years.

You can see Venice's most picturesque gondola workshop (from the outside; it's not open to the public) in the Accademia neighborhood. (Walk down the Accademia side of the canal called Rio San Trovaso; as you approach Giudecca Canal, you'll glimpse the beached gondolas on your right across the canal.) The workmen, traditionally from Italy's mountainous Dolomite region (because they need to be good with wood), maintain this refreshingly alpine-feeling little corner of Venice.

There are about 400 licensed gondoliers. When one dies, the license passes to his widow. And do the gondoliers sing, as the popular image has it? My mom asked our gondolier that very question, and he replied, "Madame, there are the lovers and there are the singers. I do not sing."

tables (allowing you to move easily on to the next orchestra when the musicians take a break), or spring for a seat and enjoy a fun and gorgeously set concert. If you sit a while, it can be €12-20 well spent (for a drink and the cover charge for music). Dancing on the square is free (and encouraged).

Streetlamp halos, live music, floodlit history, and a ceiling of stars make St. Mark's magic at midnight. You're not a tourist, you're a living part of a soft Venetian night...an alley cat with money. In the misty light, the moon has a golden hue. Shine with the old lanterns on the gondola piers, where the sloppy lagoon splashes at the Doge's Palace...reminiscing.

Entertainment

Venice has a busy schedule of events, festivals, and entertainment. Check at the TI for listings, and keep an eye out for publications such as *Shows & Events* (bilingual, available at some hotels and online at www.turismovenezia.it, click on "Venezia").

Baroque Concerts

Venice is a city of the powdered-wig Baroque era. For about €25 (prices vary), you can take your pick of traditional Vivaldi concerts in churches throughout town. Homegrown Vivaldi is as ubiquitous here as Strauss is in Vienna and Mozart is in Salzburg. In fact, you'll find frilly young Vivaldis hawking concert tickets on many corners. The TI has a list of this week's Baroque concerts. Most shows start at 20:30 and generally last 1.5 hours. You'll see posters in hotels all over town (hotels sell tickets at face-value). A one-stop shop for concerts is the Vivaldi Store, at the east end of Rialto Bridge (on Salizada del Fontego dei Tedeschi at #5537, tel. 041-522-1343). Tickets for Baroque concerts in Venice can usually be bought the same day as the concert, so don't bother with websites that sell tickets with a surcharge.

Consider the venue carefully. The general rule of thumb: Musicians in wigs and tights offer better spectacle; musicians in black-and-white suits are better performers. **San Vidal Church** (at the north end of Accademia Bridge) and the **Interpreti Veneziani orchestra** (which often plays there) are reliably top-notch (tel. 041-277-0561, www.interpretiveneziani.com). For the latest on church concerts, check any TI or visit www.turismovenezia.it.

If you're attending a concert at **Scuola San Rocco** (tickets €15-30), arrive 30 minutes early to enjoy the art (which you'd have to pay €7 to see during the day).

If you just want a quick, free Vivaldi moment, stop by the **San Maurizio Church,** which Interpreti Veneziani has turned into a bilingual exhibition on the music and instruments of Vivaldi's time (free, daily 9:30-19:00, tolerable for kids, between St. Mark's Square and the Accademia at San Marco 2603).

Other Performances

Venice's most famous theaters are **La Fenice** (grand old opera house, box office tel. 041-2424, see page 47), **Teatro Goldoni** (mostly Italian live theater), and **Teatro della Fondamenta Nuove** (theater, music, and dance).

Musica a Palazzo is a unique evening of opera at the Doge's Palace. You'll spend about 45 minutes in three sumptuous rooms as eight musicians (generally four instruments and four singers) perform. With these kinds of surroundings, under Tiepolo frescoes, you'll be glad you dressed up. As there are only 70 seats, you must book by phone or online in advance. Opera-lovers find this to be a wonderful evening (€50, nightly shows at 20:30, Palazzo Barbarigo-Minotto, Fondamenta Duodo o Barbarigo—on the Grand Canal next to the Santa Maria del Giglio vaporetto stop, mobile 340-971-7272, www.musicapalazzo.com).

Venezia is advertised as "the show that tells the great story of Venice" and "simply the best show in town." I found the performance to be slow-moving and a bit cheesy, and the venue to be disappointing (€39, nightly May-Oct at 20:00, Nov-April at 19:00; 80 minutes, Teatro San Gallo, just off St. Mark's Square on Campo San Gallo, tel. 041-241-2002, www.teatrosangallo.net).

Movies

Venetian cinema is rarely in the original language; expect to hear it in Italian. Every September, Venice's **film festival** (with some English-language films, www.labiennale.org) doubles the viewing choices and brings the stars out to Venice's Lido, a 10-minute vaporetto ride from St. Mark's Square.

Eating and Drinking

In the evening, locals and those spending the night in Venice fill the piazzas, restaurants, and bars.

Dining

The local way to spend an evening is to enjoy a slow and late dinner in a romantic canalside or piazza setting (see the Eating in Venice chapter). Another option is a fast-paced, stand-up dinner of *cicchetti* in a pub (or in several—see pub-crawl sidebar, page 280).

Zattere Neighborhood

At the south end of Dorsoduro is a canalfront strip called Zattere (near the Zattere vaporetto stop). With a fun, youthful vibe, the pizzerias, *gelaterias*, and bars do a good job of entertaining. **El Chioschetto alle Zattere,** a simple, outdoor bar, offers a free live music program right on the promenade—especially enjoyable as the sun sets over the cruise ships and sinks behind the industrial zone on the mainland in the distance (cocktails, sandwiches, and drinks; daily June-Sept 7:30-2:00 in the morning, Oct-May 7:30-18:00; just west of Zattere vaporetto dock at Zattere 1406—see map on page 256; mobile 348-396-8466).

Pubs, Clubs, and Late-Night Spots

While a pub-crawl dinner is fun and colorful, most serious eating is finished early to make way for drinking.

Near the Rialto Bridge

Located near each other in the center, these bars and jazz clubs are good spots for night owls (see map on page 252).

Bácaro Jazz Venezia wine bar, with bras upholstering its ceiling, offers food until 1:00 in the morning (on St. Mark's side of Rialto Bridge, from Campo San Bartolomeo go down street behind statue to #5546, tel. 041-528-5249).

Planet Restaurant shows sports coverage on TV while serving up pizzas (€8-12) and expensive pastas (€13-20) until midnight, and drinks until 1:00 in the morning (10 percent service charge, no cover, between St. Mark's Square and Campo Santa Maria Formosa on Calle Casselleria at #5281, tel. 041-522-0808).

Also open late are several Irish pubs, including the **Devil's Forest Pub** (fine prices, daily 11:00-24:00, pasta served 12:00-14:30 with 10 percent service charge, sandwiches available all the time, no cover or service charge at night, a block off Campo San Bartolomeo on Calle dei Stagneri at #5185, tel. 041-520-0623) and **Inishark Pub** (until 1:30 in the morning, closed Mon, on Calle del Mondo Novo, just west of Campo Santa Maria Formosa off Salizada San Lio, at #5787, tel. 041-523-5300).

Other Late-Night Haunts

The university student zone of **Campo Santa Margherita** is likely to be lively late. This square, popular with Venetians, has a good restaurant, café, and bar scene—especially May through September (Bar Rosso is particularly popular). At #2944 on the square, **Pizza al Volo** sells big, one-sixth slices for only €2 until 2:00 in the morning (see map on page 256, tel. 041-522-5430).

The **Venice Jazz Club,** between Campo Santa Margherita and Campo San Barnaba, has live music from 21:00 to 23:00 five nights a week (Mon-Wed and Fri-Sat; doors open at 19:00 and light meals are served before the music starts, €20 includes first drink, no smoking; near Ponte dei Pugni at #3102—see map on page 256; tel. 041-523-2056, www.venicejazzclub.com).

Paradiso Perduto, on Fondamenta della Sensa (on Rio della Sensa) in Cannaregio, is notorious for being noisy late at night. When locals complain, night owls say there's got to be someplace in Venice that stays open late. It's a restaurant and bar with a huge following for its good casual food and ambience (tel. 041-720-581).

Other places likely to be open after 23:00 include the touristy **American Bar** (under the Clock Tower on St. Mark's Square, tel. 041-522-2515—see map on page 75). While Irish pubs are popular with locals rather than tourists, **Harry's American Bar** is just the opposite (serving overpriced food and American cocktails to dressy tourists at the San Marco vaporetto stop—see the map on page 219, tel. 041-528-5777). But be warned: Harry's is, simply put, a rip-off.

Venice doesn't have a good dance scene, unlike other Italian cities. The close proximity of apartments means loud music isn't tolerated late at night. The few *discoteche* are overpriced, with expensive drinks and little actual dancing. Still, for a cultural experience and a throbbing techno beat, check out the incredibly soundproofed disco piano bar **Piccolo Mondo el Souk** near the Accademia art museum (daily 23:00-4:00 in the morning, Nov-March closed Mon, €10 cover charge includes one cocktail, drinks after that are all €10, locals won't show up until at least 23:30 or midnight, don't be shy—ring the bell to get in, between Accademia and recommended Pensione Accademia on Calle Corfù at Dorsoduro 1056a—see map on page 257, tel. 041-520-0371).

VENICE CONNECTIONS

This chapter addresses your arrival and departure from Venice—by train, plane, car, bus, and cruise ship.

A two-mile-long causeway (with highway and train lines) connects Venice to the mainland. Mestre, the sprawling mainland section of Venice, has fewer crowds, cheaper hotels, and plenty of inexpensive parking lots, but zero charm. Don't stop in Mestre unless you're parking your car or transferring trains.

By Train

Santa Lucia Train Station

All trains to "Venice" stop at Venezia Mestre (on the mainland). Most continue on to Santa Lucia station on the island of Venice itself. If your train only stops at Mestre, worry not. Shuttle trains regularly connect Mestre's station with Venice's Santa Lucia station (6/hour, 10 minutes, €1, buy tickets with coins from machines marked *Rete Regionale* and validate them before boarding).

Venice's Santa Lucia train station (Ferrovia) plops you right into the old town on the Grand Canal, an easy vaporetto ride or fascinating 40-minute walk to St. Mark's Square. If the station's TI is crowded when you arrive, consider visiting one of the two TIs at St. Mark's Square instead. It's not worth a long wait for a minimal TI map (buy a good one from a newsstand or pick up a free one at your hotel). Confirm your departure plan (use the machines or just study the *partenze*/departures posters on walls).

Consider storing unnecessary heavy bags, although lines for **baggage check** may be very long (at track 1, €4/5 hours, €11/24 hours, daily 6:00-23:50, no lockers, 44-pound weight limit on bags). **WCs** (€0.80) are at track 1 and in the back of the big bar/cafeteria area inside the station.

Arrival in Venice

1 Kilometer

1 Mile

MARCO POLO
AIRPORT

COVERED
SIDEWALK

DOCK

To
Padua
& Treviso
Airport

MESTRE
TRAIN STATION

Lagoon

San Marco to:
Airport = 4 miles
Mestre = 5 miles
Lido = 2 miles

Murano

MUSEO STOP

SANTA
LUCIA
TRAIN
STATION

CAUSEWAY

COLONNA
STOP

GUGLIE
BRIDGE

*Grand
Canal*

FONDAMENTA NOVE

TRONCHETTO
CAR PARK

MARIT-
TIMA

RIALTO

SAN ZACCARIA
M.V.E.

PIAZZALE
ROMA
BUS STN

SAN
MARCO

LIDO
(S.M.E.)

CRUISE
SHIP DOCK

ZATTERE

Giudecca

SAN
GIORGIO

Lido

Rail
Bus
Alilaguna Boat
(Not all stops shown)
People Mover

Minimize your time in the station—the banks of user-friendly automated ticket machines (marked *Biglietto Veloce/Fast Ticket*) are handy but cover Italian destinations only. They take euros and credit cards, display schedules, issue tickets, and even make reservations for railpass-holders. The gray-and-blue *Rete Regionale* machines are another option for tickets to nearby destinations such as Padua (coins only, push button for English). If you need international tickets or live help, the ticket windows are open from 6:00 to 20:30. Or you could take care of these tasks for a fee at downtown travel agencies (see page 29).

For more on train travel in Italy—including your ticket-buying options—see page 386.

To get from the train station to downtown Venice, walk straight out of the station to the canal. You'll see vaporetto docks and ticket booths on both sides. For vaporetto #2 (fast boat down Grand Canal), go left. For vaporetto #1 (slow boat down Grand Canal), go right. See "Getting Around Venice—By Vaporetto," on page 31, for details on vaporetto tickets and passes.

From Venice by Train to: Padua (2/hour, 30-50 minutes), **Vicenza** (2/hour, 45-75 minutes), **Verona** (2/hour, 1.25-2.25 hours), **Ravenna** (roughly hourly, 3-3.5 hours, transfer in Ferrara or Bologna), **Florence** (hourly, 2 hours, often crowded so make reservations), **Bolzano/Dolomites** (to Bolzano about hourly, 3-3.5 hours, transfer in Verona; catch bus from Bolzano into mountains), **Milan** (hourly, 2.5-3.5 hours), **Cinque Terre/Monterosso** (6/day, 6 hours, change in Milan), **Rome** (hourly, 3.75 hours, also 1 direct night train from Mestre, 6 hours), **Naples** (almost hourly, 6 hours, change in Rome), **Brindisi** (5/day, 9 hours, change in Rome or Bologna; 1 direct night train from Mestre, 10 hours), **Interlaken** (7/day, 6-7.5 hours, 2-5 changes, no pleasant overnight option), **Luzern** (7/day, 6.5-7 hours, 1 direct, others change in Milan and Arth-Goldau), **Bern** (3/day, 6 hours, change in Milan or Brig), **Munich** (4-6/day, 7 hours, change in Verona; 1 direct night train, 8 hours; most trains reservable only via www.bahn .de), **Salzburg** (4/day, 6-7 hours, 1-2 changes, 1 direct night train, 7 hours), **Paris** (3/day, 10-12 hours with change in Milan, may also transfer in Basel or Zürich; 1 direct night train, 13.5 hours, important to reserve ahead, 2 more night trains with changes), **Ljubljana** (3/day, 7.5 hours—buy ticket at train station, take bus from Piazzale Roma to Villach in Austria, then transfer to train; 1 direct night train, 4 hours, but arrives at 2:00 in the morning), and **Vienna** (3/day, 8 hours—same system as Ljubljana; 1 direct night train, 11 hours).

By Plane

Marco Polo is Venice's main airport. Some budget flights, including Ryanair, use the smaller airport in the nearby city of Treviso. (For more on budget carriers, see page 401.)

Marco Polo Airport

Venice's small, modern airport is on the mainland shore of the lagoon, six miles north of the city. There's one sleek terminal, with a TI (daily 9:00-21:00), car-rental agencies, ATMs, a bank, and a few shops and eateries. For flight information, call tel. 041-260-9260, visit www.veniceairport.com, or ask your hotel.

Transportation between Marco Polo Airport and Venice

Here are three ways to get between the airport and downtown Venice:

- Alilaguna boats—Slowest trip, medium cost
- Water taxis—Fastest trip, most expensive

• Airport shuttle buses to Piazzale Roma—Faster than Alilaguna, slower than water taxi, least expensive

Each of these options is explained in detail below. An advantage of the Alilaguna boats is that you can reach most of this book's recommended hotels very simply, with no changes—except hotels near the train station, which are better served by the bus to Piazzale Roma.

Both Alilaguna boats and water taxis leave from the airport's boat dock, an eight-minute walk from the terminal. Exit the arrivals hall and turn left, following signs along a paved, level, covered sidewalk (easy for wheeled bags).

When flying out of Venice, allow yourself plenty of time to get to the airport. Water transport is slow. Plan to arrive at the airport at least two hours before your flight, and remember that getting there can easily take another two hours. Consider alternatives ahead of time, especially if you're planning to take an Alilaguna boat (which are small and can fill up).

Alilaguna Airport Boats

These boats make the scenic (if slow) journey across the lagoon, each shuttling passengers between the airport and a number of different stops on the island of Venice (€15, €25 round-trip, 1-1.5-hour trip depending on your destination; boats leave every 30-60 minutes). Note that the Alilaguna boats are not part of the ACTV vaporetto system, so they aren't covered by city transit passes. But they do use the same docks and ticket windows as the regular *vaporetti*.

There are three Alilaguna lines (blue, red, orange), and it can get confusing. But if you know what stop you want, it's easy to find the line that goes there. Here are some key stops in Venice:

San Marco—Hotels west of St. Mark's Square

San Zaccaria—Hotels east of St. Mark's Square

Zattere—Dorsoduro hotels

Guglie—Hotels near Santa Lucia train station

Rialto—Hotels near the Rialto Bridge

Fondamente Nove—Hotels on the north side of the city, on the "fish's" back

For a full schedule, visit the TI, see the website (www.alilaguna.it), call tel. 041-240-1701, ask your hotelier, or scan the schedules posted at the docks.

From the Airport to Venice: You can buy Alilaguna tickets at the airport's TI, the ticket desk in the terminal, vending machines inside the airport terminal (cash only), or simply at the ticket booth at the dock. Any ticket-seller can tell you which line to catch to get to your destination. Boats from the airport run from roughly 7:00 to midnight.

From Venice to the Airport: Ask your hotelier what dock and what line is best. Boats start leaving Venice as early as 3:40 so that passengers can catch early flights. Scope out the dock and buy your ticket in advance to avoid last-minute stress.

Water Taxis

Luxury taxi speedboats zip directly between the airport and your hotel, getting you within steps of your final destination in about 30 minutes. The official price is €100 for up to five people; add €10 for every extra person (10-passenger limit). There's a €10 surcharge between 22:00 and 7:00. You may get a higher quote—politely talk it down. A taxi can be a smart investment for small groups and those with an early departure.

From the airport, arrange your ride at the airport's water-taxi desk or with the boat captains lounging at the dock. From Venice, book your taxi trip the day before you leave. Your hotel will help (since they get a commission), or you can book directly with the Consorzio Motoscafi water taxi association (tel. 041-522-2303, www.motoscafivenezia.it/eng).

Airport Shuttle Buses

Buses take you across the bridge from the mainland to the island, dropping you at Venice's bus station, at the "mouth of the fish" on a square called Piazzale Roma. From there, you can catch a vaporetto down the Grand Canal—convenient for hotels near the Rialto Bridge and St. Mark's Square. If you're staying near the train station, you can walk from Piazzale Roma to your hotel.

Two bus companies run between Piazzale Roma and the airport: ACTV (the local city bus company) and ATVO. Most of the day, both have departures twice an hour and cost the same (€3), although only ATVO offers a round-trip for €5.50. ATVO buses take 20 minutes and go nonstop. ACTV buses (route #5) make a few stops en route and take slightly longer (30 minutes), but are covered by Venice vaporetto passes (see page 31). Buses run from about 5:00 to 24:00; early and late, each company has just one bus an hour. Check schedules at www.atvo.it or www.actv.it.

From the Airport to Venice: Both buses leave from just outside the arrivals terminal. Buy tickets at the TI, or from ticket machines in the terminal or outside next to the buses; in a pinch at odd hours, ask the driver. Check which ticket you are buying—ATVO tickets are not valid on ACTV buses and vice versa. Double-check the destination; if taking ACTV, you want bus #5. See "By Bus," later, for directions into town from Piazzale Roma.

From Venice to the Airport: At Piazzale Roma, buy your ticket from the ACTV windows or ATVO office before heading out to the platforms. (If closed, politely ask the driver to sell you a ticket.) ACTV buses leave from platform A1; ATVO buses from platform D2. The first buses leave at around 5:00.

Private Shuttle Bus

Treviso Car Service offers a private minivan service between Marco Polo Airport and Piazzale Roma or the cruise port (minivan-€55, seats up to 8; car-€50, seats up to 3; mobile 348-900-0700 or 333-411-2840, www.tourleadervenice.com, info@tourleadervenice.com; they also offer tours—see page 38).

Treviso Airport

Several budget airlines, such as Ryanair, Wizz Air, and Germanwings, use Treviso Airport, 12 miles northwest of Venice (www.trevisoairport.it). Regular ATVO buses take you from the airport to Piazzale Roma (€6, about 2/hour, 1.25 hours, www.atvo.it). Buy your tickets at the ATVO desk in the airport and stamp them on the bus. The buses also stop at Mestre's train station. Treviso Car Service offers minivan service to Piazzale Roma (minivan-€75, seats up to 8; car-€65, seats up to 3; see private shuttle bus listing above).

By Bus

Piazzale Roma Bus Station

If you arrive in Venice at Piazzale Roma, find the vaporetto docks (by the six-story white building) and take #1 or the faster #2 down the Grand Canal to reach the Rialto, Accademia, or San Marco (St. Mark's Square) stops. If your hotel is near the train station, you can walk there from Piazzale Roma across the Calatrava Bridge.

Arriving by bus at Piazzale Roma is easy, but it can be difficult to figure out how to leave. The square is a confusing jumble of different operators, platforms, and crosswalks over busy lanes of traffic. The ticket windows for ACTV (local public buses, including #5 to Marco Polo Airport) are by the vaporetto stop. The ATVO ticket office is on the right side of the square as you face away from the canal (for express buses to Marco Polo and Treviso Airports; office open daily 7:15-19:30). The ATVO office also sells tickets for the SITA bus to Padua (1-2/hour, 45 minutes), though it's more convenient to go to Padua by train. At odd hours, you may be able to buy tickets from bus drivers. For buses to Austria run by Italian Railways, you have to buy tickets at the train station.

At Piazzale Roma, you'll also see the parking garages and the People Mover monorail to the parking-lot island of Tronchetto. A baggage-storage office is next to the monorail at #497m (€5/24 hours, daily 6:00-21:00).

By Car

Parking in Venice

The freeway dead-ends after crossing the causeway to Venice. The best balance of cost and convenience is the parking-lot island of **Tronchetto,** well-signed as you approach Venice. The rates for the multi-story Tronchetto parking garage are affordable (€3-4/hour, €21/ 24 hours, discounts for longer stays, tel. 041-520-7555, www .veniceparking.it). From the garage, head directly to the yellow-and-white vaporetto docks and take line #2, the express boat which stops at the Rialto, San Marco, Zattere, and other main points in the center. I like the approach from Tronchetto into town by sea. Don't let water taxi boatmen con you out of the relatively inexpensive €6.50 vaporetto ride. Also avoid the travel agencies masquerading as TIs; deal only with the ticket booth at the vaporetto dock or the HelloVenezia public transport office. Consider whether a local transport pass will pay off (see page 31); you can buy it here.

If you're parking at Tronchetto and staying near the train station, you can take the €1 People Mover monorail instead of paying €6.50 for the two-stop vaporetto ride. The monorail brings you from Tronchetto to the bus station at Piazzale Roma, then it's a five-minute walk across the Calatrava Bridge to the train station (buy monorail tickets with coins from machine, 3-minute trip, runs Mon-Sat 7:00-23:00, Sun 8:30-21:00).

You can park at **Piazzale Roma,** the busy square where the expressway dead-ends and which doubles as Venice's bus station. The big white building on your right is a 2,200-space public parking garage, the Autorimessa Communale (€25/24 hours, tel. 041-272-7211, www.asmvenezia.it) and in a back corner of the square is the private San Marco garage (€30/24 hours, tel. 041-523-2213, www.garagesanmarco.it). At either of these, you'll have to give up your keys. You can reserve ahead at both garages and at Tronchetto, but it's rarely necessary.

Parking in the garage across from the train station in **Mestre** (on the mainland) only makes sense if you have light bags and are staying within walking distance of the Santa Lucia train station (€8/day Mon-Fri, €12-16/day Sat-Sun; www.sabait.it).

Ask your hotel for parking advice—some can get you a small discount. For information on car rental and driving in Italy, see page 396.

By Cruise Ship

More than 1.5 million passengers visit Venice via cruise ship every year. If your trip includes cruising beyond Venice, consider my new guidebook, *Rick Steves' Mediterranean Cruise Ports.*

Venice Cruise Ship Terminals

Most cruise ships visiting Venice dock at Stazione Marittima, which is roughly between the Tronchetto parking garage and Santa Lucia train station. The terminal forms "the fish's mouth" of Venice. Ships also tie up at the Santa Marta and San Basilio docks, which are south of the main port. The Venice port website has a map of the different docks (www.port.venice.it/en/terminals .html).

Check with your cruise line to find out where your ship will moor, and give yourself plenty of time if connecting between a flight and a cruise in Venice.

Getting into Town

Venice's public transportation is convenient and affordable; for a rundown of your travel options, see page 30. The handy Alilaguna express boat #M conveniently connects Stazione Marittima directly to St. Mark's Square (San Marco-Giardinetti dock) in just 20 minutes (€6.50 one-way, €12 round-trip, €3 per big bag, 2/hour in each direction, from cruise port 8:10-16:10, from St. Mark's Square 9:10-16:10; before boarding at the cruise terminal, buy ticket at kiosk in front of building #103 at the top of the harbor; www.alilaguna.it). Because this service is understandably popular, the boats can fill up; if you're arriving on a cruise ship, get to this dock as quickly as possible.

To reach the Grand Canal (and the start of my self-guided Grand Canal Cruise) from Stazione Marittima, hop on the People Mover monorail (€1) to Piazzale Roma. Or, if money is no object, you can spring for a water taxi to anywhere in town (€80). If all of these options are jammed up (as can happen when multiple cruise ships arrive all at once), you can walk to the Grand Canal in about 15 minutes, or all the way to St. Mark's Square in about 45 minutes.

If your ship is docked outside the main port, take vaporetto #2 from San Basilio to get into Venice.

Getting to Marco Polo Airport

The shuttle buses between Piazzale Roma and the airport are quick and inexpensive (described earlier). Buses leave between 5:00 and 24:00; from Stazione Marittima, take the People Mover monorail to Piazzale Roma. You can also take a land taxi directly to the airport (€40). Keep in mind that the Alilaguna boats connecting directly to the airport have stops at Tronchetto or Piazzale Roma—but not at Stazione Marittima. From the Santa Marta or San Basilio docks, you can take a land taxi to the airport (€40).

DAY TRIPS
FROM VENICE

Venice is just one of many towns in the Italian region of Veneto (VEN-eh-toh), but few visitors venture off the lagoon. Two important towns and possible side-trips, in addition to the lakes and the Dolomites, make zipping directly from Venice to Milan (or Florence) a route strewn with temptation.

The towns of Padua and Verona are great stops, giving the visitor a low-key slice of Italy that complements the urbanity of Venice, Florence, and Rome. Visiting Padua and Verona couldn't be easier: They are roughly 30-45 minutes apart on the Venice-Milan line. Spending a day town-hopping between Venice and Milan—with stops at Padua and Verona—is exciting and efficient. Trains run frequently enough to allow flexibility and little wasted time. Architecture fans could consider a quick trip to Vicenza, located about halfway between Padua and Verona.

If you're Padua-bound, remember that you need to reserve ahead to see the Scrovegni Chapel. Mondays are not ideal for a trip to Verona, when most sights are closed (at least in the morning), or Vicenza, where the major sights are closed.

Day Trips from Venice

PADUA

Padova

Living under Venetian rule for four centuries seemed only to sharpen Padua's independent spirit. Nicknamed "the brain of Veneto," Padua (*Padova* in Italian) has a prestigious university (founded in 1222) that hosted Galileo, Copernicus, Dante, and Petrarch. Padua's old town center is elegantly arcaded, filled with students, and sprinkled with surprises. Padua's museums and churches hold their own in Italy's artistic big league—yet its hotels are reasonably priced and the city doesn't feel touristy.

Planning Your Time: Padua in Six Hours

Day-trippers can do a quick but enjoyable blitz of Padua—including a visit to the Scrovegni Chapel—in six hours. Buses and trains from Venice are cheap, take 30 to 50 minutes, and run frequently. Once in Padua, everything is a 10-minute walk or a quick tram ride apart.

Your Scrovegni Chapel reservation will dictate the order of your sightseeing (see "Reservations" on page 324). When planning your day, also consider these factors: The station has a reliable baggage check desk; the open-air markets are vibrant in the morning, dead in the evening; student life is best at the university late in the day; and the Basilica of St. Anthony is open all day, but the reliquary chapel closes from 12:45 to 14:30.

Ideally, I'd do it this way: 9:00—market action and sightseeing in town center, 11:00—Basilica of St. Anthony, 14:00—Scrovegni Chapel tour.

Orientation to Padua

Padua's main tourist sights lie on a north-south axis through the heart of the city, from the train station to Scrovegni Chapel to the market squares (the center of town) to the Basilica of St. Anthony. It's roughly a 10-minute walk between each of these sights, or about 30 minutes from end to end. I've designed this chapter around Padua's wonderful single tram line, which makes lacing things together quick and easy (see "Getting Around Padua," later).

Tourist Information

Padua has three TIs: in the **center** (in the alley behind Caffè Pedrocchi at Vicolo Cappellatto Pedrocchi 9, Mon-Sat 9:00-13:30 & 15:00-19:00, closed Sun, tel. 049-876-7927), at the **train station** (Mon-Sat 9:15-19:00, Sun 9:00-12:30, tel. 049-875-2077), and near the **Basilica of St. Anthony,** across the street on Piazza del Santo (April-Oct Mon-Sat 9:00-13:30 & 15:00-18:00, Sun 10:00-13:30 & 15:00-18:00, closed Nov-March, tel. 049-875-3087). Be aware that the TIs may have shorter hours in 2012 due to budget cuts.

At any TI, pick up a map, a list of sights, and the seasonal Padova Today entertainment listing. The TI's free I-PADova audio tour is creative and works really well. You can download it for free from their website (www.turismopadova.it), or just borrow one of their MP3 players (leave your passport) and follow any of the five routes in town.

The Padova Card gives you (and one child under 14) unlimited tram travel, free parking at Piazza Rabin, various discounts, and entry to all the recommended sights in this chapter, except the university's Anatomy Theater and the Basilica of St. Anthony's Oratory of St. George. While the card includes the Scrovegni Chapel, you still need to make a reservation to enter (which costs an extra €1). Padova Cards are also sold at all TIs, at included sights, and online at www.padovacard.it (€16/48 hours, €21/72 hours) and on the Scrovegni Chapel website (www.cappella degliscrovegni.it). If you buy the card online, bring your confirmation number and pick it up at any TI or at the Scrovegni Chapel. If you reserve a Scrovegni Chapel ticket at the same time, pick up the ticket at the chapel.

Arrival in Padua

By Train: The efficient station is a user-friendly shopping mall with whatever you might need (Despar **supermarket** open Mon-Sat 7:00-21:00, Sun 10:00-21:00). **WCs** (€0.60) and **baggage deposit** (exactly €3.87, daily 6:30-18:00, bring photo ID) are along track 1.

If you need to speak to a real person about tickets but the lines

Padua

PADUA

To A-4 Autostrada (Venice & Verona)

VIA ETA PAOLO SARPI

VIA DELLE PALME

VIA GIOVANNI VERDARA

VIA SUOR E. VENDRAMINI

VIA DELLA ROTONDA

VIALE CODALUNGA

VIA CODALUNGA

TRAIN STATION

Piazzale d. Stazione ㉓

VIA B. CAIROLI

MAIN BUS STATION

VIA N. TOMMASEO

VIA BEATO PELLEGRINO

VIA SAN PELLEGRINO

Piazza Alcide de Gasperi

VIA DEL OTOLO

V. FOSCOLO

V. DIEGO VALERI

VIA GASPARE GOZZI

VIA TRIESTE

CARMINE CHURCH

VIA DEL CARMINE

VIA GIOTTO

Trieste

OLD CITY WALLS

VIA GASO

SCROVEGNI CHAPEL

V. DOMENICO CAMPAGNOLA

VIA DEI SAVONAROLA

Piovego

PALAZZO ZUCKERMANN

CORSO GARIBALDI

CIVIC MUSEUMS (SCROVEGNI TICKETS)

Canale

VIA SAN PIETRO

V. CARLO LEONI

CORSO MILANO

VIA DANTE

Eremitani Ⓣ

ERMITAGE CHURCH

Piazza dell' Insurrezione

V. SAN FERMO

Ponti Romani

SAN GAETANO (ALTINATE CULTURAL CENTER)

V. GIUSEPPE VERDI

VIA DEI LIVELLO

S. NICOLÒ

SANTA LUCIA

VIA CAVOUR

Ponti Romani Ⓣ

VIA D. ZABARELLA

VIA ALTINATE

PATRIARCATO

② ⑱ ⑪ ⑫ ⑲ Piazza Cavour

⑬

⑳

Piazza Capitaniato

Piazza Signori

Piazza Frutta

ⓘ

VIA SAN BIAGIO

BAPTISTRY

⑩

PALAZZO RAGIONE

⑭

UNIVERSITY (PALAZZO BO)

VIA CESARE BATTISTI

VIA DEI TADI

DUOMO

Piazza Duoma

VIA MANIN

Piazza Erbe

⑧

V. S. GREGORIO BARBARIGO

V. SONCIN

⑨

SOLFERINO

㉑

Piazza Antenore

VIA DEL SANTO

VIA SAN FRANCESCO

VIA DEI VESCOVADO

MARSALA

①

VIA ROMA

Tito Livio

SAN FRANCESCO

VIA SANTA ROSA

⑫

Tito Livio

VIA SAN TOMASO

S. MARIA SERVI

⑱

RIVIERA TITO LIVIO

V. GASPARA STAMPA

VIA GALILEO GALILEI

Piazza del Castello

20 SETTEMBRE

Piazzetta Giovanni Palatucci

VIA SANTA CHIARA

⑮

⑥

Piovego

VIA DEI ROGATI

VIA UMBERTO

RIVIERA RUZANTE

VIA RUDENA

GATTAMELATA STATUE

⑤

V. CESAROTTI

Canale

R. TISO CAMPOSAMPIERO

VIA A. ALEARDI

VIA SEMINARIO

VIA ANDREA MEMMO

ⓘ

③ ④

Piazza del Santo

ST. ANTHONY

⑦

V. TORRESINO

VIA ACQUETTE

Santo

Ⓣ ⑰

VIA BELLUDI

VIA DIMESSE

Prato della Valle

Ⓣ

V. BRIOSCO

200 Meters

200 Yards

VIA ALBERTO

VIA ROBERTO MARIN

CAVALLETTO

To A-13 Autostrada (Florence)

Prato della Valle

Botanic Garden

⑯

Padua Key

1. Hotel Majestic Toscanelli
2. Albergo Verdi
3. Hotel Al Fagiano
4. Hotel Belludi 37
5. Hotel/Rist. Casa del Pellegrino
6. Hotel Al Santo
7. Ostello Città di Padova
8. Osteria dei Fabbri
9. Osteria L'Anfora
10. Ristorante alle Piazze da Giorgio
11. La Lanterna Ristorante
12. Bar dei Osei
13. Brek Cafeteria
14. PAM Supermarket & Brek
15. Pizzeria Pago Pago
16. Zairo Rist./Pizzeria
17. Pollodoro la Gastronomica
18. Gelateria Grom (2)
19. Caffè Pedrocchi
20. Internet Café
21. Feltrinelli's Intl. Bookstore
22. Launderette
23. Buses to Venice & Marco Polo Airport

PADUA

are long, go to Leonardi Viaggi-Turismo, which offers ticketing services for a small fee a block away (Mon-Fri 9:00-13:00 & 14:30-19:00, Sat 9:00-13:00, closed Sun, up the main drag in front of the station, Corso del Popolo 14, tel. 049-650-455).

The easiest way to get downtown is to simply hop on Padua's handy **tram** (see "Getting Around Padua," next page). Leaving the station, the tram stop is 30 yards to the right at the foot of the bridge (avoid the shady characters around here at night). A **taxi** into town (a good option after dark) costs about €8.

By Bus: The bus station is a few steps east of the train station, beyond the bicycle parking lot. Buses arrive here from Venice's Piazzale Roma and Marco Polo Airport.

Helpful Hints

Pronunciation: You say Padua (PAD-joo-wah), they say Padova (PAH-doh-vah).

Internet Access: Befitting a college town where every student has a laptop, Padua has few Internet cafés. The central TI offers free access for 15 minutes (if you fill out a form and show your passport). You can also walk to **Internet Point** (€2/hour, Mon-Sat 10:00-24:00, Sun 16:00-24:00, 10-minute walk east of the Ponte Romani tram stop at Via Altinate 145, tel. 049-659-292).

Bookstore: Feltrinelli's International Bookstore, with books in English, is a block from the main university building (Mon-Sat 9:00-19:30, Sun 10:00-13:00 & 15:30-19:30, Via San Francesco 7, tel. 049-875-4630).

Launderette: Lavami has only three washers and two dryers, but it's the sole option in the city center (daily 7:00-22:00, Via Marsala 22 near intersection with Via dell'Arco, tel. 049-876-4532).

Local Guide: Charming and helpful **Cristina Pernechele** is a great teacher (€110/half-day, mobile 338-495-5453, cristina @pernechele.eu).

Best Gelato: Though **Grom** is expensive (one-scoop cones: €2.20), students line up for its unusual flavors and exotic ingredients (two locations at Via Roma 101 and Piazza dei Signori 33).

Getting Around Padua

While a tangle of buses serves the city, visitors should pretend there is only the **tram** and rely on it. There's just one line, which efficiently and without stress connects everything you care about (€1.10 ticket good for 1.25 hours, buy tickets from machines at stops, departs every 8 minutes during the day Mon-Sat, every 20 minutes evenings and Sun, www.trampadova.it). The rubber-wheeled trams run on a single rail.

Before boarding, note the tram direction on posted schedules and above the front window (Pontevigodarzere is northbound, Capolinia Sud is southbound). Stops that matter include the following: Stazione FS (train and bus stations), Eremitani (Scrovegni Chapel), Ponti Romani (old town center, market squares, university), Tito Livio (ghetto, old town center, Hotel Majestic Toscanelli), Santo (Basilica of St. Anthony and neighborhood hotels), and Prato della Valle (hostel).

You'll see **hop-on, hop-off buses** at the station and around town. While these ubiquitous tourist transporters make sense in some places, they're not worth the time or money in Padua.

Sights in Padua

▲▲▲Basilica of St. Anthony

Friar Anthony of Padua, "Christ's perfect follower and a tireless preacher of the Gospel," is buried here. Construction of this

impressive Romanesque/Gothic church (with its Byzantine-style domes) started immediately after St. Anthony's death in 1231. And for nearly 800 years, his remains and this glorious church have attracted pilgrims to Padua.

Cost and Hours: The basilica is free and open April-late Oct daily 6:20-19:45; late Oct-March Mon-Fri 6:20-18:45, Sat-Sun 6:20-19:45. Note that the following sights within the basilica close around lunchtime: Chapel of the Reliquaries (daily April-late Oct 8:00-12:45 & 14:30-19:30, late Oct-March until 18:30), museum (€2.50, April-late Oct daily

---

St. Anthony of Padua
(1195-1231)

One of Christendom's most popular saints, Anthony is known as a powerful speaker, a miracle worker, and the finder of lost articles.

Born in Lisbon to a rich, well-educated family, his life changed at age 25, when he saw the mutilated bodies of some Franciscan martyrs. Their sacrifice inspired him to join the poor Franciscans and dedicate his life to Christ. He moved to Italy and lived in a cave, studying, meditating, and barely speaking to anyone.

One day, he joined his fellow monks for a service. The appointed speaker failed to show up, so Anthony was asked to say a few off-the-cuff words to the crowd. He started slowly, but, filled with the Spirit, he became more confident and amazed the audience with his eloquence. Up in Assisi, St. Francis heard about Anthony and sent him on a whirlwind speaking tour.

Anthony had a strong voice, knew several languages, had an encyclopedic knowledge of theology, and could speak spontaneously as the Spirit moved him. It's said he even stood on the shores of the Adriatic Sea in Rimini and enticed a school of fish to listen. Anthony also was known as a prolific miracle worker.

In 1230, Anthony retired to Padua, where he founded a monastery and initiated reforms for the poor. An illness cut his life short at age 36. Anthony said, "Happy is the man whose words issue from the Spirit and not from himself!"

9:00-13:00 & 14:00-18:00, late Oct-March closed Mon), and the Oratory of St. George (€2.50, daily April-late Oct 9:00-12:30 & 14:30-19:00, late Oct-March until 17:00).

Information: A modest dress code is enforced inside the basilica. A helpful information desk with Anthony-related pamphlets is in the cloisters, on the right side of the church (daily 9:00-13:00 & 14:00-18:00, public WC nearby, Santo tram stop, tel. 049-822-5652, www.basilicadelsanto.org). The information desk has free English pamphlets on the saint's life and the basilica; make a donation in the Chapel of the Reliquaries to get a more-detailed booklet. A TI is on the square facing the church.

Basilica Exterior

St. Anthony looks down from the red-brick facade and blesses all. He holds a book, a symbol of all the knowledge he accumulated as a quiet monk before starting his preaching career.

Guarding the church is Donatello's life-size equestrian statue of the Venetian mercenary general, Gattamelata. Though it looks like a thousand other man-on-a-horse statues, it was a landmark in Italy's budding Renaissance—the first life-size, secular, equestrian statue cast from bronze in a thousand years.

The church is technically outside of Italy. When you pass the banisters that mark its property line, you're passing into Vatican territory.

Interior

Entering the basilica, grab a pew in the center of the nave. Sit and appreciate the space. Gaze past the crowds and through the incense haze to Donatello's glorious crucifix rising from the altar, and realize that this is one of the most important pilgrimage sites in Christendom.

Along with the crucifix, Donatello's bronze statues—Mary with Padua's six favorite saints—grace the high altar. Late in his career, the great Florentine sculptor spent more than a decade in Padua (1444-1455), creating the altar and Gattamelata.

St. Anthony's Tomb

Head to the left side of the nave to find the gleaming marble masterpiece that is the focus of the visiting pilgrims—the tomb of St. Anthony. Pilgrims file slowly through this side chapel around the tomb, so focused on the saint that they hardly notice the nine fine marble reliefs. These Renaissance masterpieces were carved during the 16th century, and show scenes and miracles from the life of the saint. As you enjoy each scene, notice the Renaissance mastery of realism and 3-D perspective and the intricate frames, which celebrate life with a burst of exuberance.

First Relief: This depicts St. Anthony receiving the Franciscan tunic. The open door illustrates the new ability to show depth by using mathematics. The cityscape above is Padua in about 1500.

Second Relief: A jealous husband has angrily stabbed his wife. Notice the musculature, the emotion, and the determination in the faces of loved ones. Above, Anthony intercedes with God to bring the woman back to life. Notice the etchings of familiar Paduan architecture at the top of the sculptures.

Third Relief: Above this panel, which shows Anthony bringing a young man back to life, is the Palazzo della Ragione looking as it still does today.

Fourth Relief: This scene, by the famous Florentine sculptor Jacopo Sansovino, shows three generations: a dead girl, her distraught mom, and a grandmother who's seen it all. Of course, Anthony will eventually change the mood, but right now it's pretty dire. Above is a relief of this basilica.

Fifth Relief: A fisherman holds a net, sadly having retrieved a drowned boy. The mother looks at Anthony, who blesses and revives the boy. Across from here is the saint's actual tomb. Under thoughtful lighting, it reads *Corpus S. Antonii*. Prayer letters are dropped behind the iron grill.

Sixth Relief: This shows "the miracle of the miser's heart." Anthony's helper dips his hand into a moneylender's side to demonstrate the absence of his heart. At his foot, the square tray with coins and a heart illustrates the scriptural verse "for where your treasure is, there your heart will be also."

Seventh Relief: Anthony holds the foot of a young man who confessed to kicking his mother. Taking a lesson from the saint about respecting your mother a little too literally, the man has cut off his own foot. The hysterical mother implores Anthony's help, and the saint's prayers to God enable him to reattach the foot.

Stand in the corner for a moment, observing the passionate devotion that pilgrims and Paduans alike have for Anthony. Touching his tomb or kneeling in prayer, the faithful believe Anthony is their protector—a confidant and intercessor for the poor. And they believe he works miracles. Believers leave offerings, votives, and written prayers to ask for help or to give thanks for miracles they believe Anthony has performed. By putting their hands on his tomb while saying silent prayers, pilgrims show devotion to Anthony and feel the saint's presence.

Popular Anthony is the patron saint of dozens of things: travelers, amputees, donkeys, pregnant women, infertile women, flight attendants, and pig farmers. Most pilgrims ask for his help in his role as the "finder of things"—from lost car keys to a life companion. You'll see dozens of photos posted on his tomb in prayer or as thanks, including many of fervently wished-for newborns.

Eighth Relief: This scene makes the point that—unlike St. Francis, who was a rowdy youth—Anthony was holy even as a child. He tosses the glass (representing his faith), which, rather than shattering, breaks the marble floor.

Ninth Relief: An angry husband accuses his wife of cheating. The wife asks Anthony to identify her baby's father. Anthony asks the child, who speaks and says that the husband is his real dad and his mother was not messing around. Everyone is reassured—whew!

Between scenes eight and nine, go into the next room, where you'll enter the oldest part of the church—the original chapel, where Anthony was first buried in 1231. To the left of the altar, note the fine (and impressively realistic for the 14th century) view of medieval Padua, with this church outside the wall (finished by 1300 and looking just like it does today).

Below the cityscape, in a circa-1380 fresco, Anthony on his cloud promises he'll watch over his town. Because people wanted

PADUA

to be buried near a saint, graves lie all around. If you could afford it, this was about the best piece of real estate a dead person could want. (The practice was ended with Napoleonic reforms in 1806.)

Chapel of the Reliquaries

Continue your circuit of the church by going behind the altar into the apse, to the Chapel of the Reliquaries. The most prized relic is in the glass case at center stage—Anthony's tongue. When Anthony's remains were exhumed 32 years after his death (1263), his body had decayed to dust, but his tongue was found miraculously unspoiled and red in color. How appropriate for the great preacher who, full of the Spirit, couldn't stop talking about God.

Work clockwise around the chapel, starting under the dome in front of the staircase at St. Anthony's holy, and holey, tunic *(tonaca)*. His rough-hewn wood coffin is on the left wall. His pillow—a comfy rock—is up the stairs (chest level in first glass case). The center display case contains (top to bottom) the saint's lower jaw *(il mento)*, his uncorrupted tongue *(lingua)*, and, finally, his vocal chords *(apparato vocale)* discovered intact when his remains were examined in 1981. In the last display case, a fragment of the True Cross *(la croce)* is held in a precious crucifix reliquary.

Above the relics is the *Glorification of St. Anthony*. In this Baroque fantasy, a cloud of angels and giddy *putti* tumble to the left and right in jubilation as they celebrate his presence in heaven.

Cloisters

From the right side of the nave as you face the altar, follow signs to *chiostro;* from outside, find signs on the right side of the church.

The main cloister is dominated by an exceptionally bushy magnolia tree, planted in 1810, and by the graves of the most illustrious Padovans, such as Gabriel Fallopius, the scientist who gave his name to his discovery, the Fallopian tube.

Wander around the various cloisters. Picnic tables invite pilgrims and tourists to enjoy meals within the solitude of one of the cloisters (it's covered and suitable even when rainy, also has WCs). The **multimedia exhibit** on the life of St. Anthony is a bit kitschy, as pilgrimage multimedia exhibits tend to be (30 minutes, you move three times as you use headphones to listen to the story of each tableau).

At the far end, a fascinating little **museum** is filled with votives and folk art recounting miracles attributed to Anthony.

The abbreviation *PGR* that you'll see on many votives stands for *per grazia ricevuta*—for answered prayers.

Oratory of St. George

The small but sumptuous Oratory of St. George faces the little square in front of the basilica. The oratory ("ora" means prayer) is not actually a church, though it's certainly a fine place to pray—it's filled with vivid, circa-1370 frescoes showing scenes not of Anthony, but from the life of St. Catherine. Because many lovers credit St. Anthony with finding them their partners—and this is the closest place to St. Anthony where you can be married—it's popular for weddings. While you can see it all from the door, paying the entry fee lets you sit and enjoy this peaceful spot.

Near the Basilica

Prato della Valle—The square is 150 yards southwest of the basilica (down Via Luca Belludi). Once a Roman theater and later

Anthony's preaching grounds, this square claims to be the largest in Italy. It's a pleasant, 400-yard-long, oval-shaped piazza with fountains, walkways, dozens of statues of Padua's eminent citizens, and grass. It's also a lively **market** scene: fruit and vegetables (Mon-Fri 8:00-13:00), clothing, shoes, and household goods (Sat 8:00-19:00), and antiques (third Sun 8:00-19:00).

Botanic Garden (*Orto Botanico*)—Green thumbs appreciate this nearly five-acre botanical garden, which contains the university's vast collection of rare plants. Founded in 1545 to cultivate medicinal plants, it's the world's oldest academic botanical garden still in its original location. A visitors center—in a little cottage to the right of the garden's entrance—houses models of the garden's layout and computer programs that describe the history and composition of the garden in English.

Cost and Hours: Garden—€4; April-Oct daily 9:00-13:00 & 15:00-19:00; Nov-March Mon-Sat 9:00-13:00, closed Sun; entrance 150 yards south of Basilica of St. Anthony—with your back to the facade, take a hard left, Santo tram stop, tel. 049-827-2119, www.ortobotanico.unipd.it.

▲▲▲Scrovegni Chapel (*Cappella degli Scrovegni*)

You must make reservations in advance to see this glorious, recently renovated chapel (see "Reservations," next page). Wallpapered

with Giotto's beautifully preserved cycle of nearly 40 frescoes,
the chapel holds scenes depicting
the lives of Jesus and Mary.

Painted by Giotto and his
assistants from 1303 to 1305 and
considered by many to be the first
piece of modern art, this work
makes it clear: Europe was break-
ing out of the Middle Ages. A
sign of the Renaissance to come, Giotto placed real people in real
scenes, expressing real human emotions. These frescoes were radical for their 3-D nature, lively colors, light sources, emotion, and
humanism.

The chapel was built out of guilt for white-collar crimes.
Reginaldo degli Scrovegni (skroh-VEHN-yee) charged sky-high
interest rates at a time when the Church forbade the practice. He
even caught the attention of Dante, who placed him in one of the
levels of hell in his *Inferno*. When Reginaldo died, the Church
denied him a Christian burial. His son Enrico tried to buy forgiveness for his father's sins by building this superb chapel. After
seeing Giotto's frescoes for the Franciscan monks of St. Anthony,
Enrico knew he'd found the right artist to decorate the interior
(and, he hoped, to save his father's soul). The Scrovegni residence
once stood next to the chapel, but was torn down in 1824.

Cost and Hours: €13 combo-ticket with the Civic Museums
(includes the worthwhile Pinacoteca and Multimedia Room). The
chapel is open March-Oct Mon 9:00-19:00, Tue-Sun 9:00-22:00;
Nov-Feb daily 9:00-19:00. When the Civic Museums are closed—
after 19:00 and on Monday—tickets are €8.

Entry Times: Every 15 minutes (on the quarter-hour), visitors
are admitted for a 15-minute video presentation in an anteroom,
followed by 15 minutes in the chapel itself. After 19:00, visitors
can enter every 20 minutes and get 20 minutes inside (last entry
at 21:40). Daytime 20-minute visits are sometimes possible during
the slowest midwinter months.

Reservations: To protect the paintings from excess humidity,
only 25 people are allowed in the chapel at a time. Prepaid reservations are required. It's easiest to reserve online at www.cappella
degliscrovegni.it (website also sells Padova Cards—described on
page 315). If you reserve by phone, you may need to be persistent
and call several times (tel. 049-201-0020; booking office open
Mon-Fri 9:00-19:00, Sat 9:00-13:00, closed Sun, provide your
credit-card number and hotel telephone number where you can be
reached if necessary the day before your visit).

Helpful Hint: If you packed binoculars, bring them along for

Giotto di Bondone
(c. 1267-1337)

Though details of his life are extremely sketchy, we know that as a 12-year-old shepherd boy, Giotto was discovered paint-

ing pictures of his father's sheep on rock slabs. He became the wealthiest and most famous painter of his day. His achievement is especially remarkable because painters at that time weren't considered anything more than crafts-men and weren't expected to be innovators.

After making a name for himself by painting the life of St. Francis fres-coes in Assisi, the Florentine tackled the Scrovegni Chapel (c. 1303-1305).

At age 35, he was at the height of his powers. His scenes were more realistic and human than anything done for a thousand years. Giotto didn't learn technique by dissecting corpses or studying the mathematics of 3-D perspective; he had innate talent. And his personality shines through in the humanity of his art.

The Scrovegni frescoes break ground by introducing nature—rocks, trees, animals—as a backdrop for religious scenes. Giotto's people, with their voluminous, deeply creased robes, are as sturdy and massive as Greek statues, throw-backs to the Byzantine icon art of the Middle Ages. But these figures exude stage presence. Their gestures are simple but expressive: A head tilted down says dejection, an arm flung out indicates grief, clasped hands indicate hope. Giotto cre-ated his figures not just by drawing outlines and filling them in with single colors; he filled the outlines in with subtle patch-works of lighter and darker shades, and in doing so pioneered modern modeling techniques. Giotto's storytelling style is straightforward, and anyone with knowledge of the episodes of Jesus' life can read the chapel like a comic book.

The Scrovegni represents a turning point in European art and culture—away from scenes of heaven and toward a more down-to-earth, human-centered view.

a better—and more comfortable—view of the uppermost frescoes.

Ideally, book your visit at least 72 hours in advance. It's some-times possible to buy a ticket for the same day at the ticket office (especially for single visitors), but don't count on it.

Getting There: From the train station, it's a 10- to 15-minute walk, or a quick, two-stop tram ride to the Eremitani stop. You'll enter through the Civic Museums building, where you'll find the ticket counter and mandatory bag check.

Scrovegni Chapel

BLUE STARRY SKY

SOUTH

NORTH

JOACHIM

MARY

CHRIST

CHRIST

LAST JUDGEMENT

← WINDOWS

VIRTUES

VICES

SOUTH WALL

NORTH WALL

To Altar

From Anteroom (Entrance & Exit) ←

PADUA

❶ Joachim Driven from the Temple
❷ Joachim Returns to the Sheepfold
❸ Mary's Birth Announced to St. Anne
❹ Birth of Jesus
❺ Slaughter of the Innocents
❻ Jesus Astounding the Scholars
❼ Jesus Drives Out the Money Changers
❽ Last Supper
❾ Betrayal of Christ
❿ Jesus Beaten and Humiliated
⓫ Jesus Carrying the Cross
⓬ Lamentation (Deposition)
⓭ Last Judgment

Getting In: You'll be instructed to pick up your tickets at the ticket office at least an hour before your visit. In practice, I've found that you can arrive later, but give yourself a minimum of 30 minutes to weather any commotion at the desk. Present your confirmation number, verify your time, pick up your ticket, and check any bags or purses.

While waiting for your reserved time, blitz the Pinacoteca and Multimedia Room (described later). Read the chapel description (below) before you enter, since you'll only have a short time in the chapel itself.

The chapel is well-signed: From the ticket counter, go outside and walk 100 yards down the path. Be at the chapel doors at least five minutes before your scheduled visit. The doors are automatic, and if you're even a minute late, you'll forfeit your visit and have to rebook and repay to enter.

At your appointed time, you first enter an anteroom to watch a very instructive 15-minute video (with English subtitles) and to establish humidity levels before continuing into the chapel. No photos are allowed. Although you have only a short visit inside the chapel, it is divine. You're inside a Giotto time capsule, looking back at an artist ahead of his time.

Giotto's Frescoes in the Scrovegni Chapel

Giotto painted the entire chapel in 200 working days over two years, but you'll get only 15 minutes to see it.

As you enter the long, narrow chapel, look straight to the far end—the rear wall is covered with Giotto's big *Last Judgment*. Christ in a bubble is flanked by crowds of saints and by scenes of heaven and hell. This is the final, climactic scene of the story told in the chapel's 38 panels—the three-generation history of Jesus, his mother Mary, and Mary's parents.

The story begins with Jesus' grandparents, on the long south wall (with the windows) in the upper-left corner. ❶ In the first frame, a priest scolds the man who will be Mary's father (Joachim, with the halo) and kicks him out of the temple for the sin of being childless. ❷ In the next panel to the right, Joachim returns dejectedly to his sheep farm. ❸ Meanwhile (next panel), his wife is in the bedroom, hearing the miraculous news that their prayers have been answered—she'll give birth to Mary, the mother of Jesus.

From this humble start, the story of Mary and Jesus spirals clockwise around the chapel, from top to bottom. The top row (both south and north walls) covers Mary's birth and life.

Jesus enters the picture in the middle row of the south (win-

dowed) wall. ❹ The first frame shows his birth in a shed-like manger. In the next frame, the Magi arrive and kneel to kiss his little toes. Then the child is presented in the tiny temple. Fearing danger, the family gets on a horse and flees to Egypt. ❺ Meanwhile, back home, all the baby boys are slaughtered in an attempt to prevent the coming of the Messiah *(Slaughter of the Innocents)*.

Spinning clockwise to the opposite (north) wall, you see (in a badly damaged fresco) ❻ the child Jesus astounding scholars with his wisdom. Next, Jesus is baptized by John the Baptist. His first miracle, at a wedding, is turning jars of water into wine. Next, he raises a mummy-like Lazarus from the dead. Riding a donkey, he enters Jerusalem triumphantly. ❼ In the temple, he drives out the wicked money changers.

Turning again to the south wall (bottom row), we see scenes from Jesus' final days. ❽ In the first frame, he and his followers gather at a table for a Last Supper. Next, Jesus kneels humbly to wash their feet. ❾ He is betrayed with a kiss and arrested. Jesus is tried. ❿ Then he is beaten and humiliated.

❶ Finally (north wall, bottom row), he is forced to carry his own cross, is crucified, and prepared for burial, while his followers mourn (❷ *Lamentation*). Then he is resurrected and ascends to heaven, leaving his disciples to carry on.

❸ The whole story concludes on the rear wall, where Jesus reigns at the Last Judgment. The long south wall (ground level) features the Virtues that lead to heaven, while the north wall has the (always more interesting) Vices. And all this unfolds beneath the blue, starry sky overhead on the ceiling.

Some panels deserve a closer look:

Joachim Returns to the Sheepfold (south wall, upper left, second panel): Though difficult to appreciate from ground level, this oft-reproduced scene is groundbreaking. Giotto—a former shepherd himself—uses nature as a stage, setting the scene in front of a backdrop of real-life mountains, and adding down-home details like Joachim's jumping dog, frozen in midair.

Betrayal of Christ, a.k.a. *Il Bacio*, "The Kiss" (south wall, bottom row, center panel): Amid the crowded chaos of Jesus' arrest, Giotto focuses our eyes on the central action, where Judas ensnares Jesus in his yellow robe (the color symbolizing envy), establishes meaningful eye contact, and kisses him.

Lamentation, a.k.a. *Deposition* (north wall, bottom row, middle): Jesus has been crucified, and his followers weep and wail over the lifeless body. John the Evangelist spreads his arms wide and shrieks, his cries echoed by anguished angels above. Each face is a study in grief. Giotto emphasizes these saints' human vulnerability.

Last Judgment (big west wall): Christ in the center is a glorious vision, but the real action is in hell (lower right). Satan is a Minotaur-headed ogre munching on sinners. Around him, demons give sinners their just desserts in a scene right out of Dante...who was Giotto's friend and fellow Florentine. Front and center is Enrico Scrovegni, in a violet robe (the color symbolizing penitence), donating the chapel to the Church in exchange for forgiveness of his father's sins.

Before the guard scoots you out, take a look at the actual altar. Though Enrico's father's tomb is lost, Enrico Scrovegni himself is in the tomb at the altar. The three statues are by Giovanni Pisano—Mary (in the center) supports baby Jesus on her hip with a perfectly natural, maternal, S-shape. She's flanked by anonymous deacons.

Civic Museums (Musei Civici Agli Eremitani)

The Eremitani, the building next to the Scrovegni Chapel that houses these three museums, was once an Augustinian hermit's monastery. While you can skip the ground-floor Archaeological Museum (with Roman and Etruscan artifacts and no English descriptions), the Pinacoteca and the Multimedia Room are worth visiting. Another part of the museum, Palazzo Zuckermann, is across the street.

Cost and Hours: €13 combo-ticket with Scrovegni Chapel, €10 without the chapel. The Pinacoteca, Archaeological Museum, and Palazzo Zuckermann are open Tue-Sun 9:00-19:00, closed Mon. The Multimedia Room is open daily 9:00-19:00. No photos are allowed, and there's a mandatory and free bag check. The museums are on Piazza Eremitani (Eremitani tram stop, tel. 049-820-4551).

Pinacoteca

The museum's highlight is upstairs, in the Pinacoteca (picture gallery). The collection has 13th- to 18th-century paintings by Titian, Tintoretto, Giorgione, Tiepolo, Veronese, Bellini, Canova, Guariento, and other Veneto artists. But I'd make a beeline for the room with the Giotto crucifix. Ask for it: *"La Croce di Giotto?"*

Originally hung in the Scrovegni Chapel between the Scrovegni family's private zone and the public's worshipping zone, this crucifix is painted on wood by Giotto. If you actually sit on the floor and look up, the body really pops. The adjacent "God as Jesus" piece was the only painting in the otherwise frescoed chapel. (This is hung here because of preservation concerns. Its copy is the only non-original art in the chapel.) Studying these two masterpieces affirms Giotto's greatness.

Behind the crucifix room is a collection of 14th- and 15th-century art. While the works here are exquisite—and came well after Giotto—they're clearly not as modern.

Multimedia Room

The Multimedia Room, dedicated to taking a closer look at the Scrovegni Chapel, is adjacent to the Civic Museum (in the same building). To head straight from the museum entrance to the

Multimedia Room, use the entrance to the right of the main entry, step into the courtyard, make a sharp right, and head down the stairs.

Rows of computer screens offer a virtual Scrovegni Chapel visit and provide cultural insights into daily life in the Middle Ages. There are explanations of the individual panels, Giotto's fresco technique, close-ups of the art, and a description of the restoration. They show a 12-minute video (English headphones available) that is similar—but not identical—to the one that precedes your chapel visit. For me, it's worth just taking some time to enjoy a second video that features a mesmerizing, slow montage of close-ups of the Giotto frescoes.

Between the museum and the chapel are the scant remains of Roman Padua. The remnants are from the wall of an arena and nicely fitting pipes that once channeled water so that the arena could be flooded for special spectacles.

Palazzo Zuckermann

This little-visited wing of the Civic Museum, just across a busy street, is included in the same ticket. Its first two floors offer a commotion of applied and decorative arts—such as clothes, furniture, and ceramics—from the Venetian Republic (1600s-1700s). On the top floor, the Bottacin collection takes you to the 19th century with coins and delightful (but no-name) pre-Impressionist paintings.

More Sights in the Center

Palazzo della Ragione—This grand 13th-century palazzo, commonly called *il Salone* (great hall), once held the medieval law courts. The first floor consists of a huge hall—265 feet by 90 feet—that was at one time adorned with frescoes by Giotto. A fire in 1312 destroyed those paintings, and the palazzo was redecorated with the 15th-century art you see today: a series of 333 frescoes depicting the signs of the zodiac, labors of the month, symbols

representing characteristics of people born under each sign, and, finally, figures of saints to legitimize the power of the courts in the eyes of the Church.

The hall is topped with a hull-shaped roof, which helps to support the structure without the use of columns—quite an architectural feat in its day, considering the building's dimensions. The curious black stone in the corner opposite the big wooden horse is the "Stone of Shame," which was the seat of debtors being punished during the Middle Ages. It was introduced as a compassionate alternative to prison by St. Anthony in 1230. Instead of being executed or doing prison time, debtors sat upon this stone, surrendered their possessions, and denounced themselves publicly before being exiled from the city. The computer kiosks (choose "English") provide excellent information with entertaining videos.

Cost and Hours: €4, Tue-Sun March-Oct 9:00-19:00, closed Mon; Nov-Feb 9:00-18:00, closed Mon year-round. Enter through the east end of Piazza delle Erbe, and go up the long staircase. Ponti Romani tram stop, tel. 049-820-5006. The WCs are through the glass doors at the opposite end of the hall from the wooden horse.

▲▲Market Squares: Piazza delle Erbe, Piazza della Frutta, and Piazza dei Signori—The stately Palazzo della Ragione (described above) provides a dramatic backdrop for Padua's almost exotic-feeling market that fills the surrounding squares—**Piazza delle Erbe** and **Piazza della Frutta**—each morning and all day Saturday (Mon-Fri roughly 8:00-13:00, Sat 8:00-19:00, closed Sun). Second only to the produce market in Italy's gastronomic capital of Bologna, this market has

been renowned for centuries as having the freshest and greatest selection of herbs, fruits, and vegetables. As you wander, appreciate the local passion for good food: Residents can tell the month by the seasonal selections. Merchants share recipe tips with shoppers. The presentation is an art in itself. And don't miss the ground floor of the Palazzo della Ragione. Wandering through this H-shaped arcade—where you'll find various butchers, *salumerie* (delicatessens), cheese shops, bakeries, and fishmongers at work—is a sensuous experience.

Students gather in the squares after the markets have closed, spilling out of colorful bars and cafés—drinks in hand. Pizza by the slice is dirt cheap. A typical snack stand selling all kinds of fresh, hot, and ready-to-eat seafood appetizers sets up in Piazza della Frutta between 17:00 and 20:30 (daily except Sun). Belly up to the bar with your drink and try whatever's being served.

Piazza dei Signori, just a block away, is a busy clothing market in the morning and the most popular gathering place in the evening for students out for a drink. The circa-1400 clock decorates the former palace of the ruling family. The aggressive lion with unfurled wings on the column was a reminder of the Venetian determination to assert its control. Today that lion can be seen as representing the Veneto region's independence from Rome: Italy's north (Veneto and Lombardy) is tired of subsidizing the south. Grumbling about this issue continues to stir talk of splitting the country.

Drinking a Spritz with the Student Crowd—Each early evening, before dinner, students enliven Padua by enjoying a convivial drink in their favorite places. Piazza dei Signori (described above) is the favorite square. Or you could sit in front of the university, nurse your drink, and watch the graduates get roasted with their crazy gangs of friends (see "Graduation Antics in Padua" sidebar, later). The drink of choice is a *spritz,* an aperitif generally made with Campari (liquor infused with bitter herbs), white wine, and sparkling water, and garnished with a blood-orange wedge. Most Paduan women seem to prefer a lighter *spritz* made with Aperol (orange-flavored liquor, less alcohol content).

Grab a table to be part of the scene, or get your *spritz* to take away *(da portar via),* and join the young people out on the piazza. Either way, this is a classic opportunity to enjoy a real discussion with smart, English-speaking students who see tourists not as pests, but as interesting people from far away. For an instant conversation starter, ask about the current political situation in Italy, the right-wing party's policy on immigrants, or the cultural differences between Italy's north and south.

Caffè Pedrocchi—The white-columned, Neoclassical Pedrocchi building is much more than just a café on the ground floor. A complex of meeting rooms and entertainment venues, it stirs the Italian soul (at least, patriotic Italian souls). Built in 1831 during the period of Austrian rule, Caffè Pedrocchi was inaugurated for the fourth Italian Congress of Scientists, which convened during the mid-19th century to stir up nationalistic fervor as Italy struggled to become a united nation. As a symbol of patriotic hope, it was the target (no surprise) of a student uprising plot in 1848. You can still see a bullet hole (framed in silver) in the wall of the Sala Bianca, where one of the insurgents was killed. Nowadays, you get more foam than fervor.

Each of the café's three dining rooms is decorated and furnished in a different color: red, white, or green—representing the colors of the Italian flag. In the outer, unheated Sala Verde (Green Room), people are welcome to sit and relax without ordering anything or having to pay. This is where Italian gentlemen read their newspapers and gather with friends to chat about the old days. In the red room, the clock over the bar is flanked by marble reliefs of morning and night, signaling that it was once open 24 hours a day (in the 19th century). The maps of the hemispheres with south up top reflect the anti-conventional spirit of the place. The menu offers teahouse fare, including salads, sandwiches, and the writer Stendhal's beloved *zabaglione*, a creamy custard made with *marsala* wine (Sun-Thu 9:00-21:00, Fri-Sat 9:00-23:00, two entrances across from Via VIII Febbraio 14 and 20 near Ponti Romani tram stop, tel. 049-878-1231).

Piano Nobile: This upper, "noble floor" of the Pedrocchi building is more elaborate. The rooms are all in different styles, such as Greek, Etruscan, or Egyptian, with good English descriptions throughout. These rooms were intended to evoke memories of the glory of past epochs, which a united Italy had hopes of reliving.

Museum of the Risorgimento: The Piano Nobile hosts a small museum that traces Padua's role in Italian history, from the downfall of the Venetian Republic (1797) to the founding of the Republic of Italy (1948). Exhibits, a few with English descriptions, include uniforms, medals, weaponry, old artillery, Fascist propaganda posters, and a 30-minute propagandistic video (in Italian, but mostly fascinating footage without narration). The video, played on demand, is a "Luce" production (meaning a Mussolini production) and features great scenes of the town in the 1930s, including clips of Il Duce's visit and later WWII bombardments. The war and propaganda posters in the last room are haunting. An old woman pleads to those who might question the Fascist-driven war effort: "Don't betray my son." Another declares, "The Germans are truly our friends." And another asks, "And you...what are you doing?" (€4, Tue-Sun 9:30-12:30 & 15:30-18:00, closed Mon, tel. 049-820-5007). To reach the Piano Nobile, find the stairway in the far wing of the café building.

▲**Baptistery**—This richly frescoed little building was originally the private chapel of Padua's ruling family. Then, in 1405, Venice took over, killing the family, and making the building a baptistery. Located next to Padua's skippable Duomo, the Baptistery was frescoed (c. 1370) by Giusto de' Menabuoi.

While created 70 years after Giotto, the Baptistery feels older. Because the artist was working for a private family, he needed to be politically correct and not threaten or offend the family's allies, especially the Church. While still mind-blowing, the Baptistery's art seems relatively conservative compared to Giotto's Scrovegni Chapel. Giotto, supported by the powerful Scrovegni family and the Franciscans, could get away with being more progressive and bold.

The Baptistery's complex design must have made perfect and cohesive sense to the faithful in centuries past. Almighty Christ is in majesty on top, while approachable Mary and the multitude of saints provide the devout with access to God. Find the world as it was known in the 14th century (the disk below Mary's feet). It kicks off a cycle of scenes illustrating creation (clockwise from the creation of Adam). The four evangelists (Matthew, Mark, Luke, and John) with their books and symbols fill the corners. A vivid crucifixion scene faces a gorgeous annunciation. And the altar niche features a dim, blue-toned, literal Apocalypse from the book of Revelation (€2.80, daily 10:00-18:00).

University of Padua—The main building of this prestigious university, known as Palazzo Bò, is adjacent to Caffè Pedrocchi. Founded in 1222, it's one of the first, greatest, and most progressive universities in Europe. Back when the Church controlled university curricula, a group of professors and students broke free from the University of Bologna to create this liberal school, which would be independent of Catholic constraints and accessible to people of alternative faiths.

A haven for free thought, the university attracted intellectuals from all over Europe, including the great astronomer Copernicus, who realized here that the universe didn't revolve around him. And Galileo—notorious for disagreeing with the Church's views on science—called his 18 years on the faculty here the best of his life.

The gawking public is not really welcomed in the university, but you can poke into two courtyards (weekdays and Saturday mornings only; when closed, just peer through the gate). Find the entrance at Via VIII Febbraio 7, under the "Gymnasium" inscription (facing city hall, 30 yards from Caffè Pedrocchi). You'll pop into a 16th-century courtyard, the school's historic core. It's littered with the coats of arms of important faculty and leaders of the university over the ages. Classrooms, which open onto the square, are still used. Today, students gather here, surrounded by memories of illustrious alumni, including the first woman ever to receive a university degree (in 1678).

Graduation Antics in Padua

With 60,000 students, Padua's university always seems to be hosting graduation ceremonies. There's a constant trickle of happy grads and their friends and families celebrating the big event.

During the school year, every 20 minutes or so, a student steps into a formal room (upstairs, above the university courtyard) to officially meet with the leading professors of his or her faculty. When they're finished, the students are given a green laurel wreath. They pose for ceremonial group photos and family snapshots. It's a sweet scene. Then, craziness takes over.

The new graduates replace their somber clothing with raunchy outfits, as gangs of friends gather around them on Via VIII Febbraio, the street in front of the university. The roast begins. The gang rolls out a giant butcher-paper poster with a generally obscene caricature of the student and a litany of *This Is Your Life* photos and stories. The new grad, subject to various embarrassing pranks, reads the funny statements out loud. The poster is then taped to the university wall for all to see. (Find the plastic panels to the right of the main entry, facing Via VIII Febbraio. Graduation posters are allowed to stay there for 24 hours. The panels are emptied each morning, but by nighttime a new set of posters is affixed to the plastic shields.)

During the roast, the friends sing the catchy but obscene local university anthem, reminding their newly esteemed friend not to get too huffy: *Dottore, dottore, dottore del buso del cul. Vaffancul, vaffancul* (loosely translated: "Doctor, doctor. You're just a doctor of the a-hole...go f-off, go f-off"). After you've heard this song (with its fanfare and oom-pah-pah catchiness) and have seen all the good-natured fun, you can't stop singing it.

The crazy show is usually staged late in the afternoon. Outdoor café tables afford great seats to enjoy the spectacle.

A passageway leads from here to an adjacent second courtyard from the Fascist era (c. 1938). The relief celebrates heroic students in World War I. Off of this courtyard, notice the richly decorated stairway, frescoed in the 1930s with themes celebrating art, science, and the pursuit of knowledge.

The big attraction among tourists is Europe's first great **Anatomy Theater** (from 1594), which you can visit only on a guided tour (explained below). Try to get a ticket, but keep in

PADUA

mind that it's not worth any hero-
ics to see. The first two rooms of
the tour are underwhelming: One
features the supposed "pulpit of
Galileo" (c. 1550) and portraits
of 40 famous alums. The second
is the Aula Magna, a ceremonial
room for festivities. The historic
Anatomy Theater itself is more
impressive. Despite the Church's
strict ban on autopsies, more than 300 students would pack this
theater to watch professors dissect human cadavers (the bodies of
criminals from another town). This had to be done in a "don't ask,
don't tell" kind of way, because the Roman Catholic Church only
started allowing the teaching of anatomy through dissection in the
late 1800s.

Cost and Hours: While it's free to visit the university, you
must sign up for a 30-minute tour (€5) to see the Anatomy Theater.
Only 30 people may enter at a time. Tours run three times a day
(March-Oct Mon, Wed, and Fri at 15:15, 16:15, and 17:15; Tue,
Thu, and Sat at 9:15, 10:15, and 11:15; no tours on Sun, reduced
schedule Nov-Feb—call number below, Ponti Romani tram stop,
www.unipd.it). School groups often book the entire visit, and
many of the guides speak no English.

Confirm tour times and availability by calling 049-827-3047
or stopping by the ticket window (opens 15 minutes before each
tour, located just inside the palace, in the hall reached from the
Fascist-era courtyard described above). The bar there is fun for a
cheap drink and to see photos of university life.

Sleeping in Padua

Rooms in Padua's hotels are more spacious and a better value than
those in Venice. Keep in mind that when large conventions take
over the town—several times a year—all hotels raise prices. I've
listed two hotels in the center and a group of accommodations near
the basilica. All are reachable from the station by the tram; only
Albergo Verdi is more than a five-minute walk from the nearest
tram stop.

In the Center
$$$ Hotel Majestic Toscanelli is a central, fancy hotel with 34
pleasant, air-conditioned rooms and a touch of charm, buried in a
characteristic ghetto with wonderful cobbled ambience. This area
is popular with students at night, and it can be noisy until about
1:00 in the morning; as the hotel's windows are single-paned,

Sleep Code

(€1 = about $1.40, country code: 39)

S = Single, **D** = Double/Twin, **T** = Triple, **Q** = Quad, **b** = bathroom, **s** = shower only. Unless otherwise noted, credit cards are accepted, breakfast is included, and English is spoken.

To help you easily sort through these listings, I've divided the accommodations into three categories based on the price for a standard double room with bath:

$$$ Higher Priced—Most rooms €130 or more.

$$ Moderately Priced—Most rooms between €90-130.

$ Lower Priced—Most rooms €90 or less.

Prices can change without notice; verify the hotel's current rates online or by email. For other updates, see www .ricksteves.com/update.

request a quiet room on the back side (Sb-€95-110, Db-€150-160, ask for 10 percent Rick Steves discount, superior rooms and suites available at extra cost, check website for special discounts, includes a wonderful breakfast, free Wi-Fi, parking-€19/day, Via dell'Arco 2, Tito Livio tram stop, tel. 049-663-244, fax 049-876-0025, www .toscanelli.com, majestic@toscanelli.com). From the tram stop, follow the passageway next to #26 (locked after 20:30), then jog left down Via Marsala and turn right on Via dell'Arco.

$$ Albergo Verdi, a modern little place, is crammed into an old building on a small back street beyond Piazza dei Signori. While public spaces are very tight, the 14 rooms are comfortable (Sb-€70, Db-€90-100, extra person-€30, air-con, elevator—could be Padua's smallest, pay Wi-Fi, Via Dondi dall'Orologio 7, Ponti Romani tram stop, tel. 049-836-4163, fax 049-878-0175, www .albergoverdipadova.it, info@albergoverdipadova.it). From Piazza dei Signori, walk through the arch under the clock tower and go to the far end of Piazza del Capitaniato; the hotel is on the side street to your right.

Near Basilica of St. Anthony

Santo is the nearest tram stop for the following hotels. Use the Prato della Valle tram stop for the hostel.

$$ Hotel Al Fagiano feels like an art gallery with crazy, sexy, modern art everywhere. The hotel is all about the union of a man and a woman (quite romantic). They rent 40 bright and cheery air-conditioned rooms, each uniquely decorated with Rossella Fagiano's canvases (Sb-€64, Db-€100, Tb-€115, ask for 5 percent Rick Steves discount, €7 per person less without breakfast, free

Wi-Fi, parking-€10/day, 50 yards from the Santo tram stop at Via Locatelli 45, tel. & fax 049-875-3396, www.alfagiano.com, info @alfagiano.com).

$$ Hotel Belludi 37 is a slick, borderline-pretentious place renting 15 modern rooms shoehorned into an old building. The decor is dark, woody, fresh, and stylish (S-€80, Sb-€100, Db-€120, bigger Db-€135, ask for 10 percent Rick Steves discount, €7 less per person without breakfast, air-con, Wi-Fi, a block from the Santo tram stop at Via Luca Belludi 37, tel. 049-665-633, fax 049-658-685, www.belludi37.it, info@belludi37.it).

$ Hotel Casa del Pellegrino, with 150 spotless, cheap, institutional rooms and straight pricing, is home to the pilgrims who come to pay homage to St. Anthony in the basilica next door. But any visitor to Padua is welcome (S-€51, Sb-€69, D-€72, Db-€89, Tb-€106, Qb-€128, family rooms-€145, ask for a room off the street, €7 less per person without breakfast, air-con, elevator, free Wi-Fi, parking-€5/day, Via Cesarotti 21, tel. 049-823-9711, fax 049-823-9780, www.casadelpellegrino.com, info@casadel pellegrino.com). For better accommodations, request one of the 24 "superior" rooms in the *dipendenza,* the hotel's modern wing (€5 extra/night).

$ Hotel Al Santo, run with charm by Valentina and Antonio, offers 15 spacious rooms with all the comforts on two floors above their restaurant, a few steps from the basilica (Sb-€65-70, Db-€90, Tb-€120, Qb-€135, double-paned windows, quieter rooms off street, some rooms have views of basilica, air-con, elevator, free Wi-Fi, parking-€14/day, Via del Santo 147, tel. 049-875-2131, fax 049-878-8076, www.alsanto.it, alsanto@alsanto.it).

Hostel: **$ Ostello Città di Padova,** near Prato della Valle, is well-run and has 80 beds in 4-, 6-, and 9-bed rooms (beds with sheets and breakfast-€19; family rooms-€90; free Wi-Fi, laundry-€5.50/load, lockers, reception open 7:00-9:30 & 15:30-23:30, rooms locked during afternoon but reception staffed if you need to leave bags, 23:30 curfew; Via Aleardi 30, Prato de Valle tram stop, tel. 049-875-2219, fax 049-654-210, www.ostellopadova.it, ostello padova@ctgveneto.it). From the tram stop, exit the square ahead of you to the right and make an immediate left down Via Memmo; after the church, continue straight one block on Via Torresini and turn right on Via Aleardi.

Eating in Padua

The university population means cheap, good food abounds. For picnic shopping, see "Market Squares," on page 331. My recommended restaurants are all centrally located in the historic core. You'd think there would be fine dining on the charming market squares, but on the piazzas it's a take-out-pizza-and-casual-bar scene (dominated by students after dark). La Lanterna, at the neighboring Piazza dei Signori, is the best on-square option I've found—but it's still basically pizza. The dreamily atmospheric ghetto neighborhood (just two blocks off the market squares) thrives after dark with trendy bars and a lively student *spritz* scene.

Fine Dining near the Center

Osteria dei Fabbri, with shared rustic tables, offers a good mix of class and accessibility, quality, and price. The dining room is spacious, and the dishes are traditional Venetian (€9 pastas, €14 *secondi*, €2.50 cover, Mon-Sat 12:30-14:30 & 19:30-22:30, closed Sun, Via dei Fabbri 13, on a side street on south side of Piazza Erbe, tel. 049-650-336).

Osteria L'Anfora is a classic place serving classic dishes in an informal, fun-loving space. Don't be put off by the woody, ruffian decor and the fact that it's a popular hangout for a pre-meal drink. They take food seriously and serve it at good prices, and the energy and commotion add to a great dining experience (€9 pastas, €14-16 *secondi*, €2 cover, meals served Mon-Sat 12:30-15:00 & 19:30-22:30, closed Sun, no reservations taken, Via dei Soncin 13, tel. 049-656-629).

Ristorante alle Piazze da Giorgio is a respected fixture in town for its dressy white-tablecloth dining. They are passionate about their vegetarian dishes and proud of their bean soup, fish soup, cod, and squid. Reservations are smart at night (€9-11 pastas, €18-24 *secondi*, €3 cover, save with €14-18 single-plate specials and €20-28 three-course lunches, meals served 12:00-15:00 & 19:00-24:00, closed Sun, Via Daniele Manin 8, tel. 049-836-0973).

Cheap Eats near the Center

La Lanterna has a forgettable interior, but a pizza here on Piazza dei Signori includes a rare-in-Padua chance to sit in a grand square under the stars, surrounded by great architecture. Its pizzas are a local favorite—takeaway available—and reservations are recommended (€6.50-8.50 pizzas, €8 pastas, €14 *secondi*, €1.60 cover, Fri-Wed 12:00-14:30 & 18:00-24:00, closed Thu, Piazza dei Signori 39, tel. 049-660-770).

Bar dei Osei, on Piazza della Frutta, is a very simple sandwich bar with some of the best outdoor seats in town. While Paduans love their delicate *tremazzini*—white bread sandwiches with crusts cut off (€1.30/€1.80 with table service), I'd choose their *porchetta*—savory roasted sandwiches (€3.50/€3.80). The two-foot-long mother lode awaits on the counter for you to say how big a slice you'd like. Wines are listed on the board (Mon-Sat 7:00-21:00, closed Sun, Piazza della Frutta 1, tel. 049-875-9606). With a fast, cheap meal and drink in hand, grab a seat and enjoy the market scene.

Brek, with one entrance next to the Ponti Romani tram stop and another tucked into a corner of Piazza Cavour at #20, is an easy self-service chain *ristorante* with healthy and affordable choices. It's big, bright, practical, and family-friendly (pastas €4-5, no cover, daily 11:30-15:00 & 18:30-22:00, tel. 049-875-3788).

Brek Foccacceria (part of the same chain), across from Caffè Pedrocchi and next door to the PAM supermarket, is a café selling big sandwiches and slices of pizza that you can eat at outdoor tables (daily 8:00-22:00, Piazzetta della Garzeria 6, tel. 049-876-1651).

Stock up on picnic items at the outdoor markets, or visit the **PAM supermarket,** in the tiny *piazzetta* east of Caffè Pedrocchi (Mon-Sat 8:00-21:00, closed Wed after 14:00 and all day Sun, Piazzetta Garzeria 3).

Near the Basilica of St. Anthony

Pizzeria Pago Pago dishes up wood-fired Neapolitan pizzas (a local favorite) and daily specials depending on what's in season. Get there early for dinner or wait (€5.50-7.50 pizzas, €2.50 cover, Wed-Mon 12:00-14:00 & 19:00-24:00, closed Tue; 2 blocks from Basilica of St. Anthony, up Via del Santo and right onto Via Galileo Galilei to #59; tel. 049-665-558, Gaetano and Modesto).

Casa del Pellegrino Ristorante caters to St. Anthony pilgrims with simple, basic, and hearty meals, served in a cheery dining room just north of the basilica. *Baccalà* (cod) is a favorite here (€4-6 pastas, €7.50-9.50 *secondi*, €14 fixed-price meal includes water and coffee, €1.70 cover, daily 12:00-14:00 & 19:30-21:30, Via Cesarotti 21, tel. 049-876-0715).

Zairo is a huge indoor/outdoor *ristorante*/pizzeria with reasonable prices, delicious homemade pastas, Veneto specialties, snappy service, and a local clientele (€6-8 pastas, Tue-Sun 12:00-14:30 & 19:00-24:00, closed Mon, east side of the vast Prato della Valle square at #51, tel. 049-663-803).

Pollodoro la Gastronomica, my pick of the take-out delis near the basilica, sells roast chicken, pastas, pizza, and veggies, and will make sandwiches (Wed-Sat and Mon 9:00-14:00 & 17:00-20:00, Sun 9:00-14:00 only, closed Tue, 100 yards from basilica at Via Belludi 34, tel. 049-663-718). You can picnic at the nearby cloisters of the basilica.

Padua Connections

From Padua by Train to: Venice (2/hour, 30-50 minutes), **Vicenza** (2/hour, fewer on weekends, 15-25 minutes), **Milan** (1-2/hour, 2-3 hours), **Verona** (2/hour, 40-60 minutes), **Ravenna** (roughly hourly, change in Bologna or Ferrara, 2.5-3 hours).

By Bus to: Venice (45 minutes, €3.70, hourly at :25 past the hour from 5:25 to 22:25, also at :55 past the hour from 5:55 to 8:55 and 13:55 to 18:55) and Venice's **Marco Polo Airport** (65 minutes, €4.30 plus €1.10 per piece of luggage, same departure times). Buses depart from platform 11 at Padua's bus station, next to the train station; recheck times at www.sitabus.it. If flying into the airport, take this bus to get directly to Padua (buy tickets at windows in arrivals hall or at airport TI).

By Minibus to Airports: A minibus service runs from Padua to **Marco Polo Airport** (€28/person) or **Treviso Airport** (€39/person, reservations required, tel. 049-870-4425, www.airservice padova.it).

Near Padua: Vicenza

To many architects, Vicenza (vih-CHEHN-zah) is a pilgrimage site. Entire streets look like the back of a nickel. This is the city of Andrea Palladio (1508-1580), the 16th-century Renaissance architect who gave us the Palladian style that is so influential in countless British country homes. But as grandiose as Vicenza's Palladian facades may feel, there is little marble here. The city lacked the wealth to build with much more than painted wood and plaster.

If you're an architecture buff, Vicenza merits a quick day trip on any day but Monday, when major sights are closed. If you're packing light, it's an easy stop, located on the same train line as Padua, Verona, and Venice. But because you can't store bags at the train station, it's not worth stopping if you have lots of luggage.

Tourist Information: Vicenza has two TIs. The larger one is next to the Olympic Theater at Piazza Matteotti 12 (daily 9:00-13:00 & 14:00-18:00, tel. 0444-320-854, www.vicenzae.org) and the other is at Piazza dei Signori 8 (daily 9:00-14:00 & 14:30-18:30). Ask for the free brochure on Palladio's buildings. Architecture fans appreciate the €2.50 *Vicenza and the Villas of Andrea Palladio.*

Arrival in Vicenza: From the **train station,** I'd head straight for the most distant sight, the Olympic Theater (with a TI next door), and then see other sights on the way back. Go straight out the train station's front door, and use the crosswalk on the right side of the roundabout. From here, it's a 5-minute walk straight ahead up wide Viale Roma to the PAM supermarket at the bottom of Corso Palladio; turn right through the gate and then it's a good 10 minutes more down the Corso to the Olympic Theater (a taxi costs €8). **Drivers** can park in one of the cheap parking lots (Parcheggio Bassano and Parcheggio Cricoli), and catch a free

Vicenza

shuttle bus to the center.

Helpful Hints: All of the sights mentioned (except the villas outside of town) are covered by the **Card Musei** combo-ticket (€8.50/3 days, sold at Olympic Theater and Palazzo Leoni Montanari). In a pinch, the TIs may be willing to store bags for you while you walk around town.

Sights in Vicenza

Helpful bilingual signs in front of Palladio's buildings explain their history. Arrows around town point you to his major works, and you can also pick up a map from the TI.

▲▲**Olympic Theater (Teatro Olimpico)**—Palladio's last work, one of his greatest, shouldn't be missed. This indoor theater is a wood-and-stucco festival of classical columns, statues, and an oh-wow stage bursting with perspective tricks

Cost and Hours: Entry only with €8.50 Card Musei, which covers other Vicenza sights; audioguide available, Tue-Sun 9:00-17:00, closed Mon, last entry 30 minutes before closing, very

occasionally closed when theater is in use, entrance to left of TI at Piazza Matteotti 11, tel. 0444-222-800, www.comune.vicenza .it. When you step back outside, look up the town's main drag—named after Palladio. It's the same main street you saw on the stage of his theater.

▲**Church of Santa Corona**—A block away from the Olympic Theater and currently being restored, this "Church of the Holy Crown" was built in the 13th century to house a thorn from the Crown of Thorns, given to the Bishop of Vicenza by the French King Louis IX. The church has two artistic highlights: the art embellishing its high altar and Giovanni Bellini's fine painting, *Baptism of Christ*. During restoration, its paintings are on display at the Diocesan Museum.

Cost and Hours: €5, Tue-Sun 10:00-13:00 & 14:00-18:00, closed Mon, Piazza Duomo 12, tel. 0444-226-400, www.museo diocesanovicenza.it.

Archaeological and Natural History Museum—Located next door to the Church of Santa Corona, this museum has a ground floor featuring Roman antiquities (mosaics, statues, and artifacts excavated from Rome's Baths of Caracalla, plus swords) and a barbarian warrior skeleton complete with sword and helmet. Prehistoric scraps are upstairs. Look for English description sheets near exhibit entryways throughout.

Cost and Hours: Covered by Card Musei, Tue-Sun 9:00-17:00, closed Mon, Contrà Santa Corona 4, tel. 0444-222-811, www.museicivicivicenza.it.

Palazzo Leoni Montanari—Across the street from the Church of Santa Corona, this small museum is a palatial riot of Baroque, with cherub-cluttered ceilings jumbled like a preschool in heaven. A quick stroll shows off Venetian paintings and a floor of Russian icons.

Cost and Hours: €5, Tue-Sun 10:00-18:00, closed Mon, last entry 30 minutes before closing, Contrà Santa Corona 25, tel. 800-578-875, www.palazzomontanari.com.

Piazza dei Signori—Vicenza's main square has been the center of town ever since it was the site of the ancient Roman forum. The commanding **Basilica Palladiana,** with its 270-foot-tall, 13th-century tower, dominates the square (may be under renovation during your visit). It was a meeting place for local big shots. It was young Palladio's proposal—to redo Vicenza's dilapidated Gothic palace of justice in the Neo-Greek style—that established him as the city's favorite architect. The rest of Palladio's career was a one-man construction boom. When the basilica reopens sometime in 2012, it'll host special exhibitions that sometimes involve a fee, but you can often pop in for a free look.

Villas on the Outskirts of Vicenza—Vicenza is surrounded by dreamy Venetian villas. Venice's commercial empire receded in the 1500s when trade began to pick up along the Atlantic seaboard and dwindle in the Mediterranean. Venice redirected its economic agenda to agribusiness, which led to the construction of lavish country villas, such as **Villa la Rotonda** (the inspiration for Thomas Jefferson's Monticello) and **Villa Valmarana ai Nani** (www.villavalmarana.com). Located southeast of the town center, both houses are furnished with period pieces and come with good English descriptions (closed Mon). Pick up the free English brochure on Palladio's villas from the TI if you plan to visit.

Vicenza Connections

From Vicenza by Train to: Venice (2/hour, 45-75 minutes), **Padua** (2/hour, fewer on weekends, 15-25 minutes), **Verona** (2/hour, 30-60 minutes), **Milan** (1-2/hour, 1.75-2.5 hours). Unless you crave speed or need to burn a railpass day, you'll save a lot of money by taking the slow *R* trains to Vicenza instead of the fast *ES* trains.

VERONA

Romeo and Juliet made Verona a household word. Alas, a visit here has nothing to do with those two star-crossed lovers. You can pay to visit the house that falsely claims to be Juliet's (with an almost believable balcony and a courtyard swarming with tour groups), join in the tradition of rubbing the breast of Juliet's statue to help find a lover (or to pick up the sweat of someone who can't), and even make a pilgrimage to what isn't "La Tomba di Giulietta."

Fiction aside, Verona—Italy's fourth-most-visited city—has been an important crossroads for 2,000 years and is therefore packed with genuine history. R and J fans will take some solace in the fact that two real feuding families, the Montecchi and the Cappellos, were the models for Shakespeare's Montagues and Capulets. And, if R and J had existed and were alive today, they would still recognize much of their "hometown."

Verona's main attractions are its wealth of Roman ruins; the remnants of its 13th- and 14th-century political and cultural boom; its 21st-century, quiet, pedestrian-only ambience; and its world-class opera festival, held each summer (www.arena.it). After Venice's festival of tourism, Veneto's second city (in population and in artistic importance) is a cool and welcome sip of pure Italy, where dumpsters are painted by schoolchildren as class projects and public spaces are the domain of locals, not tourists. If you like Italy but don't need blockbuster sights, this town is a joy.

Orientation to Verona

Verona's old town fills an easy-to-defend bend in the River Adige. The vibrant and enjoyable core of Verona is along Via Mazzini between Piazza Brà (pronounced "bra") and Piazza Erbe, Verona's market square since Roman times. Via Mazzini attracts mob scenes during the *passeggiata* (evening stroll), so don't neglect the parallel Corso Porta Borsari. Across the river, to the east of the old town, the quieter neighborhood of Veronetta offers a few sights and accommodations. For a good day trip to Verona, visit the Roman Arena and then take my self-guided walk.

Tourist Information

Verona's TI is just off **Piazza Brà**—from the square, head behind the big yellow building with columns and cross the street to Via degli Alpini 9 (Mon-Sat Feb-Nov 9:00-19:00, Dec-Jan 9:00-18:00; Sun 10:00-16:00 year-round, tel. 045-806-8680, www.tourism .verona.it). Pick up the free city map for a list of sights and opening hours, and confirm the walking-tour schedule. If you're staying the night, ask about concerts or pick up the monthly entertainment guide, *Carnet Verona* (free at TI, €1 at newsstands).

Verona Card: This tourist card covers bus transportation and entrance to all the recommended Verona sights, except the manicured Giusti Garden (€15/2 days or €20/5 days, sold at TIs and at participating sights). If you visit the Roman Arena (€6), climb Torre dei Lamberti (€6), explore Castelvecchio (€6), tour two churches (€5), and take a bus ride (€1.10), you'll pay €24.10. At €15, the card saves a day-tripper intent on blitzing the city almost 40 percent.

The €6 **Church Card**, sold at four churches (San Zeno, Duomo, Sant'Anastasia, and San Fermo) that require admission, pays off if you visit at least three (www.chieseverona.it). There's no need to get both tourist cards.

Arrival in Verona

By Train: Get off at the Verona Porta Nuova station. You'll emerge into the station from one of two passages. In the main hall, you'll find WCs (€0.80) and a baggage check office (€4/5 hours, €11/24 hours, daily 7:00-23:00, 44 pounds maximum). Buses and taxis are immediately outside.

Avoid the boring 15-minute walk from the station to Piazza Brà by catching a **city bus.** Before boarding, buy an individual ticket from the tobacco shop inside the station (€1.10/1 hour, €3.50 day pass valid until midnight). Now find platform A in front of the station and hop on bus #11, #12, or #13. After 20:00 and all day Sunday, though, you'll want bus #90, #92, or #98. If in doubt, confirm that your bus is headed to the city center by asking, *"Per il centro?"* (pehr eel CHEN-troh). Validate your ticket by stamping it in the machine on the bus. (For public transport information, visit www.atv.verona.it.)

Drivers don't announce stops, but you'll know Piazza Brà because of the can't-miss-it Roman Arena. The TI is just a few steps beyond the bus stop (keep walking along the medieval walls). You can catch return buses to the station (same numbers) from the stop on the piazza side of the street, or from another bus stop just outside the city wall on Corso Porta Nuova (on the right).

Taxis pick up only at taxi stands (at Piazza Brà and train station) and cost about €8 for the quick ride between the train station and the center of town.

By Car: The town center is closed to traffic, but if you're staying here, your hotel can get you permission to drive in—ask when you book. Otherwise your license plate could be photographed, and a €100 ticket might be waiting in the mail when you get home.

Drivers will find reasonably priced parking in well-marked lots and garages just outside the center. The underground **Cittadella garage,** at Piazza Cittadella (a block off Piazza Brà, behind the TI), is huge, convenient, and easy to find (€1.90/hour, €12/24 hours). The lot in front of the train station costs less (€9.40/24 hours), but you'll spend your savings on the bus to the center. Street parking costs €1.50 per hour (buy ticket at a tobacco shop to put on dashboard, spaces marked with blue lines, maximum two hours).

By Plane: Efficient buses connect Verona's airport (known as Catullo or Verona-Villafranca, 12 miles southwest of the city) with its train station (€5, buy tickets on board or at tobacco shop, daily about 5:40-23:00, 3/hour, 15 minutes, bus stop is by front door of train station, www.aeroportoverona.it).

From Brescia Airport, 40 miles west of Verona, a bus meets Ryanair flights and takes passengers to the train station (€11, buy tickets on board, bus schedule is coordinated with Ryanair arrivals and departures).

Helpful Hints

Sightseeing Schedules: Many sights are closed on Mondays, at least in the morning.

Opera: From mid-June through early September, Verona's opera festival brings the city to life, with 15,000 music fans filling the Roman Arena for almost nightly performances. The city is packed and festive—restaurants have prescheduled seatings for dinner and hotels jack up their prices (cheap upper-level seats about €27, book tickets either online at www.arena.it or by calling 045-800-5151; box office open Mon-Fri 9:00-12:00 & 15:15-17:45, Sat-Sun 9:00-12:00; during opera season, open daily 10:00-17:45, or until 21:00 on performance days; Via Dietro Anfiteatro 6B).

Internet Access: Try **Verona Web** (Mon-Fri 10:00-20:00, Sat-Sun 14:00-20:00, a couple of blocks off Piazza Brà toward Castelvecchio at Via Roma 17A, tel. 045-801-3394) or **Internet**

Etc. (€5.50/hour, Tue-Sat 10:00-19:45, Sun-Mon 15:30-19:45, off Via Mazzini on Via Quattro Spade 3B, tel. 045-800-0222).

Tours in Verona

Walking Tours—The TI organizes 1.5-hour tours in English (March-Oct Fri-Sun 11:30, no tours off-season, €10 per person). Tours meet inside the Piazza Brà TI and stroll all the way through the old town (call to confirm schedule, no reservation necessary, tel. 045-806-8680).

Private Guides—Two excellent and enthusiastic Verona guides enjoy giving private tours of the town and region to readers of this book (€105/2 hours and €210/5 hours per group, tours tailored to your interests—villas, wine tasting, and so on). They are **Marina Menegoi** (tel. 045-801-2174, mobile 328-958-1108, mmenegoi @gmail.com) and **Valeria Biasi** (€65/hour, ask for Rick Steves discount, mobile 348-903-4238, www.aguideinverona.com, valeria @aguideinverona.com). For families with children, Valeria offers an interactive game in the city called Safari (€130/2.5 hours).

Self-Guided Walk

Welcome to Verona Town Walk

This walk covers the essential sights in the town core, starting at Piazza Brà and ending at the cathedral. Allow 1.5 hours (including the tower climb and dawdling, more with the optional detours).

❶ Piazza Brà

If you're wondering about the name, it comes from the local dialect and means "open space." A generation ago this piazza was noisy with cars. Now it's open and people friendly—it's become the community family room and natural festival grounds.

Grab a bench near the central fountain called "The Alps." This was a gift from Verona's sister city Munich, which is just over the mountains to the north. You'll see in the middle of the fountain the symbols of the two cities with the peaks carved out of pink marble from this region.

The ancient Arena looming over the piazza is a reminder that the city's history goes back to Roman times. On this walk, we'll meander across what was the ancient city, from the Arena on this side to the theater across the river.

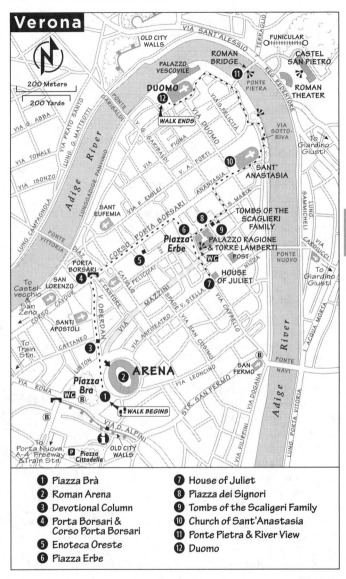

Verona

200 Meters
200 Yards

1. Piazza Brà
2. Roman Arena
3. Devotional Column
4. Porta Borsari &
   Corso Porta Borsari
5. Enoteca Oreste
6. Piazza Erbe
7. House of Juliet
8. Piazza dei Signori
9. Tombs of the Scaligeri Family
10. Church of Sant'Anastasia
11. Ponte Pietra & River View
12. Duomo

With the fall of Rome in the fifth century, Verona became a favored capital of barbarian kings. In the Middle Ages, noble families had to choose sides in the civil struggles between emperors (Ghibellines) and popes (Guelphs). During this time, the town bristled with San Gimignano-type towers, built by different families to symbolize their power. When the Scaligeri family rose to power here in the 14th century, they established stability on their terms and made the other noble families lop off their proud tow-ers—only the Scaligeris were allowed to keep theirs. But inter-family feuds made it impossible for the Scaligeris to maintain a stable government, and in 1405 the town essentially gave itself to Venice, which ruled Verona until Napoleon stopped by in 1796. During the 19th century, a tug-of-war between France and Austria actually divided the city for a time, with the river marking the border of each country's domain. Eventually Verona, like Venice, fell into Austrian hands. The huge yellow Neoclassical city hall facing Piazza Brà (look for the flags) was built by the Austrians to serve as their 19th-century military headquarters. The big statue is of Italy's first king, Victor Emmanuel II, and celebrates Italian independence and unity, won in the 1860s.

Apart from all its history, Piazza Brà is about strolling... the evening *passeggiata* is a national sport in Italy. The broad, shiny sidewalk was named the "Liston" (ribbon) by 17th-century Venetians, who made it big and wide so that promenading social-ites could see and be seen in all their finery.

VERONA

❷ Roman Arena

The Romans built this stadium outside their town walls, just as modern stadiums are usually located outside downtown districts. With 72 aisles, this elliptical 466-by-400-foot amphitheater is the third largest in the Roman world (and it was originally 50 percent taller). Most of the stone you see is original. Dating from the first century A.D., it looks great in its pink marble. Over the cen-turies, crowds of up to 25,000 spectators have cheered Roman gladiator battles, medieval executions, and modern plays—including the popular opera festival (held every sum-mer), which takes advantage of the Arena's famous acoustics. While there's little to see inside except for the impressive stonework, it

is memorable to visit a Roman arena that is still a thriving concert venue. If you climb to the top, you'll enjoy great city views.

Cost and Hours: €6, don't bother with the combo-ticket that includes the unimpressive Maffei Museum, Tue-Sun 8:30-19:30, Mon 13:30-19:30, closes at 14:00 during opera season from mid-June through early Sept, last entry one hour before closing, WC near entry, tel. 045-800-3204.

• *As you exit the Arena, look to your right. Where the street splits you'll see a column.*

❸ Devotional Column

In the Middle Ages, this column blessed a marketplace held here. Ten yards in front of it, a bronze plaque in the sidewalk shows the Roman city plan—a town of 20,000 placed strategically in the bend of the river, which provided protection on three sides. A wall enclosed the peninsula. The center of the grid was the forum, today's Piazza Erbe. (If you look down Via Mazzini, the busy main pedestrian drag, the bell tower in the distance marks Piazza Erbe.)

• *After viewing the bronze plaque, turn around so your back is to the Arena. Head straight down Via Oberdan and continue a couple of blocks until you see an ancient gate, the Porta Borsari. Walk up to it.*

❹ Porta Borsari and Corso Porta Borsari

You're standing before the main entrance to Roman Verona; back in the day, this gate functioned as a toll booth (*borsari* means purse,

referring to the collection of tolls here). Below the spiral, fluted columns (which parents nickname *"tortiglioni"*—a pasta kids can relate to), you'll see the names of patrons ("this arch was brought to you by the generous support of..."). Outside the adjacent Caffè Rialto, the stone on the curb is from a tomb—in Roman times, the roads outside the walls were lined with tombstones, because burials were not allowed within the town itself. Step into the café. A glass panel in the floor shows the original Roman foundations and pavement stones.

Now head into the ancient city and walk down Corso Porta Borsari, the Roman main drag, toward what was the forum. Make it a scavenger hunt. As you walk, discover bits of the town's illustrious past—chips of Roman columns, medieval reliefs, fine old facades, fossils in marble—as well as its elegant present of fancy shops, in a setting that prioritizes pedestrians over cars.

• *Between Corso Porta Borsari 13 and 15, detour right down Vicolo San Marco in Foro, following the* Pozzo dell'Amore *sign. Twenty yards ahead on your right, you'll find...*

❺ Enoteca Oreste

This funky wine and grappa bar is still run by Oreste (with his Chicagoan wife,

Beverly) like a 1970s, old-style *enoteca*. Browse and sample. This historic *enoteca* was once the private chapel of the archbishop of Verona. Traces of the past hide between the bottles—ask Beverly to tell you the story (Tue-Sun 8:00-20:00, closed Mon, Vicolo San Marco in Foro 7, tel. 045-803-4369).

• *Return to Corso Porta Borsari and continue one block until you hit a big square.*

❻ Piazza Erbe

This bustling market square is a photographer's delight. Its pastel buildings corral the fountains, pigeons, and people who have congregated here since Roman times, when this was a forum. Notice the Venetian lion hovering above the square atop a column, reminding locals of the conquest of 1405. During medieval times, the stone canopy in the center of the square held the scales where merchants measured the weight of goods they bought and sold,

such as silk, wool, and wood. A fountain has bubbled here for 2,000 years. The original Roman statue lost its head and arms. After a sculptor added a new head and arms, the statue became Verona's Madonna. She holds a small banner that reads, "I want justice and I bring peace."

If you were standing here in the Middle Ages, you would have been surrounded by proud noble family towers. Medieval nobles showed off with towers. Renaissance nobles showed off with finely painted facades on their palaces. If you look carefully, you can see remnants of the 16th-century days when Verona was nicknamed "the painted city."

Locals like to start their evening with an *aperitivo* here. It's a trendy scene, as young Veronans fill the bars to enjoy their refreshing *spritz* drinks, olives, and chips.

• *At the far end of Piazza Erbe is a market column featuring St. Zeno, the patron of Verona, who looks at the crazy crowds flushing into the city's silly claim to touristic fame: the House of Juliet (100 yards down Via Cappello to #23—just follow the crowds). Side-trip there now (but watch your wallet—it's a pickpocket's haven).*

❼ House of Juliet

The tiny, admittedly romantic courtyard is a spectacle in itself, with tourists from all over the world posing on the balcony, Nebraskans polishing Juliet's bronze breast, and amorous graffiti everywhere. Residents marvel that each year, about 1,600 Japanese tour groups break their Venice-Milan ride for an hour-long stop in Verona just to see this courtyard. Hang out and savor the scene. The information boxes (€1 for two people) offer a good story: "While no documentation has been discovered to prove the truth of the legend, no documentation has disproved it either." The "museum," which displays art inspired by the love story, plus costumes and the bed from Franco Zeffirelli's film *Romeo and Juliet,* is certainly not worth the €6 entry fee (Tue-Sun 8:30-19:30, Mon 13:30-19:30, tel. 045-803-4303).

Was there a Juliet Capulet? You just walked down Via Cappello, the street of the cap makers. Above the courtyard entry (looking out) is a coat of arms featuring a hat—representing a family that made hats and which would be named, logically, Capulet.

The world does love Juliet. Upstairs (through the embroidery store on the left as you enter the courtyard) is the home of Verona's Juliet Club (www.julietclub.com). Every day, volunteers respond to countless letters addressed simply to Juliet, Verona, Italy. You can see them at work and read a smattering of love letters (9:00-20:00). There's also a fine view of the courtyard from here.

• *Return to Piazza Erbe. From the middle of the piazza, head right on Via della Costa—look for the whale's rib suspended under an arch. It was likely a souvenir brought home by a traveling merchant, reminding the townspeople that there was a big world out there. Walk down Via della Costa, into the big square.*

❽ Piazza dei Signori

Literally the "Lords' Square," this is Verona's sitting room, quieter and more harmonious than Piazza Erbe. The buildings—which span five centuries—define the square and are all linked by arches. The long portico on the left is inspired by Brunelleschi's Hospital of the Innocents (considered the first Renaissance building) in Florence.

Locals call the square Piazza Dante for the statue of the Italian poet Dante Alighieri that dominates it. Dante—always pensive, never smiling—seems to wonder why the tourists choose Juliet over him. Dante was expelled from Florence for political reasons and was granted asylum in Verona by the Scaligeri family. With the whale's rib behind you, you're facing the brick, crenellated, 14th-century Scaligeri residence. Behind Dante is the yellowish, 15th-century Venetian Renaissance-style Portico of the Counsel. In front of Dante to his right is the 12th-century Romanesque **Palazzo della Ragione.**

Follow the white *WC* signs into the courtyard of the Palazzo della Ragione. The impressive stairway is the only surviving Renaissance staircase in Verona. For a grand city view, you can climb to the top of the palazzo's 13th-century **Torre dei Lamberti** (€6 for stairs or elevator, daily June-Sept 8:30-20:30, Oct-May 8:30-19:30, ticket office next to staircase). The elevator saves you 245 steps—but you'll still need to climb about 45 more to get to the first viewing platform. It's not worth continuing up the endless spiral stairs to the second viewing platform.

• *Exit the courtyard the way you entered and turn right, continuing downhill. Within a block, you'll find the...*

❾ Tombs of the Scaligeri Family

These exotic and very Gothic 14th-century tombs, with their fine, original, wrought-iron protective cages, evoke the age when one family ruled Verona. The Scaligeri were to Verona what the Medici family was to Florence. These were powerful people. They changed the law so that they could be buried within the town. They forbade the presence of any towers but their own. And, by building tombs atop pillars, they arranged to be looked up to even in death.

• *Continue 15 yards to the next corner and take a left on Vicolo Cavalletto. At the first corner, turn right along Corso Sant'Anastasia toward the big, unfinished brick facade of Verona's largest church. For a fragrant and potentially tasty diversion, pop into the recommended* **Albertini** *and* **Gastronomia,** *two classic, family-run alimentari, both located on your left in the next block. Either can rustle up tasty sandwiches (about €3-4), and Albertini sells cold beers and juices.*

⑩ Church of Sant'Anastasia

This church was built from the late 13th century through the 15th

century. Although the facade was never finished (the builders ran out of steam), the interior was—and still is—brilliant. Step inside to see the delightful way this region's medieval churches were painted. Note the grimacing hunchbacks holding basins of holy water on their backs (near main entrance at base of columns). And don't miss Pisanello's fresco of *St. George and the Princess of Trebizond* (1438; at the tip of the arch, high above chapel to right of altar). Once color-ful, it has oxidized over time to its current monochrome state. For a closer look at its wonderful detail, check out the images on the com-puter terminal below. Ask for the English brochure, which describes the story of the church

Cost and Hours: €2.50, March-Oct Mon-Sat 9:00-18:00, Sun 13:00-18:00; Nov-Feb closes daily at 17:00, www.chieseverona.it.

• *Leaving the church, make two lefts, and walk along the right side of the church to Via Sottoriva. To the right, the Sottoriva arcade was once busy with colorful wine bars and osterie, some of which still exist (see "Eating in Verona," later). But for now, head to the left on Via Sottoriva. In a block, you'll reach a small riverfront area with stone benches that usually have a few modern-day Romeos and Juliets gazing at each other rather than at the view. Belly up to the river view.*

⑪ Ponte Pietra and a River View

The white stones of the Ponte Pietra footbridge are from the origi-nal Roman bridge that stood here. After the bridge was bombed in World War II, the Veronese fished the marble chunks out of

the river to rebuild it. From here, you can see across the river to the Roman Theater, built into the hillside behind the green hedge (see page 358). Way above the the-ater (behind the cypress trees) is the fortress, Castello San Pietro.

Continue up the river toward the bridge. You'll pass Gelateria

Ponte Pietra (daily 14:30-20:00, until 23:00 in summer, at #23, no sign because of city codes), where Mirko and Stefano dish out fine gelato—try the *riso* flavor. Walk to the high point on the bridge and enjoy the view. For some exercise, break away, cross the bridge to the Veronetta neighborhood: Visit the Roman Theater or head up to the Castello for an expansive city view (at the end of the bridge, go up the little road called Scalone Castello San Pietro, or climb the stairs to the left of the theater).

• *From the bridge, look back 200 yards at the tall spire...that's where you're heading.*

⑫ Duomo

Started in the 12th century, this church was built over a period of several hundred years. Before enter-ing, note the fine Romanesque carvings on its facade. Also notice the elevated tomb (high above on the left)—a donor was buried this way at his request. Step inside, and pick up the leaflet that explains the church's highlights.

Directly ahead is Titian's 16th-century *Assumption of the Virgin* (Mary calmly rides a cloud—direction up—to the shock and bewilderment of the crowd below). To the right of the Titian (through the last wooden door, left of high altar) are the ruins of an older church. These are the 10th-century foundations of the Church of St. Elena, turned intrigu-ingly into a modern-day chapel featuring exposed fourth-century mosaic floors from the Roman church that originally stood here. Don't miss the adjacent baptistery, with its clean Romanesque lines, hanging 14th-century crucifix, and fine marble font. Try to identify the eight biblical scenes carved on its panels before refer-ring to my answers. (Answers: Annunciation; first Christmas, with animals licking baby Jesus and giving him a barnyard welcome; announcement to shepherds of Jesus' birth; Epiphany, with the Three Kings giving their gifts to Baby Jesus; Herod commanding to have firstborn sons killed; Slaughter of the Innocents; flight to Egypt; and finally, facing the entry door, John the Baptist baptiz-ing Christ.) The peaceful Romanesque cloister is to the right as you leave the church, with mosaics from a fifth-century Christian church exposed below the walk.

Cost and Hours: €2.50; March-Oct Mon-Fri 10:00-17:30, Sat 10:00-16:00, Sun 13:30-17:30; off-season Tue-Sun closes half-hour earlier and also closes 13:00-13:30, closed Mon; www.chiese verona.it.

Sights in Verona

▲▲**Evening *Passeggiata***—For me, the highlight of Verona is the *passeggiata* (stroll)—especially in the evening. Make a big circle from Piazza Brà through the old town on Via Mazzini (one of Europe's many "first" pedestrian-only streets) to the colorful Piazza Erbe, and then back down Corso Porta Borsari to Piazza Brà. This is a small town, where people know each other, and they're all out on parade. Like peacocks, the young and nubile spread their wings. The classy shop windows are integral to the *passeggiata* as, for the ladies, shopping is a sport. Their never-finished wardrobes are considered a work in progress, and this is when they gather ideas. If you're going to complement your stroll with a sit in a café or bar, the best plan is to enjoy a *spritz* drink on Piazza Erbe (the oldest and most elegant bars are on the end farthest from Juliet's balcony).

▲**Castelvecchio**—Verona's powerful Scaligeri family built this castle (1343-1356) as both a residence and a fortress. Today, it's a museum showing off Verona's glory days. The extensive collection of Verona's finest art is well displayed throughout the huge building. The religious statues, once brightly painted, were the city's medieval forte. The paintings were the city's Renaissance forte. You'll also find armor and have a chance to roam the ramparts with fine views of the city and river. Info sheets with good English descriptions are available throughout, but the audio-guide (€4, or €6/2 people) is worthwhile (€6, Tue-Sun 8:30-19:30, Mon 13:30-19:30, Corso Castelvecchio 3, see map on page 360 for location).

Next to Castelvecchio, the **Fortress Bridge** (Ponte Scaligero) is free, open to the public, and fun to stroll across. Destroyed by the Germans in World War II, it was rebuilt in the 1950s. Today it's understandably a favorite for wedding-day photos.

▲**Basilica of San Zeno Maggiore**—This church, outside the old center, is dedicated to the patron saint of Verona, whose remains are buried in the crypt under the main altar. In addition to being a fine example of Italian Romanesque, the basilica features Mantegna's *San Zeno Triptych* (1456-1459) with its marvelous perspective, peaceful double-columned cloisters, and a set of 48 paneled 11th-century bronze doors nicknamed "the poor man's Bible." Pretend you're an illiterate medieval peasant and do some reading. Facing the altar, on the walls of the right-side aisle, you can see frescoes painted on top of other frescoes and graffiti dating from the 1300s. These were done by people who fled into the church in times of war or flooding and scratched prayers into the walls. Druidic-looking runes are actually decorated letters typical of the Gothic period, like those in illuminated manuscripts.

Cost and Hours: €2.50, March-Oct Mon-Sat 8:30-18:00, Sun 12:30-18:00; Nov-Feb Tue-Sat 10:00-13:00 & 13:30-17:00, Sun 12:30-17:00, closed Mon; located on Piazza San Zeno, a good 15-minute walk upriver beyond Castelvecchio; www.chiese verona.it.

Roman Theater (Teatro Romano)—Dating from the first century A.D., this ancient theater was discovered in the 19th century

and restored. Admission includes the Roman Museum, located high in the building above the theater (reach it via elevator—start at the stage and walk up the middle set of stairs, then continue straight on the path through the bushes).

The museum displays a model of the theater, a small Jesuit chapel, and Roman artifacts, including mosaic floors, busts and other statuary, clay and bronze votive figures, and architectural fragments. You'll find helpful English information sheets throughout.

Cost and Hours: €4.50, Tue-Sun 8:30-19:30, Mon 13:30-19:30, last entry 45 minutes before closing, theater located across the river near Ponte Pietra footbridge, tel. 045-800-0360. From mid-June through August, the theater stages Shakespeare plays—only a little more difficult to understand in Italian than in Elizabethan English.

Giusti Garden (Giardino Giusti)—If you'd enjoy a Renaissance garden with manicured box hedges and towering cypress trees, you might find this worth the walk and fee.

Cost and Hours: €6, daily April-Sept 9:00-20:00, Oct-March 9:00-17:00; cross river at Ponte Nuovo, continue up Via Carducci, and turn left on Via Giardino Giusti, or take bus #72 from Piazza Brà and get off at Via Carducci.

Sleeping in Verona

I've listed rates you'll pay in the regular season—most of April through May, and September through October. Prices soar (at least €20-30 more per night) from mid-June through early September (opera season), in early April (during the Vinitaly wine festival—see "The Wines of Verona" sidebar later), and during big trade fairs or major holidays. Unless your goal is opera, consider coming before mid-June or after early September. Prices are lower from November to March. Hotel websites clearly explain their rates.

Near Piazza Erbe

$$$ Hotel Aurora, at the corner of Piazza Erbe and Via Pelliciai, has friendly family management, a terrace overlooking the piazza, and 19 fresh, air-conditioned rooms (S-€70, Sb-€125, Db-€140, Tb-€160, Qb-€200, elevator, free Wi-Fi, Piazzetta XIV Novembre 2, tel. 045-594-717, fax 045-801-0860, www.hotelaurora.biz, info @hotelaurora.biz, Rita). Coming from the train station, stay on the bus until the San Fermo stop (two stops past Piazza Brà) to get within an easy walk of the hotel.

$ Casa della Giovane, run by an association that houses poor women, also rents rooms and dorm beds to female tourists (and their children up to age 10). Buried deep in the old town and up several flights of stairs, the place offers 55 cheap beds in a clean, institutional, and peaceful setting (women only, €22/bed in 11-bed dorm, Sb-€35, Db-€60, Tb-€90, no breakfast, free Wi-Fi,

---

Sleep Code

(€1 = about $1.40, country code: 39)

S = Single, **D** = Double/Twin, **T** = Triple, **Q** = Quad, **b** = bathroom, **s** = shower only. Hotels accept credit cards and provide breakfast unless otherwise noted. Everyone speaks English.

To help you easily sort through these listings, I've divided the accommodations into three categories, based on the price for a standard double room with bath:

$$$ Higher Priced—Most rooms €120 or more.
$$ Moderately Priced—Most rooms between €90-120.
$ Lower Priced—Most rooms €90 or less.

Prices can change without notice; verify the hotel's current rates online or by email. For other updates, see www .ricksteves.com/update.

Verona Hotels & Restaurants

VERONA

1 Hotel Aurora
2 Casa della Giovane
3 Hotel Milano & Hotel Giulietta e Romeo
4 Hotel Europa
5 Hotel/Ristorante Torcolo
6 Albergo Arena
7 To L'Ospite Apartments
8 To Villa Francescatti Hostel
9 Enoteca Can Grande
10 Osteria al Duca
11 Bottega del Vin
12 Osteria le Vecete & Pizzeria Du de Cope
13 Osteria Sottoriva
14 Trattoria al Pompiere
15 Brek Cafeteria
16 PAM Supermarket
17 Albertini & Gastronomia
18 Internet Cafés (2)

reception open 9:00-23:00, Via Pigna 7, tel. 045-596-880, fax 045-088-5449).

Near Piazza Brà

You'll find several options in the quiet streets just off Piazza Brà, within 200 yards of the bus stop. From the square, yellow signs point you to the hotels. The first three are big, business-class places with the service and formality you'd expect. The Torcolo is more homey and friendly.

$$$ Hotel Giulietta e Romeo is on a quiet side street just 50 yards behind the Roman Arena. Nine of its 40 well-designed rooms have balconies (Sb-€110, Db-€120, bigger Db-€150, prices shoot up to €200/€230 during opera season, non-smoking, air-con, elevator, free Wi-Fi, free loaner bikes, fitness room, garage €19/day, Vicolo Tre Marchetti 3, tel. 045-800-3554, fax 045-801-0862, www.giuliettaeromeo.com, info@giuliettaeromeo.com).

$$$ Hotel Milano, a few doors from Hotel Giulietta e Romeo, is an arty hotel with 52 rooms. The lobby and fancier rooms are tricked out in black and chrome (rates vary wildly— see website—generally about Sb-€75-100, Db-€120-150, air-con, elevator, free Wi-Fi, garage €20/day, Vicolo Tre Marchetti 11, tel. 045-591-692, fax 045-801-1299, www.hotelmilano-vr.it, info @hotelmilano-vr.it).

$$$ Hotel Europa offers sleek, modern comfort in spring-time colors. Most of its 46 rooms are non-smoking, and a few rooms have little balconies overlooking the *piazzetta* below (Db-€120-180, 10 percent discount if you mention this book when reserving direct, air-con, elevator, free Wi-Fi, a couple of blocks off Piazza Brà at Via Roma 8, tel. 045-594-744, fax 045-800-1852, www.veronahoteleuropa.com, info@veronahoteleuropa.com).

$$ Hotel Torcolo offers 19 comfortable, lovingly maintained, non-smoking rooms with Grandma's furnishings (Sb-€65, Db-around €100, €8-14 for breakfast—optional except during opera season, air-con, fridge in room, elevator, pay Wi-Fi, garage €20/day; from Piazza Brà promenade, head down the alley to the right of #16 and walk to Vicolo Listone 3; tel. 045-800-7512, fax 045-800-4058, www.hoteltorcolo.it, hoteltorcolo@virgilio.it, well-run by Silvia, Diana, and helpful Caterina).

Near Castelvecchio

$ Albergo Arena, while borderline dreary, is a good value for those on a budget. Located in a peaceful courtyard off a busy street a few blocks from Piazza Brà, it offers 17 very basic, institutional, quiet rooms (S-€45, Sb-€60, D-€75, Db-€85, no air-con, free Wi-Fi, just west of Castelvecchio at Stradone Porta Palio 2, tel. & fax 045-803-2440, www.albergoarena.it, info@albergoarena.it, Beatrice).

Across the River

$$ L'Ospite, a 10-minute walk across the river from Piazza Erbe, has six cozy, immaculate, fully equipped apartments and lots of stairs. The rooms, warmly managed by English-speaking Federica De Rossi, sleep from two to four, with air-conditioning and free Wi-Fi (Db-€95, Tb/Qb-about €40-55/person, discounts for cash and longer stays, no reception or daily cleaning; Via XX Settembre 3; tel. 045-803-6994, mobile 329-426-2524, www.lospite.com, info@lospite.com). Coming from the station by bus, get off three stops past Piazza Brà at the XX Settembre stop (across the street from the apartments).

$ Villa Francescatti is a good, church-affiliated hostel in a pretty hillside setting (€18/bed in 6- or 8-bed sex-segregated rooms with hall bath, €20/bed in family rooms with private bathrooms, includes breakfast, €8 dinners, laundry €5/load, free Wi-Fi in common areas, rooms closed from 9:00 to 17:00 but reception open all day, 24:00 curfew; Salita Fontana del Ferro 15, bus #73 or #91 from station to Piazza Isolo plus short steep walk, tel. 045-590-360, fax 045-800-9127, www.ostelloverona.it, info@villafrancescatti.it).

Eating in Verona

The restaurants I list are mostly small and intimate, and found along side streets. It's tempting to grab a table next to the *passeggiata* action along Piazza Brà, but you may be sacrificing service, value, and quality for your view of the floodlit Roman Arena and Verona on parade. Except for Brek Cafeteria, restaurants on the piazza tend to charge a cover and service fee, making even pizza a pricey choice.

Finer Dining

Enoteca Can Grande is enthusiastically run by Giuliano and Corrina, who enjoy turning people on to great, well-matched food and wine. Their star offering is a €40 set menu including an aperitif, a festival of *antipasti* treats, an imaginative pasta, your choice of a meat or fish course, and dessert. They also offer a junior version at lunch (except Sun) for €20: a pasta and your choice of salad or dessert, plus water, coffee, and a glass of wine (Wed-Mon 12:00-15:30 & 18:00-24:00, closed Tue, closed Mon instead of Tue during opera season; a block off Piazza Brà at Via Dietro Liston 19D—if the equestrian statue jogged slightly right, he'd head straight here; tel. 045-595-022).

Osteria al Duca is a fun, family-run place with a lively atmosphere and good traditional dishes. Locals line up for its affordable, two-course, €16 fixed-price meal. I much prefer their ground

The Wines of Verona

Wine connoisseurs love the high-quality wines of the Verona area. The hills to the east are covered with grapes to make Soave; to the north is Valpolicella country; and Bardolino comes from vineyards to the west.

Valpolicella grapes, which are used to make the fruity, red Valpolicella table wine (found everywhere), are also the basis for full-bodied red Amarone and the sweet dessert wine Recioto. To produce Amarone, grapes are partially dried (*passito*) before fermentation, then aged for a minimum of four years in oak casks, resulting in a rich, velvety, full-bodied red. Recioto, which in local dialect means "ears," uses only the grapes from the top of the cluster (so they sort of look like the "ears" of the cluster's "head"). Because these grapes get the most sun, they mature the fastest and have the highest concentration of sugar. Before pressing, the grapes are dried for months until all moisture has gone out; the wine is then aged for one to three years.

Bardolino, from the vineyards near Lake Garda, is a light, fruity wine, like a French Beaujolais. It's a perfect picnic wine.

Soave, which might be Italy's best-known white wine, goes well with seafood and risotto dishes. While Soave can vary widely in quality, the best are called "Soave Classico" and come from the heart of the region, near the Soave Castle. Soave is sometimes aged in oak casks, giving it a mellow, rounded flavor.

Sample these and many others at the numerous *enoteche* (wine-tasting bars) or at any restaurant around town. In early April, Verona hosts Vinitaly, the most important international convention of domestic and international wines. Vintners vie for prestigious awards for the past year's vintage. Tourists are welcome to attend at the end of the week, and are shuttled to the convention hall from Piazza Brà. Hotels book up months in advance. Check with the TI and www.vinitaly.com for details.

If you're visiting the area in the fall, consider a day trip to nearby Monteforte d'Alpone, east of Verona. The town hosts a fun, raucous wine festival in September—ask at the TI for more information on this and other regional wine festivals.

floor (*piano terra*—worth requesting). Reservations are advised (Mon-Sat 10:00-15:00 & 18:30-24:00, closed Sun, half-block east of Scaligeri family tombs at Via Arche Scaligere 2, tel. 045-594-474, Alessandro or Daniele).

Ristorante Torcolo is a warm family restaurant, with mom (Paola) running the kitchen, and father and son (Roberto and Luca) serving. It's dressy but without pretense, and the service is professional yet fun-loving. There's a happy energy, stoked by carts of tempting boiled meat and desserts rolling through the dining room. They serve all the classic dishes, with an accessible menu and an extensive wine list (€9 pastas, €15 *secondi*, €3 cover, closed Mon, just behind the Piazza Brà scene on a quiet street, Via Carlo Cattaneo 11, tel. 045-803-3730).

Bottega del Vin is pricey, venerable, and proud to have a sister establishment in New York City. Under a high ceiling and walls of wine bottles, brisk black-vested waiters match traditional dishes (polenta, duck, game) with glasses of fine wine. Choose from 100 open bottles—glasses range from €1 to €15. The waitstaff, ambience, and food have deep roots in local culture. I like their front room best (€13 pastas, €18-22 *secondi*, good daily specials, daily 12:00-24:00; take third left off Via Mazzini as you're coming from Piazza Erbe, Via Scudo di Francia 3; tel. 045-800-4535, reservations smart for dinner).

Osteria le Vecete, just one room under open beams with walls of wine, has an enjoyable, intimate pub ambience. Slide up to the bar for wine and *tartine* (elaborate little open-faced sandwiches), or sit down and order a meal. Choose from daily specials of home-made pastas and Veronese dishes—as well as €10 salad plates. The blackboard lists plenty of wines by the glass (€9-12 pastas, €16-20 *secondi*, daily 12:30-15:30 & 18:30-23:00, drinks and snacks served between mealtimes and until late; from Piazza Erbe, put your back to the whalebone arch and walk down Via Pelliciai to #32A; tel. 045-594-748, Karen).

Pizzeria Du de Cope is a high-energy, informal place (with paper placemats) that buzzes with smartly attired young waiters and locals who consider the pizza here to be the best in town (big €11 salads, €9-13 pizzas, daily 12:00-14:00 & 19:00-23:00, flamboyant desserts, family friendly, no reservations, a few doors past Osteria le Vecete at Galleria Pelliciai 10, tel. 045-595-562).

Osterie *on Via Sottoriva:* Historically, Verona's river served as the thoroughfare through town. Business deals could be made over a glass of wine at places along the river, set in a fine old covered arcade (the portico of Via Sottoriva). Several of these survive as rustic, characteristic eateries serving finger food. Browse around and consider the wonderful **Osteria Sottoriva,** with simple soups and pastas, and both indoor and outdoor seating (open from 18:30, behind the Church of Sant'Anastasia in the covered arcade, Via Sottoriva 9, tel. 045-801-4323).

Trattoria al Pompiere, which has a commitment to regional traditions, is a favorite of foodies and has earned its huge local following. Amid the bustle (contained by walls plastered with photos of local big shots), Stefano and his gang serve gourmet meats and cheeses as *antipasti*, ideal for a mixed plate to complement the huge selection of fine wines. Reservations are wise (€12-13 pastas, €16-17 *secondi*, lunch from 12:30, dinner from 19:30, closed Sun and at lunch time on Mon, chivalry lives—ladies' menus come without prices; find Via Cappello 8, across from Juliet statue, and head down side street to Vicolo Regina d'Ungheria 5; tel. 045-803-0537).

Cheaper Eats

Brek Cafeteria, a well-run and modern chain, has a location at Piazza Brà with self-service prices (€5 pastas, €6 *secondi*, cheap salad plates, daily 9:30-15:00 & 18:30-22:00, full menu from 11:30, indoor/outdoor seating, facing equestrian statue at Piazza Brà 20, tel. 045-800-4561).

Supermarket near Piazza Brà: **PAM supermarket** is just outside the historic gate on Piazza Brà (Mon-Sat 8:00-21:00, Sun 9:00-20:00, exit Piazza Brà through the gate and take the first right to Via dei Mutilati 3).

The *döner kebab* place by Hotel Europa is cheap, fast, and not Italian (great €4 meals, daily 11:30-late; from Piazza Brà, walk down Via Roma and turn right before Hotel Europa toward Via Teatro Filharmonico 6).

Delicatessens near Piazza Erbe: You'll find two family-run *alimentari* on Corso Sant'Anastasia, between the end of Vicolo Cavoletto and the Church of Sant'Anastasia. One is under the **Gastronomia** sign at Corso Sant'Anastasia 33 (Mon-Sat 8:00-20:00, Sun 9:00-13:30). A few doors down at #41 is **Albertini** (Mon-Sat 8:00-20:00, closed Sun). Either can sell you a €3-4 sandwich. Bakeries also sell sandwiches and pizza by the slice.

A list of "official" picnicking spots can be picked up at the TI—freelance picnicking in Verona is strongly discouraged. One good spot is along the river by Ponte Pietra.

Verona Connections

From Verona by Train to: Venice (2/hour, 1.25-2.25 hours), **Padua** (2/hour, 40-60 minutes), **Vicenza** (2/hour, 30-60 minutes), **Florence** (listed as *Firenze* on train schedules, about hourly, 1.5 hours direct or 2.5 hours with transfer in Bologna), **Bologna** (hourly, 1.5 hours, a few faster trains), **Milan** (2/hour, 1.5-2 hours, a few faster trains), **Rome** (at least hourly, 4-5 hours, often with transfer in Bologna), **Bolzano** (2/hour, 1.75-2.25 hours, avoid "fast" trains that take the same amount of time but cost much more). For more information, visit www.trenitalia.com.

VENETIAN HISTORY

In the Middle Ages, the Venetians became Europe's clever middlemen for East-West trade, creating a great trading empire ruled by a series of doges. By smuggling in the bones of St. Mark, Venice gained religious importance as well. But after the discovery of America and new trading routes to the Orient, Venetian power ebbed. Yet as Venice fell, her appetite for decadence grew. Throughout the 17th and 18th centuries, Venice partied on the wealth accumulated in earlier centuries as a trading power.

That's Venetian history in a seashell. Want more? Read on.

500: Rome Falls, Venice Rises

In A.D. 476, the last Roman emperor abdicated, the infrastructure was crumbling, and Italy was crawling with barbarians. Hoping these Visigoths, Huns, and Lombards didn't like water, mainland farmers took refuge on the marshy, uninhabited islands of the lagoon.

The refugees squatted on this wet and miserable land. They sank pilings in the mud to

build on, channeled water into canals, and built bridges to lace together the motley collection of about 120 natural islands that would eventually become Venice.

500-1000: Medieval Growth

These former farmers, the first Venetians, now harvested salt and fish for their livelihood, and traded it on the mainland. Though Venice's islands were desolate, the area—known to the Romans as the "Seven Seas"—was strategically important. In 540 A.D., the

Byzantine Emperor Justinian reconquered Italy from the barbarians and briefly reunited the Roman Empire. He established a capital at Ravenna, bringing the Venetian islands under Byzantine influence.

In 726, Venice elected a local ruler, a "doge"—the first of many who would rule for the next 1,100 years. (Though "doge" is linguistically related to our word "duke," Venetian rulers were more like constitutional monarchs, elected by their fellow nobles and expected to govern according to the rule of law.) The first doge established his capital in the settlement of Rivo Alto ("High Bank"), near today's Rialto Bridge.

Under Byzantine protection, Venetians became prosperous seagoing merchants. Acting as middlemen, they bought goods from the sophisticated Byzantine and Islamic lands to the East and sold them to consumers in the West.

Venice's merchant economy boomed while the rest of Europe languished under land-based feudalism. Charlemagne, the Holy Roman Emperor who'd conquered much of Italy (c. 800), eyed the region hungrily. But Venetians, wanting to keep their independence, deposed Charlemagne's bishop and chose one who was loyal to (distant) Byzantium.

To legitimize their new bishop, the Venetians managed to smuggle the holy relics of St. Mark from Egypt in 828, thus becoming a religious power overnight. To seal the city's oriental orientation, Venetian leaders had the grand St. Mark's Basilica built in a distinctly Eastern style. By the 10th century, tiny Venice had effectively established itself as an independent, self-ruling country.

Representative Sights
- Gondolas and the network of canals
- Old crypt under San Zaccaria Church
- San Moisè Church
- Church on Torcello Island

1000-1500:
A Seafaring Power
Well-located between northern Europe and the eastern Mediterranean, Venetian sea traders established trading outposts in Byzantine and Muslim territories to the east. At home, a stable, constitutional government ran an efficient, state-operated

Venice in the 15th Century

Black area shows Venetian Empire at its peak—the 15th Century

London
•Bruges
Paris
•Vienna
Atlantic Ocean
✪ Venice
Genoa
Ravenna
Adriatic Sea
Pisa
Florence
Rome
Constantinople
Mediterranean Sea
Gibraltar
•Corfu
Lepanto
To Holy Land & Alexandria
Crete

multinational corporation. The shallow lagoon was easily defended against attack. Grand buildings reflected Venice's wealth.

Venetian merchants ran a profitable trading triangle: timber from Venice's mainland to Egypt for gold to Byzantium for luxury goods to Venice. Its merchant fleet was the biggest in the Mediterranean, backed by powerful warships.

By 1104, Venice was running Europe's first industrial complex, the Arsenale. With more than 1,000 workers using an early form of assembly-line production, the Arsenale could produce about one warship a day. This put the "fear of Venice" into visiting rulers. When France's King Henry III dropped by the Arsenale, Venice entertained him with a shipbuilding spectacle: from ribs to finished product in four hours.

When Europe launched its Crusades to the Holy Land (1095-1272), Venice transported soldiers and defended Byzantine and Crusader ports in return for free-trade privileges. This made the eastern Mediterranean a virtual free-trade zone for a very aggressive Venetian trading community to exploit.

Wealthy Venetian nobles built lavish palaces. With a natural lagoon defense, these were not fortified castles like the rest of Europe but luxurious palazzos, complete with loading docks, warehouses, and chandeliered ballrooms. The streets were paved. And by the 12th century, the government provided oil and required that streets be lit—a first in Europe.

Besides sea trade, Venice established strong local industries. Having mastered the art of making glass, Venice was on the cutting edge of the new science of grinding lenses for eyeglasses and telescopes. Understanding medicine as a chemical rather than an herbal pursuit, the city developed Europe's first real pharmaceutical industry. They made Europe's first affordable paper, from rags rather than from sheepskin (parchment). As the city offered the world's first copyright protection, its printing and bookmaking industry boomed, and Venice became a center for new (secular, scientific, democratic) ideas. With mountains of capital and a sophisticated trade system of insurance, joint ventures, and money drafts, Venice's merchants eventually became bankers, loaning money at interest—making them early capitalists.

They were also on the forefront of a budding democracy not seen in feudal Europe. Constitutional limits were placed on the doges, and the Republic was ruled by a voting body of wealthy families.

By the 13th century, Venice was fast becoming a Mediterranean superpower. During the Fourth Crusade (1204), Venetian troops joined other Crusaders in attacking and looting Christian Constantinople. The haul of booty enriched the city, and Venice could now stand up to its former Byzantine protectors. When Venetian ships routed the fleet of their Genoan rivals at Chioggia (on the south end of the lagoon, 1381), Venice became the undisputed master of the eastern Mediterranean. Next, they launched attacks on the mainland, conquering much of northern Italy. By 1420, Venice was at the height of its power, with mainland possessions and a powerful overseas trading empire to the east.

Representative Sights
- Doge's Palace
- St. Mark's Basilica
- Frari Church
- Buildings decorated in ornate Venetian Gothic style
- Doge paraphernalia and city history at Correr Museum
- Glass and lace industries
- Arsenale shipbuilding complex

Noteworthy Residents
Enrico Dandolo (r. 1192-1205): Doge during the Fourth Crusade,

Church Architecture

History comes to life when you visit a centuries-old church. Even if you wouldn't know your apse from a hole in the ground, learning a few simple terms will enrich your experience. Of course, not every church has every feature. It's worth noting that a "cathedral" (*duomo* in Italian) isn't a type of church architecture, but rather a designation for a church that's a governing center for a local bishop.

Aisles: The long, generally low-ceilinged arcades that flank the nave.

Altar: The raised area with a ceremonial table (often adorned with candles or a crucifix), where the priest prepares and serves the bread and wine for Communion.

Apse: The space beyond the altar, generally bordered with small chapels.

Barrel Vault: A continuous round-arched ceiling that resembles an upside-down "U".

Choir: A cozy area, often screened off, located within the church nave and near the high altar, where services are sung in a more intimate setting.

Cloister: A square-shaped series of hallways surrounding an open-air courtyard, traditionally where monks and nuns got fresh air.

Facade: The outer wall of the church's main (west) entrance, viewable from outside and generally highly decorated.

Groin Vault: An arched ceiling formed where two equal barrel vaults meet at right angles. Also: a medieval jock strap.

Narthex: The area (portico or foyer) between the main entry and the nave.

Nave: The long, central section of the church (running west to east, from the entrance to the altar) where the congregation stood through the service.

Transept: The north-south part of the church, which crosses (perpendicularly) the east-west nave. In a traditional Latin cross-shaped floor plan, the transept forms the "arms" of the cross.

West Portal: The main entry to the church (on the west end, opposite the main altar).

when Venetian crusaders looted Constantinople, helping to enrich Venice.

Marco Polo (1254-1324): Traveler to faraway China whose journal, *The Book of Marvels*, was dismissed by many as fiction.

Paolo Veneziano (1310-1358): Painter who mastered the Byzantine gold-icon style, then added touches of Western realism.

Francesco Foscari (1373-1457): Doge at Venice's peak of power, whose ill-advised wars against Milan and the Ottoman Turks started the Republic's slow fade.

Jacopo Bellini (c. 1400-1470): Father of painting family. His training in Renaissance Florence brought 3-D realism to Venice.

Gentile Bellini (c. 1429-1507): Elder son of painting family, known for straightforward, historical scenes of Venice.

1500-1600: Renaissance and Seeds of Decline

In 1500, Venice was a commercial powerhouse—among the six biggest cities in Europe. Of its estimated 180,000 citizens, nearly 1,000 were of Rockefeller-esque wealth and power. Europe's richest city-state poured money into the arts. Titian, Tintoretto, Sansovino, the Bellini family, and Palladio called Venice home. St. Mark's Square became the gathering place for merchants and nobles from Venice's vast trading empire. Across Europe, Venice had a reputation as a luxury-loving, exotic, cosmopolitan playground.

But Venice's power was declining. The seeds had been sown in the 15th century. In 1492, Columbus sailed the ocean blue, and established trade in a World that was New. In 1498, Vasco da Gama circled Africa's Cape of Good Hope, finding a new sea-trade route to eastern markets. Venice's sea-trade monopoly was broken.

On the Italian mainland, Venice became locked in draining wars against its economic rivals Milan, Pisa, and Amalfi. Meanwhile, Ottomans were expanding in the East, encroaching on Venice's former monopoly on trade. Venetians and Ottomans became wary trade partners, sometimes dealing peacefully but sometimes battling over strategic ports. In 1453, the Ottomans took Constantinople, and Venice suddenly lost one of its best customers. Venice (and its European allies) scored a temporary victory over the Ottomans at the Battle of Lepanto (1571), but Venice's navy suffered major damage, and the city lost more trading rights. Spain, England, and Holland, with their oceangoing vessels, emerged as superior traders in a more global economy.

Representative Sights

- St. Mark's Square facades and other work by Sansovino
- Palladio's classical facades (San Giorgio Maggiore and Il Redentore churches)
- Masterpiece paintings by Titian, Giovanni Bellini, Giorgione, and Tintoretto (Accademia, Frari Church, Doge's Palace, San Zaccaria Church, Correr Museum, Scuola San Rocco)
- Jewish Ghetto and Jewish Museum

Noteworthy Residents

Giovanni Bellini (c. 1430-1516): The most famous son in the painting family, whose glowing, colorful, 3-D Madonna-and-Childs started the Venetian Renaissance. Teacher of Titian and Giorgione.

Vittore Carpaccio (c. 1460-1525): Painter of realistic, secular scenes and the impressive Scuola Dolmata di San Giorgio.

Giorgione (c. 1477-1511): Innovative painter whose moody realism influenced Bellini (his teacher) and Titian (his friend and fellow painter).

Jacopo Sansovino (1486-1570): Renaissance architect who redid the face of Venice (especially St. Mark's Square), introducing sober, classical columns and arches to a city previously full of ornate Gothic.

Titian (Tiziano Vecellio, 1488-1576): Premier Venetian Renaissance painter. Master of many styles, from teenage Madonnas to sober state portraits to exuberant mythological scenes to centerfold nudes.

Andrea Palladio (1508-1580): Influential architect whose classical style was much imitated around the world, resulting in villas, government buildings, and banks that look like Greek temples.

Tintoretto (Jacopo Robusti, c. 1518-1594): Painter of dramatic religious scenes, using strong 3-D, diagonal compositions, twisting poses, sharp contrast of light and shadow, and bright, "black velvet" colors (late Renaissance/Mannerist style).

Paolo Veronese (1528-1588): Painter of big, colorful canvases, capturing the exuberance and luxury of Renaissance Venice.

1600-1800: Elegant Decline

New trade routes, new European powers, and belligerent Ottomans drained Venice's economy and shrank its trading empire. At home, however, Venice's reputation for luxury—and decadence—still made it a popular tourist destination for Europe's gentry. In some ways, this is the period that most defines Venice: the city of Baroque monuments, masked balls at Carnevale, velvet-dressed nobles at opera debuts, and the roguish debauchery of Casanova.

Venice dwindled economically and politically. In 1669, its last

major outpost, Crete, fell to the Ottomans. Several devastating plagues
gutted the population at home. The
once-enlightened government gained
a nasty reputation for corruption
and for locking away dissidents in
the notorious prisons in the Doge's
Palace. In 1797, Napoleon Bonaparte
rolled into Venice and toppled the
final doge. A thousand-year era of
independent rule was over.

Representative Sights

- Ca' Rezzonico (Museum of 18th-Century Venice)
- La Salute Church
- Masks of the Carnevale tradition
- Old cafés (e.g., the Florian and the Quadri, both on St. Mark's Square)
- La Fenice Opera House
- Baroque interiors in many churches
- Canova sculptures (Correr Museum, Frari Church)
- G. B. Tiepolo paintings (Accademia, Doge's Palace, Ca' Rezzonico)
- Paintings of Canaletto, Guardi, and G. D. Tiepolo (Ca' Rezzonico)

Noteworthy Residents

Claudio Monteverdi (1567-1643): The composer and *maestro di capella* at St. Mark's Basilica who wrote in a budding new medium—opera.

   Baldassare Longhena (1598-1682): Architect of the Baroque La Salute Church.

   Antonio Vivaldi (1678-1741): Composer of *The Four Seasons* ("Dah dunt-dunt-duh dutta dah-ah-ah").

   G. B. Tiepolo (Giovanni Battista, 1696-1770): Painter of mythological subjects in colorful Rococo ceilings.

   Antonio Canaletto (1697-1768): Painter of photo-realist Venice views.

   Carlo Goldoni (1707-1793): Comic playwright who brought refinement to commedia dell'arte buffoonery.

   Francesco Guardi (1712-1793): Painter of proto-Impressionist Venice views.

   Giacomo Casanova (1725-1798): Gambler, womanizer, and adventurer whose exaggerated memoirs inspired Romantics.

   G. D. Tiepolo (Giovanni Domenico, 1727-1804): Painter son of the famous G. B. Tiepolo.

VENETIAN HISTORY

Lorenzo Da Ponte (1749-1838): Mozart's librettist, who popularized Venice's sophisticated and decadent high society.

Antonio Canova (1757-1822): Neoclassical sculptor whose beautiful polished-white statues were especially popular in Napoleon's France.

1800 to the Present: Modern Venice

After Napoleon was defeated at Waterloo, the European allies placed Venice under Austrian rule. Sophisticated Venetians chafed against their bourgeois masters. However, Venice was still a key stop on any traveler's Grand Tour, as Europe's young aristocrats visited the city to complete their education. Venice and Italy became a political backwater as Austrian, French, and British culture dominated.

In 1866, Austria was defeated by Prussia, and rebellious Venetians seized the moment to join Italy's Risorgimento movement, annexing itself to the newly unified, democratic nation of Italy.

Venice joined the Industrial Revolution only reluctantly. The island city became connected to the mainland with a two-mile railroad causeway (1846), which was later paralleled by a highway for cars (1932). On the mainland, unbridled industrialization produced pollution (mainly sulfuric acid) that threatened Venice's stone monuments. In 1966, Venice suffered a disastrous flood, which prompted many plans and projects to control future flooding—some have been enacted, while others are still on the drawing board.

Inside Venice proper, however, there has been little new building for centuries. Today, Venice remains a museum piece for foreigners—one increasingly threatened by mainland pollution, global warming, floods, and hordes of tourists. Venice's leaders face the dilemma of having to pay for essential upkeep by allowing billboard advertising. Local and UNESCO regulations try to preserve Venice as a cultural landmark. When Venice's venerable La Fenice Opera House burned down in 1996, it was rebuilt

gloriously in 2003 in the old style. The Punta della Dogana, a museum devoted to contemporary art, opened in 2009, continuing Venice's legacy as a world arts capital. While keeping up with what's new, Venice remains a historic wonderland. Venice is timeless—a place where visitors can easily blink away elements of the modern world and find themselves transported back in time.

Representative Sights
- Correr Museum's Risorgimento wing
- Statue of Daniele Manin (between St. Mark's Square and Rialto Bridge)
- Motorized *vaporetti* and taxis
- Train station (1954)
- Peggy Guggenheim Collection
- Biennale International Art Exhibition (held in odd years)
- Pollution from the mainland city of Mestre
- Calatrava Bridge (2008)
- Burger King

Noteworthy Residents
Daniele Manin (1804-1857): Rebel who led 1848 Venetian revolt against the city's Austrian rulers, eventually allowing Venice to join a united, democratic, modern Italy.

    Peggy Guggenheim (1898-1979): American-born art collector, gallery owner, and friend of modern art and artists.

APPENDIX

Contents

Tourist Information 377
Communicating 378
Transportation 386
Resources 402
Holidays and Festivals 406
Conversions and Climate. 409
Hotel Reservation Form. 412
Packing Checklist 413
Italian Survival Phrases 414

Tourist Information

The Italian national tourist offices **in the US** are a wealth of information. Before your trip, scan their website (www.italiantourism .com) or contact the nearest branch to briefly describe your trip and request information. They'll mail you a general interest brochure, and you can download many other brochures free of charge at their website. If you have a specific problem, they're a good source of sympathy.

In New York: tel. 212/245-5618, brochure hotline tel. 212/245-4822, fax 212/586-9249, newyork@enit.it; 630 Fifth Ave. #1565, New York, NY 10111

In Illinois: tel. 312/644-0996, brochure hotline tel. 312/644-0990, fax 312/644-3019, chicago@enit.it; 500 N. Michigan Ave. #506, Chicago, IL 60611

In California: tel. 310/820-1898, brochure hotline tel. 310/820-0098, fax 310/820-6357, losangeles@enit.it; 12400 Wilshire Blvd. #550, Los Angeles, CA 90025

In Venice, your best first stop is generally the tourist information office (abbreviated **TI** in this book). There are several in Venice (listed on page 23). A TI is a good place to get a city map, advice on public transportation, walking-tour information, tips on special events, and recommendations for nightlife. While the TI is eager to book you a room, use its room-finding service only as a last resort. They are unable to give hard opinions on the relative value of one place over another. The accommodations stakes are too high to go potluck through the TI. Even if there's no "fee," you'll save yourself and your host money by going direct with the listings in this book.

Useful websites are www.turismovenezia.it (Tourist Board of Venice), www.hellovenezia.com (vaporetto and event schedules), www.museiciviciveneziani.it (civic museums in Venice), www.venicexplorer.net (interactive maps), www.veniceforvisitors.com, and www.aguestinvenice.com.

Websites on Italy: In addition to the Italian Tourist Board site listed above, you may find the following sites useful: www.museionline.it (museums in Italy) and www.trenitalia.com (train info and schedules).

Communicating

Hurdling the Language Barrier

Many Italians—especially those in the tourist trade and in big cities such as Venice—speak English. Still, you'll get better treatment if you learn and use Italian pleasantries. In smaller, non-touristy towns, Italian is the norm. For a list of survival phrases, see page 414.

Note that Italian is pronounced much like English, with a few exceptions, such as: c followed by e or i is pronounced *ch* (to ask, *"Per centro?"*—To the center?—you say, pehr CHEHN-troh). In Italian, ch is pronounced like the hard *c* in Chianti (*chiesa*—church—is pronounced kee-AY-zah). Give it your best shot. Italians appreciate your efforts.

Telephones

Smart travelers use the telephone to reserve or reconfirm rooms, get tourist information, reserve restaurants, confirm tour times, or phone home. Generally the easiest, cheapest way to call home is to use an international phone card purchased in Italy. This section covers dialing instructions, phone cards, and types of phones (for more in-depth information, see www.ricksteves.com/phoning).

How to Dial

Calling from the US to Italy, or vice versa, is simple—once you break the code. The European calling chart later in this chapter will walk you through it.

Dialing Domestically Within Italy

Italy has a direct-dial phone system (no area codes). To call anywhere within Italy, just dial the number. For example, the number of one of my recommended Venice hotels is 041-520-5764. That's the number you dial whether you're calling it from Venice's train station or from Rome.

Land lines start with 0; mobile lines start with 3; toll-free lines start with 80; and expensive toll lines begin with 8 and then any number other than 0. Keep in mind that Italian phone numbers vary in length; a hotel can have, say, an eight-digit phone number and a nine-digit fax number.

Dialing Internationally to or from Italy

If you want to make an international call, follow these steps:

• Dial the international access code (00 if you're calling from Europe, 011 from the US or Canada).

• Dial the country code of the country you're calling (39 for Italy, or 1 for the US or Canada).

• Dial the local number. Note that in most European countries, you have to drop the zero at the beginning of the local number—but in Italy, you dial it. (The European calling chart lists specifics per country.)

Calling from the US to Italy: To call the Venice hotel from the US, dial 011 (the US international access code), 39 (Italy's country code), then 041-520-5764.

Calling from any European country to the US: To call my office in Edmonds, Washington, from anywhere in Europe, I dial 00 (Europe's international access code), 1 (the US country code), 425 (Edmonds' area code), and 771-8303.

Note: You might see a + in front of a European number. When dialing the number, replace the + with the international access code of the country you're calling from (00 from Europe, 011 from the US or Canada).

Public Phones and Hotel-Room Phones

To make calls from public phones, you'll need a prepaid phone card. There are two different kinds of phone cards: international and insertable. (Both types of phone card work only in Italy. If you have a live card at the end of your trip, give it to another traveler to use up.) Coin-op phones are virtually extinct.

Insertable Phone Cards: This type of card can only be used at a pay phone. These Telecom cards, considered "official" since they're sold by Italy's state phone company, give you the best deal

APPENDIX

European Calling Chart

Just smile and dial, using this key:
AC = Area Code, LN = Local Number.

European Country	Calling long distance within ...	Calling from the US or Canada to ...	Calling from a European country to ...
Austria	AC + LN	011 + 43 + AC (without the initial zero) + LN	00 + 43 + AC (without the initial zero) + LN
Belgium	LN	011 + 32 + LN (without initial zero)	00 + 32 + LN (without initial zero)
Bosnia-Herzegovina	AC + LN	011 + 387 + AC (without initial zero) + LN	00 + 387 + AC (without initial zero) + LN
Britain	AC + LN	011 + 44 + AC (without initial zero) + LN	00 + 44 + AC (without initial zero) + LN
Croatia	AC + LN	011 + 385 + AC (without initial zero) + LN	00 + 385 + AC (without initial zero) + LN
Czech Republic	LN	011 + 420 + LN	00 + 420 + LN
Denmark	LN	011 + 45 + LN	00 + 45 + LN
Estonia	LN	011 + 372 + LN	00 + 372 + LN
Finland	AC + LN	011 + 358 + AC (without initial zero) + LN	999 (or other 900 number) + 358 + AC (without initial zero) + LN
France	LN	011 + 33 + LN (without initial zero)	00 + 33 + LN (without initial zero)
Germany	AC + LN	011 + 49 + AC (without initial zero) + LN	00 + 49 + AC (without initial zero) + LN
Gibraltar	LN	011 + 350 + LN	00 + 350 + LN
Greece	LN	011 + 30 + LN	00 + 30 + LN
Hungary	06 + AC + LN	011 + 36 + AC + LN	00 + 36 + AC + LN
Ireland	AC + LN	011 + 353 + AC (without initial zero) + LN	00 + 353 + AC (without initial zero) + LN

European Country	Calling long distance within ...	Calling from the US or Canada to ...	Calling from a European country to ...
Italy	LN	011 + 39 + LN	00 + 39 + LN
Montenegro	AC + LN	011 + 382 + AC (without initial zero) + LN	00 + 382 + AC (without initial zero) + LN
Morocco	LN	011 + 212 + LN (without initial zero)	00 + 212 + LN (without initial zero)
Netherlands	AC + LN	011 + 31 + AC (without initial zero) + LN	00 + 31 + AC (without initial zero) + LN
Norway	LN	011 + 47 + LN	00 + 47 + LN
Poland	LN	011 + 48 + LN (without initial zero)	00 + 48 + LN (without initial zero)
Portugal	LN	011 + 351 + LN	00 + 351 + LN
Slovakia	AC + LN	011 + 421 + AC (without initial zero) + LN	00 + 421 + AC (without initial zero) + LN
Slovenia	AC + LN	011 + 386 + AC (without initial zero) + LN	00 + 386 + AC (without initial zero) + LN
Spain	LN	011 + 34 + LN	00 + 34 + LN
Sweden	AC + LN	011 + 46 + AC (without initial zero) + LN	00 + 46 + AC (without initial zero) + LN
Switzerland	LN	011 + 41 + LN (without initial zero)	00 + 41 + LN (without initial zero)
Turkey	AC (if there's no initial zero, add one) + LN	011 + 90 + AC (without initial zero) + LN	00 + 90 + AC (without initial zero) + LN

APPENDIX

- The instructions above apply whether you're calling a land line or mobile phone.
- The international access codes (the first numbers you dial when making an international call) are 011 if you're calling from the US or Canada, or 00 if you're calling from virtually anywhere in Europe (except Finland, where it's 999 or another 900 number, depending on the phone service you're using).
- To call the US or Canada from Europe, dial 00, then 1 (the country code for the US and Canada), then the area code and number. In short, 00 + 1 + AC + LN = Hi, Mom!

for calls within Italy and are reasonable for international calls. You can buy Telecom cards in denominations of €5 or €10 at tobacco shops, post offices, and machines near phone booths (many phone booths have signs indicating where the nearest phone-card sales outlet is located).

Rip off the perforated corner to "activate" the card, and then physically insert it into a slot in the pay phone. It displays how much money you have remaining on the card. Then just dial away. The price of the call is automatically deducted while you talk.

International Phone Cards: These are the cheapest way to make international calls from Europe—with the best cards, it costs literally pennies a minute. They can also be used to make local calls, and work from any type of phone, including your hotel-room phone. To use the card, dial a toll-free access number, then enter your scratch-to-reveal PIN code. If you're calling from a hotel, be sure to dial the *freephone* number (starts with "80") provided on your card rather than the "local access" number (which would incur a charge).

You can buy the cards at small newsstand kiosks, tobacco shops, Internet cafés, hostels, and hole-in-the-wall long-distance phone shops. Ask for an international phone card (*carta telefonica prepagata internazionale,* KAR-tah teh-leh-FOHN-ee-kah pray-pah-GAH-tah in-ter-naht-zee-oh-NAH-lay). Tell the vendor where you'll be making most calls (*"per Stati Uniti"*—to America), and he'll select the brand with the best deal.

Buy a lower denomination in case the card is a dud. I've had good luck with the Europa card, which offers up to 350 minutes from Italy to the US for €5.

Hotel-Room Phones: Calling from your hotel room can be cheap for local calls (ask for the rates at the front desk first), but is often a rip-off for long-distance calls, unless you use an international phone card (explained above). Some hotels charge a fee for dialing supposedly "toll-free" numbers, such as the one for your international phone card—ask before you dial. Incoming calls are free, making this a cheap way for friends and family to stay in touch (provided they have a good long-distance plan for calls to Europe—and a list of your hotels' phone numbers).

US Calling Cards: These cards, such as the ones offered by AT&T, Verizon, or Sprint, are the worst option. You'll save money by using an international phone card purchased in Italy.

Metered Phones: In Italy, some call shops have phones with meters. You can talk all you want, then pay the bill when you leave—but be sure you know the rates before you have a lengthy conversation. Note that charges can be "per unit" rather than per minute; find out the length of a unit.

Mobile Phones

Many travelers enjoy the convenience of traveling with a mobile phone.

Using Your Mobile Phone: Your US mobile phone works in Europe if it's GSM-enabled, tri-band or quad-band, and on a calling plan that includes international calls. Phones from AT&T and T-Mobile, which use the same GSM technology that Europe does, are more likely to work overseas than Verizon or Sprint phones (if you're not sure, ask your service provider). Most US providers charge $1.29-1.99 per minute while roaming internationally to make or receive calls, and 20-50 cents to send or receive text messages.

You'll pay cheaper rates if your phone is electronically "unlocked" (ask your provider about this); then in Europe, you can simply buy a tiny **SIM card,** which gives you a European phone number. SIM cards are sold at mobile-phone stores and some newsstand kiosks for about $5-15, and generally include several minutes' worth of prepaid domestic calling time. When you buy a SIM card, you may need to show ID, such as your passport. Insert the SIM card in your phone (usually in a slot on the side), and it'll work like a European mobile phone. When buying a SIM card, always ask about fees for domestic and international calls, roaming charges, and how to check your credit balance and buy more time. When you're in the SIM card's home country, domestic calls are reasonable, and incoming calls are free. You'll pay more if you're roaming in another country.

Many **smartphones,** such as the iPhone, Android, and BlackBerry, work in Europe (note that you can use the AT&T iPhone—but not the Verizon model—in Europe). For voice calls and text messaging, smartphones work the same as other US mobile phones (explained earlier). But beware of sky-high fees for data downloading (checking email, browsing the Internet, streaming videos, and so on). To avoid this expense, you can disable data roaming entirely, and get online at Wi-Fi hotspots instead. You can ask your mobile-phone service provider to cut off your account's data roaming capability, or you can manually turn it off on your phone (look under the "Network" menu). If you want Internet access without being limited to Wi-Fi, you'll need to keep data roaming on—but you can take steps to reduce your charges. Consider paying extra for a limited international data-roaming plan through your carrier, then use data roaming selectively (if a particular task gobbles bandwidth, wait until you're on Wi-Fi). In general, ask your provider in advance how to avoid unwittingly roaming your way to a huge bill. If your smartphone is on Wi-Fi, you can use certain apps to make cheap or free voice calls (see "Calling over the Internet," later).

Buying a European Mobile Phone: Mobile-phone shops all over Europe sell basic phones. The mobile phone desk in a big department store is another good place to check. Phones that are "locked" to work with a single provider start around $40; "unlocked" phones (which allow you to switch out SIM cards to use your choice of provider) start around $60. You'll also need to buy a SIM card and prepaid credit for making calls. TIM and Vodafone are the two largest Italian mobile-phone operators.

Renting a European Mobile Phone: Car-rental companies and mobile-phone companies offer the option to rent a mobile phone with a European number. Some hotels even rent or loan phones. While this seems convenient, hidden fees (such as high per-minute charges or expensive shipping costs) can really add up—which usually makes it a bad value. One exception is Verizon's Global Travel Program, available only to Verizon customers.

Calling over the Internet

Some things that seem too good to be true...actually are true. If you're traveling with a laptop, you can make calls using VoIP (Voice over Internet Protocol). With VoIP, two computers act as the phones, and the Internet-based calls are free (or you can pay a few cents to call from your computer to a telephone). If both computers have webcams, you can even see each other while you chat. The major providers are Skype (www.skype.com) and Google Talk (www.google.com/talk).

For people traveling with a smartphone, various apps allow you to make VoIP calls from a Wi-Fi hotspot. A Skype app is available for most smartphones (including the iPhone, Android, and BlackBerry), while Fring (www.fring.com) allows you to use other VoIP providers—including Google Talk—on your smartphone. These apps also work on the iPod Touch (if you have an older model, you'll need to attach an external microphone).

Useful Phone Numbers

Italy's toll-free numbers start with 80. These numbers—called *freephone* or *numero verde* (green number)—can be dialed free from any phone without using a phone card. Note that you can't call Italy's toll-free numbers from America, nor can you count on reaching America's toll-free numbers from Italy.

Any Italian phone number that starts with "8" but isn't followed by a "0" is a toll call, generally costing €0.10-0.50 per minute.

Emergencies
English-speaking police help: tel. 113
Ambulance: tel. 118
Road Service: tel. 116

Embassies and Consulates
Nearest US Consulate: tel. 02-290-351 (Via Principe Amedeo 2/10, Milan, http://milan.usconsulate.gov)
US Embassy: 24-hour emergency line—tel. 06-46741, non-emergency—tel. 06-4674-2406 (Via Vittorio Veneto 121, Rome, www.usembassy.it)
Canadian Embassy: tel. 06-854-441 (Via Zara 30, Rome, www.italy.gc.ca)

Travel Advisories
US Department of State: tel. 202/647-5225, www.travel.state.gov
Canadian Department of Foreign Affairs: Canadian tel. 800-267-6788, www.dfait-maeci.gc.ca
US Centers for Disease Control and Prevention: tel. 800-CDC-INFO (800-232-4636), www.cdc.gov/travel

Directory Assistance
Telephone Help: tel. 170 (in English; free directory assistance)
Directory Assistance: tel. 12 (€0.50, an Italian-speaking robot gives the number twice, very clearly)

Internet Access
It's useful to get online periodically as you travel—to confirm trip plans, check train or bus schedules, get weather forecasts, catch up on email, blog or post photos from your trip, or call folks back home (explained earlier, under "Calling over the Internet").

Many hotels offer a computer in the lobby with Internet access for guests. Smaller places may sometimes let you sit at their desk for a few minutes just to check your email, if you ask politely. If your hotel doesn't have access, ask your hotelier to direct you to the nearest place to get online.

Traveling with a Laptop or Tablet: You can get online if your hotel has Wi-Fi (wireless Internet access) or a port in your room for plugging in a cable. Some hotels offer Wi-Fi for free; others charge by the minute or hour. A cellular modem—which lets your laptop access the Internet over a mobile phone network—provides more extensive coverage, but is much more expensive than Wi-Fi (in Italy, www.wind.it and www.tim.it offer pay-as-you-go mobile broadband).

Warning: While using a public Internet terminal or free Wi-Fi is convenient, it can come with security risks. Some computers are loaded with damaging "malware," such as "key logger" programs that keep track of what you're typing—including passwords. You can ask the Internet café or hotel what sort of security software their machines and Wi-Fi routers are running. If you're not convinced it's secure, don't access any sites (such as online

APPENDIX

banking) that could be sensitive to fraud. Be careful about storing personal information (such as passport and credit-card numbers) online.

Mail

While you can arrange for mail delivery to your hotel (allow 10 days for a letter to arrive), phoning and emailing are so easy that I've dispensed with mail stops altogether. Mail service in Italy has improved over the last few years, but even so, mail nothing precious from an Italian post office. Federal Express makes pricey two-day deliveries.

You can mail one package per day to yourself worth up to $200 duty-free from Europe to the US (mark it "personal purchases"). If you're sending a gift to someone, mark it "unsolicited gift." For details, visit www.cbp.gov and search for "Know Before You Go."

Transportation

By Car or Train?

If your trip will cover more of Italy than just Venice, you'll need to decide whether to rent a car or take trains. Cars are best for three or more traveling together (especially families with small kids), those packing heavy, and those scouring the countryside. Trains and buses are best for solo travelers, blitz tourists, and city-to-city travelers. While a car gives you the ultimate in mobility and freedom, enables you to search for hotels more easily, and carries your bags for you, the train zips you effortlessly from city to city, usually dropping you in the center and near the TI.

Trains

To travel by train cheaply in Italy, you can simply buy tickets as you go. Ticket machines work well and are easy to use (see "Buying Tickets," later), so you can usually avoid long lines at ticket windows. Pay all ticket costs in the station before you board, or you'll pay a penalty on the train.

Types of Trains: Since ticket prices depend on the speed of

the train, it pays to know the different types of trains in Italy: pokey R *(regionali)*, medium-speed RV *(regionali espresso)*, and E *(espresso)*; fast IC (Intercity) and EC (Eurocity); and super-fast ES (Eurostar Italia, including Alta Velocità and Frecciarossa). If you're traveling with a rail-pass, note that reservations are

Italy's Public Transportation

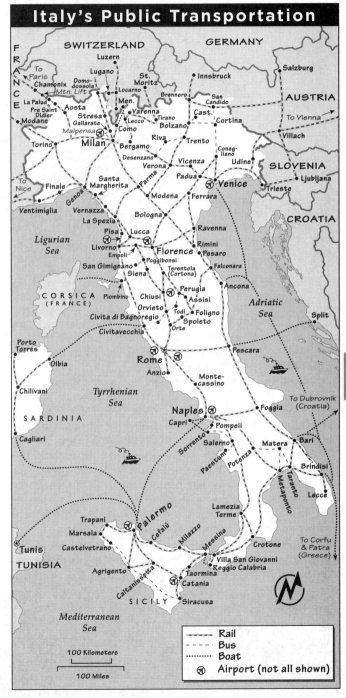

Rail
Bus
Boat
✈ Airport (not all shown)

100 Kilometers

100 Miles

Train Costs in Italy

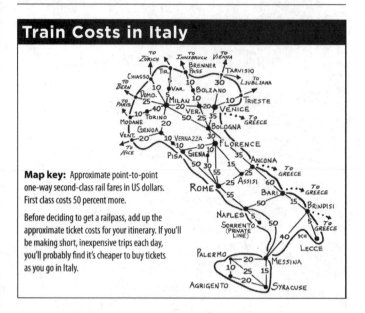

Map key: Approximate point-to-point one-way second-class rail fares in US dollars. First class costs 50 percent more.

Before deciding to get a railpass, add up the approximate ticket costs for your itinerary. If you'll be making short, inexpensive trips each day, you'll probably find it's cheaper to buy tickets as you go in Italy.

optional for IC trains, but required for EC and international trains (€5) and ES trains (€10). You can't make reservations for regional trains. A new high-speed rail service in Italy—*Nuovo Trasporto Viaggiatori* or NTV—will probably have launched its Italo trains by the time you visit. For details, see www.ntvspa.it.

Schedules: At the train station, the easiest way to check schedules is at a handy automated ticket machine (described next page, under "Buying Tickets"). Enter the desired date, time, and destination to view all your options. Printed schedules are also posted at the station (departure posters are always yellow).

Newsstands sell up-to-date regional and all-Italy timetables (€5, ask for the *orario ferroviario*). On the Web, check www.tren italia.it (domestic journeys only); for international trips, use http://bahn.hafas.de/bin/query.exe/en (Germany's excellent all-Europe train-schedule website). There is also a single all-Italy telephone number for train information (24 hours daily, toll tel. 892-021, Italian only, consider having your hotelier call for you).

TRENI IN PARTENZA

DESTINAZIONE	INDICAZIONE SUSSIDIARIA	CATEGORIA	ORARIO	BINARIO		DESTINAZIONE	INDICAZIONE SUSSIDIARIA	CATEGORIA	ORARIO	BINARIO	
DEPARTS		DEPARTURES				SALIDAS			ABFAHRTEN		
NETTUNO		REG.	14.45	14		NAPOLI C.LE		IR	15.15	15	
CASSINO		REG.	14.55	18		FIUMICINO A.		DIR.	15.15	22	
ANCONA		2	14.55	3		NAPOLI C.LE		DIR.	15.20	12	
FRASCATI		REG.	15.05	19							
MILANO C.LE		X	15.05	8		ANCONA		IR	15.25	5	
TARANTO			15.05	13		CASSINO		REG.	15.30	17	
NAPOLI C.LE			15.10	9		FIUMICINO A.		DIR.	15.35	21	
UDINE		1	15.15	6							

Point-to-Point Tickets

Train tickets are a good value in Italy. Fares are shown on the map on page 388, though fares can vary for the same journey, mainly depending on the speed of the train. **First-class** tickets cost 50 percent more than **second-class.** While second-class cars go as fast as their first-class neighbors, Italy is one country where I would consider the splurge of first class. The easiest way to "upgrade" a second-class ticket once on board a crowded train is to nurse a drink in the snack car.

Speed vs. Savings: For point-to-point tickets, you'll pay more the faster you go. Spending a modest amount of extra time in transit can save money. For example, a round-trip ticket between Padua and Venice costs €25 on a Eurocity train (15 minutes each way), but only €6 on a regional train (25 minutes each way). On longer, mainline routes, fast trains save more time and provide most of the service. For example, super-fast Venice-Rome trains run hourly, cost €76 in second class, and make the trip in 3.75 hours, while less-frequent InterCity options cost €46 and take 6.5 hours.

Discounts: Families with young children can get price breaks—kids ages 4 and under travel free; ages 4-11 at half-price. Sometimes the parents get a 20 percent price break. Ask for the "Offerta Familia" deal when buying tickets at a counter (or, at a ticket machine, choose "Yes" at the "Do you want ticket issue?" prompt, then choose "Familia"). With the discount, families of three to five people with at least one kid (age 12 or under) get 50 percent off the child fare and 20 percent off the adult fare. The deal doesn't apply to all trains at all times, but it's worth checking out.

Discounts for youths and seniors require purchase of a separate card (Carta Verde for ages 12-26 costs €40; Carta Argento for ages 60 and over is €30), but the discount on tickets is so minor (10-15 percent respectively for domestic travel), it's not worth it for most.

Buying Tickets: Avoid train station ticket lines whenever possible by using the automated ticket machines in station halls. You'll be able to easily purchase tickets for travel within Italy (not international trains), make seat reservations, and even book a *cuccetta* (koo-CHEHT-tah; overnight berth).

Red-white-and-green **automated ticket machines** (marked *Biglietto Veloce/Fast Ticket*) are user-friendly and found in all but the tiniest stations in Italy. You can pay by cash (they give change) or by debit or credit card (even for small amounts). Select English, then your destination. If you don't immediately see the city you're traveling to, keep keying in the spelling until it's listed. You can choose from first- and second-class seats, request tickets for more than one traveler, and (on high-speed Eurostar Italia trains) choose

APPENDIX

Open or Non-Reserved Ticket—Need to Validate

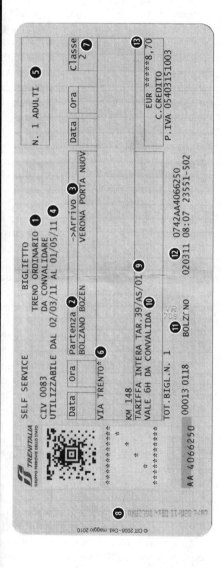

1 Open ticket for non-express trains, must be validated
2 Point of departure
3 Destination
4 Validity of ticket (use once within 2 months of purchase)
5 Number of passengers
6 Route
7 Class of travel (1 = 1st, 2 = 2nd)
8 Validation stamp
9 Full fare for non-express train
10 Once stamped, ticket is good for 1 trip within 6 hours
11 Location of ticket sale
12 Date ticket was purchased
13 Ticket cost

Reserved Ticket (Fast Train)—Need Not Validate

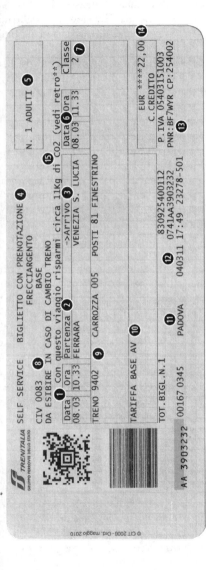

1. Departure date & time
2. Point of departure
3. Destination
4. "Ticket with reservation"
5. Number of passengers
6. Arrival date & time
7. Class of travel (1 = 1st; 2 = 2nd)
8. "Present to official if changing trains"
9. Train #, train car # & seat # (finestrino = window seat)
10. Fast-train fare (other types of trains can be cheaper and don't require reservations)
11. Location of ticket sale
12. Date ticket was purchased
13. Booking ID
14. Ticket cost
15. Amount of CO_2 usage reduced by this train trip

an aisle or window seat. If the machine prompts you—"Fidelity Card?"—choose no. Don't select a discount rate without being sure that you meet the criteria (for example, Americans are not eligible for certain EU or resident discounts). Railpass-holders can use the machines to make seat reservations. If you need to validate your ticket, you can do it in the same machine if you're boarding your train right away.

Tickets to nearby destinations only (including Mestre, Padua, and Verona) can also be bought from the older, gray-and-blue machines marked *Rete regionale* (cash only, push button for English).

Note that you can't buy international tickets from machines; for this and anything else that requires a real person, try a local travel agency, a good alternative to the ticket windows at the station. They also sell domestic tickets and make reservations. The cost is only a little more (agencies charge a small fee); it can be more convenient (if you find yourself near a travel agency while sightseeing); and the language barrier can be smaller than at the station's ticket windows.

Validating Tickets: If your ticket includes a seat reservation on a specific train, you are all set and can just get on board. However, many tickets (especially for slower trains) are flexible—not tied to a particular train or specific reserved seat—and so must be validated before you board. You always need to validate the small, paper-slip tickets that you buy from newsstands or older ticket machines. Tickets from the newer machines must also be validated if they say *"Da convalidare"* near the top. To validate your ticket, stamp it in the yellow box near the platform. Once you validate a ticket, you must complete your trip within the timeframe shown on the ticket (within 6 hours for medium-distance trips; within 1.25 hours for short rides under 6 miles). If you forget to validate your ticket, go right away to the train conductor—before he comes to you—or you'll pay a fine. Note that you don't need to validate a railpass.

Railpasses

The **Italy Pass** for Italian State Railways may save you money if you're taking three long train rides or prefer first-class travel, but don't count on it for hop-on convenience on every train. Use the price map on the next page to add up your ticket costs (ticket prices on the map are for the fastest trains on a given route, many of which have reservation costs built in).

Railpass travelers must make separate seat reservations for the fastest trains between major Italian cities (€10-15 each). Railpass travelers can just hop on InterCity trains (optional €5 reservation) and regional trains (no reservations possible). Making a reservation

APPENDIX

Railpasses

Prices listed are for 2011 and are subject to change. For the latest prices, details, and train schedules (and easy online ordering), see my comprehensive *Guide to Eurail Passes* at www.ricksteves.com/rail.

"Saver" prices are per person for two or more people traveling together. "Youth" means under age 26. The fare for children 4–11 is half the adult individual fare or Saver fare. Kids under age 4 travel free.

ITALY PASS

	Individual 1st Class	Individual 2nd Class	Saver 1st Class	Saver 2nd Class	Youth 2nd Class
3 days in 2 months	$278	$227	$237	$192	$183
Extra rail days (max 7)	30-33	23-27	24-29	21-23	20-23

ITALY RAIL & DRIVE PASS

Any 3 rail days and 2 car days in 2 months.

Car Category	1st Class	2nd Class	Extra Car Day
Economy 2-Door	$348	$295	$66
Economy 4-Door	357	304	75
Compact	377	324	95
Intermediate	404	352	122
Economy Automatic	386	333	104
Premium	508	455	226
Extra rail days (max 7)	31	25	

Prices are per person, two traveling together. Solo travelers pay about 20 percent more. To order a Rail & Drive pass, call your travel agent or Rail Europe at 800-438-7245. *This pass is not sold by Europe Through the Back Door.*

FRANCE–ITALY PASS

	Individual 1st Class	Individual 2nd Class	Saver 1st Class	Saver 2nd Class	Youth 2nd Class
4 days in 2 months	$403	$343	$343	$292	$261
Extra rail days (max 6)	46-49	39-42	39-42	33-37	29-33

Be aware of your route. Many daytime connections from Paris to Italy pass through Switzerland (an additional $60 2nd class or $90 1st class if not covered by your pass). Routes via Nice, Torino, or Modane will bypass Switzerland. Direct Paris–Italy day or night trains are covered by the pass, regardless of their route.

GREECE–ITALY PASS

	Individual 1st Class	Individual 2nd Class	Saver 1st Class	Saver 2nd Class	Youth 2nd Class
4 days in 2 months	$384	$306	$326	$260	$250
Extra rail days (max 6)	38-40	32-33	33-35	26-28	25-27

Covers deck passage on overnight Superfast Ferries between Patras, Greece and Bari or Ancona, Italy (starts use of one travel day). Or 30-50% discount on Hellenic Mediterranean Line ferry with basic cabin Patras-Corfu-Brindisi (does not use a travel day). Does not cover travel to or on Greek islands, except a 30% discount on Blue Star Ferries.

SELECTPASS

This pass covers travel in three adjacent countries. Please visit **www.ricksteves.com/rail** for four- and five-country options.

	Individual 1st Class	Saver 1st Class	Youth 2nd Class
5 days in 2 months	$489	$416	$319
6 days in 2 months	540	459	352
8 days in 2 months	638	543	416
10 days in 2 months	740	630	482

at a train station or travel agency is the same as the process to buy a ticket, so you may need to stand in line either way. Reservations for berths on overnight trains cost extra, aren't covered by railpasses, and aren't reflected on the ticket cost map.

A 22-country **Eurail Global Pass** can work well for an all-Europe trip, but is a bad value for travel exclusively in Italy. A cheaper version, the **Eurail Select Pass,** allows you to tailor a pass to your trip, provided you're traveling in three, four, or five adjacent countries directly connected by rail or ferry. For instance, with a three-country pass allowing 10 days of train travel within a two-month period (about $700 for a single adult in 2011), you could choose France-Italy-Greece or Germany-Austria-Italy. A **France and Italy Pass** combines just those two countries and covers night trains to and from Paris via Switzerland (but if your route crosses Switzerland by day, you'll pay extra—so the Selectpass is a better choice if you want to see the Alps). Before you buy a Selectpass or France and Italy Pass, consider how many travel days you'll really need. Use the pass for travel days that involve long hauls or several trips. Pay out of pocket for tickets on days you're taking only short, cheap rides.

For a summary of railpass deals and the latest prices, check my Guide to Eurail Passes at www.ricksteves.com/rail. If you decide to get a railpass, this guide will help you know you're getting the right one for your trip.

Train Tips

This section contains more information on making seat reservations, storing baggage, avoiding theft, and dealing with strikes.

Seat Reservations: Trains can fill up, even in first class. If you're on a tight schedule, you'll want to reserve a few days ahead for fast trains (see "Types of Trains," earlier). Purchasing tickets or passholder seat reservations onboard a train comes with a nasty penalty. Buying them at the station can be a time-waster unless you use the automatic ticket machines.

If you don't need a reservation, and if your train originates at your departure point (e.g., you're catching the Venice-Florence train in Venice), arriving at least 15 minutes before the departure time will help you snare a seat.

Some major stations have train composition posters on the platforms showing where first- and second-class cars are located when the trains arrive (letters on the poster are supposed to correspond to letters posted over the platform—but they don't always). Since most trains now allow you to make reservations up to the time of departure, conductors are no longer marking reserved seats with a card—instead, they simply post a list of the reservable and non-reservable seat rows (sometimes in English) in each train car's

Deciphering Italian Train Schedules

At the station, look for the big yellow posters labeled *Partenze*—Departures (ignore the white posters, which show arrivals).

Schedules are listed chronologically, hour by hour, showing the trains leaving the station throughout the day. Each schedule has columns:

- The first column *(Ora)* lists the time of departure.
- The next column *(Treno)* shows the type of train.
- The third column *(Classi Servizi)* lists the services available (first- and second-class cars, dining car, *cuccetta* berths, etc.) and, more importantly, whether you need reservations (usually denoted by an R in a box). Note that all Eurostar Italia (ES) and Alta Velocita (AV) trains, many InterCity (IC) and EuroCity (EC) trains, and most international trains require reservations.
- The next column lists the destination of the train *(Principali Fermate Destinazioni),* often showing intermediate stops, followed by the final destination, with arrival times listed throughout in parentheses. Note that your final destination may be listed in fine print as an intermediate destination. For example, if you're going from Venice to Verona, scan the schedule and you'll notice that regional trains that go to Milan usually stop in Verona en route. Travelers who read the fine print end up with a far greater choice of trains.
- The next column *(Servizi Diretti e Annotazioni)* has pertinent notes about the train, such as "also stops in..." *(ferma anche a...),* "doesn't stop in..." *(non ferma a...),* "stops in every station" *(ferma in tutte le stazioni),* "delayed..." *(ritardo...),* and so on.
- The last column lists the track *(Binario)* the train departs from. Confirm the *binario* with an additional source: a ticket-seller, the electronic board that lists immediate departures, TV monitors on the platform, or the railway officials who are usually standing by the train unless you really need them.

For any odd symbols on the poster, look at the key at the end. Some of the phrasing can be deciphered easily, such as *servizio periodico* (periodic service—doesn't always run). For the trickier ones, ask a local or railway official, try your *Rick Steves' Italian Phrase Book & Dictionary,* or simply take a different train.

You can also check schedules—for trains anywhere in Italy, not just from the station you're currently in—at the handy ticket machines. Enter the date and time of your departure (to or from any Italian station), and you can view all your options.

vestibule. This means that if you board a crowded train and get one of the last seats, you may be ousted when the reservation-holder comes along.

Baggage Storage: Many stations have *deposito bagagli* where you can safely leave your bag for about €8 per 12-hour period (payable when you pick up the bag, double-check closing hours). Due to security concerns, no Italian stations have lockers.

Theft Concerns: Italian trains are famous for their thieves. Never leave a bag unattended. Police do ride the trains, cutting down on theft. Still, for an overnight trip, I'd feel safe only in a *cuccetta* (a bunk in a special sleeping car with an attendant who keeps track of who comes and goes while you sleep—approximately €20 in a six-bed compartment, €25 in a less-cramped four-bed compartment, €50 in a more-private double compartment).

Strikes: Strikes, which are common, generally last a day. Train employees will simply explain, *"Sciopero"* (strike). But in actuality, sporadic trains, following no particular schedule, lumber down the tracks during most strikes. When a strike is pending, travel agencies (and Web-savvy hoteliers) can check the Internet for you to see when the strike goes into effect and which trains will continue to run. Revised schedules may be posted in Italian at stations, and station personnel still working can often tell you what trains are expected to run. If I need to get somewhere and know a strike is imminent, I leave early (before the strike, which often begins at 9:00), or I just go to the station with extra patience in tow and hop on anything rolling in the direction I want to go.

Renting a Car

If you're renting a car in Italy, bring your driver's license. You're also technically required to have an International Driving Permit—a translation of your driver's license (sold at your local AAA office for $15 plus the cost of two passport-type photos; see www.aaa.com). While that's the letter of the law, I've often rented cars in Italy without having—or being asked to show—this permit.

Rental companies require you to be at least 18 years old and have held your license for one year. Drivers under the age of 25 may incur a young-driver surcharge, and some rental companies do not rent to anyone 75 and over. If you're considered too young or old, look into leasing, which has less-stringent age restrictions.

Research car rentals before you go. It's cheaper to arrange most car rentals from the US. Call several companies and look online to compare rates, or arrange a rental through your home-town travel agent.

Most of the major US rental agencies (such as Alamo/National, Avis, Budget, Dollar, Hertz, and Thrifty) have offices in Italy. It can be cheaper to use a consolidator, such as Auto Europe (www.autoeurope.com) or Europe by Car (www.ebctravel.com), which compares rates at several companies to get you the best deal. My readers, however, have reported problems with consolidators, ranging from misinformation to unexpected fees; because you're going through a middleman, it can be more challenging to resolve disputes that arise with the rental agency.

Regardless of the car-rental company you choose, always read the contract carefully. The fine print can conceal a host of common add-on charges—such as one-way drop-off fees, airport surcharges, or mandatory insurance policies—that aren't included in the "total price," but can be tacked on when you pick up your car.

For the best rental deal, rent by the week with unlimited mileage. To save money on gas, ask for a diesel car. I normally rent the smallest, least-expensive model with a stick shift (cheaper than an automatic). Almost all rentals are manual by default, so if you need an automatic, you must request one in advance; beware that these cars are usually larger models (not as maneuverable on narrow, winding roads). An automatic transmission adds about 50 percent to the car-rental cost over a manual transmission. Roads and parking spaces are narrow in Italy, so you'll do yourself a favor by renting the smallest car that meets your needs.

For a three-week rental, allow $900 per person (based on two people sharing a car), including insurance, tolls, gas, and parking. For trips of this length, look into leasing; you'll save money on insurance and taxes. Compare pick-up costs (downtown can be cheaper than the airport) and explore drop-off options.

You can sometimes get a GPS unit with your rental car or leased vehicle for an additional fee (around $15/day; be sure it's set to English and has all the maps you need before you drive off). Or, if you have a portable GPS device at home, consider taking it with you to Europe (buy and upload European maps before your trip). GPS apps are also available for smartphones, but roaming charges in Europe could lead to exorbitant charges.

When you pick up the rental car, check it thoroughly and make sure any damage is noted on your rental agreement. Find out how your car's lights, turn signals, wipers, and gas cap function, and know what kind of gas the car takes.

Returning a car at a big-city train station can be tricky; get precise details on the car drop-off location and hours. Note that rental offices usually close from midday Saturday until Monday morning. When you return the car, make sure the agent verifies its condition with you.

If you want a car for only a couple of days, a rail-and-drive pass (such as a EurailDrive, Selectpass Drive, or Italy Rail and Drive) can be put to thoughtful use. The basic Italy Rail and Drive Pass, which includes theft insurance and CDW (described below), comes with two days of car rental and three days of rail travel in two months. While rail-and-drive passes are convenient, they're also pricey, particularly for solo travelers.

Car Insurance Options

Accidents can happen anywhere, but when you're on vacation, the last thing you need is stress over car insurance. When you rent a car, you're liable for a very high deductible, sometimes equal to the entire value of the car. Limit your financial risk in case of an accident by choosing one of these two options: Buy Collision Damage Waiver (CDW) coverage from the car-rental company, or get coverage through your credit card (free, but more complicated).

In Italy, most car-rental companies' rates automatically include CDW coverage (which you sometimes can't decline). Even if you try to decline CDW when you reserve your Italian car, you may find when you show up at the counter that you must buy it after all.

While each rental company has its own variation, basic CDW costs $15-35 a day and reduces your liability, but does not eliminate it. When you pick up the car, you'll be offered the chance to "buy down" the basic deductible to zero (for an additional $15-30/day; this is sometimes called "super CDW").

If you opt for credit-card coverage, there's a catch. You'll technically have to decline all coverage offered by the car-rental company; this means they can place a hold on your card (which can be up to the full value of the car). In case of damage, it can be time-consuming to resolve the charges with your credit-card company. Before you decide on this option, quiz your credit-card company about how it works.

For more on car-rental insurance, see www.ricksteves.com /cdw.

Theft Insurance: Note that theft insurance (separate from CDW insurance) is mandatory in Italy. The insurance usually costs about $15-20 a day, payable when you pick up the car.

Leasing

For trips of three weeks or more, consider leasing (which automatically includes zero-deductible collision and theft insurance). By technically buying and then selling back the car, you save lots of money on tax and insurance. Leasing provides you a new car with unlimited mileage and a 24-hour emergency assistance program. You can lease for as little as 17 days to as long as six months. Car leases must be arranged from the US. One of many companies offering affordable lease packages is Europe by Car (US tel. 800-223-1516, www.ebctravel.com).

Driving in Italy

*(Map labels:)*

AUSTRIA

SWITZERLAND

Brenner Pass

Villach

Dolomites (Bolzano)

SLOVENIA

Mt. Blanc Tunnel

Lake Como

70m·2h

Trieste

145m·2.5h

30m·.75h

260m·5h

100m·2.25h

155m·2.5h

95m·1.75h

200m·4h

255m·4.5h

175m·3h

Milan

170m·3h

Venice

185m·3.25h

85m·2h

CROATIA

175m·2.75h

135m·2.5h

225m·4h

230m·3.5h

Ravenna

160m·2.75h

155m·2h

115m·2h

Cinque Terre (La Spezia)

90m·1.75h

Florence

Ventimiglia

50m·1h

70m·1.5h

100m·2h

125m·2.25h

Pisa

45m·1h

80m·2h

Assisi

Siena

100m·1h

75m·1.75h

55m·1.5h

115m·2.25h

210m·4h

75m·1.5h

Orvieto

75m·1.5h

Rome

155m·2.5h

30m·.5h

Note: Your times may vary based on traffic, construction, and road conditions.

Naples

Salerno

30m·.75h

30m·1h

Sorrento

60m·3h

m = miles
h = hours

Paestum

APPENDIX

Driving

Driving in Italy can be scary—a video game for keeps, and you only get one quarter. Italian drivers can be aggressive. They drive fast and tailgate as if it were required. They pass where Americans are taught not to—on blind corners and just before tunnels. Roads have narrow shoulders or none at all. Driving in the countryside is less stressful than driving through urban areas, but stay alert. On one-lane roads, larger vehicles have the right-of-way. If you're on a truckers' route, stifle your Good Samaritan impulse when you see provocatively dressed women standing by camper-vans at the side of the road; they're not having car trouble.

Road Rules: Stay out of restricted traffic zones or you'll risk huge fines. Car traffic is restricted in many city centers. Don't drive or park anywhere with signs reading *Zona Traffico Limitato* (ZTL, often shown above a red circle, see image). If you do, your license plate

ZONA TRAFFICO LIMITATO

red

will likely be photographed and a hefty (€100-plus) ticket mailed to your home without your ever having met a cop. Bumbling in and out of these zones can net you multiple fines. If your hotel is within a restricted area, it's best to ask your hotelier to direct you to parking outside the zone. (Although your hotelier can register your car as an authorized vehicle permitted to enter the zone, this usually isn't worth the hassle.)

As for other road rules, seatbelts are mandatory, kids 12 and under need a child-safety or booster seat, and you should keep headlights on at all times outside of urban areas. It's illegal to use your mobile phone without a hands-free headset while driving. Ask your car-rental company about additional rules, or check the US State Department website (www.travel.state.gov, click on "International Travel," then specify your country of choice and click "Traffic Safety and Road Conditions").

Tolls: Italy's freeway system, the autostrada, is as good as our interstate system, but you'll pay about a dollar for every 10 minutes of use. While I favor the freeways because I feel they're safer, cheaper (saving time and gas), and less nerve-racking than smaller roads, savvy local drivers know which toll-free *superstradas* are actually faster and more direct than the autostrada. For more information, visit www.autostrade.it.

Fuel: Gas is expensive—often about $6 per gallon. Diesel cars are more common in Europe than back home, so be sure you know what type of gas your car takes before you fill up. Gas pumps are color-coded for unleaded *(senza piombo)* or diesel *(gasolio)*. Autostrada rest stops are self-service stations open daily without a siesta break. Many 24-hour-a-day stations are entirely automated. Small-town stations are usually cheaper and offer full service but shorter hours.

Maps and Signage: A good map is essential. Learn the universal road signs (explained in charts in most road atlases and at service stations). Although roads are numbered on maps, actual road signs don't list route numbers. Instead, roads are indicated by blue signs with a city name on them (for

STOP **AND LEARN THESE ROAD SIGNS**

- (50) Speed Limit (km/hr)
- ▽ Yield
- No Passing
- End of No Passing Zone
- ⟶ One Way
- ⊗ Intersection
- ◆ Main Road
- Freeway
- ⚠ Danger
- No Entry
- No Entry for cars
- ◯ All Vehicles Prohibited
- **P** Parking
- No Parking
- ⊖ Customs
- ☮ Peace

example, if you want to take a road heading east out of Venice—marked route S-11 on your map—you'd follow signs to Padua, the next town along this road). The signs are inconsistent: They may direct you to the nearest big city or simply the next town along the route.

Theft: Cars are routinely vandalized and stolen. Thieves easily recognize rental cars and assume they are filled with a tourist's gear. Try to make your car look locally owned by hiding the "tourist-owned" rental-company decals and putting an Italian newspaper in your back window. Be sure all of your valuables are out of sight and locked in the trunk, or even better, with you or in your room.

Parking: White lines generally mean parking is free. Blue lines mean you'll have to pay—usually €1 per hour (use machine, leave time-stamped receipt on dashboard). If there's no meter, there's probably a roving attendant who will take your money. Study the signs. Often the free zones have a 30- or 60-minute time limit. Signs showing a street cleaner and a day of the week indicate which day the street is cleaned; there's a €100 tow-fee incentive to learn the days of the week in Italian.

Zona disco has nothing to do with dancing. Italian cars come equipped with a time disk (a cardboard clock), which you set at your arrival time and lay on the dashboard so the attendant knows how long you've been parked. This is a fine system that all drivers should take advantage of. (If your rental car doesn't come with a *zona disco*, pick one up at a tobacco shop or just write your arrival time on a piece of paper and place it on the dashboard.)

Garages are safe, save time, and help you avoid the stress of parking tickets. Take the parking voucher with you to pay the cashier before you leave.

Cheap Flights

If you're traveling beyond Venice, you might want to look into flying one of the affordable intra-European airlines. While trains are still the best way to connect places that are close together, a flight can save both time and money on long journeys. When comparing a flight versus a train trip, consider the time it takes to get to the airport and how early you'll need to arrive to check in before the flight. Most flights make sense only as an alternate to a train ride of five or more hours in length.

One of the best websites for comparing inexpensive flights is www.skyscanner.com. Other comparison search engines include www.wegolo.com and www.whichbudget.com. Many budget airlines—such as easyJet, Ryanair, and Jet Blue—serve Venice. Airport websites may list small airlines that serve your destination.

Be aware of the potential drawbacks of flying on the cheap: nonrefundable and nonchangeable tickets, minimal or nonexistent customer service, treks to airports far outside of town, and pricey baggage fees. Especially if you're traveling with lots of luggage, a cheap flight can quickly become a bad deal. To avoid unpleasant surprises, read the small print before you book.

Resources

Resources from Rick Steves

Books: *Rick Steves' Venice 2012* is one of many books in my series on European travel, which includes country guidebooks, city

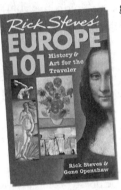

guidebooks (Rome, Florence, Paris, London, etc.), Snapshot guides (excerpted chapters from my country guides), Pocket Guides (full-color little books on big cities), and my budget-travel skills handbook, *Rick Steves' Europe Through the Back Door*. Some of my books are available in electronic format. My phrase books—for Italian, French, German, Spanish, and Portuguese—are practical and budget-oriented. My other books include *Europe 101* (a crash course on art and history), *Mediterranean Cruise Ports* (how to make the most of your time in port), and *Travel as a Political Act* (a travelogue sprinkled with tips for bringing home a global perspective). A more complete list of my titles appears near the end of this book.

Video: My public television series, *Rick Steves' Europe*, covers European destinations in 100 shows, with 14 episodes on Italy, including 2 on Venice. To watch episodes, visit www.hulu.com /rick-steves-europe; for scripts and other details, see www.rick steves.com/tv.

Audio: My weekly public radio show, *Travel with Rick Steves*, features interviews with travel experts from around the world. I've also produced free, self-guided audio tours of the top sights in Venice. All of this audio content is available for free at Rick Steves Audio Europe, an extensive online library organized by destination. Choose whatever interests you, and download it for free to your computer or mobile device via www.ricksteves.com/audio europe, iTunes, or the Rick Steves Audio Europe smartphone app.

Begin Your Trip at www.ricksteves.com

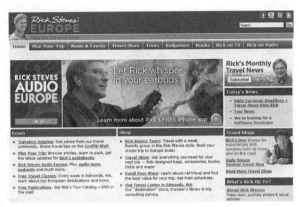

At www.ricksteves.com, you'll discover a wealth of free information on European destinations, including fresh monthly news and helpful tips from thousands of fellow travelers. You'll find my latest guidebook updates (www.ricksteves.com/update), a monthly travel e-newsletter (easy and free to sign up), my personal travel blog, and my free Rick Steves Audio Europe smartphone app (if you don't have a smartphone, you can access the same content via podcasts). You can even follow me on Facebook and Twitter.

Our **online Travel Store** offers travel bags and accessories specially designed by me and my staff to help you travel smarter and lighter. These include my popular carry-on bags (roll-aboard and backpack versions), money belts, totes, toiletries kits, adapters, other accessories, and a wide selection of guidebooks, planning maps, and DVDs.

Choosing the right **railpass** for your trip—amid hundreds of options—can drive you nutty. We'll help you choose the best pass for your needs and ship it to you for free, plus give you a bunch of free extras.

Rick Steves' Europe Through the Back Door travel company offers **tours** with more than three dozen itineraries and 450 departures reaching the best destinations in this book...and beyond. Our Italy tours include "the best of" in 17 days, Village Italy in 14 days, South Italy in 13 days, Venice-Florence-Rome in 10 days, the Heart of Italy in 9 days, Sicily in 10 days, and a week-long Rome tour. You'll enjoy great guides, a fun bunch of travel partners (with small groups of generally around 24-28), and plenty of room to spread out in a big, comfy bus. You'll find European adventures to fit every vacation length. For all the details, and to get our Tour Catalog and a free Rick Steves Tour Experience DVD (filmed on location during an actual tour), visit www.ricksteves.com or call us at 425/608-4217.

APPENDIX

Maps

The black-and-white maps in this book are concise and simple, designed to help you locate recommended places and get to local TIs, where you can pick up more in-depth maps of cities or regions (usually free). Better maps are sold at newsstands and bookstores. Before you buy a map, look at it to be sure it has the level of detail you want. Drivers will want to pick up a good, detailed map in Europe (I'd recommend a 1:200,000- or 1:300,000-scale map).

Other Guidebooks

If you're like most travelers, this book is all you need. But if you're heading beyond my recommended neighborhoods and destinations, $40 for extra maps and books can be money well spent.

The following books are worthwhile, though they are not updated annually; check the publication date before you buy. Focusing mainly on sights, Eyewitness' colorful *Venice and the Veneto* guide is fun for its great graphics and photos, but it's relatively skimpy on content and weighs a ton. (Their *Top 10 Venice* book, which features top-10 lists, is lighter, as is Rough Guide's *Pocket Rough Guide Venice*.) Frommer's publishes *24 Great Walks in Venice* and Lonely Planet offers *Venice Encounter*. You can buy these in Venice (no more expensive than in the US) or simply borrow them for a minute from other travelers at certain sights to make sure you're aware of that place's highlights. In Venice, local guidebooks (sold at kiosks) are cheap and give you a map and a decent commentary on the sights.

If you'll be traveling elsewhere in Italy, consider these books in the Rick Steves series: *Italy, Rome,* and *Florence & Tuscany.*

Recommended Books and Movies

To learn more about Venice past and present, check out a few of these books or films.

Non-Fiction

A History of Venice (Norwich) covers the city from its beginnings until Napoleon ended the Republic's independence. *Venice: A Maritime Republic* (Lane) explains how dominance on the high seas brought in piles of riches. *Venice: Lion City* (Wills), another city history, has a more academic tone. *Francesco's Venice* (da Mosto), based on a BBC series, balances history with coffee tablebook illustrations. *The Venetian Empire* (Morris) is an easy read and shows the city's place on a larger historical canvas.

Filled with stories of a woman abroad, *Venice Observed* rings with Mary McCarthy's engaging voice. *The City of Falling Angels,* by best-selling author John Berendt, hinges on a devastating fire at La Fenice Opera House. Based on once-hidden letters found in a palazzo, *A Venetian Affair* (di Robilant) tells a true love story. *Venice: A Cultural and Literary Companion* (Garrett) also covers the nearby islands, while *A Literary Companion to Venice* (Littlewood) includes walking tours of the city, as does *Strolling Through Venice* (Freely). For a traveler's insight into Venice, consider picking up Barrie Kerper's *Venice: The Collected Traveler.* Kids of all ages enjoy the whimsical impressions of the city in Miroslav Sasek's classic picture-book *This is Venice.*

For a fun, critical perspective on tourism in Venice, get *Venice: The Tourist Maze* (Davis and Martin). Jane da Mosto's *The Science of Saving Venice* is a readable introduction to the ecology and future of Venice's lagoon.

Fiction

Henry James set many of his best books in Venice, including *The Wings of the Dove, Italian Hours,* and *The Aspern Papers and Other Stories.* Thomas Mann also chose this city for his doomed tale *Death in Venice.*

Invisible Cities (Calvino) takes place during the era of Genghis Khan and Marco Polo, while *The Palace: A Novel* (St. Aubin de Terán) has the Italian Risorgimento as its backdrop. Set in the Napoleonic era, *The Passion* (Winterson) is both a complex love story and a work of literary fiction. *In the Company of the Courtesan* (Dunant), *The Glassblower of Murano* (Fiorato), and *The Rosseti Letter* (Phillips) novelize the drama and romance of Venice.

Venice's murky waters make a perfect setting for intrigue. Mystery fans will enjoy *Dead Lagoon* (Dibdin), *Dirge for a Doge* (Eyre), *Stone Virgin* (Unsworth), and *The Haunted Hotel* (Collins). In *Death at La Fenice,* one of a dozen of her novels set in Venice, Donna Leon chronicles the adventures of detective Guido Brunetti and his wife Paola. Fans of the series will enjoy *Brunetti's Venice* (Sepeda) that leads visitors on intimate walks through the city, highlighting Brunetti's haunts and settings from Leon's novels.

Films

Summertime (1955) sends melancholy Katherine Hepburn to Venice for romance. *Death in Venice* (1971), based on the book (see above), shows the devastating impact of a troubling infatuation. *Don't Look Now* (1973), based on a novel by Daphne du Maurier, uses Venice as a mysterious backdrop for a haunting tale.

Only You (1994) is a cute (and even sappy) love story, while *Bread and Tulips* (2000)—equally romantic, but firmly grounded in reality—shows the power of Venice in reviving a wounded soul. *Dangerous Beauty* (1998), meanwhile, keeps love out of the picture in the story of a 16th-century prostitute. *Wings of the Dove* (1997), based on the Henry James novel, is a tale of desire that takes full

APPENDIX

advantage of its Venetian locale.

The 2003 version of *The Italian Job* begins its fluffy, fun crime caper in Venice. Shakespeare fans will appreciate *The Merchant of Venice* (2004), which won raves for Al Pacino. The Woody Allen musical *Everyone Says I Love You* (1997) is partially set in Venice. And the climax of the James Bond thriller *Casino Royale* (2006) takes place along—and under—the canals of Venice. For more Venetian eye-candy, try *Casanova* (2005), starring Heath Ledger as the master of *amore*, or *The Tourist* (2010), with Johnny Depp and Angelina Jolie.

Holidays and Festivals

Holidays seem to strike without warning, and every town has a festival honoring its patron saint. Venice is always busy with special musical and artistic events. The free monthly *Un Ospite di Venezia* lists all the latest in English (free at fancy hotels, or check www .aguestinvenice.com).

This list includes many—but not all—major festivals in Venice, plus national holidays observed throughout Italy. Many sights and banks close on national holidays—keep this in mind when planning your itinerary. Before gearing your trip around a festival, make sure you verify its dates by checking the festival's website or TI sites (www.italiantourism.com and www.turismo venezia.it).

In Venice, hotels get booked up on Carnevale, Easter weekend, Liberation Day/St. Mark's Day, Labor Day, Feast of the Ascension Day, the Feast and Regatta of the Redeemer, the Historical Regatta, All Saint's Day, the Feast of our Lady of Good Health, Christmas, and New Year's Eve, and on Fridays and Saturdays year-round. Some hotels require you to book the full three-day weekend around a holiday.

Jan 1	New Year's Day
Jan 6	Epiphany
Feb 11-21	Carnevale
April 8	Easter Sunday
April 9	Easter Monday
April 25	Italian Liberation Day, St. Mark's Day (Venetian patron saint)
May 1	Labor Day
May 17	Feast of the Ascension Day
Late May-Early June	Vogalonga Regatta (www.vogalonga.it)
June 2	Anniversary of the Republic
June 7	Feast of Corpus Christi
July 21-22	Feast and Regatta of the Redeemer
Aug 15	Assumption of Mary (Ferragosto)

2012

JANUARY
S	M	T	W	T	F	S
1	2	3	4	5	6	7
8	9	10	11	12	13	14
15	16	17	18	19	20	21
22	23	24	25	26	27	28
29	30	31				

FEBRUARY
S	M	T	W	T	F	S
			1	2	3	4
5	6	7	8	9	10	11
12	13	14	15	16	17	18
19	20	21	22	23	24	25
26	27	28	29			

MARCH
S	M	T	W	T	F	S
				1	2	3
4	5	6	7	8	9	10
11	12	13	14	15	16	17
18	19	20	21	22	23	24
25	26	27	28	29	30	31

APRIL
S	M	T	W	T	F	S
1	2	3	4	5	6	7
8	9	10	11	12	13	14
15	16	17	18	19	20	21
22	23	24	25	26	27	28
29	30					

MAY
S	M	T	W	T	F	S
		1	2	3	4	5
6	7	8	9	10	11	12
13	14	15	16	17	18	19
20	21	22	23	24	25	26
27	28	29	30	31		

JUNE
S	M	T	W	T	F	S
					1	2
3	4	5	6	7	8	9
10	11	12	13	14	15	16
17	18	19	20	21	22	23
24	25	26	27	28	29	30

JULY
S	M	T	W	T	F	S
1	2	3	4	5	6	7
8	9	10	11	12	13	14
15	16	17	18	19	20	21
22	23	24	25	26	27	28
29	30	31				

AUGUST
S	M	T	W	T	F	S
			1	2	3	4
5	6	7	8	9	10	11
12	13	14	15	16	17	18
19	20	21	22	23	24	25
26	27	28	29	30	31	

SEPTEMBER
S	M	T	W	T	F	S
						1
2	3	4	5	6	7	8
9	10	11	12	13	14	15
16	17	18	19	20	21	22
23/30	24	25	26	27	28	29

OCTOBER
S	M	T	W	T	F	S
	1	2	3	4	5	6
7	8	9	10	11	12	13
14	15	16	17	18	19	20
21	22	23	24	25	26	27
28	29	30	31			

NOVEMBER
S	M	T	W	T	F	S
				1	2	3
4	5	6	7	8	9	10
11	12	13	14	15	16	17
18	19	20	21	22	23	24
25	26	27	28	29	30	

DECEMBER
S	M	T	W	T	F	S
						1
2	3	4	5	6	7	8
9	10	11	12	13	14	15
16	17	18	19	20	21	22
23/30	24/31	25	26	27	28	29

Sept 1-2	Historical Regatta
Nov 1	All Saints' Day
Nov 21	Feast of Our Lady of Good Health
Dec 8	Feast of the Immaculate Conception
Dec 25	Christmas
Dec 26	St. Stephen's Day

Festivals in Venice

Venice's most famous festival is **Carnevale,** the celebration Americans call Mardi Gras (Feb 11-21 in 2012, www.carnevale .venezia.it). Carnevale, which means "farewell to meat," originated centuries ago as a wild two-month-long party leading up to the austerity of Lent. In Carnevale's heyday—the 1600s and 1700s—you could do pretty much anything with anybody from any social class if you were wearing a mask. These days it's a tamer 10-day celebration, culminating in a huge dance lit with fireworks on St. Mark's Square. Sporting masks and costumes, Venetians from kids to businessmen join in the fun. Drawing the biggest crowds of the year, Carnevale has nearly been a victim of its own success, driving away many Venetians (who skip out on the craziness to go skiing in the Dolomites).

Every odd year (next in 2013), the city hosts the **Venice Biennale International Art Exhibition,** a world-class contemporary art fair spread over the Arsenale and sprawling Castello Gardens. Artists representing 70 nations from around the world offer the latest in contemporary art forms: video, computer art, performance art, and digital photography, along with painting and sculpture (take vaporetto #1 or #2 to Giardini-Biennale; for details and an events calendar, see www.labiennale.org). The actual exhibition usually runs from June through November, but other events—film, dance, theater—loosely connected with the Biennale are held throughout the year (starting as early as Feb) in various venues on the island.

Other typically Venetian festival days filling the city's hotels with visitors and its canals with decked-out boats are **Feast of the Ascension Day** (May 17 in 2012), **Feast and Regatta of the Redeemer** (third Sun in July and the preceding evening, June 20-21 in 2012), and the **Historical Regatta** (old-time boats and pageantry, first Sat and Sun in Sept, Sept 1-2 in 2012). **Vogalonga** is a colorful regatta that attracts more than 1,500 human-powered watercraft; teams of often-costumed participants follow a 20-mile course through the canals and lagoon (late May-early June, www.vogalonga.it). Smaller regattas include the **Murano Regatta** (early July) and the **Burano Regatta** (mid-Sept).

Venice's patron saint, **St. Mark,** is commemorated every April 25. Venetian men celebrate the day by presenting roses to the women in their lives (mothers, wives, and lovers).

Every November 21 is the **Feast of Our Lady of Good Health.** On this local "Thanksgiving," a bridge is built over the Grand Canal so that the city can pile into La Salute Church and remember how Venice survived the gruesome plague of 1630. On this day, Venetians eat smoked lamb from Dalmatia (which was the cargo of the first ship admitted when the plague lifted).

Conversions and Climate

Numbers and Stumblers

- Europeans write a few of their numbers differently than we do. 1 = 1, 4 = 4, 7 = 7.
- In Europe, dates appear as day/month/year, so Christmas is 25/12/12.
- Commas are decimal points and decimals commas. A dollar and a half is 1,50, and there are 5.280 feet in a mile.
- When pointing, use your whole hand, palm down.
- When counting with fingers, start with your thumb. If you hold up your first finger to request one item, you'll probably get two.
- What Americans call the second floor of a building is the first floor in Europe.
- On escalators and moving sidewalks, Europeans keep the left "lane" open for passing. Keep to the right.

Metric Conversions (approximate)

A kilogram is 2.2 pounds, and 1 liter is about a quart, or almost four to a gallon. A kilometer is six-tenths of a mile. I figure kilometers to miles by cutting them in half and adding back 10 percent of the original (120 km: 60 + 12 = 72 miles, 300 km: 150 + 30 = 180 miles).

1 foot = 0.3 meter	1 square yard = 0.8 square meter
1 yard = 0.9 meter	1 square mile = 2.6 square kilometers
1 mile = 1.6 kilometers	1 ounce = 28 grams
1 centimeter = 0.4 inch	1 quart = 0.95 liter
1 meter = 39.4 inches	1 kilogram = 2.2 pounds
1 kilometer = 0.62 mile	32°F = 0°C

Roman Numerals

In the US, you'll see Roman numerals—which originated in ancient Rome—used for copyright dates, clocks, and the Super Bowl. In Italy, you're likely to observe these numbers chiseled on statues and buildings. If you want to do some numeric detective work, here's how: In Roman numerals, as in ours, the highest numbers (thousands, hundreds) come first, followed by smaller numbers. Many numbers are made by combining numerals into sets: V = 5, so VIII = 8 (5 plus 3). Roman numerals follow a subtraction principle for multiples of fours (4, 40, 400, etc.) and nines (9, 90, 900, etc.); the number four, for example, is written as IV (1 subtracted from 5), rather than IIII. The number nine is IX (1 subtracted from 10).

Rick Steves' Venice 2012—written in Roman numerals—would translate as *Rick Steves' Venice MMXII*. Big numbers such as dates can look daunting at first. The easiest way to handle them is to read the numbers in discrete chunks. For example, Michelangelo was born in MCDLXXV. Break it down: M (1,000) + CD (100 subtracted from 500, or 400) + LXX (50 + 10 + 10, or 70) + V (5) = 1475. It was a very good year.

M = 1000	XL = 40
CM = 900	X = 10
D = 500	IX = 9
CD = 400	V = 5
C = 100	IV = 4
XC = 90	I = duh
L = 50	

Clothing Sizes

When shopping for clothing, use these US-to-European comparisons as general guidelines (but note that no conversion is perfect).

- Women's dresses and blouses: Add 30
  (US size 10 = European size 40)
- Men's suits and jackets: Add 10
  (US size 40 regular = European size 50)
- Men's shirts: Multiply by 2 and add about 8
  (US size 15 collar = European size 38)
- Women's shoes: Add about 30
  (US size 8 = European size 38-39)
- Men's shoes: Add 32-34
  (US size 9 = European size 41; US size 11 = European size 45)

Venice's Climate

First line, average daily high; second line, average daily low; third line, days of no rain. For more detailed weather statistics for destinations in this book (as well as the rest of the world), check www .worldclimate.com.

J	F	M	A	M	J	J	A	S	O	N	D
42°	46°	53°	62°	70°	76°	81°	80°	75°	65°	53°	46°
33°	35°	41°	49°	56°	63°	66°	65°	61°	53°	44°	37°
25	21	24	21	23	22	24	24	25	24	21	23

Temperature Conversion: Fahrenheit and Celsius

Europe takes its temperature using the Celsius scale, while we opt for Fahrenheit. For a rough conversion from Celsius to Fahrenheit, double the number and add 30. For weather, remember that 28°C is 82°F—perfect. For health, 37°C is just right.

Hotel Reservation

To: _____   _____
              hotel   *email or fax*

From: _____   _____
              name   *email or fax*

Today's date: _____ /_____ /_____
                    day   *month*   *year*

Dear Hotel _____ ,
Please make this reservation for me:

Name: _____

Total # of people: _____   # of rooms: _____   # of nights: _____

Arriving: _____ /_____/ _____   My time of arrival (24-hr clock): _____
              day *month* *year*   (I will telephone if I will be late)

Departing: ____/____ /_____
                day *month* *year*

Room(s): Single___   Double ___   Twin ___   Triple ___   Quad___

With: Toilet _____   Shower _____ Bath _____   Sink only ___

Special needs: View___ Quiet ___ Cheapest ___ Ground Floor___

Please email or fax confirmation of my reservation, along with the type of room reserved and the price. Please also inform me of your cancellation policy. After I hear from you, I will quickly send my credit-card information as a deposit to hold the room. Thank you.

_____
Name

_____
Address

_____
City   *State*   *Zip Code*   *Country*

APPENDIX

Before hoteliers can make your reservation, they want to know the information listed above. You can use this form as the basis for your email, or you can photocopy this page, fill in the information, and send it as a fax (also available online at www.ricksteves.com/reservation).

Packing Checklist

Whether you're traveling for five days or five weeks, here's what you'll need to bring. Pack light to enjoy the sweet freedom of true mobility. Happy travels!

- ❑ 5 shirts: long- and short-sleeve
- ❑ 1 sweater or lightweight fleece
- ❑ 2 pairs pants
- ❑ 1 pair shorts
- ❑ 1 swimsuit
- ❑ 5 pairs underwear and socks
- ❑ 1 pair shoes
- ❑ 1 rainproof jacket with hood
- ❑ Tie or scarf
- ❑ Money belt
- ❑ Money—your mix of:
  - ❑ Debit card (for ATM withdrawals)
  - ❑ Credit card
  - ❑ Hard cash (in easy-to-exchange $20 bills)
- ❑ Documents plus photocopies:
  - ❑ Passport
  - ❑ Printout of airline eticket
  - ❑ Driver's license
  - ❑ Student ID and hostel card
  - ❑ Railpass/car rental voucher
  - ❑ Insurance details
- ❑ Daypack
- ❑ Electronics—your choice of:
  - ❑ Camera (and related gear)
  - ❑ Mobile phone or smartphone
  - ❑ iPod (or other MP3 player)
  - ❑ Laptop/netbook
  - ❑ ebook reader
  - ❑ Chargers for each of the above
  - ❑ Plug adapter

- ❑ Empty water bottle
- ❑ Wristwatch and alarm clock
- ❑ Earplugs
- ❑ Toiletries kit
  - ❑ Toiletries
  - ❑ Medicines and vitamins
  - ❑ First-aid kit
  - ❑ Glasses/contacts/sunglasses (with prescriptions)
- ❑ Sealable plastic baggies
- ❑ Laundry soap
- ❑ Clothesline
- ❑ Small towel
- ❑ Sewing kit
- ❑ Travel information (guidebooks and maps)
- ❑ Address list (for sending postcards)
- ❑ Postcards and photos from home
- ❑ Notepad and pen
- ❑ Journal

If you plan to carry on your luggage, note that all liquids must be in 3.4-ounce or smaller containers and fit within a single quart-size sealable baggie. For details, see www.tsa.gov/travelers.

Italian Survival Phrases

Good day.	Buon giorno.	bwohn JOR-noh
Do you speak English?	Parla inglese?	PAR-lah een-GLAY-zay
Yes. / No.	Sì. / No.	see / noh
I (don't) understand.	(Non) capisco.	(nohn) kah-PEES-koh
Please.	Per favore.	pehr fah-VOH-ray
Thank you.	Grazie.	GRAHT-seeay
You're welcome.	Prego.	PRAY-go
I'm sorry.	Mi dispiace.	mee dee-speeAH-chay
Excuse me.	Mi scusi.	mee SKOO-zee
(No) problem.	(Non) c'è un problema.	(nohn) cheh oon proh-BLAY-mah
Good.	Va bene.	vah BEHN-ay
Goodbye.	Arrivederci.	ah-ree-vay-DEHR-chee
one / two	uno / due	OO-noh / DOO-ay
three / four	tre / quattro	tray / KWAH-troh
five / six	cinque / sei	CHEENG-kway / SEHee
seven / eight	sette / otto	SEHT-tay / OT-toh
nine / ten	nove / dieci	NOV-ay / deeAY-chee
How much is it?	Quanto costa?	KWAHN-toh KOS-tah
Write it?	Me lo scrive?	may loh SKREE-vay
Is it free?	È gratis?	eh GRAH-tees
Is it included?	È incluso?	eh een-KLOO-zoh
Where can I buy / find...?	Dove posso comprare / trovare...?	DOH-vay POS-soh kohm-PRAH-ray / troh-VAH-ray
I'd like / We'd like...	Vorrei / Vorremmo...	vor-REHee / vor-RAY-moh
...a room.	...una camera.	OO-nah KAH-meh-rah
...a ticket to ___.	...un biglietto per ___.	oon beel-YEHT-toh pehr
Is it possible?	È possibile?	eh poh-SEE-bee-lay
Where is...?	Dov'è...?	DOH-veh
...the train station	...la stazione	lah staht-seeOH-nay
...the bus station	...la stazione degli autobus	lah staht-seeOH-nay DAYL-yee OW-toh-boos
...tourist information	...informazioni per turisti	een-for-maht-seeOH-nee pehr too-REE-stee
...the toilet	...la toilette	lah twah-LEHT-tay
men	uomini, signori	WOH-mee-nee, seen-YOH-ree
women	donne, signore	DON-nay, seen-YOH-ray
left / right	sinistra / destra	see-NEE-strah / DEHS-trah
straight	sempre diritto	SEHM-pray dee-REE-toh
When do you open / close?	A che ora aprite / chiudete?	ah kay OH-rah ah-PREE-tay / keeoo-DAY-tay
At what time?	A che ora?	ah kay OH-rah
Just a moment.	Un momento.	oon moh-MAYN-toh
now / soon / later	adesso / presto / tardi	ah-DEHS-soh / PREHS-toh / TAR-dee
today / tomorrow	oggi / domani	OH-jee / doh-MAH-nee

In an Italian Restaurant

I'd like...	**Vorrei...**	vor-REHee
We'd like...	**Vorremmo...**	vor-RAY-moh
...to reserve...	**...prenotare...**	pray-noh-TAH-ray
...a table for one / two.	**...un tavolo per uno / due.**	oon TAH-voh-loh pehr OO-noh / DOO-ay
Non-smoking.	**Non fumare.**	nohn foo-MAH-ray
Is this seat free?	**È libero questo posto?**	eh LEE-bay-roh KWEHS-toh POH-stoh
The menu (in English), please.	**Il menù (in inglese), per favore.**	eel may-NOO (een een-GLAY-zay) pehr fah-VOH-ray
service (not) included	**servizio (non) incluso**	sehr-VEET-seeoh (nohn) een-KLOO-zoh
cover charge	**pane e coperto**	PAH-nay ay koh-PEHR-toh
to go	**da portar via**	dah POR-tar VEE-ah
with / without	**con / senza**	kohn / SEHN-sah
and / or	**e / o**	ay / oh
menu (of the day)	**menù (del giorno)**	may-NOO (dayl JOR-noh)
specialty of the house	**specialità della casa**	spay-chah-lee-TAH DEHL-lah KAH-zah
first course (pasta, soup)	**primo piatto**	PREE-moh peeAH-toh
main course (meat, fish)	**secondo piatto**	say-KOHN-doh peeAH-toh
side dishes	**contorni**	kohn-TOR-nee
bread	**pane**	PAH-nay
cheese	**formaggio**	for-MAH-joh
sandwich	**panino**	pah-NEE-noh
soup	**minestra, zuppa**	mee-NEHS-trah, TSOO-pah
salad	**insalata**	een-sah-LAH-tah
meat	**carne**	KAR-nay
chicken	**pollo**	POH-loh
fish	**pesce**	PEH-shay
seafood	**frutti di mare**	FROO-tee dee MAH-ray
fruit / vegetables	**frutta / legumi**	FROO-tah / lay-GOO-mee
dessert	**dolci**	DOHL-chee
tap water	**acqua del rubinetto**	AH-kwah dayl roo-bee-NAY-toh
mineral water	**acqua minerale**	AH-kwah mee-nay-RAH-lay
milk	**latte**	LAH-tay
(orange) juice	**succo (d'arancia)**	SOO-koh (dah-RAHN-chah)
coffee / tea	**caffè / tè**	kah-FEH / teh
wine	**vino**	VEE-noh
red / white	**rosso / bianco**	ROH-soh / beeAHN-koh
glass / bottle	**bicchiere / bottiglia**	bee-keeAY-ray / boh-TEEL-yah
beer	**birra**	BEE-rah
Cheers!	**Cin cin!**	cheen cheen
More. / Another.	**Ancora un po.' / Un altro.**	ahn-KOH-rah oon poh / oon AHL-troh
The same.	**Lo stesso.**	loh STEHS-soh
The bill, please.	**Il conto, per favore.**	eel KOHN-toh pehr fah-VOH-ray
tip	**mancia**	MAHN-chah
Delicious!	**Delizioso!**	day-leet-seeOH-zoh

For more user-friendly Italian phrases, check out *Rick Steves' Italian Phrase Book & Dictionary* or *Rick Steves' French, Italian, and German Phrase Book*.

INDEX

A

Abstract art: 182
Accademia: eating, 256–257, 284–286; general information, 49, 70–71; maps, 133, 135, 137, 143, 256–257; sleeping, 255–259; tour, 132–145
Adoration of the Magi (Brueghel): 129
The Adoration of the Shepherds (Tintoretto): 161–162
Airport boats: 307–308
Airports: Marco Polo, 306–309; shuttle buses, 308–309; Treviso, 309
Air travel: baggage restrictions, 7; cheap flights, 401–402; cost, 5
Almanac: 9
Anatomy Theater (Padua): 335–336
The Angel of the City (Marini): 187
The Annunciation (Tintoretto): 156
Anthony of Padua, Saint: 319
The Antipope (Ernst): 184
Apartments. *See* Sleeping
The Apotheosis of Venice (Veronese): 115
Archaeological and Natural History Museum (Vicenza): 343
Architecture of churches: 370
Armory Museum: 113–114
Arrival at San Marco of Dogaressa Morosina Grimani (Michieli): 124
Assumption of the Virgin (Giordano): 192
The Assumption of the Virgin (Titian): 148–149
ATMs: 10–12
Audio tours: Accademia, 133; Ca' Rezzonico, 165; Doge's Palace, 105; Frari Church, 147; Grand Canal Cruise, 61; Peggy Guggenheim Collection, 177; Rick Steves' Audio Europe, 7, 21; Scuola San Rocco, 154; St. Mark's Basilica, 85; St. Mark's Square, 74

B

Bacchus and Ariadne (Tintoretto): 111
Back Door travel philosophy: 19
Baggage restrictions: 7–8
Baggage storage: 396
Bancomats. *See* ATMs
Baptistery (Padua): 333–334
Bars: 35–36. *See also* eating
Basilica of San Zeno Maggiore (Verona): 357–358
Basilica of St. Anthony (Padua): 318–323
Basilica Palladiana (Vicenza): 343–344
The Battle of Lepanto: 125–126
Bellini, Gentile: Accademia, 144–145; Correr Museum, 130
Bellini, Giovanni: Accademia, 136–137, 138–139; Church of San Pietro Martire, 209; Church of San Zaccaria, 233–234; Correr Museum, 130, 131; Frari Church, 150–151
Bellini, Jacopo: 130
Bell tower (Burano): 213
Bell tower (San Giorgio Maggiore): 199–201
Betrayal of Christ (Giotto): 328
Billboards: 43
Birth of John the Baptist (Tintoretto): 234
The Birth of Liquid Desires (Dalí): 184–185
Birth of the Virgin (Giordano): 192
Boating: 213. *See also* Cruise ships; Gondolas; Traghetti; Vaporetti; Water buses; Water taxis
Bondone, Giotto di: 325
Books, recommended: 404–405
Bookstores: Padua, 317; Venice, 28
Botanic Garden (Padua): 323
The Break of Day (Delvaux): 184
Bridge of Sighs: 47–48, 72, 83, 117, 232, 236
Bronze Horses: 101–102

Burano: 59, 212–214
Buses: 309
Buses, airport shuttle: 308–309
Buses, water: 306–308
Business hours: 8, 24, 49
Byzantium: 92–93

C
Ca' d'Oro: 56–57, 66–67
Cafés: 78, 268–270. *See also* eating
Caffè Florian: 9, 78, 80
Caffè Pedrocchi (Padua): 332–333
Ca' Foscari: 69–70
Calatrava Bridge: 56, 64
Campanile: 46–47, 73, 79–80
Campo Manin: 221–222
Campo San Giacomo: 225–227
Campo San Polo: 229
Canaletto (Giovanni Antonio Canal): 143, 169, 172–173
Cannaregio Canal: 65
Cannaregio District: 53–57
Canova, Antonio: Correr Museum, 121; general information, 169; monument, 152–153
Ca' Pesaro International Gallery of Modern Art: 51
Ca' Rezzonico: 50, 70, 164–175
Car leasing: 398
Car rental: 7, 396–398
Carriera, Rosalba: 167–168
Car travel: distance and time map, 399; driving tips, 399–401; fuel, 400; insurance, 396–398; maps and signage, 400–401; parking, 310, 341–342, 401; road rules, 399–400; theft, 401; tolls, 400; *vs.* trains, 386
Casanova, Giacomo: 169, 171
Casinò: 65–66
Castello District: 57–58
Castelvecchio (Verona): 357
Cell phones. *See* Telephones
Children, traveling with: 288–291
Chip and PIN: 12. *See also* Debit cards
Chorus pass: 26
Christ as Pantocrator: 90
Christ Before Pilate (Tintoretto): 158
Christ Crowned with Thorns (Tintoretto): 158

Church Card: 346
Churches: architecture, 370; Basilica of San Zeno Maggiore, 357–358; Basilica of St. Anthony, 318–323; chorus pass, 26; Church Card, 346; Church of San Pietro Martire, 209; Church of San Polo, 53, 229–230; Church of Santa Corona, 343; Church of Sant'Anastasia, 355; Church of San Zaccaria, 48, 233–235; Church of the Scalzi, 64–65; dress code, 17, 27, 85; English services, 29; Frari Church, 52, 146–153; La Salute Church, 50, 70, 80, 189–193; San Giorgio Maggiore Church, 48, 72, 195–199; San Maurizio Church, 300; San Moisè Church, 219–220; San Simeone Piccolo Church, 64; San Stae Church, 66; Santa Maria Assunta Church, 215–216; Santa Maria e San Donato Church, 210; San Vidal, 300; San Zulian Church, 29; Scrovegni Chapel, 323–329; St. George's Anglican Church, 29; St. Mark's Basilica, 42–43, 84–102
Church of San Pietro Martire: 209
Church of San Polo: 53, 229–230
Church of Santa Corona: 343
Church of Sant'Anastasia: 355
Church of San Zaccaria: 48, 233–235
Church of the Scalzi: 64–65
Cimitero: 58
The Circumcision (Tintoretto): 163
Civic Museums (Padua): 329–330
Climate: 6, 411
Clock Tower: 39, 42, 72, 73, 77, 79
Clothing sizes: 410
Composition with Red (Mondrian): 181
Concerts: Baroque, 300; Frari Church, 52, 147. *See also* Music
Constantinople: 92–93
Consulates: 385
Coronation of the Virgin in Paradise (Fiore): 136

Correr Museum: 46, 80, 118–131
Corso Porta Borsari (Verona): 351
Costs: 5–6. *See also* Discounts;
    Money; Shopping; Sightseeing
Credit cards: 7, 8, 11–13
Crime: 8, 26, 85, 396
Crowds: 24, 80
Crucifix (Brunelleschi): 198
Crucifixion (Giovanni Bellini): 130
Crucifixion (Jacopo Bellini): 130
The Crucifixion (Tintoretto):
    158–159
Cruise ships: 310–311
Culture: 53
Cupid and Psyche (Canova): 122
Customs: 15
Customs House: 71

D

Daedalus and Icarus (Canova):
    121–122
Day trips: general information,
    313; map, 313; Padua, 314–341;
    Verona, 345–365; Vicenza,
    341–344
*The Dead Christ Supported by Two
    Angels* (Giovanni Bellini): 131
Debit cards: 7, 8, 11–13. *See also*
    ATMs
Devotional column (Verona):
    351
Discounts: Card Musei, 342;
    Church Card, 346; museum,
    8–9; Padova Card, 315;
    railpasses, 392–394; vaporetto
    passes, 34; Verona Card, 346;
    youth pass, 26, 34. *See also* Costs
Discovery of the True Cross
    (Tiepolo): 142–143
Districts: map, 22. *See also*
    individual districts
Doges: 123
Doge's Palace: 43, 46, 72, 82–83,
    103–117, 301
Donatello: 150
Dorsoduro District: 49–51
Dress code: 17, 27, 85
Driving. *See* Car travel
Duomo (Verona): 356
*Dynamism of a Speeding Horse +
    Houses* (Boccioni): 180

E

Eating: Accademia Bridge area,
    256–257, 284–286; bars and
    cafés, 35–36, 268–270; Campo
    San Barnaba area, 286; Campo
    Santa Maria Nova area, 287;
    canalside settings, 284–285;
    cheap meals, 267–271; cicchetti,
    9, 272, 280–281; costs, 5; in
    Dorsoduro district, 284–286;
    Fondamente Nove area, 286–
    287; gelato, 287; Padua, 338–
    340; picnics, 270–271; pizzerias,
    268; pub-crawl (progressive
    dinner), 280–281; pubs, clubs
    and late-night spots, 302–303;
    restaurant maps, 246–247,
    252–253, 256–257; restaurant
    phrases, 415; restaurants, 265–
    267, 276–287; Rialto Bridge
    area, 252–253, 276–282, 302;
    seasonal foods, 266; St. Mark's
    Square area, 246–247, 282–284;
    tipping, 13, 267; train station
    area, 287; Venetian cuisine,
    272–276; Verona, 360, 362–365;
    wine bars, 9; Zattere area, 301.
    See also cafés
Electricity: 8
Embassies: 385
Emergencies: 8
Empire of Light (Magritte): 184
Enchanted Forest (Pollock): 185
Enoteca Oreste (Verona): 351–352
Entertainment: 5, 296–303
Enthroned Madonna with Child
    (Giovanni Bellini): 136–137
Etiquette: 27
Exchange rate: 11

F

The Fall of Manna in the Desert
    (Tintoretto): 161
Feast of the House of Levi
    (Veronese): 139–140
Feedback: 17
Ferrovia: 64–65
Festivals: 407–408
Figures and Episodes of Saints
    (Veneziano): 128
Films: 301

Flamboyant Gothic style: 128
The Flight into Egypt (Tintoretto): 163
Flooding: 6–7
Flooring, flexible: 251
Fortress Bridge (Verona): 357
Frari Church: 52, 146–153. *See also* walking tours

G
Gelato: 287
Giardinetti Reali: 80
Giotto di Bondone: 325
Giusti Garden (Verona): 358
Glass: 294. *See also* Murano
Glassblowing demonstrations: 290
Glass Museum (Murano): 59, 210
Golden Altarpiece: 98–99
Golden Staircase (Doge's Palace): 107
Goldoni, Carlo: 169
Gondolas: 297–299; tipping, 13
Gothic style, Flamboyant: 128
Gothic style, International: 128–129
Grand Canal Cruise: 60–72
Grand Canal from Palazzo Balbi to Rialto (Canaletto): 172
Guardi, Francesco: 143, 169, 174
Guggenheim, Peggy: 176, 178–179, 180–181, 181–182, 183, 186. *See also* Peggy Guggenheim Collection
Guidebooks: 404; Rick Steves, 402

H
Haircuts: 29–30
Harry's American Bar: 218
History of Venice: 366–375
Holidays: 7, 406–407
Hotels. *See* Sleeping
House of Juliet (Verona): 352–353

I
Il Merletto: 80
Il Ridotto di Palazzo Dandolo (Guardi): 174
Insurance: 396–398
International Gothic style: 128–129
Internet access: general information, 28, 385–386; Padua, 317; Venice, 28, 385–386; Verona, 347–348; VoIP, 384
Islands: Burano, 59, 212–214; Murano, 59, 208–212; San Giorgio Maggiore, 48, 72, 80, 194–201; San Michele, 58, 204–205, 208; Torcello, 59, 214–216
Itineraries: 21–23

J
Jewish Ghetto: 53–56, 65
Jewish Museum: 55–56
Jews in Venice's Ghetto: 55
Joachim Returns to the Sheepfold (Giotto): 328
John the Baptist (Donatello): 150
Jupiter Descending from Heaven to Strike Down the Vices (Veronese): 113
Justice Presenting the Sword and Scales to Doge Girolamo Priuli (Tintoretto): 109

K
Key to this book: 3

L
La Biennale: 58
Lace: 80, 213–214. *See also* Burano
Lace Museum: 59, 214
La Fenice Opera House: 47, 220–221, 300
Lagoon: general information, 58–59; maps, 203, 206–207; tour, 202–216; transportation, 202. *See also* Islands
Lamentation (Giotto): 328
Language: general information, 378; restaurant phrases, 415; survival phrases, 414
La Salute Church: 50, 70, 80, 189–193
Last Judgment (Giotto): 328–329
The Last Supper (Tintoretto): San Giorgio Maggiore, 197–198; Scuola San Rocco, 162–163
Laundry: Padua, 317; Venice, 29
Lazzarini, Gregorio: 170
Lido: 72
Longhi, Pietro: 174–175

M

Madonna and Child (Giovanni Bellini): 131

Madonna and Child between St. Catherine and Mary Magdalene (Giovanni Bellini): 138–139

Madonna and Child with Doge Francesco Dandolo (Veneziano): 151–152

Madonna and Child with Saints (Giovanni Bellini): 233–234

Madonna and Child with Saints and Angels (Giovanni Bellini): 150–151

Madonna and Child with Two Donors (Veneziano): 135–136

Madonna of Ca' Pesaro (Titian): 153

Maiastra (Brancusi): 180

Mail: 386. *See also* Post office

Manin, Daniele: 221–222

Manna from Heaven (Tintoretto): 198

Mantegna, Andrea: 137–138

Maps: Accademia, 133, 135, 137, 143; book legend, 2; Burano, 207; Ca' Rezzonico, 166; Correr Museum, 120, 128; Doge's Palace, 104, 110, 113, 115; driving distance and time, 399; Frari Church, 148; general information, 404; Grand Canal, 62–63; hotels in Verona, 360; hotels near Accademia Bridge, 256–257; hotels near Rialto Bridge, 252–253; hotels near St. Mark's Square, 246–247; hotels near the train station, 260–261; Jewish Ghetto, 54; lagoon, 203; lagoon tour, 206–207; La Saluted Church, 191; Murano, 206; Padua, 316; Peggy Guggenheim Collection, 177; restaurants in Verona, 360; restaurants near Accademia Bridge, 256–257; restaurants near Rialto Bridge, 252–253; restaurants near St. Mark's Square, 246–247; Rialto to Frari Church walk, 226–227; San Giorgio Maggiore Church, 196; Scrovegni Chapel, 326; Scuola San Rocco, 155; St. Mark's Basilica, 87; St. Mark's Square, 75; St. Mark's to Rialto walk, 219; St. Mark's to San Zaccaria walk, 232; Torcello, 207; train costs in Italy, 388; Venice, 40–41; Venice in the 15th century, 368; Venice's districts, 22; Verona, 349; Verona hotels and restaurants, 360; Vicenza, 342; view from San Giorgio Maggiore, 200; where to buy, 25

Marciana National Library: 127

Marco Polo Airport: 306–309

Markets: Ca' D'Oro, 67; fish, 228; Padua, 323; produce, 228; Rialto, 51, 228, 271; St. Mark's Square, 271

Mark, Saint: 96

Mars and Neptune with Campanile and Lion (Veronese): 112

Masks: 230, 293

Medical help: 8, 26–27

Mercato Rialto: 67–68

Metric conversion: 409

The Miracle of the Bronze Serpent (Tintoretto): 160

Money: ATMs, 10–12; cash, 10–11; credit/debit cards, 7, 8, 11–13; customs, 15; exchange rate, 11; tipping, 13–14; VAT refunds, 14–15; what to bring, 10

Monument to Titian (Canova): 121

Mosaics: general information, 91; St. Mark's Basilica, 86, 88–93, 100

Moses Strikes Water from the Rocks (Tintoretto): 160–161

Mouth of Truth (Doge's Palace): 107

Movies: 301; recommended, 405–406

Multimedia Room (Padua): 329–330

Murano: 59, 208–212

Museum of the Risorgimento (Padua): 333

Museums: Accademia, 49, 70–71, 132–145, 255–259, 284–286; Archaeological and Natural

History Museum (Vicenza), 343; Armory Museum, 113–114; Ca' d'Oro, 56–57, 66–67; Ca' Pesaro International Gallery of Modern Art, 51; Ca' Rezzonico, 50, 70, 164–175; Civic Museums (Padua), 329–330; Correr Museum, 46, 80, 118–131; Glass Museum (Murano), 59, 210; Jewish Museum, 55–56; Museum of the Risorgimento (Padua), 333; National Archaeological Museum, 127; Palazzo Mocenigo Costume Museum, 51–52; passes, 25–26; Peggy Guggenheim Collection, 50, 70, 176–188; Punta della Dogana, 50–51; San Marco Museum, 99–102; Scuola Dalmata di San Giorgio, 57–58; Scuola San Rocco, 52–53, 154–163, 300; Treasury (St. Mark's Basilica), 95–98

Music: 300–301, 302–303. *See also* Concerts

N

National Archaeological Museum: 127

Nativity and Adoration of the Shepherds (Bassano): 198

News: 9–10

New World (Tiepolo): 173

Nightlife: general information, 296; gondola rides, 297–298; late-night eating, 301–303; movies, 301; music, 300–301, 302–303; sightseeing, 296; St. Mark's Square, 298–299

Nude (Study), Sad Young Man on a Train (Duchamp): 179

Numbers: 409–410

O

Off-season traveling: 6–7, 31

Olympic Theater (Vicenza): 342–343

On the Beach (Picasso): 178

Opera: 220–221, 300–301, 347

Orpheus and Eurydice (Canova): 119–120

P

Packing checklist: 413

Padova Card: 315

Padua: eating, 338–340; general information, 314; Internet access, 317; laundry, 317; maps, 316; planning time, 314; sightseeing, 318–336; sleeping, 336–338; tourist information, 315; transportation, 315, 317, 340–341

Palazzo Balbi: 69

Palazzo della Ragione (Padua): 330–331

Palazzo della Ragione (Verona): 354

Palazzo Grassi: 70

Palazzo Leoni Montanari (Vicenza): 343

Palazzo Mocenigo Costume Museum: 51–52

Palazzo Zuckermann (Padua): 330

Paradise (Tintoretto): 115

Paris (Canova): 122

Parking: 401

Parks: 290

The Parlor (Guardi): 174

Passeggiata (Verona): 357

Passes: 25–26. *See also* Discounts

Passports: 7, 8

Peggy Guggenheim Collection: 50, 70, 176–188

Pentecost (Titian): 193

Perspective View of Venice (Barbari): 129

Perspective with Portico (Canaletto): 144

Phones. *See* Telephones

Photography: 85

Piano Nobile (Padua): 333

Piazza Brà (Verona): 348–350

Piazza dei Signori (Padua): 331–332

Piazza dei Signori (Verona): 353–354

Piazza dei Signori (Vicenza): 343–344

Piazza Erbe (Verona): 352

Piazzale Roma Bus Station: 309

Piazzetta (St. Mark's Square): 81–82

Piazzetta dei Leoni: 231–232

Picnics: 214, 270–271. *See also* Eating

Pietà (Messina): 129–130

Pietà (Titian): 140–141

Pigeons: 27, 289–290

Pinacoteca (Padua): 329

Pizzerias: 268. *See also* Eating

Planning: costs, 5–6; general information, 4–5, 7–10; itineraries, 21–23; packing checklist, 413; sightseeing, 15–17; tipping, 13–14; when to go, 6–7. *See also* Money

The Poet (Picasso): 179

Pollock, Jackson: 185

Ponte de la Verona: 221

Ponte della Costituzione: 56

Ponte Pietra (Verona): 355–356

Population: 9, 53

Porta Borsari (Verona): 351

Portrait of a Young Man (Crevalcore): 129

Portrait of Clement XIII: 167

Portrait of Doge Francesco Foscari (Bastiani): 122–123

Portrait of Doge Mocenigo (Gentile Bellini): 130

Portrait (Ritratto) of Sister Maria Caterina (Carriera): 167–168

Post office: 28. *See also* Mail

Pound, Ezra: 205

Prato della Valle (Padua): 323

Presentation of the Virgin (Titian): 134–135

Presentation of the Virgin in the Temple (Giordano): 193

Prisons (Doge's Palace): 117

Procession in St. Mark's Square (Gentile Bellini): 144–145

Public toilets: 27, 74, 85

Pubs: bars, 35–36; cafés, 78, 268–270; tours, 35–36. *See also* Eating

Punta della Dogana: 50–51

R

Rain (Chagall): 180

The Rape of Europa (Veronese): 110–111

The Removal of St. Mark's Body (Tintoretto): 141–142

Renaissance: 136, 139–140, 371

Resources: 402–406

Restaurants. *See* Eating

Rest rooms: 27, 74, 85

The Resurrection (Tintoretto): 162

Rialto: 68

Rialto Bridge: 51, 68, 223. *See also* walking tours

Rick Steves' resources: 402–403

Riva (waterfront promenade): 72, 235

Riva de Biasio: 65

Robusti, Domenico: 115–116, 198

Rolling Venice pass: 26, 34

Roman arena (Verona): 350

Roman numerals: 409–410

Roman theater (Verona): 358

Room and board. *See* Costs; Sleeping

S

Sala dei Banchetti: 100–101

Salute: 71. *See also* La Salute Church

Salviati building: 71

San Giorgio Maggiore: 48, 72, 80, 194–201

San Giorgio Maggiore and the Giudecca (Guardi): 144

San Giorgio Maggiore Church: 48, 195–199

San Marco district: 39, 42–43, 46–48, 72

San Marco Museum: 99–102

San Marcuola: 65–66

San Maurizio Church: 300

San Michele: 58, 204–205, 208

San Moisè Church: 219–220

San Polo District: 52–53

San Silvestro: 68–69

San Simeone Piccolo Church: 64

San Stae: 66

San Stae Church: 66

Santa Croce District: 51–52

Santa Elena: 58

Santa Lucia train station: 64, 304–306

Santa Maria Assunta Church: 215–216

Santa Maria del Giglio: 71

Santa Maria e San Donato Church: 210

Sant'Angelo: 69
San Tomà: 69–70
San Vidal Church: 300
San Zaccaria: 72
San Zulian Church: 29
Scala Contarini del Bovolo: 222
Scala dei Giganti (Doge's Palace): 106
Scala d'Oro (Doge's Palace): 107
Scrovegni Chapel (Padua): 7, 323–329
Scuola Dalmata di San Giorgio: 57–58
Scuola San Rocco: 52–53; concerts, 300; tour, 154–163
Secret Itineraries Tour: 46, 104–105
Self-guided walk (Verona): 348–356
Shopping: clothing sizes, 410; costs, 5–6; customs, 15; general information, 292–295; glass, 294; masks, 293; Murano, 209; souvenirs, 294–295; VAT refunds, 14–15
Shuttle buses: 308–309
Siege of Constantinople (Robusti): 115–116
Sightseeing: with children, 288–291; in churches, 17; costs, 5; early and late, 49; general information, 15–17; itineraries, 21–23; at night, 49; off-season, 6–7, 31; passes, 25–26; planning, 15–17; Venice, 39, 42–59; *See also specific location*
Six Saints (Veneziano): 127
Sleep code: 239
Sleeping: Accademia Bridge area, 255–259; air conditioning, 243; apartments, 244; costs, 5; dormitory accommodations, 263–264; general information, 237–242; hostels, 244; hotel reservation form, 412; hotels, 242–244, 263; making reservations, 240–241; Padua, 336–338; rates and deals, 238, 242, 263; Rialto Bridge area, 251–255; St. Mark's Square area, 245–251; train station area, 259–263; Verona, 359–362

Soccer games: 290
Souvenirs: 294–295
Stairway of Giants (Doge's Palace): 106
St. Anthony of Padua: 319
St. Benedict and Other Saints (Robusti): 198
St. George (Mantegna): 137–138
St. George's Anglican Church: 29
St. Mark: 96
St. Mark's Basilica: 42–43, 72, 76–77, 84–102
St. Mark's Square: eating, 246–247, 282–284; general information, 39, 42, 72; nightlife, 298–299; sleeping, 245–251; tour, 73–83. *See also* walking tours
The Stoning of St. Stephen (Robusti): 198
Story of Alatiel: 128–129
St. Roch in Glory (Tintoretto): 157–158
St. Zachariah: 233
The Sun in its Jewel Case (Tanguy): 182–183
Surrealism: 183–184

T
Tanguy, Yves: 182–183
Tapestries: 168
Teatro della Fondamenta Nuove: 300
Teatro Goldoni: 222, 300
Telephones: European calling chart, 380–381; general information, 378; hotel-room phones, 382; how to dial, 378–379; metered phones, 382; mobile phones, 383–384; phone cards, 379, 382; public phones, 379, 382; useful phone numbers, 384–385; VoIP, 384
The Tempest (Giorgione): 139
Tetrarchs: 82
Theater: 222, 300–301
Theft: 8, 26, 85, 396
Theft insurance: 398
Three Apples (Tintoretto): 159
Tiepolo, Cecilia Guardi: 168
Tiepolo, Giovanni Battista: Accademia, 142–143;

Ca' Rezzonico, 169–170; Doge's Palace, 110; general information, 169

Tiepolo, Giovanni Domenico: 169, 173

Time zones: 8

Tintoretto, Jacopo Robusti: Accademia, 141–142; Church of San Zaccaria, 234; Correr Museum, 125; Doge's Palace, 108, 109, 111, 112, 115; La Salute Church, 192; San Giorgio Maggiore Church, 197–198; Scuola San Rocco, 156–163

Tipping: 13–14

TIs. *See* Tourist information

Titian (Tiziano Vecellio): Accademia, 134, 140–141; Doge's Palace, 108; Frari Church, 148–149, 153; La Salute Church, 192, 193; *Monument to Titian* (Canova), 121; tomb, 152

Toilets: 27, 74, 85

Tomb of Doge Foscari: 149–150

Tomb of St. Anthony: 320–322

Tomb of Titian: 152

Tombs of the Scaligeri Family (Verona): 354

Torcello: 59, 214–216

Tourist information: general information, 23, 25, 377–378; Padua, 315; Verona, 346; Vicenza, 341

Tours: Accademia, 132–145; Ca' Rezzonico, 164–175; Correr Museum, 118–131; Doge's Palace, 103–117; Frari Church, 146–153; Grand Canal Cruise, 60–72; La Salute Church, 189–193; Murano, 211; Peggy Guggenheim Collection, 176–188; San Giorgio Maggiore, 194–201; Scuola San Rocco, 154–163; Secret Itineraries, 46, 104–105; St. Mark's Basilica, 84–102; St. Mark's Square, 73–83; Venice, 35–38; Venice's lagoon, 202–216; Verona, 348. *See also* Walking tours

Traghetti: 34–35; tipping, 13

"Tragicomica" Mask Shop: 230, 293

Train travel: baggage storage, 396; costs, 388; general information, 386; maps, 387, 388; point-to-point tickets, 389–392; railpasses, 392–394; Santa Lucia station, 64, 304–306; schedules, 388–389, 395; tips, 394–396; travel tips, 7; types of trains, 386, 388; *vs.* car travel, 386

Transportation: car *vs.* train, 386; costs, 5; maps, 305, 387; passes, 26; tipping, 13. *See also* Airports; Parking; Santa Lucia train station; *specific modes of transportation*

Travel agencies: 29

Travel insurance: 7

Treasury (St. Mark's Basilica): 95–98

Treviso Airport: 309

Triumph of Venice (Tintoretto): 112

Turkish "Fondaco" Exchange: 65

Two Venetian Gentlewomen (Carpaccio): 131

U

University of Padua: 334–336

V

Vaporetti: 31–34

VAT refunds: 14–15

Venetian Gothic style: 81

Veneziano, Lorenzo: 128

Veneziano, Paolo: Accademia, 135–136; Correr Museum, 127; Frari Church, 151–152

Venice at a glance: 44–45

Venice Receiving Neptune (Tiepolo): 110

Verona: eating, 360, 362–365; general information, 345–348; Internet access, 347–348; maps, 349; self-guided walk, 348–356; sightseeing, 357–358; sleeping, 359–362; tourist information, 346; tours, 348; transportation, 346–347, 365; wines, 363

Veronese, Paolo: Accademia, 139–140; Doge's Palace, 108, 110–111, 112, 113, 115

Vicenza: general information,
341–342; map, 342; sightseeing,
342–344; tourist information,
341; transportation, 344
View of Rio dei Mendicante
(Canaletto): 172–173
Views: 27
Villa la Rotonda (Vicenza): 344
Villa Valmarana ai Nani (Vicenza):
344
*Virgin Enthroned with Mark and
a Kneeling Doge* (Giovanni
Bellini): 209
VoIP: 384

W
Walking in Venice: 30–31
Walking tours: Rialto to Frari
Church, 224–230; St. Mark's to
Rialto, 217–223; St. Mark's to
San Zaccaria, 231–236; Verona,
348–356

Water buses: 306–308
Water, drinking: 27–28
Water taxis: 35, 308; tipping, 13
The Way to Calvary (Tintoretto):
158
WCs. *See* toilets
Weather: 6, 411
Websites: on Italy, 378; Rick
Steves, 403
White Cross (Kandinsky): 181
Wines: 274–275, 276, 363

Z
Zachariah, Saint: 233
Zattere neighborhood: 301

MAP INDEX

Color Maps
Venice: ii-iii
St. Mark's Area: iv-v
Rialto Area: vi-vii
Italy: viii

Introduction
Venice Overview: xii

Orientation
Venice's Districts: 22
Handy Vaporetti: 33

Sights in Venice
Venice: 40
Jewish Ghetto: 54

Grand Canal Cruise
Grand Canal: 62

St. Mark's Square Tour
St. Mark's Square: 75

St. Mark's Basilica Tour
St. Mark's Basilica: 87
Byzantine Empire: 93

Doge's Palace Tour
Doge's Palace: 104
Executive & Legislative Rooms:
110
Judicial Rooms: 113
Hall of the Grand Council: 115

Correr Museum Tour
Correr Museum—First Floor: 120
Correr Museum—Second Floor:
128

Accademia Tour
Accademia: 133
Accademia—Medieval Art: 135
Accademia—Early Renaissance:
137
Accademia—High Renaissance:
141

Accademia—Elegant Decay: 143

Frari Church Tour
Frari Church: 148

Scuola San Rocco Tour
Scuola San Rocco: 155

Ca' Rezzonico Tour
Ca' Rezzonico—First Floor: 166
Ca' Rezzonico—Second Floor: 173

**Peggy Guggenheim Collection
    Tour**
Peggy Guggenheim Collection: 177

La Salute Church Tour
La Salute Church: 191

San Giorgio Maggiore Tour
San Giorgio Maggiore: 196
View from San Giorgio Maggiore:
    200

Venice's Lagoon Tour
Venice's Lagoon: 203
Lagoon Tour: 206

St. Mark's to Rialto Walk
St. Mark's to Rialto Walk: 219

Rialto to Frari Church Walk
Rialto to Frari Church Walk: 226

St. Mark's to San Zaccaria Walk
St. Mark's to San Zaccaria Walk:
    232

Sleeping in Venice
Hotels & Restaurants near St.
    Mark's Square: 246
Hotels & Restaurants near the
    Rialto Bridge: 252
Hotels & Restaurants near the
    Accademia Bridge: 256
Hotels near the Train Station: 260

Venice Connections
Arrival in Venice: 305

Day Trips From Venice
Day Trips from Venice: 313
Padua: 316
Scrovegni Chapel: 326
Vicenza: 342

Verona
Verona: 349
Verona Hotels & Restaurants: 360

Venetian History
Venice in the 15th Century: 368
Church Architecture: 370

Appendix
Italy's Public Transportation: 387
Train Costs in Italy: 388
Driving in Italy: 399

Audio Europe

RICK STEVES AUDIO EUROPE

Rick's free app and podcasts

The FREE **Rick Steves Audio Europe**™ app for iPhone, iPad and iPod Touch gives you 29 self-guided audio tours of Europe's top museums, sights and historic walks—plus more than 200 tracks filled with cultural insights and sightseeing tips from Rick's radio interviews—all organized into geographic-specific playlists.

Let **Rick Steves Audio Europe**™ amplify your guidebook.

With Rick whispering in your ear, Europe gets even better.

Thanks Facebook fans for submitting photos while on location! From top: John Kuijper in Florence, Brenda Mamer with her mother in Rome, Angel Capobianco in London, and Alyssa Passey with her friend in Paris.

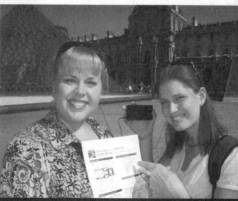

Find out more at ricksteves.com

Join a Rick Steves tour

Enjoy Europe's warmest welcome... with the flexibility and friendship of a small group getting to know Rick's favorite places and people. It all starts with our free tour catalog and DVD.

Great guides, small groups, no grumps.

Start your trip at

Free information and great gear to

▸ Plan Your Trip

Browse thousands of articles and a wealth of money-saving tips for planning your dream trip. You'll find up-to-date information on Europe's best destinations, packing smart, getting around, finding rooms, staying healthy, avoiding scams and more.

▸ Eurail Passes

Find out, step-by-step, if a railpass makes sense for your trip—and how to avoid buying more than you need. Get free shipping on online orders

▸ Graffiti Wall & Travelers Helpline

Learn, ask, share—our online community of savvy travelers is a great resource for first-time travelers to Europe, as well as seasoned pros.

Rick Steves' Europe Through the Back Door, Inc.